LIMITATIONS AND FUTURE TRENDS IN NEURAL COMPUTATION

NATO Science Series

A series presenting the results of scientific meetings supported under the NATO Science Programme.

The series is published by IOS Press and Kluwer Academic Publishers in conjunction with the NATO Scientific Affairs Division.

Sub-Series

I.	Life and Behavioural Sciences	IOS Press
II.	Mathematics, Physics and Chemistry	Kluwer Academic Publishers
III.	Computer and Systems Sciences	IOS Press
IV.	Earth and Environmental Sciences	Kluwer Academic Publishers
V.	Science and Technology Policy	IOS Press

The NATO Science Series continues the series of books published formerly as the NATO ASI Series.

The NATO Science Programme offers support for collaboration in civil science between scientists of countries of the Euro-Atlantic Partnership Council. The types of scientific meeting generally supported are "Advanced Study Institutes" and "Advanced Research Workshops", although other types of meeting are supported from time to time. The NATO Science Series collects together the results of these meetings. The meetings are co-organized by scientists from NATO countries and scientists from NATO's Partner countries – countries of the CIS and Central and Eastern Europe.

Advanced Study Institutes are high-level tutorial courses offering in-depth study of latest advances in a field.
Advanced Research Workshops are expert meetings aimed at critical assessment of a field, and identification of directions for future action.

As a consequence of the restructuring of the NATO Science Programme in 1999, the NATO Science Series has been re-organized and there are currently five sub-series as noted above. Please consult the following web sites for information on previous volumes published in the series, as well as details of earlier sub-series:

http://www.nato.int/science
http://www.wkap.nl
http://www.iospress.nl
http://www.wtv-books.de/nato_pco.htm

Series III: Computer and Systems Sciences - Vol. 186

ISSN 1387-6694

Limitations and Future Trends in Neural Computation

Edited by

Sergey Ablameyko

Institute of Engineering Cybernetics,
National Academy of Sciences of Belarus, Belarus

Marco Gori

Department of Information Engineering,
University of Siena, Italy

Liviu Goras

Department of Fundamental Electronics,
Technical University of Iasi, Romania

and

Vincenzo Piuri

Department of Information Technologies,
University of Milan, Italy

IOS
Press

Ohmsha

Amsterdam • Berlin • Oxford • Tokyo • Washington, DC

Published in cooperation with NATO Scientific Affairs Division

Proceedings of the NATO Advanced Research Workshop on
Limitations and Future Trends in Neural Computation
22–24 October 2001
Siena, Italy

ISBN 1 58603 324 7 (IOS Press)
ISBN 4 274 90581 0 C3055 (Ohmsha)
Library of Congress Control Number: 2003101038

Publisher
IOS Press
Nieuwe Hemweg 6B
1013 BG Amsterdam
Netherlands   .
fax: +31 20 620 3419
e-mail: order@iospress.nl

Distributor in the UK and Ireland
IOS Press/Lavis Marketing
73 Lime Walk
Headington
Oxford OX3 7AD
England
fax: +44 1865 75 0079

Distributor in the USA and Canada
IOS Press, Inc.
5795-G Burke Centre Parkway
Burke, VA 22015
USA
fax: +1 703 323 3668
e-mail: iosbooks@iospress.com

Distributor in Germany, Austria and Switzerland
IOS Press/LSL.de
Gerichtsweg 28
D-04103 Leipzig
Germany
fax: +49 341 995 4255

Distributor in Japan
Ohmsha, Ltd.
3-1 Kanda Nishiki-cho
Chiyoda-ku, Tokyo 101-8460
Japan
fax: +81 3 3233 2426

Preface

In the last fifteen years neural computation has become a fundamental paradigm used for either learning or problem solving. Apart from its chequered story, Backpropagation – developed independently in different contexts, but mainly brought to the attention of the scientific community by the PDP research group – made learning from examples possible in feedforward neural networks, a problem that could not be faced by classical Rosenblatt's PC algorithm. At the end of the eighties this raised a fundamental debate on the actual progress of the new connectionist wave mainly based on continuous optimization. In the expanded edition of his seminal book *Perceptrons*, Minsky raised a number of fundamental questions either related to architectural issues or to the optimization-based learning approach. Ten years later the publication of Minsky's intriguing epilogue on open issues related to the new connectionist wave, some questions have been partially answered, others, however, are still waiting for a satisfactory response. The massive application of connectionist models to many different fields has given rise to successes and failures which are often not clearly understood.

This book collects the contributions of the invited speakers at the NATO Advanced Research Workshop on "Limitations and Future Trends in Neural Computation", held in Siena (Italy), 22–24 October 2001. The Workshop was held immediately after the NATO Advanced Study Institute on NIMIA (Neural networks for Instrumentation, Measurement, and related Industrial Applications), held in Crema (Italy), 9–20 October 2001.

The major aim of the workshop was that of providing a critical assessment of the new connectionist wave roughly began in the middle eighties. Either theoretical foundation or future research were core of the workshop. The book reports critical analyses on complexity issues in the continuum setting and on generalization to new examples, which are two basic milestones of learning from examples in connectionist models. The problem of loading the weights of neural networks, which is often framed as continuous optimization, has been the target of many criticisms, since the potential solution of any learning problem is severely limited by the presence of local minima in the error function. The maturity of the field requires to convert the quest for a general solution to all learning problem into the understanding of which learning problems are likely to be solved efficiently. Likewise, the notion of efficient solution needs to be formalized so as to provide useful comparisons with the traditional theory of computational complexity in the discrete setting. The book covers these topics focussing also attention on recent developments in computational mathematics, where interesting notions of computational complexity emerge in the continuum setting (see e.g. Cucker-Blum-Smale-Shub's book (1998)). New computational frameworks are foreseen which seem to be adequate for understanding the structural complexity of the loading problem in artificial neural networks as well as problem solving methodologies with Hopfield networks. Continuous optimization can in fact be hard either because of the inherent complexity of the problem at hand or because of the way the problem is framed in the context of optimization. A wrong choice of the numerical algorithm may also affect the computational complexity significantly. The complexity of the optimization can be due to a spurious formulation of the problem, but can have also a structural nature, in the sense that the complexity can be inherently associated with the problem at hand.

The book includes also critical issues on real-world applications, aimed at spotting those applications that benefit considerably from connectionist models. In particular, some interesting models of data clustering are proposed especially for problems in high dimensional spaces. More than addressing very specific problems, the book is expected to activate a constructive discussions on successes and failures of connectionist models in the context of real-world applications so as to identify the actual advances deriving from the adoption of these models. The analysis of the most significant applications is integrated with the proposal of adopting hybrid systems, capable of incorporating symbolic prior knowledge on the problem at hand.

The critical analyses of some of the book chapters are expected to serve as the basis for the proposal of fundamental research guidelines for the next few years. The exploration of the links with brain sciences, the integration with knowledge-based models, and broadly speaking, the search for more unified theories of learning are foreseen as promising research directions. Although interesting and effective in some cases, the hybrid structure of some of the proposed models seems to be just a straightforward way of bridging purely symbolic and sub-symbolic models. Unfortunately, in addition to obvious criticisms of biological plausibility, when using these models many challenging and important engineering tasks have not been solved satisfactorily yet.

The book is organized as follows:

Chapter 1, by Marco Gori, provides a unified framework for problem solving the continuum setting of computation which is based on the notion of action, a sort of continuous algorithm running on an abstract machine, referred to as the deterministic terminal attractor machine (DTAM), somehow related to discrete computational counterparts. The proposed framework represents a first step towards the construction of solid computational foundations to neural networks learning algorithms and problem solving using Hopfield networks.

Chapter 2, by Hava Siegelmann, aims to incorporate concepts of mathematical analysis into complexity theory, thus enlarging its scope to encompass continuous algorithms defined by differential equations. The purpose of the analysis is that of providing insights for the foundation of an algorithmic and complexity analysis of flows that converges to fixed points.

Chaper 3, by Jiří Šíma, proposes a unified approach for the analysis of computational aspects of symmetric Hopfield nets which is based on the concept of energy source. Interestingly enough, some computational classes are introduced which are somehow related to the discrete counterpart.

Chapter 4, by Marcello Pelillo, presents a continuous optimization frameworks for solving various combinatorial problems. The approach is based on an equivalent maximum clique formulation and is centered around a fundamental result provided by Motzin and Straus in the mid-1960s.

Chapter 5, by Simon Haykin, discusses the impact of neural computation in signal processing and communications. Special attention is placed on adaptive filtering algorithms and to the contribution of different neural networks architectures to improve the traditional linear models.

Chapter 6, by Joachim Buhmann, discusses data clustering by proposing a twofold formulation. The traditional density estimation techniques are proposed in conjunction with combinatorial optimization depending on the data representation as vectors, proximity relations or histograms.

Chapter 7, by Michel Verleysen, covers the problem of learning high-dimensional data. It is pointed out that many intuitions gained for two or three dimensional problems are misleading for high dimensional data. In particular, some neural networks design techniques are proposed to face the "curse of dimensionality".'

Chapter 8, by Nathan Intrator, basically deals with the same problem of learning high-dimensional data. A survey of the existing methods is given and it is shown that multiple networks can reduce the over all error of a system by simple ensamble averaging.

Chapter 9, by Tamás Roska, discusses the cellular neural networks paradigm with emphasis on architectural issues and on the implementation by massively parallel analog array processors. A Universal Machine is introduced which is based on a stored programmable spatial–temporal computer. It is pointed out that recent silicon implementations, as a focal plane array visual microprocessor show an unprecedented supercomputer speed on a single chip (a few TeraOPS).

Chapter 10, by Liviu Goras, deals also with cellular neural networks, but the emphasis is on theoretical issues and, particularly, on pattern formation. A detailed description of the Turing pattern formation mechanism is given for CNN, and the theory is also extended to other architectures based on similar or different cells and various types of couplings.

Chapter 11, by Mirko Novák, addresses the problem of the reliability of interactions in complicated artificial systems involving the combination of artificial- and human-based functional blocks. Such composed systems are typical for many real-world applications.

Finally, Chapter 12, by Vladmir Golovko, examines different approaches to the design of neural network systems and shows applications for chaotic time series processing and intelligent system for control of a mobile robot.

Sergey Ablameyko, Marco Gori, Liviu Goras, and Vincenzo Piuri

Contents

Preface   v

Chapter 1. Continuous Problem Solving and Computational Suspiciousness,
Marco Gori   1

Chapter 2. The Complexity of Computing with Continuous Time Devices,
Asa Ben-Hur, Hava Siegelmann and Shmuel Fishman   23

Chapter 3. Energy-Based Computation with Symmetric Hopfield Nets,
Jiří Šíma   45

Chapter 4. Computational Complexity and the Elusiveness of Global Optima,
Marcello Pelillo   71

Chapter 5. Impact of Neural Networks on Signal Processing and Communications,
Simon Haykin   95

Chapter 6. From Clustering Data to Traveling as a Salesman: Empirical Risk
Approximation as a Learning Theory, *Joachim M. Buhmann*   115

Chapter 7. Learning High-dimensional Data,
Michel Verleysen   141

Chapter 8. The Curse of Dimensionality and the Blessing of Multiply Hybrid
Networks, *Nathan Intrator*   163

Chapter 9. A Kind of Neural Computing Goes Practical: TeraOPS, Stored
Programmable, Analog-and-Logic Visual Microprocessors – a Review,
Tamás Roska   177

Chapter 10. On Pattern Formation in Cellular Neural Networks,
Liviu Goras   185

Chapter 11. Reliability of Man-System Interaction and Theory of Neural Networks
Operations, *Mirko Novák and Zdeněk Votruba*   207

Chapter 12. From Neural Networks to Intelligent Systems: Selected Aspects of
Training, Application and Evolution, *Vladimir Golovko*   219

Author Index   245

Limitations and Future Trends in Neural Computation
S. Ablameyko et al. (Eds.)
IOS Press, 2003

Continuous Problem Solving and Computational Suspiciousness

Marco Gori
Dipartimento di Ingegneria dell'Informazione

Abstract

Continuous optimization seems to be the ubiquitous formulation of an impressive number of different problems in science and engineering. In this chapter, a unified framework for problem solving is proposed in the continuum setting which is based on the notion of *action*, a sort of continuous algorithm running on an abstract machine, referred to as the deterministic terminal attractor machine (DTAM), somehow related to discrete computational counterparts.

A number of examples are given which illustrate how continuous algorithms can be devised. The proposed general computational scheme incorporates most interesting supervised and unsupervised learning schemes in artificial neural networks as well as the problem solving approach based on Hopfield networks. Finally, a general discussion on computational complexity issues indicates some intriguing links between the presence of local minima in the error surface of the energy function and the complexity of the solution.

1   Introduction

Nature seems to obey harmoniously to elegant optimization laws that like Fermat's minimum time principle in optics and least action in mechanics rely on the minimization of proper functions. One might wonder whether this ubiquitous formulation as continuous optimization is man's trend to unify or is instead the inherent solution of most natural problems. No matter what the true answer is, there is no doubt that a similar elegance and generality can also be gained for the solution of an impressive number of different problems, not necessarily related to natural phenomena. In spite of the generality of optimization-based approaches, however, it seems that not all problems are well-suited for solutions based on continuous optimization.

In the last fifteen years, the renewal of interest in neural networks, that rely hardly on continuous optimization, witnesses the attention that the scientific community has been paying on problem solving by continuous optimization. By and large, continuous optimization is regarded as the natural framework for neural computation, which has been challenging traditional symbolic approaches in many interesting real-world problems. One of the common belief that seems to drive the research in that field is that neural networks give rise to a general problem solving methodology that is likely to be applied successfully to many different cases. Optimization-based problem solving has also been applied successfully to a number of other fields like numerical analysis, computational geometry, and information retrieval.

The solution of a given problem in the framework of continuous optimization takes place by constructing a function that, once optimized, makes it possible to determine the solution. Basically, determining such function seems to be related to the creative process of designing algorithms in the classic discrete setting of computation.

The elegance and generality of solutions based on continuous optimization, however, seems to represent also the main source of troubles that typically arise when approaching *complex* problems. The process of function optimization can either be hard because of the inherent complexity of the problem at hand or because of the way the problem is framed in the context of optimization. A wrong choice of the numerical algorithm may also affect the computational complexity significantly. The complexity of the optimization can be due to a *spurious* formulation of the problem, but can have also a *structural* nature, in the sense that the complexity can be inherently associated with the problem at hand. In the last case the problem gives rise to a sort of *suspiciousness* concerning the actual possibility to discover its solution under reasonable computational constraints. Whereas most practitioners use to accept without reluctance the flavor of suspiciousness arising from the approach and use to be proud of their eventual experimental achievements, most theoreticians are instead quite skeptical on problem solving by continuous optimization. As a matter of fact, the success of these methods is related to the problem at hand and, therefore, one can expect an excellent performance for a class of problems, whereas can raise serious suspects about the solution of others. To the best of our knowledge, however, so far, this practical evidence has no general theoretical explanation, and there is no satisfactory theoretical support to this intuitive concept of suspiciousness.

This chapter proposes a general framework for problem solving using continuous optimization of an energy function and gives some theoretical foundations on the intuitive notion of suspiciousness by relating it to the theory of computational complexity. The concept of *action* is introduced as a sort of continuous algorithm running on an abstract machine, referred to as the deterministic terminal attractor machine (DTAM), which performs a terminal attractor gradient descent on the energy. This machine is conceived for running actions. For any instance of a given problem, the corresponding action runs on the DTAM and is guaranteed to yield a solution whenever the energy is local minima free, regardless of the problem dimension. In this case there is no need to initialize the DTAM. Problems with associated a local minima free energy with a polynomially bounded number of parameters in the problem dimension are referred to as *unimodal problems*. For complex problems one may require a *guessing module* for an appropriate initialization of the gradient descent. The corresponding machine is referred to as the non-deterministic terminal attractor machine (NDTAM), which suggests the introduction of non-deterministic unimodal problems. A fundamental consequence of the proposed approach is that actions for unimodal problems can be conceived which give rise to optimal algorithms in the problem dimension. Examples to the problem of solving linear systems and to the problem of linear separation in computational geometry are presented, along with the corresponding complexity evaluation.

1.1 Related research

Continuous problem solving is a fundamental issue at the cross-road of many disciplines. The idea of conceiving the process of computation as the evolution of the state of a dynamical system has been explored with different approaches by many researchers (see e.g. [1, 2]). The computation with real numbers has an old history originated with Turing's seminal paper [3]. Register machines [4] and RAM (real random access machines) [5] were conceived for integers, but with an algebraic approach which makes them good candidates for an extension to real values (see e.g. the real RAM proposed in [6].

Specific contributions to the area of continuous problem solving can be properly grouped depending on whether the continuous computational scheme concerns the solution of a specific problem or is instead the proposal for a general computational model for a class of problems.

Continuous optimization has been used successfully for linear and non-linear systems of equations [7], sorting [8], and for many problems in the area of computational geometry [6].

Interestingly enough, continuous approaches have been devised also for approaching simple and complex optimization problems like N-Queens [9] and the traveling salesman [10, 11, 12].

A general framework for understanding continuous computational models has been recently proposed by Blum, Chucker, Shub, and Smale [13]. Their theory, however, is based on framing problems in the context of non-linear equations more than on continuous function optimization. On the other hand, in-depth computational analyzes aimed at understanding the actual breakthrough of neural computation were stimulated by Marvin Minsky in the epilogue of the expanded edition of seminal book Perceptrons [14].

One of the closest related approach is the one proposed by Hava Siegelmann in Chapter 2, where many motivations and basic ideas are very related. Some of the ideas presented in this chapter are also discussed in [15], where the notion of problem reduction is also introduced. For previous work on the computational capabilities of continuous-time systems see the surveys by Cris Moore [16] and by Pekka Orponen [17]. This chapter presents a step into the direction of creating a general framework for a complexity theory of continuous-time systems as outlined in [17].

2   Continuous problem solving

In computer science, the attention is commonly focused on decision problems. One important reason for considering decision problems is that they have the concept of formal language as a very suitable counterpart, and the theory of complexity can nicely be grounded in that framework. In science and engineering, many problems which involve naturally real numbers, however, can be given a more appropriate formulation.

2.1   Problems and actions

Let us begin with the definition of a problem. One needs to define the *instance space* $D_\pi^n \subseteq I\!R^n$ and the corresponding closure $\mathcal{D}_\pi^\star \doteq \lim_{n\to\infty} \mathcal{D}_\pi^n \doteq \bigoplus_{i\geq 0} D_\pi^n$ which can be regarded as a real counterpart of Σ^* for finite alphabets Σ. In the special interesting case in which $\forall n,\ D_\pi^n = I\!R^n$, we consider problem instances in $I\!R^\infty := \bigoplus_{i\geq 0} I\!R^i$. Likewise, forall $n \in I\!N$ we define $\mathcal{T}_\pi^n := \bigoplus_{i\geq 0} T_\pi^n\ (T_\pi^n \subseteq I\!R^n)$ as the set of admissible problem solutions.

Definition 2.1 *A* PROBLEM Π *is a relation in* $I\!\!R^\infty \times I\!\!R^\infty$. SOLVING A PROBLEM *means that on input* $\boldsymbol{d} \in I\!\!R^n$, *for some* $n \in I\!\!N$, *a vector* $\boldsymbol{y} \in I\!\!R^k$, *for some* $k \in I\!\!N$, *is computed such that* $\pi \doteq (\boldsymbol{d}, \boldsymbol{y}) \in \Pi$. *Here, we require the output dimension* k *be polynomially related to* n, *i.e. there exists a polynomial* p *such that* $k = p(n)$ *for all* $n \in I\!\!N$. *We will frequently write* $\Pi(\boldsymbol{d})$ *to denote a(!) solution* $\boldsymbol{y}$ *such that* $(\boldsymbol{d}, \boldsymbol{y}) \in \Pi$, *even though* Π *might not be a function.*

It is worth mentioning that since $D_\pi^n \subseteq I\!\!R^n$, a problem Π might not be defined for all the element in $I\!\!R^\infty$; that is for some $\boldsymbol{d} \in I\!\!R^\infty$ one could simply construct the don't care pair $(\boldsymbol{d}, -)$ and make the assumption that $(\boldsymbol{d}, -) \notin \Pi$. In the case the relation Π is a function $\Pi : \mathcal{D}_\pi^\star \subseteq I\!\!R^\infty \to I\!\!R^\infty$ than only one solution $\Pi(d)$ exists for the given instance $\boldsymbol{d}$. Of course, for a given $\boldsymbol{d} \in \mathcal{D}_\pi^\star$ one might not be able to find any solution $\boldsymbol{y}$; hence the solution space might be augmented with the `null` element so as $(\boldsymbol{d}, \texttt{null}) \in \Pi$.

Problem 2.1 - Π_{stab}
Let $\dot{\boldsymbol{x}} = \boldsymbol{F}(\boldsymbol{x}(t))$ *be a dynamical system in which* $\boldsymbol{F}$ *is a rational function and consider the problem of finding an asymptotically stable equilibrium point. This can be formalized in different ways. One possibility is to consider* $\boldsymbol{F}$ *as the first component of a problem* Π *and to look for a* $\boldsymbol{y}$ *which is an equilibrium point of* $\boldsymbol{F}$. *Thus*

$$\Pi_{stab} = \{(\boldsymbol{F}, \boldsymbol{y}) \in I\!\!R^\infty \times I\!\!R^\infty \mid y \text{ is an asymptotically stable equilibrium of } \dot{\boldsymbol{x}} = \boldsymbol{F}(\boldsymbol{x}(t))\} \ .$$

In the above definition $\boldsymbol{F}$ *is supposed to be representable in a certain way by a point in* $I\!\!R^\infty$, *which can easily be done under the assumption that* $\boldsymbol{F}$ *is a rational function. Note that* Π_{frac} *is not a function, since* $\boldsymbol{F} \in I\!\!R^\infty$ *can easily be found which admits multiple asymptotically stable equilibrium points.*

Problem 2.2 - Π_{lin}
We want to find the solution of the linear system

$$\boldsymbol{Aw} = \boldsymbol{b}, \tag{1}$$

where $\boldsymbol{A} \in I\!\!R^{n,n}$, *and* $\boldsymbol{w}, \boldsymbol{b} \in I\!\!R^n$, *under the assumption* $\det \boldsymbol{A} \neq 0$.
For any $n \in I\!\!N$, *let* $\boldsymbol{A}_e \doteq [\boldsymbol{A}, \boldsymbol{b}] \in I\!\!R^{n,n+1}$ *be and consider the problem*

$$\Pi_{lin} = \{(\boldsymbol{A}_e, \boldsymbol{y}) \in I\!\!R^\infty \times I\!\!R^\infty \mid \boldsymbol{y} = \boldsymbol{A}^{-1}\boldsymbol{b}\}$$

Since there exists only one solution for (1), Π_{lin} *is a function. If* $\det \boldsymbol{A} = 0$ *then* Π *can be relation since a linear subspace of solutions might be admissible. However, if* $rank \boldsymbol{A} \neq rank \boldsymbol{A}_e$ *then* Π *does not admit solution, that is* $(\boldsymbol{A}_e, \texttt{null}) \in \Pi$.

The solution of a problem might not necessarily require the full knowledge of the instances. In general, one can use oracle operators to attach the INFORMATION [18] $\boldsymbol{d}_{inf} \doteq \mathcal{I}(\boldsymbol{d}) = [L_1(\boldsymbol{d}), L_2(\boldsymbol{d}), \ldots, L_k(\boldsymbol{d})]$ to each instance $\boldsymbol{d}$ of a given problem Π. The interesting aspect of dealing with information-based problem representations is that $k << n$ might hold in many interesting problems and, therefore, one can look for the solution by dealing with $\boldsymbol{d}_{inf}$ instead of $\boldsymbol{d}$.

For a given problem Π one can associate a corresponding infinite family of energy functions $\{E_n\}_{n \in I\!\!N}$. Here, every E_n is a function depending on two blocks $\boldsymbol{d}$ and $\boldsymbol{w}$ of variables. The block $\boldsymbol{w} \in \Omega_n \subseteq I\!\!R^m$ will be related to a solution $\boldsymbol{y}$ of Π for input $\boldsymbol{d}$.

Definition 2.2 ENERGIES: *For any set A we begin introducing the modifier $\diamond$: $\mid \diamond A := A$ or $\diamond A := \emptyset$. Moreover, given any Π, throughout this paper, the operator $\triangleright$ will be used to denote a sampled version of countable sets. For example given Π, we denote by $\triangleright\Pi$ any finite subset of Π.*

1. *Given any instance $\pi \doteq (\boldsymbol{d}, \Pi(\boldsymbol{d})) \in \Pi$, an INSTANCE ENERGY is any $\boldsymbol{C}^1$ function $e_n : (D_\pi^n \subseteq I\!\!R^n) \times (\diamond I\!\!R) \times (\Omega_n \subseteq I\!\!R^m) \to I\!\!R : (\boldsymbol{d}, \diamond\boldsymbol{y}, \boldsymbol{w}) \to e_n(\boldsymbol{d}, \diamond\boldsymbol{y}, \boldsymbol{w})$, being $m = q(n)$. In the case the modifier $\diamond$ returns the empty set than the instance energy simply outputs a real value for any pair $(\boldsymbol{d}, \boldsymbol{w}) \in D_\pi^n \times \Omega_n$.*

2. *A LEARNING ENERGY for $\Pi \subset I\!\!R^\infty \times I\!\!R^\infty$ is any $\boldsymbol{C}^1$ additive function [1]*
$$E_n : 2^{\triangleright(D_\pi^n \times (\diamond R))} \times \Omega_n \to I\!\!R. \; If \diamond I\!\!R = I\!\!R \; then \; E_n = \sum_{\pi \in \triangleright\Pi} e_n(\pi).$$

3. *$\mathcal{E} := \{E_n\}_{n \in I\!\!N}$ is called the ENERGY FAMILY associated with Π. The family can either be created by learning or instance energies.*

Likewise we can define the *network functions* as follows

Definition 2.3 NETWORK FUNCTIONS:

1. *For any instance $\pi \doteq (\boldsymbol{d}, \Pi(\boldsymbol{d})) \in \Pi$ we define the corresponding NETWORK FUNCTION $N_n : (D_\pi^n \subseteq I\!\!R^n) \times (\Omega_n \subseteq I\!\!R^m) \to I\!\!R : (\boldsymbol{d}, \boldsymbol{w}) \to N_n(\boldsymbol{d}, \boldsymbol{w})$, being $m = q(n)$.*

2. *$\mathcal{N} := \{N_n\}_{n \in I\!\!N}$ is called the NETWORK FUNCTION FAMILY associated with Π*

Definition 2.4 ACTIONS: *Given any $\Pi \subset I\!\!R^\infty \times I\!\!R^\infty$, let P_d be the probability distribution of the problem instances and consider a sampling[2] $\triangleright\Pi$ $\mid$ $\mid \triangleright \Pi\mid \leq s(n)$, being $s(n)$ a polynomial. A pair $\mathcal{C}_a(\Pi) \doteq \{\mathcal{E}(\Pi), \mathcal{N}(\Pi)\}$ is called a LEARNING ACTION [3] for Π if $\forall n, \epsilon_p^\star(n) > 0, \triangleright\Pi, \delta > 0, \; \exists \epsilon_e(n) > 0 \mid$*
$\forall \boldsymbol{w} \mid \; |E_n(\triangleright\Pi, \boldsymbol{w}) - min_{\boldsymbol{w} \in \Omega_n} E_n(\triangleright\Pi, \boldsymbol{w})| < \epsilon_e(n):$

$$\mathcal{P}_{r \; \triangleright\Pi \in EX(\Pi)} \left(\int_{\boldsymbol{d} \in D_\pi^n} \| \Pi(\boldsymbol{d}) - N_n(\boldsymbol{d}, \boldsymbol{w}) \| \; P_d(\boldsymbol{d}) \; d\boldsymbol{d} \; < \epsilon_p^\star(n) \right) \; > \; 1 - \delta \qquad (2)$$

The function $q : I\!\!N \to I\!\!N : n \to m = q(n)$ will also be referred to as the DIMENSION OF THE ACTION.

According to this definition, learning actions yields ONE PROBABLY APPROXIMATELY COR-RECT SOLUTION, following a framework which is related to PAC learning.

---

[1] Given any finite set $\mathcal{X}$, we denote by $2^\mathcal{X}$ the power set of $\mathcal{X}$.

[2] When setting Π in the probabilistic framework, it turns out to be useful to regard problems as concepts in machine learning.

[3] The name was inspired from the concept of *action* in mechanics while reading occasionally Feynman's prologue on the principle of minimum action (see The Feynman Lectures of Physics[19], 1963): *When I was in high school, my physics teacher - whose name was Mr. Bader - called me down one day after physics class and said, "You look bored; I want to tell you something interesting". Then he told me something which I found absolutely fascinating. Everytime the subject comes up, I work on it... The subject is this - the principle of least action.*

Definition 2.5 INSTANCE ACTIONS*: Given any problem Π, an important case is that in which the energy can be constructed by trivial sampling, that is $\triangleright\Pi \mid \; \mid \triangleright \Pi\mid = 1$ and the precision requirement (2) holds regardless of the chosen sampling of Π. In addition if $\forall n \diamond T_\pi^n \equiv \emptyset$ then the energy reduces to a function $E_n : D_n \times \Omega_n \to \mathbb{R}$ which yields real values for any pair $(\boldsymbol{d}, \boldsymbol{w})$. All actions for which one can provide energies with the previous property are called* INSTANCE ACTIONS.

For action-feasible problems the precision requirement (2) can be rewritten by stating that

$$\forall n, \epsilon_p(n) > 0, \boldsymbol{d} \in D_\pi^n, \; \exists \epsilon_e(n) > 0 \mid$$
$$\forall \boldsymbol{w} \mid \; |E_n(\boldsymbol{d}, \boldsymbol{w}) - min_{\boldsymbol{w} \in \Omega_n} E_n(\boldsymbol{d}_n, \boldsymbol{w})| < \epsilon_e(n) : \| \Pi(\boldsymbol{d}_n) - N_n(\boldsymbol{d}_n, \boldsymbol{w}) \| < \epsilon_p(n).$$

Note that in this case we focus attention on single instances by imposing an uniform error bound, that is errors are not tolerated on single instance which exceeds a given threshold.

Remark 2.1 *Note that actions can only provide* ONE SOLUTION *for a given problem Π, thus failing the task of discovering all solutions in the case in which Π is a relation.*

If the previous condition can be guaranteed for $\epsilon_p(n) \equiv 0$ then we say that the action $C_a(\Pi)$ yields an EXACT SOLUTION[4] for Π.

The degree of approximation of the given problem $\epsilon_p(n)$ is a very important concern. The admissible error $\epsilon_p(n)$ is generally related to the problem dimension.

Definition 2.6 *Let $\Pi \in \mathbb{R}^\infty \times \mathbb{R}^\infty$ be. We say that Π* CAN BE GIVEN A SOLUTION WITH APPROXIMATION *$\mathcal{T}(h(n))$, and denote this fact by $\Pi \in \mathcal{T}(h(n))$, provided that there exists $\epsilon_p > 0$, and a polynomial $h(n)$ such that $\epsilon_p(n) \leq \epsilon_p/h(n)$. In particular we say that Π is a* UNIFORM PROBLEM, *and use the notation $(\mathcal{T}(1))$, provided that we can find an action $C_a(\Pi)$ such that an approximate solution can be found with $h(n) \equiv 1$.*

Of course, the strongest constraint is that which requires the exact solution. Note that, whereas to establish that $\Pi \in \mathcal{T}(h(n))$ is generally quite an easy task, finding the *lower bound* is more involved, since this requires to exhibit an action giving rise to the lower $h(n)$ value for which $C_a(\Pi)$ makes it possible to solve Π exactly or with a given degree of approximation given by the pair $(\hat{\epsilon}_p, h_p(n))$. We denote the case in which the lower bound is found by $\Pi \in \mathcal{T}_\Theta(h(n))$. Note that in the case in which we require an exact solution we use conventionally the notation $\mathcal{T}(\infty)$.

Remark 2.2 *The analogy with action in mechanics and other minimum principles in physics is very intriguing. In physics the minimization of the action yields the law of the motion of a given particle. In our framework, the time becomes the general instance $\boldsymbol{d} \in \mathcal{D}_\pi^\star$ and the "temporal law" is the problem solution expressed by means of the network function $N_n(\boldsymbol{d}_n, \boldsymbol{w})$.*

---

[4]On the opposite, the default condition considered in this paper is the one in which one is interested in an APPROXIMATE SOLUTION for Π.

2.2 Computational models for $\mathcal{C}_a(\Pi)$

As will be clear in the remainder of the paper, it turns out to be useful to impose restrictions either on the class of energy functions or on the class of network functions.

Definition 2.7 *Given an action $\mathcal{C}_a(\Pi)$ for $\Pi \in I\!\!R^\infty \times I\!\!R^\infty$ we say that functions E and N are* ADMISSIBLE OVER THE SET OF OPERATORS $\mathcal{O}$ *provided that, for all problem dimensions n, both functions can be represented by means of directed acyclic graph expressions, denoted $\mathcal{G}^n_E$ and $\mathcal{G}^n_N$, respectively. The leaves are either instances $\boldsymbol{d}_n \in D^n_\pi$ or parameters $\boldsymbol{w} \in \Omega_n$, whereas the nodes are operators in $\mathcal{O}$.*

When forcing such restriction, functions E_n and N_n can be fully represented by the corresponding graphs $\mathcal{G}^n_E$ and $\mathcal{G}^n_N$, respectively. An important example of operators are those considered in real RAM machines [6]. Throughout this paper we rely on the assumption that the cost of the computation of functions like E_n and N_n is independent of the operators in $\mathcal{O}$, but simply on the size of graphs $\mathcal{G}_E$, $\mathcal{G}_N$. Let m_E and m_N be the size required to store graphs $\mathcal{G}^n_E$ and $\mathcal{G}^n_N$. Note that in general $m_E \neq q(n)$ and $m_N \neq q(m)$, since the same parameters can be shared on several edges [5]. The dependence on the problem dimension is expressed by functions $n_E = \gamma_E(n)$ and $n_N = \gamma_N(n)$. The $\{m_E$ and $m_N\}$ will be referred to as the CIRCUIT COMPLEXITY of the energy and network functions, respectively. This notion is related to that used for Boolean functions represented by directed acyclic graphs [20]. More closer thoughts about circuit complexity for real-valued functions are given in [21]. A special interesting case is the one in which $\gamma_E(\cdot):\ m = \gamma_N(n)$ are polynomials.

2.3 Topics in action design

Actions are a counterpart of algorithms in the continuous setting of computation. In this section we look into the structure of actions and emphasize their most relevant features. We also give some design guidelines and provide corresponding examples to highlight the essence of the creative process behind the construction of actions.

2.3.1 Trivial actions

Let $\Pi \in I\!\!R^\infty \times I\!\!R^\infty$ and consider any extracted function [6] $I\!\!R^\infty \to I\!\!R^\infty : \boldsymbol{d} \to \Pi(\boldsymbol{d})$ There always exists at least the TRIVIAL INSTANCE ACTION $\mathcal{C}^t_a(\Pi) \doteq \{\mathcal{E}^t(\Pi), \mathcal{N}^t(\Pi)\}$ for Π which yields an approximate solution over all the instances of Π, where $\forall n \in I\!\!N$:

$$
\begin{aligned}
m &= q(n) = n \\
E^t_n(\boldsymbol{d}, \boldsymbol{w}) &= \alpha \cdot \parallel \boldsymbol{M}\,(\boldsymbol{w} - \Pi(\boldsymbol{d})) \parallel^2 \\
N^t_n(\boldsymbol{d}, \boldsymbol{w}) &= \boldsymbol{w}
\end{aligned}
$$

where $\boldsymbol{M}$ is any non-singular matrix and $\alpha := 1/\parallel \boldsymbol{M} \cdot \Pi(\boldsymbol{d}) \parallel^2$. Let $\epsilon_p(n)$ be the precision required for any instance and consider the energy stopping criterion $\alpha \cdot \parallel \boldsymbol{M}(\boldsymbol{w} - \Pi(\boldsymbol{d})) \parallel^2 < \epsilon_e$. We have

---

[5] Note that there are cases in which $m_C = m$. This holds in those cases in which a different parameter is associated with each arc of the graph (see e.g. Problem 2.2).

[6] For the sake of simplicy, we use the same notation for the relation Π and for the extracted function.

$$\| \, M^{-1} \, \| \cdot \| \, M(w - \Pi(d)) \, \| \; < \; \| \, M^{-1} \, \| \cdot \sqrt{\frac{\epsilon_e}{\alpha}}$$

which yields

$$\| \, w - \Pi(d) \, \| \; < \; \| \, M^{-1} \, \| \sqrt{\frac{\epsilon_e}{\alpha}}$$

Hence, if we set set

$$\epsilon_e \leq \left(\frac{\epsilon_p}{\| \, M^{-1} \, \| \cdot \| \, M \cdot \Pi(d) \, \|} \right)^2 \tag{3}$$

we conclude that $\mathcal{C}_a^t(\Pi)$ is an action for Π.

Remark 2.3 *Note that this trivial energy may not be admissible over the chosen set of operator $\mathcal{O}$. One straightforward solution is to use for the energy a set of operators which includes Π's.*

$\mathcal{C}_a^t$ is trivial in the sense that it requires one to be able to express $\Pi(d)$ with a given set of operators. However, it may still turn out to be useful, since the solution of the problem is turned to a different setting[7].

As an example consider Problem 2.2 concerning the solution of linear systems and set $M := A$. We immediately conclude that $\mathcal{C}_a^t(\Pi_{lin})$ is an action for Π_{lin}. In this case $d := A_c$ and $\Pi(A_c) = A^{-1}b$ and the energy stopping criterion requires setting

$$\epsilon_e \leq \left(\frac{\epsilon_p}{\| \, A^{-1} \, \| \cdot \| \, b \, \|} \right)^2 \tag{4}$$

Note that given action yields the problem solution also in presence of singular matrixes A; however, only one admissible solution is provided.

There are cases in which a trivial action can be given also for exact solutions

Problem 2.3 Π^{hash}: *Let us consider the problem of constructing a* PERFECT HASH FUNC-TION *according to Cichelli's scheme [22]:*

$$\begin{aligned}
h(key) = \; &(code \; of \; the \; key's \; first \; character) + \\
&(code \; of \; the \; key's \; last \; character) + \\
&(key \; length).
\end{aligned} \tag{5}$$

---

[7]In the following, it will be proven that the formalization of linear systems in the framework of actions turns out to be useful for well-conditioned equations.

This function can be given a simple algebraic representation if we represent any key by a permutation matrix which indicated which character is located in a given position. For instance, if we use the characters $\{A, B, C, D\}$ the key ACD is represented by

$$ACD \equiv \begin{pmatrix} 1\ 0\ 0 \\ 0\ 0\ 0 \\ 0\ 1\ 0 \\ 0\ 0\ 1 \end{pmatrix}$$

Let $\boldsymbol{P}_\sigma$ be any permutation matrix having s rows (number of characters) and p columns (maximum key's length) representing key σ. Consider a p-dimensional integer weight vector $\boldsymbol{\gamma} \in I\!N^p$ and the vector of real codes $\boldsymbol{w} \in I\!R^s$. The address where key σ is mapped to is $\boldsymbol{y}_\sigma = \boldsymbol{\gamma}' \boldsymbol{P}'_\sigma \boldsymbol{w}$. Let $\boldsymbol{\omega}_\sigma \doteq \boldsymbol{P}_\sigma \boldsymbol{\gamma}$ and $\boldsymbol{\Omega}_\Gamma \doteq [\boldsymbol{\omega}'_1, \ldots, \boldsymbol{\omega}'_m]$ be. The problem of mapping n keys to the n-dimensional address vector $\boldsymbol{y}$ is converted to finding a real-valued vector code $\boldsymbol{w}$ which satisfies $\boldsymbol{y} = \boldsymbol{\Omega}_\Gamma \boldsymbol{w}$.

Let $\psi \in I\!R$ be such that $\psi \geq p\gamma_{max}$, being $\gamma_{max} = \max_i \gamma_i$ and denote by $[\cdot] : I\!R \to I\!N$ the roundoff operator. $\forall n \in I\!N$, let us consider the following family of functions $\mathcal{C}_a(\Pi_{hash}) \doteq \{\mathcal{E}(\Pi_{hash}), \mathcal{N}(\Pi_{hash})\}$

$$
\begin{aligned}
E_n(\boldsymbol{d}, \boldsymbol{w}) &= \parallel \boldsymbol{y} - \boldsymbol{\Omega}_\Gamma \boldsymbol{w} \parallel^2 \\
N_n(\boldsymbol{d}, \boldsymbol{w}) &= [\psi^{-1} \boldsymbol{\Omega}_\Gamma [\psi\ \boldsymbol{w}]]
\end{aligned}
$$

Proposition 2.1 $\mathcal{C}_a(\Pi_{hash})$ *is an instance action which yields exact solutions for* Π_{hash}

Proof: Trivial consequence from [23]. $\square$

2.3.2   Actions for continuous optimization

Actions for optimization in unconstrained domains can be constructed straightforwardly. When the domain $\Omega \subset I\!R^m$ (in a strict sense) one can always reduce to the case of unconstrained optimization. The following is a noticeable example.

Problem 2.4 LPO: LINEAR PROGRAMMING OPTIMIZATION *Given* $\boldsymbol{c} \in I\!R^n - \{\boldsymbol{0}\}$, *an* $n \times$ *p real matrix* $\boldsymbol{A}$, *and a real vector* $\boldsymbol{b} \in I\!R^p$ *consider the Linear Programming Optimization problem*

$$minimize\ \ \boldsymbol{c} \cdot \boldsymbol{w}$$
$$subject\ to\ \ \boldsymbol{Aw} \geq \boldsymbol{b}.$$

This is a problem in the sense of Definition 2.1, that is

$$\Pi_{lpo} \doteq \{((\boldsymbol{A}, \boldsymbol{b}, \boldsymbol{c}), \boldsymbol{w}^\star) \mid \forall \boldsymbol{w} \mid \boldsymbol{Aw} \geq \boldsymbol{b} : \boldsymbol{c}(\boldsymbol{w}^\star - \boldsymbol{w}) \geq 0\}$$

Let us denote $Int \doteq \{\boldsymbol{x} \in I\!R^n \mid \boldsymbol{aw} > \boldsymbol{b}\}$. Let us also assume that Int is bounded and non-empty. Π_{lpq} can be solved by converting the constrained optimization using the

BARRIER METHOD. $\forall n \in I\!N$, $\boldsymbol{w} \in Int$, let us consider the following family of functions $\mathcal{C}_a(\Pi_{lpo}) \doteq \{\mathcal{E}(\Pi_{lpo}), \mathcal{N}(\Pi_{lpo})\}$ for LPO

$$E_n(\boldsymbol{d}, \boldsymbol{w}) = \boldsymbol{c} \cdot \boldsymbol{w} - t \cdot \sum_{i=1}^{p} \ln(\boldsymbol{A}_i \boldsymbol{w} - \boldsymbol{b}_i) \tag{6}$$

$$N_n(\boldsymbol{d}, \boldsymbol{w}) = \boldsymbol{w} \tag{7}$$

where $\boldsymbol{A}_i$ are the rows of $\boldsymbol{A}$. We know that $\forall t > 0$ the function h_t is strictly convex on Int and, therefore, it has a unique minimum which we denote by ζ_t

Proposition 2.2 $\mathcal{C}_a(\Pi_{lpo})$ *is a* INSTANCE ACTION *for LPO.*

Proof: This yields as a direct consequence of

$$\boldsymbol{c} \cdot (\zeta_t - \boldsymbol{w}^\star) \leq tp$$

(see [13] (p. 279)). being $(\boldsymbol{d}, \boldsymbol{w}^\star) \in \Pi_{lpo}$. $\forall \epsilon_p > 0$, it suffices to set $\epsilon_e := \epsilon_p$ and $t := \epsilon_p/p$.
$\square$

Note that $\mathcal{C}_a(\Pi_{lpo})$ is an non-zero minimum action, that is $\min_{\boldsymbol{w}}(\boldsymbol{cw})$ is unknown. However, we know that $\forall i : \ \boldsymbol{A}_i \boldsymbol{w} - \boldsymbol{b}_i \to 0$, which turns out to be very useful to discover the minimum. The idea shown for LPO can be extended to general constrained optimization in the case in which the minimum is on the frontier.

Problem 2.5 CONSTRAINT OPTIMIZATION ON THE FRONTIER   *Given* $\boldsymbol{w} \in I\!R^n$, *consider the non-linear constraint optimization problem*

$$minimize \ \ \phi(\boldsymbol{w})$$
$$subject \ to \ \ \boldsymbol{\psi}(\boldsymbol{w}) \geq \boldsymbol{0}; \ \ \ \boldsymbol{\psi}(\boldsymbol{w}) \in I\!R^p$$

in which any solution $\boldsymbol{w}^\star \ | \ \boldsymbol{\psi}(\boldsymbol{w}^\star) = \boldsymbol{0}$. *This is an obvious extension of LPO.*

Like for LPO, let us consider the following family of functions $\mathcal{C}_a(\Pi_{frn}) \doteq \{\mathcal{E}(\Pi_{frn}), \mathcal{N}(\Pi_{frn})\}$.

$$E_n(\boldsymbol{d}, \boldsymbol{w}) = \phi(\boldsymbol{w}) - t \cdot \sum_{i=1}^{p} \ln\psi_i(\boldsymbol{w}) \tag{8}$$

$$N_n(\boldsymbol{d}, \boldsymbol{w}) = \boldsymbol{w} \tag{9}$$

Proposition 2.3 $\mathcal{C}_a(\Pi_{frn})$ *is a* INSTANCE ACTION *for FRN.*

2.3.3   Universal actions

Let $\Pi \in I\!R^\infty \times I\!R^\infty$ be and consider any extracted function $I\!R^\infty \to I\!R^\infty : \boldsymbol{d} \to \Pi(\boldsymbol{d})$. The following property states the possibility of constructing a learning action only using an appropriate sample (learning set) of Π.

Proposition 2.4 *Let* $\Pi \in \mathcal{N}_n^m$ *be. There always exists at least a* UNIVERSAL LEARNING ACTION $\mathcal{C}_a^u(\Pi) = \{\mathcal{E}^u(\Pi), \mathcal{N}^u(\Pi)\}$ *which returns one probably approximately correct solution, where*

$$
\begin{aligned}
N_n^u(\boldsymbol{d}, \boldsymbol{w}) \ &= \ F_m; \\
E^u(\triangleright\Pi, \boldsymbol{w}) \ &= \ \sum_{(\boldsymbol{d}_n, \Pi(\boldsymbol{d}_n)) \in \triangleright\Pi} e_q^u(\triangleright\Pi, \boldsymbol{w}) = \sum_{(\boldsymbol{d}_n, \Pi(\boldsymbol{d}_n)) \in \triangleright\Pi} \| \Pi(\boldsymbol{d}_n) - N_n^u(\boldsymbol{d}_n, \boldsymbol{w}) \|^2 \ .
\end{aligned}
$$

Problem 2.6 *Let us consider the problem of learning with Rosenblatt's perceptron [14] in the case of sigmoidal units.*

This problem is very much related to discovering a linear separation hyperplane for a given set of points.

Definition 2.8 LINEARLY-SEPARABLE SETS
Let $\mathcal{X}^+ \doteq \{\boldsymbol{x}_q \in I\!\!R^p : \ q = 1, \dots, n^+\}$ (POSITIVE SET) *and* $\mathcal{X}^- \doteq \{\boldsymbol{x}_q \in I\!\!R^p : \ q = 1, \dots, n^-\}$ (NEGATIVE SET) *be two set of* $n = n^+ + n^-$ *points. Let us assume that there exists a vector* $\boldsymbol{a} \in I\!\!R^{p+1}$ *and a thickness parameter* $\delta > 0$ *such that*

$$
\begin{aligned}
\left[\boldsymbol{x}_q', 1\right] \boldsymbol{a} &> \delta \quad \forall \boldsymbol{x}_q \in \mathcal{X}^+ \\
\left[\boldsymbol{x}_q', 1\right] \boldsymbol{a} &< \delta \quad \forall \boldsymbol{x}_q \in \mathcal{X}^-
\end{aligned}
$$

If these conditions hold we say that sets $\mathcal{X}^+$ *and* $\mathcal{X}^-$ *are* LINEARLY SEPARABLE.

Problem 2.7 Π^{lsp} LINEAR SEPARATION: *Let* $\mathcal{X}_\delta \doteq \mathcal{X}^+ \cup \mathcal{X}^- \cup \{\delta\}$ *be and consider the problem*

$$
\Pi^{lsp} = \left\{ (\mathcal{X}_\delta, \boldsymbol{a}) \in I\!\!R^\infty \times I\!\!R^\infty \ | \ \forall \boldsymbol{x}_q \in \mathcal{X}^+ : \ \left[\boldsymbol{x}_q', 1\right] \boldsymbol{a} > \delta, \ \forall \boldsymbol{x}_q \in \mathcal{X}^- : \ \left[\boldsymbol{x}_q', 1\right] \boldsymbol{a} < \delta \right\}
$$

A solution to this problem can be given in a number of different ways (see e.g. [14, 6]). We formulate this problem in the framework of function optimization using the classical artificial neural ([24]) in which an activation $\zeta \in I\!\!R$ is attached to each neuron which is calculated by

$$
\begin{aligned}
\zeta &= [\boldsymbol{x}', 1] \cdot \boldsymbol{w} & (10) \\
z &= \sigma(\zeta) & (11)
\end{aligned}
$$

where

$$
\sigma(\zeta) = \frac{1}{1 + \exp\left(-\zeta\right)}.
$$

Let us associate the targets $d^+ = +1$ and $d^- = -1$ with the points in $\mathcal{X} = \mathcal{X}^+ \cup \mathcal{X}^-$ and consider the following family of functions $\forall n \in I\!\!N : \mathcal{C}_a^{lsp} \doteq \{\mathcal{E}_n, \mathcal{N}_n\}_{n \in I\!\!N}$

$$N_n(\boldsymbol{x}, \boldsymbol{w}) \;\dot{=}\; \sigma\left([\boldsymbol{x}', 1] \cdot \boldsymbol{w}\right)$$

$$E(\boldsymbol{d}_n, \boldsymbol{w}) \;\dot{=}\; \sum_{q \in \triangleright \mathcal{X}^-} \beta_-(N_n(\boldsymbol{x}, \boldsymbol{w}) - d^-) + \sum_{q \in \triangleright \mathcal{X}^+} \beta_+(N_n(\boldsymbol{x}, \boldsymbol{w}) - d^+)$$

being[8]

$$\beta_+(\alpha) \;=\; 0 \quad if \;\; \alpha \geq 0 \tag{12}$$

$$\beta_+(\alpha) \;>\; 0, \;\; \beta'_+(\alpha) < 0 \quad if \;\; \alpha < 0 \tag{13}$$

$$\beta_-(\alpha) \;=\; 0 \quad if \;\; \alpha \leq 0 \tag{14}$$

$$\beta_-(\alpha) \;>\; 0, \;\; \beta'_-(\alpha) > 0 \quad if \;\; \alpha > 0 \tag{15}$$

This energy is referred to as an LEAST MINIMUM SQUARE THRESHOLD FUNCTION and was introduced in [25]. It is defined on $I\!R^m$, but we can restrict the domain to

$$\Omega_{thr} := \{\boldsymbol{w} \in I\!R^m \mid \sum_{q \in \triangleright \mathcal{X}^-} \beta_-(N_n(\boldsymbol{x}, \boldsymbol{w}) - d^-) + \sum_{q \in \triangleright \mathcal{X}^+} \beta_+(N_n(\boldsymbol{x}, \boldsymbol{w}) - d^+) > 0\} \tag{16}$$

Proposition 2.5 $\mathcal{C}_a^{lsp}$ *is an action for* Π_{lsp}.

In the optimization one can impose two different constraints depending on whether an exact or approximate separation is desired.

In the first case, the stopping criterion can be formulated by imposing the condition $E(\boldsymbol{d}_n, \boldsymbol{w}) < \epsilon_e/n$. In fact, this condition implies that $\forall q = 1, \ldots, n$, $E_q < \epsilon_e$, which guarantees a given degree of approximation for all the examples of the training set. Whether an example q is positive or negative can be established using the criterion:

If $x(\boldsymbol{w}, q) > (\ell + +\ell^-)/2$ then $q \in \mathcal{C}^+$ else $q \in \mathcal{C}^-$,
whenever $\epsilon_e \doteq (\ell^+ - \ell^-)/2$.

In the second case the condition $E(\mathcal{D}_{\Pi^{lsp}}, \boldsymbol{w}) < \epsilon_e$ only guarantees that the *average error* is below the chosen threshold. Hence, these continuous algorithms are $\mathcal{T}(n)$ and $\mathcal{T}(1)$, respectively. Finally, note that Π^{lsp} is a direct problem, that is its solution is expressed directly in terms of the parameters $\boldsymbol{w}$.

2.3.4 Linear and superlinear actions

Now, let us consider the following line segment intersection problem from computational geometry.

Problem 2.8 Π_{seg} LINE SEGMENT INTERSECTION
Let $\mathcal{S} \doteq \left\{ s_k \equiv \left(\boldsymbol{x}_k^{(1)}, \boldsymbol{x}_k^{(2)}\right) \mid \boldsymbol{x}_k \in I\!R^2, k = 1, n \right\}$ *be a set of segments in* $I\!R^2$, *defined by*

---

[8]d^+ and d^- are typically set to 1 and 0, respectively.

extremes $\boldsymbol{x}_k^{(1)}, \boldsymbol{x}_k^{(2)}$ *and consider the problem of establishing whether or not there are at least two intersecting segments. When adopting our nation* $\boldsymbol{d} \doteq [\boldsymbol{x}_1^{(1)}, \boldsymbol{x}_1^{(2)}, \ldots, \boldsymbol{x}_n^{(1)}, \boldsymbol{x}_n^{(2)}] \in I\!R^{4n}$ *and the solution space can simply consists of* $\{0,1\}$ *to report intersection (no intersection); hence* $\pi = (\boldsymbol{d}, y) \in I\!R^{4n+1}$.

Let $\boldsymbol{w} \in I\!R^2$ be and denote by $d_E(\boldsymbol{w}, s_k)$ the ordinary Euclidean distance of $\boldsymbol{w}$ from segment s_k. Moreover, let $d(\boldsymbol{w}, s_k)$ denote the following distance:

$$d(\boldsymbol{w}, s_k) \doteq \frac{d_E(\boldsymbol{w}, \boldsymbol{x}_k^{(1)}) + d_E(\boldsymbol{w}, \boldsymbol{x}_k^{(2)})}{d_E(\boldsymbol{x}_k^{(1)}, \boldsymbol{x}_k^{(2)})} - 1. \tag{17}$$

It can easily be checked that $d(\boldsymbol{w}, s_k) = 0 \iff \boldsymbol{w} \in s_k$.

Definition 2.9 *Let* $s_k \equiv \left\{ (\mathbf{x}_k^{(1)}, \mathbf{x}_k^{(2)}) : \quad k = 1,2 \right\}$ *be two segments. We define the distance* $d_s(s_1, s_2)$ *as*

$$d_s(s_1, s_2) \doteq min \left\{ d(\boldsymbol{x}_1^{(1)}, s_2), d(\boldsymbol{x}_1^{(2)}, s_2), d(\boldsymbol{x}_2^{(1)}, s_1), d(\boldsymbol{x}_2^{(2)}, s_1) \right\}. \tag{18}$$

Definition 2.10 Π *will be analyzed under the two following important assumptions*

1. *Let* $\epsilon > 0$ *be. Given any two segments* $s_1, s_2 \in I\!R^4$ *we says that there an* ϵ-*intersection, and use the notation* $s_1 \bowtie_\epsilon s_2$ *whenever* $d_s(s_1, s_2) < \epsilon$.

2. *The segments will be assumed to belong to a ball of diameter* D

The line ϵ-*intersection problem defined in a ball of radius* D *will be denoted by* $\Pi_{lin}^\epsilon(D)$.

Searching the cross $\boldsymbol{w} \in I\!R^2$

Let us consider the following familiy of functions $\forall n \in I\!N : \mathcal{C}_a^{cs} \doteq \{\mathcal{E}_n, \mathcal{N}_n\}_{n \in I\!N}$

$$q(n) \equiv 2 \quad, \quad \boldsymbol{w} \in I\!R^2;$$

$$E_n(\boldsymbol{d}, \boldsymbol{w}) = \prod_{k=1}^{n} (a_n + d(\boldsymbol{w}, s_k))$$

$$N_n(\boldsymbol{d}, \boldsymbol{w}) = sgn \left[\left(a_n + \frac{\epsilon}{2} \right)^n - E_n(\boldsymbol{d}, \boldsymbol{w}) \right]$$

Proposition 2.6 *If we choose*

$$a_n < \frac{\epsilon^2}{4(D - \epsilon)} \tag{19}$$

then $\{\mathcal{E}_n, \mathcal{N}_n\}_{n \in I\!N}$ *is an instance action for* $\Pi_{lin}^\epsilon(D)$.

Proof: Since any segment is a ball of diameter D, for any instance $\boldsymbol{d}^+ \mid \pi(\boldsymbol{d}^+, 1) \in \Pi_{lin}^\epsilon(R)$ with at least one line segment intersection we have the upper bound $\forall n : \ E_n(\boldsymbol{d}^+, \boldsymbol{w}^\star) \leq a_n^2(a^2 + D)^{n-2}$, being $\boldsymbol{w}^\star$ a minimizer for $E_n(\boldsymbol{d}^+, \boldsymbol{w})$.

Now let us consider any negative instance $\boldsymbol{d}^-$, that is $\boldsymbol{d}^- \mid \pi(\boldsymbol{d}^-, 0) \in \Pi^\epsilon_{lin}(R)$ and look for a lower bound of $E_n(\boldsymbol{d}^-, \boldsymbol{w})$. Let $a_n < \epsilon/4$ be [9]. Then a lower bound for E_n is surely obtained[10]

by considering $d(\boldsymbol{w}, s_k) \equiv \epsilon/2$, that is $(a_n + \epsilon/2)^n$.

When choosing a_n according to the hypothesis (equation 19) $\forall n \in I\!N, \boldsymbol{d}^+, \boldsymbol{d}^- \in \mathcal{D}^\star_\pi$:

$$
\begin{aligned}
E_n(\boldsymbol{d}^+, \boldsymbol{w}^\star) \quad &< \\
&< \quad a_n^2 (a_n + D)^{n-2} \\
&< \quad \left(a_n + \frac{\epsilon}{2}\right)^n \\
&< \quad E_n(\boldsymbol{d}^-, \boldsymbol{w}^\star)
\end{aligned}
$$

Of course, we can always find $\mathcal{I}_{\boldsymbol{w}^\star}$ such that $\forall \boldsymbol{w} \in \mathcal{I}_{\boldsymbol{w}^\star}$:

$$
\begin{aligned}
E_n(\boldsymbol{d}^+, \boldsymbol{w}^\star) \quad &< \quad E_n(\boldsymbol{d}^+, \boldsymbol{w}) < \\
\left(a_n + \frac{\epsilon}{2}\right)^n \quad &< \quad E_n(\boldsymbol{d}^-, \boldsymbol{w}) < \\
&\qquad\quad E_n(\boldsymbol{d}^-, \boldsymbol{w}^\star)
\end{aligned}
$$

Finally, from the last inequalities

$$
\begin{aligned}
N_n(\boldsymbol{d}, \boldsymbol{w}) \quad &= \\
&= \quad sgn\left[\left(a_n + \frac{\epsilon}{2}\right)^n - E_n(\boldsymbol{d}, \boldsymbol{w})\right] \\
&= \quad \begin{cases} 1 & \boldsymbol{d} := \boldsymbol{d}^+ \\ 0 & \boldsymbol{d} := \boldsymbol{d}^- \end{cases}
\end{aligned}
$$

$\square$

Pairwise check

A straightforward way to construct an action for $\Pi^\epsilon_{lin}(D)$ is that of operating on $\Omega = I\!R^{n^2}$ by associating an internal point $\boldsymbol{w}_k$ for any given segment. We can easily verify that the following pair of family of functions $\forall n \in I\!N : \mathcal{C}^{pw}_a \doteq \{\mathcal{E}_n, \mathcal{N}_n\}_{n \in I\!N}$, $w_i \in [0,1]$:

$$
\begin{aligned}
q(n) \quad &= \quad n^2 \\
E_n(\boldsymbol{d}, \boldsymbol{w}) \quad &= \quad \prod_{(i \neq j)} \left(\boldsymbol{x}_i^{(1)} + w_i \boldsymbol{x}_i^{(2)} - \boldsymbol{x}_j^{(1)} - w_j \boldsymbol{x}_j^{(2)}\right)^2 \\
N_n(\boldsymbol{d}, \boldsymbol{w}) \quad &= \quad \frac{1}{2} sgn\left[\frac{1}{2}\epsilon^{\frac{n(n-1)}{2}} - E(\boldsymbol{d}, \boldsymbol{w})\right]
\end{aligned}
$$

is an instance action for $\Pi^\epsilon_{lin}(D)$.

---

[9]Note that this can always be done by choosing $D > 2\epsilon$. This is in fact guaranteed by hypothesis (19).

[10]This can easily be checked for $n = 2$; for a higher number of segments n the property holds as well.

2.4   Actions with unknown energy minimum

In problems like Π_{lin} and Π_{lsp} we can find actions with known minimum of the energy, which is null in both cases. These actions will be referred to as ZERO-MINIMUM ACTIONS. For this problems, one can always reduce to the case in which $E_{min} = 0$ by simply replacing $E \leftarrow E - E_{min}$. For other problems, finding actions with this property can be very difficult (see e.g. Π_{lpo}). However, if only an nonzero-minimum action is known for a given problem Π, one can always construct an associated zero-minimum action as follows

1. Choose $a \in I\!\!R \mid \forall w \in \Omega : E(w) + a > 0$ and set $E := E + a$

2. Set $E_z := E \cdot \parallel \nabla E \parallel^2$.

Proposition 2.7 *Let us assume that* $\forall w \in \Omega : \quad D^2 E(w) > 0.$ *Then*

$$\nabla E_z(w) = 0 \iff \nabla E(w) = 0$$

Proof: We start reducing $E := E + a$ which guarantees that $\forall w \in \Omega : \quad E > 0$. From straightforward calculus

$$\nabla E_z = \parallel \nabla E \parallel^2 \cdot \nabla E + 2E \cdot D^2 E \cdot \nabla E$$

If we left-multiply by ∇E:

$$(\nabla E)' \cdot \nabla E_z = \parallel \nabla E \parallel^4 + 2E \cdot (\nabla E)' \cdot D^2 E \cdot \nabla E$$

Hence, $(\nabla E)' \cdot \nabla E_z = 0 \iff \nabla E = 0$, which, in turn, yields the thesis. $\square$

2.4.1   Actions for problems on discrete domains

In the given formulation PROBLEM Π is a relation in $I\!\!R^\infty \times I\!\!R^\infty$. The cases in which $\Pi \subset I\!\!N^\infty \times I\!\!N^\infty$, $\Pi \subset I\!\!R^\infty \times I\!\!N^\infty$, and $\Pi \subset I\!\!R^\infty \times I\!\!N^\infty$ give rise to different methods to construct actions.

2.4.2   Actions for dynamic data types

Assume d as DOAG an mention how actions can be created on such dynamical objects. In particular, if d is any graph, it does not make sense to talk about its dimension. However, one can create a correspondent static representation based on recursive computation. The methods for constructing actions on static domains can then be used. Here we describe how to convert dynamic to static data.

Actions exhibit different features, which makes it possible to classify them accordingly. The notion of APPROXIMATE and EXACT actions have been introduced which are related to the error ϵ_p. The concept of UNIFORM ACTIONS has been introduced to express the possibility of representing the action by SLP independently of the problem dimension. Another concept of uniformity arises when considering the problem instances. Hence we consider UNIFORM ACTIONS WRT THE INSTANCES those for which $d \in D_\pi^n \subseteq I\!\!R^n$. The actions introduced in subsection 2.4.2 are not uniform, in the sense that we cannot express instances as points of a metric space of fixed dimension.

Depending on the instance and solution space, actions can be CONTINUOUS ($\Pi \in I\!R^\infty \times I\!R^\infty$) and COMBINATORIAL ($\Pi \in I\!R^\infty \times I\!N^\infty$). In the last case we can have also $\Pi \in I\!N^\infty \times I\!N^\infty$. The examples given in the previous subsection motivate also the following additional definitions.

Definition 2.11 *We say that an action* $C_a(\Pi)$ *for* Π *is* DIRECT *provided that*

$$\forall n \in I\!N : \quad N_n(\boldsymbol{d}, \boldsymbol{w}) = \boldsymbol{w}.$$

Definition 2.12 *An action* $C_a(\Pi)$ *for* Π *is of* FINITE DIMENSION *if*

$$\max_{n \in I\!N} q(n) = \hat{m} < \infty.$$

3 Computational suspiciousness in the continuum

Given a problem Π and a corresponding action $C_a(\Pi)$, the most significant step for finding the solution is to determine $\min_{\boldsymbol{w} \in \Omega} E(\boldsymbol{d}, \boldsymbol{w})$. We can consider the associated differential equation

$$\frac{d\boldsymbol{w}}{dt} = \boldsymbol{f}(\Pi, t, \boldsymbol{w}), \tag{20}$$

which is expected to reach a stable point corresponding to $\min_{\boldsymbol{w} \in \Omega} E(\boldsymbol{d}, \boldsymbol{w})$. A fundamental question arises which concerns the choice of function $\boldsymbol{f}$. In particular, one may wonder how efficiently can such a function lead to the solution. The efficiency can reasonably be assessed by the time required to determine the solution. Of course, one can conceive different actions for the same problem. Running these actions is likely to require different time. Note that there are two different levels of freedom, which reside in the choice of the action and of the function $\boldsymbol{f}$ to optimize the energy. As will be put forward in the following, however, problems can be found for which these two levels of freedom collapse.

3.1 Continuous terminal attractor machines

According to our formulation of problems solving which is based on the concept of action, the field of equation (20) comes from the gradient of an energy function, that is $\nabla \times \boldsymbol{f} = \boldsymbol{0}$. The solution of a given problem Π can be performed by the following abstract machine.

Definition 3.1 DTAM - DETERMINISTIC TERMINAL ATTRACTOR MACHINE
A DETERMINISTIC TERMINAL ATTRACTOR MACHINE *is a map which takes an action* $C_a(\Pi) = \{\mathcal{E}_n(\Pi), \mathcal{N}_n(\Pi)\}_{n \in I\!N}$ *for a given problem* Π *and an instance* $\boldsymbol{d} \in D_\pi^n$ *and returns* $\boldsymbol{y} = \mathcal{N}_n(\boldsymbol{d}, \boldsymbol{w}_{ta})$, *which is the solution of* Π. *The parameter* $\boldsymbol{w}_{ta}$ *is the* TERMINAL VALUE *of differential equation*

$$\frac{d\boldsymbol{w}}{dt} = -\frac{E_o}{\sigma} \frac{\nabla_w E}{\| \nabla_w E \|^2}. \tag{21}$$

determined while checking the condition $\nabla E(\boldsymbol{w}_{ta}) = \boldsymbol{0}$. In this equation $\sigma > 0$ and $E_o \doteq E(0)$ corresponds with $\boldsymbol{w}_o \doteq \boldsymbol{w}(0)$, which is the DETERMINISTIC INITIALIZATION *of the machine.*

Of course, one can decide to stop the computation of the DTAM before reaching $\boldsymbol{w}_{ta}$. For instance, if the energy is local minima free and we stop the computation for $\hat{\boldsymbol{w}}$ such that the condition $|E_n(\boldsymbol{d}_n, \hat{\boldsymbol{w}}) - E_n(\boldsymbol{d}_n, \boldsymbol{w}_{ta})| < \epsilon_e(n)$ is sufficient to guarantee that $\forall \boldsymbol{d}_n \in D_\pi^n$: $\| \Pi(\boldsymbol{d}_n) - N_n(\boldsymbol{d}_n, \hat{\boldsymbol{w}}) \| < \epsilon_p(n)$, as required by the definition of action $\mathcal{C}_a$. Note that if there are suboptimal local minima then the returned value $\boldsymbol{w}_{ta}$ might not yield the desired solution. However, one can straightforwardly verify whether the reached point $\boldsymbol{w}_{ta}$ yields the desired solution just by inspecting the corresponding value of the energy. This property does not held when relying on fields for which $\nabla \times \boldsymbol{f} \neq \boldsymbol{0}$.

Proposition 3.1 *Let $E(\boldsymbol{d}, \cdot) \mid E(\boldsymbol{d}, \boldsymbol{w}) \geq 0$ be [11] and assume that there are no local minima apart from $E_{min} \doteq \min_{\boldsymbol{w} \in \Omega} E(\boldsymbol{d}, \boldsymbol{w})$ (global minimum). Then the terminal value of the DTAM is reached for $t \leq \sigma$ regardless of the energy $E(\boldsymbol{d}, \cdot)$ and regardless of the initial point $\boldsymbol{w}_o$. In particular, if $E_{min} \neq 0$ (non-zero minimum actions) then $t \leq \sigma$, while $t = \sigma$ holds for zero minimum actions.*

Proof: From the chain rule

$$\frac{dE}{dt} = (\nabla_w E)' \cdot \frac{d\boldsymbol{w}}{dt} \tag{22}$$

$$= -\frac{E_o}{\sigma}(\nabla_w E)' \cdot \frac{\nabla_w E}{\| \nabla_w E \|^2} \tag{23}$$

$$= -\frac{E_o}{\sigma}. \tag{24}$$

Hence,

$$E(t) = E_o(1 - \frac{t}{\sigma}) \tag{25}$$

For non-zero minimum actions the terminal values $E_{min} \neq o$ is reached for $t < \sigma$, while for zero-minimum actions the terminal attractor dynamics ends up with $E(t = \sigma) = 0$. $\square$

Whereas for local minima free energies $\boldsymbol{w}_{ta} = \hat{\boldsymbol{w}}$ yields a global minimum, this is not necessarily true for multimodal energies. Under the hypothesis of Proposition 3.1, the DTAM has a deterministic behavior and always returns the solution $\boldsymbol{y}(\mathcal{C}_a, \boldsymbol{d})$ in a fixed time $\sigma(E_o - E_{min})/E_o$, which is either independent of the problem Π or of the action $\mathcal{C}_a(\Pi)$. Moreover, note that the DTAM machine runs the given action regardless of the initial configuration $\boldsymbol{w}_o$.

It turns out to be convenient to define the circuit complexity of the action as follows:

Definition 3.2 *Let Π be a problem and $\mathcal{C}_a(\Pi)$ be a corresponding action. Let $\mathcal{G}_{\nabla E}$ be the graph corresponding to ∇E and denote by $g(n)$ the circuit complexity of $\mathcal{G}_{\nabla E}$. The* CIRCUIT COMPLEXITY OF ACTION $\mathcal{C}_a(\Pi)$, *denoted $CC(\mathcal{C}_a)(\Pi)$, is defined as $\Gamma(n) \doteq g(n) + \gamma_E(n) + \gamma_N(n))$.*

---

[11] We can easily reduce to this case whenever one knows a lower bound of E.

Note that for Problem 1 and 2.7 the given action has circuit complexity $\gamma(n)$ since the gradient can optimally be represented by its graph $\mathcal{G}_{\nabla E}$.

Definition 3.3 NON-SUSPECT ACTION
An action $\mathcal{C}_a(\Pi)$ for Π is called (WEAKLY/STRONGLY) NON-SUSPECT *provided that* $\forall n \in \mathbb{N}$, $\boldsymbol{d} \in D_\pi^n$:

    1. $E_n(\boldsymbol{d}, \cdot)$ is a (LOCAL MINIMA FREE FUNCTION/GLOBAL MINIMUM FUNCTION)*;*

    2. $CC(\mathcal{C}_a) = \Gamma(n)$ is polynomially bounded.

On the opposite, actions which violate at least one of the two conditions of Definition 3.3 are referred to as SUSPECT ACTIONS.

Definition 3.4 *A problem $\Pi \in \mathbb{R}^\infty \times \mathbb{R}^\infty$ is* UNIMODAL *provided that there exists a non-suspect action $\mathcal{C}_a(\Pi)$ for Π. The class of unimodal problems is denoted by U.*

Unimodal problems can also be regarded as those problems which can be solved by DTAM. For unimodal problems, DTAM machines offer a very natural way of expressing the complexity of either actions or problems, which is strictly related to the dimension m of the action.

When the energy is not local minima free, the DTAM is not guaranteed to yield the desired solution. Hence, when using DTAM for problems with unknown complexity, the suspect arises that the machine gets trapped into a sub-optimal minimum. For a given problem $\Pi \in U$ might not discover non-suspect actions. In general, the run of suspect actions on DTAM machines does not guarantee that the terminal value $\boldsymbol{w}_t$ yields the solution of Π. The following generalization of DTAM is strongly inspired to Non-Determinist Turing machines.

Definition 3.5 NDTAM - NON-DETERMINISTIC TERMINAL ATTRACTOR MACHINE
An NON-DETERMINISTIC TERMINAL ATTRACTOR MACHINES (NDTAM) *is a DTAM augmented with a* GUESSING MODULE, *which takes the action $\mathcal{C}_a(\Pi)$ and any instance $\boldsymbol{d} \in D_\pi^n$ as inputs and returns the initial value $\boldsymbol{w}_o = \boldsymbol{w}(0)$ for differential equation (21) such that the dynamics ends up to the terminal attractor $\boldsymbol{w}_{ta}$. The point $\boldsymbol{w}_o$ guessed by the NDTAM is called a* GOOD POINT.

The following concept of Nondeterministic Unimodal problems is directly inspired to the class NP.

Definition 3.6 *A problem Π belongs to the class* NON-DETERMINISTIC UNIMODAL PROBLEMS ($\Pi \in NU$) *provided that it can be solved by an NDTAM.*

Of course, $U \subseteq NU$. The relationship between U and NU resembles the links between P and NP.

In some special cases, a random guess in the NDTAM is sufficient to determine a good initial point $\boldsymbol{w}_o$ with probability one ($\mathcal{P} = 1$). This happens if the singular points are saddles with null Lebesgue measure in the Ω.

3.2 The universal action

Now we prove that the universal action $\mathcal{C}_a^u$ can be designed in such a way to become unimodal. Let $T \doteq |\triangleright \Pi|$ be the cardinality of the sample set used for the training set $\triangleright\Pi$ Let N be a network function with the associated graph $\mathcal{G}_N^n$. Let $\boldsymbol{x}_v \in I\!\!R^T$ be the output variable attached to node v which contains the outputs x_v corresponding to all instances $\boldsymbol{d}_n \in \triangleright D_\pi^n$. Likewise we use the notation $\boldsymbol{a}_v$ for the activation variable such that $\boldsymbol{x}_v = \boldsymbol{\sigma}(\boldsymbol{a}_v)$. Furthermore, denote by

$$\boldsymbol{\delta}_v \doteq \left[\frac{\partial e_1^u}{\partial a_v}, \ldots, \frac{\partial e_T^u}{\partial a_v}\right] \in I\!\!R^T \tag{26}$$

and denote by $pa[v]$ the parents of node v in $\mathcal{G}_N^n$. Let

$$\boldsymbol{X}_{pa[v]} \doteq \left[q_1^{-1}\boldsymbol{x}_v, \ldots, q_{pa[v]}^{-1}\boldsymbol{x}_v\right].$$

Lemma 3.1 *The gradient*

$$\boldsymbol{G}_v = \left[\frac{\partial E}{\partial w_{v,1}}, \ldots, \frac{\partial E}{\partial w_{v,|pa[v]|}}\right]$$

can be calculated by

$$\boldsymbol{G}_v = \boldsymbol{X}'_{pa[v]} \cdot \boldsymbol{\delta}_v \tag{27}$$

Proof: The proof is straightforward calculus. We just need to use the chain rule for each term e_q^u

$$\frac{\partial e_q^u}{\partial w_{v,u}} = \delta_v(q) \cdot x_u(q)$$

and sum up over all the training set $\triangleright\Pi$. $\square$

Lemma 3.2 BACKPROPAGATION
If $v = s$ (supersource node) then

$$\delta_s(q) = \frac{\partial e_q^u}{\partial a_s(q)} \tag{28}$$

$$= 2\sigma'(a_s(q))\left(N(\boldsymbol{d}_n, \boldsymbol{w}) - \Pi(\boldsymbol{d}_n)\right) \tag{29}$$

else

$$\boldsymbol{\delta}_v = \sigma'(\boldsymbol{a}_v) \sum_{\mu \in pa[v]} w_{\mu,v}\boldsymbol{\delta}_\mu \tag{30}$$

Proof: The proof is straightforward calculus. $\square$

Lemma 3.3 *Let $\boldsymbol{w} \in \Omega$ such that $\boldsymbol{\delta}_v(\boldsymbol{w}) = \boldsymbol{0}$ be. Then the condition $\nabla_{\boldsymbol{w}} E = 0$ yields $E(\boldsymbol{w}) = 0$.*

Proposition 3.2 [12] *Let Π be a problem with input length n. Then the corresponding universal action $\mathcal{C}_a^u$ is unimodal if*

$$\texttt{outdegree } \mathcal{G}_N \geq |\mathcal{D}_\pi^n|.$$

The proof of these results can be gained from the results given in [26] In the case in which $\mathcal{G}_N$ has a multilayer architecture the number of required hidden nodes must be at least $|\mathcal{D}_\pi^n|$.

Note that the construction of such an unimodal action is of theoretical interest only. In practice, the effective construction of actions requires a creative process that, to some extent, resembles the one required for conceiving classic discrete algorithms. The situation in which no other actions apart from $\mathcal{C}_a^u$ are known for a given problem seems to be very much related to the situation occurring in classical computational complexity theory when only trivial exponential algorithms can be exhibited.

4   Conclusions

This chapter has given some computational complexity insights about the continuous optimization approach to problem solving. In the last few years, there has been a growing attention to this computational approach particularly in the field of in artificial neural networks. When comparing symbolic and sub-symbolic approaches the need for unified frameworks for judging these different computational models becomes of crucial importance.

In chapter paper we have introduced the concept of suspiciousness that provides a "bridge" between the ways the complexity is evaluated in the continuous and the discrete setting. The notion of computational suspiciousness is formulated in the framework of continuous function optimization and is related to the presence of local minima in the error function associated to the problem.

The ideas introduced in this chapter gives a preliminary contribution towards the construction of a general computational framework to understand learning algorithms and problem solving methods developed in the last few years in neural computation.

5   Acknowledgments*

I thank Monica Bianchini, Stefano Fanelli, Paolo Frasconi, Marco Maggini, Marco Protasi, Franco Scarselli, Hava T. Siegelmann, and Ah Chung Tsoi for fruitful discussions and comments on earlier drafts of this paper. Special thanks to Klaus Meer who has provided many constructive comments and has been contributing to provide rigorous foundations to the ideas reported in this chapter.

---

[12]See related result in [26].

References

[1] R. Brockett, "Hybrid models for motion control systems," in *Essays in Control: Perspectives in the Theory and its Applications* (H. Trentelman and J. Willems, eds.), (Boston, MA), pp. 29–53, Birkhauser, 1993.

[2] M. Branicky, "Analog computation with odes," in *Proc. of the IEEE Workshop on Physics and Computation*, (Dallax, TX), pp. 265–274, 1994.

[3] A. Turing, "On computable numbers, with applications to the entscheidungsproblem," in *Proc. of the london Mathematical Society*, pp. 230–265, 1936.

[4] J. Sheperdson and H. Sturgis, "Computability of recursive functions," *Journal of the ACM*, vol. 10, pp. 217–225, 1963.

[5] A. Aho, J. Hopcroft, and J. Ullman, *The Design and Analysis of Computer Algorithms*. Addison-Wesley, 1974.

[6] F. Preparata and M. Shamos, *Computational Geometry - An Introduction*. Springer-Verlag, 2nd ed., 1985.

[7] D. Luemberger, *Linear and non-linear programming*.

[8] J. Wang, "Analysis and design of an analog sorting network," *IEEE Transactions on Neural Networks*, vol. 6, no. 4, pp. 962–971, 1995.

[9] J. Mándziuk, "Solving the n-queens problems with a binay hopfield-type network," *Biological Cybernetics*, no. 72, pp. 439–445, 1995.

[10] J. Hopfield, "Neural networks and physical systems with emergent collective computational abilities," *Proceedings of the National Academy of Sciences, USA*, vol. 79, pp. 2554–2558, 1982. Also in *Neurocomputing*, The MIT Press, 1988.

[11] J. Hopfield and D. Tank, ""neural" computation of decisions in optimization problems," *Biological Cybernetics*, vol. 52, pp. 141–152, 1985.

[12] J. Hopfield and D. Tank, "Computing with neural circuits: A model," *Science*, vol. 233, pp. 625–633, 1986.

[13] L. Blum, F. Cucker, M. Shub, and S. Smale, *Complexity and real computation*. Springer, 1997.

[14] M. Minsky and S. Papert, *Perceptrons - Expanded Edition*. Cambridge: MIT Press, 1988.

[15] M. Gori and K. Meer, "A step towards a complexity theory for analog systems," *Mathematical Logic Quarterly*, vol. 48, pp. 45–59, 2002.

[16] C. Moore, "Finite-dimensional analog computers: Flows, maps, and recurrent neural networks," in *1st International Conference on Unconventional Models of Computation*, (Auckland), Springer, 1998.

[17] P. Orponen, "A survey of continuous-time computation theory," in *Advances in Algorithms, Languages, and Complexity* (D.-Z. Du and K.-I. Ko, eds.), pp. 209–224, Dordrecht: Kluwer Academic Publishers, 1997.

[18] J. Taub, G. Wasilkowski, and H. Wo'zniakoski, *Information-based complexity*. Academic Press, Inc, 1988.

[19] R. Feynman, *The Feynman Lectures of Physics*. 1973.

[20] R. Boppana and M. Sipser, "The complexity of finite functions," in *Handbook of Theoretical Computer Science* (J. van Leeuwen, ed.), ch. 14, pp. 759–804, Elsevier Science Publisher B.V., 1990.

[21] J. Shave-Taylor, M. Anthony, and W. Kern, "Classes of feedforward neural networks and their circuit complexity," tech. rep., 1990.

[22] R. Cichelli, "Perfect hash function made simple," *Communication of the ACM*, vol. 23, pp. 17–19, January 1980.

[23] M. Gori and G. Soda, "An algebraic approach to cichelli's perfect hashing," *BIT*, vol. 29, pp. 2–13, 1989.

[24] D. Rumelhart, G. Hinton, and R. Williams, "Learning internal representations by error propagation," in *Parallel Distributed Processing* (D. Rumelhart and J. McClelland, eds.), vol. 1, ch. 8, pp. 318–362, Cambridge: MIT Press, 1986. Reprinted in [27].

[25] E. Sontag and H. Sussman, "Backpropagation separates when perceptrons do," in *International Joint Conference on Neural Networks*, vol. 1, (Washington DC), pp. 639–642, IEEE Press, June 1989.

[26] M. Bianchini, P. Frasconi, M. Gori, and M. Maggini, "Optimal learning in artificial neural networks: A theoretical view," in *Optimization Techniques. Neural Systems and Applications* (C. T. Leondes, ed.), ch. 1, pp. 1–52, Academic Press, 1998.

[27] J. Anderson and E. Rosenfeld, eds., *Neurocomputing: Foundations of Research*. Cambridge: MIT Press, 1988.

The complexity of computing with continuous time devices

Asa Ben-Hur
BioWulf Technologies
2030 Addison st. suite 102
Berkeley, CA 94704, USA

Hava Siegelmann
Lab for Inf. & Decision Systems
MIT
Cambridge, MA 02139, USA

Shmuel Fishman
Department of Physics
Technion, Israel Institute of Technology
Haifa 32000, Israel

Abstract.
The theory of complexity, one of the cornerstones of theoretical computer science, has logic and discrete mathematics as its mathematical foundations. In its basis is the Turing machine, the mathematical abstraction of a digital computer. A Turing machine is essentially a discrete time dynamical systems in a discrete configuration space. In this chapter we aim to incorporate concepts of mathematical analysis into complexity theory, thus enlarging its scope to encompass continuous algorithms defined by differential equations. We provide the foundations for an algorithmic and complexity analysis of flows that converge to fixed points. This way the efficiency of a large class of continuous algorithms defined by differential equations can be compared against discrete algorithms. Time complexity of continuous time systems is a delicate issue that is hard to define in a meaningful way. By interpreting differential equations as models of physical systems we connect time as measured in the laboratory with time complexity, making it a well defined concept. We show examples of efficient problemsolving for finding the maximum of n number, maximum network flow and linear programming. We define a continuous P complexity class and conjecture that a subclass of the continuous P is equivalent to the classical P.

1 Introduction

In recent years scientists have developed new approaches to computation, some of them based on continuous time analog systems. Analog VLSI devices, often described by differential equations, have applications in the fields of signal processing and optimization. Many of these devices are implementations of neural networks [1, 2, 3], or the so-called neuromorphic systems [4], which are hardware devices whose structure is directly motivated by the workings of the brain. Applications in vision for example are found in [5, 6]. In addition there is an increasing number of theoretical studies of differential equations that solve problems such as sorting [7], linear programming [8] and algebraic problems such as singular value decomposition and finding of eigenvectors (see [9] and references therein). Despite the interest in computation with continuous time systems, no theory exists for their algorithmic analysis. The standard theory of computation and computational complexity [10] deals with computation in discrete time and in a discrete configuration space, and is inadequate for the description of such systems. In the engineering literature we have found reference to continuous time systems as "real time" computing devices [11, 3].

In this chapter we aim to capture the problem solving paradigm employed by people implementing continuous time systems in hardware into a computational model with a notion of computational complexity. Our model is based on ordinary differential equations that converge to fixed points. This facilitates a definition of the attracting fixed points as the possible outputs of a computation. Convergence to attractors (fixed points, limit cycles or chaotic attractors) is a property of the class of dissipative dynamical systems which describe most small-scale classical physical systems [12]. We thus aim our model to be a computational model for realizable analog devices: a differential equation in our model is viewed as describing a concrete physical system. Thus, our theory can be used not only in the analysis of fabricated systems, but also promotes the view of computation in nature: it allows the interpretation of various physical and biological phenomena, often described by differential equations, as processes of computation.

A continuous time parameter can be used in ways that make a computational model unrealizable. Consider for example the model in [13] where the user can set the amount of time required to execute each instruction. In this model *any* computation can be performed in finite "time". The computation time of a differential equation, as measured by its time parameter can also be decreased by reparameterizing the equation (see Section 2). We avoid such pitfalls by the assumption that a given differential equation describes a concrete physical system, and its time parameter thus takes on the role of "physical" time. Time complexity thus reflects the convergence time of the underlying system.

The computation of a digital computer, and its mathematical abstraction, the Turing machine can be described by a map on a discrete configuration space: the program of a computer or the transition function of a Turing machine describes how its configuration should change at each computational step. However, expressing computation in terms of dynamical systems does not prove to be fruitful in this case, since most of the theory of dynamical systems is applicable to the study of *continuous* dynamical systems. In this context we use the often quoted words of von Neumann who stated the need for "a detailed, highly mathematical, and more specifically *analytical* theory of automata and of information" [14]. The framework introduced here is an effort in this direction; we believe it strengthens the connection between the theory of computational complexity and the field of continuous dynamical systems. In fact, we propose a subclass of analytically solvable ODEs as a counterpart for the classical complexity class P. This suggests a correspondence between tractability in the realm of dynamical systems and tractability in the Turing model.

Another work in this direction is the BSS model of computation over the real numbers [15, 16]. There are two important distinctions to be made between this work and the BSS model. The first is that the BSS model deals with maps, whereas we use differential equations; the second distinction is related to the type of the input. The BSS model is a model of computation *over* the real numbers: the input is real with operations on real numbers, including comparisons between real numbers at unit cost. In our model the parameters of an ODE are the input of the computational machine. In principle, these can be real numbers, but we consider mainly rational inputs in order to have a model that can be compared with the Turing model. Our model *uses* the real numbers since the evolution of an ODE occurs in a continuum. However, this does not add computational power to the model: the fixed points of the equations considered in this chapter can be obtained by simulating the dynamics on a Turing machine by numerical integration. Complexity in the real number model and in our model are related by the appearance of condition numbers that relate ill-conditioning of an instance and the complexity of solving it [16, 17, 18, 19].

Most of the work connecting computation and dynamical systems is aimed at simulating discrete automata. First we note that continuous low dimensional *maps* in $\mathbb{R}^2$ can be used to simulate the computation of a Turing machine. Simulations with piecewise linear systems were shown in [20, 21], and by analytic functions in [22]. ODEs were used to simulate various discrete time models, thus providing lower bounds on their computational power. Brockett demonstrated how to simulate finite automata by ODEs [23]; Branicky generalized this result to simulate Turing machines [24], thus proving their computational universality. Simulation with piecewise constant functions was shown in [25]. Such constructions retain the discrete nature of the simulated map, in that they follow its computation step by step by a continuous equation. In this work on the other hand, we consider continuous systems as is, and interpret their dynamics as a non-symbolic process of computation.

The interest in the theory of computation in continuous time is not new. A survey of some of the previous work appears in [26]. A seminal contribution is the work of Shannon [27] and Pour-El [28] on the so called General Purpose Analog Computer (GPAC) which was shown to be equivalent in its computational power to a class of differential equations. For a recent extension of this work see [29]. The output of a GPAC computation is determined by the state at a time that is the input of the machine, whereas here output is determined by the asymptotical behavior. Moore's theory of recursive functions over the reals [30] which is an "analog" of classical recursive functions, also uses continuous time. In our model we have in mind a physical realization of a differential equation, whereas Moore's approach and the approach of [13], that enables to "squeeze" infinite computations into a finite time span, are not realizable.

Analog computation can be utilized to test possible theoretical limitations of the "physical Church-Turing thesis" [31]. Some theoretical analog models of computation have the capability of computing beyond the Turing limit [32, 33], but no realizable "super-Turing" system has been proposed. We do not suggest the current work as a step towards the identification of realizable super-Turing systems. Rather, we have the goal of providing an alternative view of computability that has its roots in continuous mathematics, and suggest physical systems as readily available special purpose analog computers.

2   Time and time complexity

We begin this section with a discussion of the issue of defining time complexity for continuous time systems. We are interested in ODEs as models of physical systems. For such dynamical systems, the state $x(t)$ represents the state of the corresponding physical system at time t. The time parameter is then time as measured in the laboratory, and has a well defined meaning. Since it is reasonable to associate time with complexity, we suggest to use it as a measure of the time complexity of a computation. However, for non-autonomous ODEs (systems with a time dependent vector field $F(x, t)$) that are not directly associated with physical systems, the time parameter seems to be arbitrary: if the time variable t of a non-autonomous vector field is replaced by another variable s where $t = g(s)$, and $g(s)$ is strictly monotonic, we obtain another non-autonomous system

$$\frac{dx}{ds} = F(x, g(s))g'(s) \,. \tag{1}$$

The above system will be called the time transformed version of F. If we take for example, $t = \exp(s)$, then the transformed system computes exponentially faster. This way arbitrary speed-up can be achieved in principle. However, the time transformed system is a *new* system. Only once it is constructed does its time parameter takes on the role of physical time, and is no longer arbitrary (up to a linear change of the time unit). Therefore speed-up is a relevant concept only within the bounds of physical realizability. We stress the distinction between linear and non-linear transformations of the time parameter: a linear transformation is merely a change of the units with which time is measured; a nonlinear transformation effectively changes the system itself.

This discussion shows the problem in taking the time parameter of non-autonomous systems as a measure of complexity. We now point out that the class of exponentially convergent autonomous systems is not closed under nonlinear transformations of the time parameter, if we further assume that the vector field is analytic. For autonomous analytic vector fields *convergence to a fixed point is either exponential or polynomial*. When a non-linear speed-up transformation is applied to an exponentially convergent vector field, a non-autonomous system results, which converges faster than exponential. If one is successful in making the system into an autonomous one, keeping the faster than exponential convergence rate, then it is no longer analytic. The analyticity property rules out systems such as

$$\frac{dx}{dt} = -(x - x^*)^{1/3},$$

and

$$\frac{dx}{dt} = -\frac{f(x)}{|f(x)|},$$

where $|\cdot|$ is the absolute value. These systems converge in *constant time* to a fixed point due to the fact that these vector fields are not Lipschitz. These are known as *terminal attractors*, and were suggested as an efficient model for associative memory [34].

3   Examples of problem solving with dynamical systems

In this section we present several examples that demonstrate an approach to problem solving by continuous dynamical systems; this approach will be formulated into a computational model in the next section. We begin with a flow for the MAX problem which is the problem of finding the maximum of n numbers. First we formulate it as an optimization problem: Let the numbers be $c_1, \ldots, c_n$, and define the linear cost function

$$h(x) = c^T x \,. \tag{2}$$

The MAX problem can be cast as a constrained optimization problem: find the maximum of h subject to the constraints

$$\sum_{i=1}^{n} x_i = 1, \quad x_i \geq 0 \,. \tag{3}$$

This is recognized as the linear programming problem on the $n - 1$ dimensional simplex $\{x \in \mathbb{R}^n : x_i \geq 0, \sum_{i=1}^{n} x_i = 1\}$. We use the vector field

$$F_i = (c_i - \sum_{j=1}^{n} x_j c_j)\, x_i \, , \tag{4}$$

which is the gradient of the function h on the simplex relative to a Riemannian metric which enforces the positivity constraints [9]. This flow is a special case of the Faybusovich vector field [8], which is introduced in section 6. It is easy to verify that the vertices of the simplex are the fixed points of this flow, and it converges to the vertex with the largest c_i. Thus the system converges to the solution to the problem, i.e. the attracting fixed point can be used to read off the solution; the parameters of the vector field, the vector c, are the input numbers, and the initial condition is an initialization that facilitates fast computation (see Section 5).

Now, consider solving a set of m equations in n unknowns, with $m \leq n$ in the form $Ax = b$. Define the cost function

$$h(x) = ||Ax - b||^2 \, .$$

The linear system $\dot{x} = -\nabla h = (AA^T)^{-1}(Ax - b)$ is a linear system that converges to a solution of $Ax = b$. Its rate of convergence depends on the eigenvalues of $(AA^T)^{-1}A$. A complexity analysis of this system would be based on showing the problem size dependence of the eigenvalues. This is the type of "analytical complexity analysis" that we study here. A problem which leads to similar behavior is the problem of finding a dominant eigenvector of a symmetric matrix A. The flow

$$\dot{x} = (I - xx^T)Ax$$

converges to a dominant eigenvector at a rate which is $1/(\lambda_1 - \lambda_2)$, where λ_1 and λ_2 are the first and second largest eigenvalues of A, respectively [9]. Other examples are found in [9].

The general idea is to find a cost function $E(x)$ whose minimum or maximum corresponds to a solution to the problem, and use a gradient flow as a continuous device for solving the problem. Actual implemetations by neural network type devices are found in [3, 2, 11]. In these cases the parameters that specify the vector field are the inputs, and the system converges to a state from which the solution to the problem can be read from.

Another possiblity is to take the initial condition as the input, as for example in models of associative memory [1, 35]. An example of this paradigm is the continuous version of the Hopfield network:

$$\dot{x}_i = \sigma \left(\sum_{j} w_{ij} x_j \right) ,$$

When the weight matrix is constructed according to a Hebb like rule, the system converges to one of the memories encoded by W. With the initial condition serving as input, it was shown that the continuous Hopfield network can simulate a class of Turing machines [36]. In the case of the initial condition as input, the fixed point corresponding to the minimum of the Lyapunov functional associated with the flow is the solution of an NP-complete optimization problem. However, the system has many local minima, so it cannot be used as the basis for an efficient problem solving device.

4   The computational model

In this section we formulate the examples treated in the previous section into a computational model. The model we are about to define is based on a set of autonomous ODEs

$$\frac{dx}{dt} = F(x), \tag{5}$$

where $x \in \mathbb{R}^d$ and F is a d-dimensional vector field whose dynamics converge exponentially to fixed points. We put special emphasis on gradient flows since their dynamics is simpler to analyze, and they provide a convenient problem solving framework, with many useful examples (see [9]). The use of attractor systems provides a natural way to define the output, as opposed to arbitrary halting regions that arise when simulating a Turing machine by a continuous dynamical system (see [21, 22] for example). The motivation for focusing on flows which converge exponentially is as follows:

- Polynomial convergence is slow compared to exponential convergence, so polynomially convergent vector fields are unlikely to produce computationally efficient systems (see section 4.5).

- Exponentially convergent systems also have tolerance to noise, or in mathematical terms, they are structurally stable, i.e. there exists an ϵ such that for all perturbations g of norm less than ϵ, $f + g$ and f are topologically equivalent (there exists a homeomorphism ϕ s.t. $f + g = \phi^{-1} \circ f \circ \phi$). In addition, exponential convergence is the typical convergence scenario in dynamical systems [37].

   In the following we describe our interpretation of the dynamics as a process of computation. We consider parameters that specify the vector field as the input to the computational device. In our framework the initial condition is part of the continuous algorithm, and its role is to initiate a trajectory in the basin of attraction of the solution to the problem, and the output of a computation is the attractor of the dynamics. For a given problem F takes on the *same* mathematical form, and only the size of the objects in it (vectors, matrices) depend on the size of the instance. This corresponds to the concept of uniformity in the standard computational complexity theory; its role is to ensure that the computational power of the model is not simply due to the complexity of the vector field, but is rather the result of the dynamics. For example, all maximum problems are solved with the same formula: $F_i(x_1, \ldots, x_n) = (c_i - \sum_{j=1}^{n} c_j x_j) x_i$. The n parameters c_i are the inputs, and it is seen that a single formula specifies the vector field for all n. Also note that the vector field has a dimensionality $d(n) = n$, but this may not be the case in general. Following this example, we formulate the vector field as a fixed *formula* for inputs of all sizes where only the length of the various objects in it (vectors, matrices etc.) varies with the number of inputs.

   In the definition of a formula we assume that the vector field does not contain any real numbers in its defining formula, and that it is computable in NC.[1] This limitation on the vector field ensures that the computational power of the system is based purely on its structure, and does not depend for example on constants which serve to increase the computational power,

---

[1] NC is a parallel computation complexity class. A computation is in NC if it can be performed using a polynomial number of processing units in polylogarithmic time. NC is contained in the polynomial class P. See also [10].

as it is known that neural networks with real weights can compute non-recursive functions [32].

Now we are ready to define our concept of a computational machine:

Definition 4.1. A continuous time computer (CTC) is a tuple $(F, \Pi, x_0, T(L))$ where F is a formula for a vector field which converges exponentially to fixed points. Π are the parameters of the vector field which constitute the input. These are taken to be integer or rational (real inputs can be considered as well, but minor changes in some definitions are required). x_0 is an NC computable initial condition for the flow. $T(L)$ is a bound on the time required to reach a sufficiently close vicinity of the attracting fixed point on input of size L (see Section 4.2). As a shorthand we will denote a CTC by the vector field F.

Remark 4.1. We did not impose restrictions on the relation between the number of variables used to solve a problem instance and its size. This will be done when defining complexity classes. In the example given above for finding the maximum of n numbers, n variables are be used.

Remark 4.2. The size (precision) of the initial condition need not be restricted since all initial conditions in a basin of attraction are equivalent in the sense that they produce the same output (possibly with varying computation times), so specifying the initial condition with very high (possibly infinite) precision gives no computational advantage.

4.1 The output of a CTC

In our framework we postulate the attractor, or a simple function that is associated with the flow as the output of a computation. In the case of a gradient flow for example, the output can be taken to be the state which optimizes the cost function or the value of the function itself. In section 5 we analyze a CTC for finding the maximum of n numbers. This problem can be expressed as a linear programming problem on the simplex: given n numbers represented by a vector c, find the maximum of $c^T x$ subject to $\sum_{i=1}^{n} x_i = 1$ and $x_i \geq 0$. We have shown a gradient flow whose fixed points are the vertices of the simplex. These serve as *pointers* to the possible solutions, while the value of the cost function at each vertex represent the possible values of the solution. A gradient flow for the general linear programming problem whose fixed points are exactly the vertices of the solution polytope was introduced in [8] (see Sections 6 and 6.2).

The evolution of a CTC reaches an attractor only in the infinite time limit. Therefore for any finite time we can only compute it to some precision. A computation will be halted when the attractor is computed with enough precision to infer a solution to the associated problem by rounding. When the inputs are integer or rational, the set of fixed points (the possible solutions) will in general be distributed on a grid of some finite precision defined as follows:

Definition 4.2. A CTC F is said to *require precision* $\epsilon_p(L)$ if for every instance Π of size L, every ball of radius $\epsilon_p(L)$ around the attractor associated with input Π does not contain any other fixed point of F.

Equivalently, a precision $\epsilon_p(L)$ is required if the attractor associated with every instance of size L can be written as an irreducible rational number/vector with denominator/s less than $1/\epsilon_p(L)$.

When the dynamics of a CTC for a problem requiring precision $\epsilon_p(L)$ reaches the ϵ_p-vicinity of the attractor, the solution is obtained by rounding the state space variables to the nearest grid point. It is possible to generalize this to allow for the output to be some function of the attractor.

Remark 4.3. For a problem in P with a CTC it is straightforward to show that the required precision is polynomial, i.e. for a problem of size L there exists $k > 0$ such that $\epsilon_p(L) \leq 2^{-L^k}$. In the CTC for the maximum problem the fixed points are the vertices of the simplex which have integer coordinates (see section 5), and therefore its required precision is $O(1)$.

4.2   Halting and the computation time

The phase space evolution of a trajectory may be rather complicated, and a major problem is to know when a point approached by the trajectory is indeed the attractor of the dynamics, and not a saddle point. To facilitate this decision we define:

Definition 4.3. Let F be a CTC with an attracting fixed point x^*. A *trapping region* of x^* a set U containing x^* such that if $x(t) \in U$, then for all $t' > t$, $x(t') \in U$. A trapping region U is said to be *attracting* if there exists a norm $||\cdot||$ such that for all $t, t', t' > t$ and $x(t), x(t') \in U$ we have that $||x(t') - x^*|| < ||x(t) - x^*||$.

The attracting region is a region in the phase space in which the distance from the attractor is monotonically decreasing relative to some norm.

Remark 4.4. An attracting region as defined above exists for every CTC [38]. When the stability matrix is diagonalizable and has real eigenvalues e.g., for gradient flows [38], the norm in the definition is the regular Euclidean norm.

We define the convergence time to an attracting region:

Definition 4.4. Let F be a CTC with an attracting region U, the *convergence time* to the attracting region, $t_c(U)$ is the infimum over all t such that $x(t) \in U$.

When the computation has reached the attracting region of a fixed point, and is also within ϵ_p of it, namely in $B(x^*, \epsilon_p)$, a ball of radius ϵ_p around x^*, then we can say that the dynamics is near an attracting fixed point and that it is computed with a high enough precision. Thus we define:

Definition 4.5. Given a CTC F, let U be an attracting region of an attracting fixed point x^*. Its *halting region*, H is

$$H = U \cap B(x^*, \epsilon_p) \,. \tag{6}$$

We can now define the computation time:

Definition 4.6. Let F be a CTC with a halting region H. Its *computation time* is the convergence time to the halting region, $t_c(H)$.

The convergence time to the halting region is given by:

$$t_c(H) = \max(t_c(\epsilon_p), t_c(U)) \,, \tag{7}$$

where $t_c(\epsilon_p)$ is the convergence time to the ϵ_p-vicinity of the attractor, and $t_c(U)$ is the convergence time to its attracting region, U.

The attracting region of a CTC F on input Π is some vicinity of the attractor $x^*(\Pi)$ which is associated with the solution to the problem. Thus computing the attracting region is not easier than solving the problem. Not knowing the attracting region, we do not know when to halt the computation, i.e. that the dynamics has reached $H(\Pi)$. Instead, we specify halting by a bound on the computation time of all instances of size L:

$$T(L) = \max_{|\Pi|=L} t_c(H(\Pi)) \,. \tag{8}$$

For integer or rational inputs we will consider the *bit-size* measure, denoted by L, which is the number of bits required to encode the input in binary. When real inputs are considered the size of the input is the number of inputs, n. In practice, one can only obtain a bound on $T(L)$, and efficiency depends on finding tight bounds. Considering systems with an analytical solution allows us to find such bounds (see next section for an example). This halting criterion yields worst case performance on all instances. A halting condition which senses proximity to a fixed point is described in [39].

4.3　Time complexity

The upper bound $T(L)$ is an upper bound on the computation time. Unlike the number of steps complexity measure it is not a dimensionless number. Moreover, by changing the time parameter from t to $t' = at$ for $0 < a < 1$ we obtain a system that computes faster by a factor a. This is equivalent to the the transformation $F' = \frac{1}{a}F$. The computation time in the system F' is smaller than in F, only because it is measured in different units. We can make $T(L)$ independent of the chosen time unit by turning it into a dimensionless number. To achieve this, we express the time parameter as a multiple of some time unit inherent to the system, and choose the *characteristic time scale* that is defined by the rate of convergence to the fixed point.

Let $x^*(\Pi)$ be the attracting fixed point of $\dot{x} = F(x)$ on input Π. In the vicinity of x^* the following linearization approximation holds:

$$\dot{\delta x} = DF|_{x^*}\, \delta x \,, \tag{9}$$

where $\delta x = x - x^*$, and $DF|_{x^*}$ is the matrix of partial derivatives at the point x^*. Let λ_i be the real part of the ith eigenvalue of $DF|_{x^*}$. We define:

$$\lambda = \min_i |\lambda_i| \,. \tag{10}$$

λ determines the rate of convergence to the attractor, since in its vicinity

$$|x(t) - x^*| \sim \exp(-\lambda t) \,, \tag{11}$$

leading to the definition of the characteristic time

$$\tau_{ch} = \frac{1}{\lambda} \,. \tag{12}$$

When the approximation (9) holds (the linear regime), in a time $\tau_{ch} \ln 2$ an additional bit of the attractor is computed. Note that $\tau_{ch} = \tau_{ch}(\Pi)$. We now define:

$$T'(L) = \frac{T(L)}{\tau_{ch}(\Pi_0)} \,, \tag{13}$$

where Π_0 are the parameters of a fixed instance of the problem, independent of L. Next we show that $T'(L)$ is indeed invariant under a linear transformation of the time parameter:

Proposition 4.1. Let F, F' be two CTCs related by $F' = \frac{1}{a}F$ for some constant $a > 0$, then they have the same time complexity.

Proof. We denote by primes properties of the the system F'. Multiplying the vector field by $\frac{1}{a}$ is equivalent to multiplying the time parameter by a. Therefore the computation times in the two systems are related by: $t'_c(\Pi) = at_c(\Pi)$, for every input Π. Let M, M' be the stability operators of F, F' on input Π, respectively. Clearly $M' = \frac{1}{a}M$ so that $\tau'_{ch}(\Pi) = a\tau_{ch}(\Pi)$, and in particular for Π_0. We conclude:

$$\frac{t_c(H(\Pi))}{\tau_{ch}(\Pi_0)} = \frac{t'_c(H(\Pi))}{\tau'_{ch}(\Pi_0)} \,.$$

This holds when taking the maximum as well. $\qquad\qquad\square$

Remark 4.5. We now indicate the relation between exponential convergence and efficient computation. We noted that when a system is in the linear regime, in a time $\tau_{ch} \ln 2$ a digit of the attractor is computed. Thus to compute L digits requires a time which is $O(\tau_{ch}L)$. We compare this with the case of non-exponential convergence. To get non-exponential convergence at least one eigenvalue of the stability matrix must be zero. Then there is a direction such that $\dot{y} \sim (y - y^*)^\beta$, where $\beta \geq 2$. This yields polynomial convergence: $|x(t) - x^*| \sim t^{-\beta+1}$. In order to compute x^* with L significant digits, we need to have $|x(t) - x^*| < 2^{-L}$, or $t > 2^{L/(\beta-1)}$, for an exponential time complexity. Note that requiring the vector field to be analytic rules out convergence which is faster than exponential.

5 A CTC for the maximum problem

5.1 Analysis of the flow

In this section we give a detailed analysis of the flow for the MAX problem introduced in Section 3:

$$F_i = \left(c_i - \sum_{j=1}^{n} x_j c_j\right) x_i \,, \tag{14}$$

We denote by $e^1, \ldots, e^n$ the standard basis of $\mathbb{R}^n$. It is easy to verify that the only fixed points of F are the n vertices of the simplex $e^1, \ldots, e^n$. We begin with the case of a unique maximum. For the purpose of analyzing the flow suppose that $c_1 > c_2$ and $c_2 \geq c_j$, $j = 3, \ldots, n$. Under this assumption the flow converges exponentially to e^1 as witnessed by the solution to the equations $\dot{x} = F$:

$$x_i(t) = \frac{\exp(c_i t)x_i(0)}{\sum_{j=1}^{n} \exp(c_j t)x_j(0)} \,, \tag{15}$$

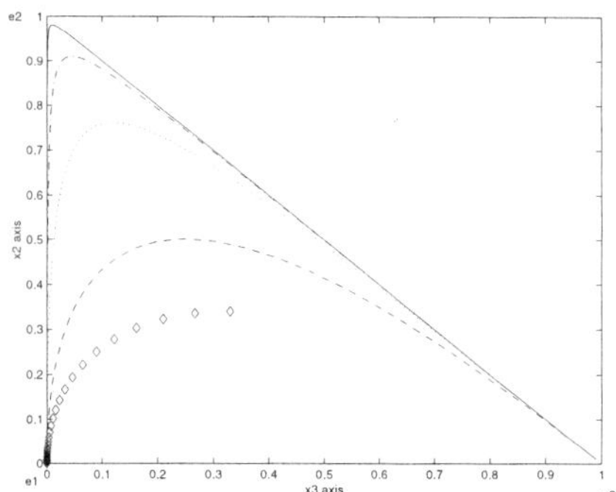

Figure 1: Phase space behavior of the flow generated by (4) on the two dimensional simplex with $c_1 > c_2 > c_3$. A projection onto the plane of the x_2 and x_3 coordinates is shown. A number of trajectories which start near the minimum vertex e^3 are plotted. Such trajectories reach a vicinity of the saddle point e^2 before flowing in the direction of the maximum which is projected onto the origin. The trajectory of the interior initial condition $e/3 = \frac{1}{3}(1, 1, 1)$ is denoted by diamonds.

where $x_i(0)$ are the components of the initial condition. It is important to notice that the analytical solution does not help in determining which of the fixed points is the attractor of the system: one needs the solution to the specific instance of the problem for that. Thus the analytical solution is only a formal one, and one has to follow the dynamics with the vector field (4) to find the maximum.

To avoid the problem of flow near saddle points exemplified in Figure 1 we choose an initial condition at the center of the simplex:

$$\frac{e}{n} = \frac{1}{n}(1, \ldots, 1)^T. \tag{16}$$

This subsection can be summarized by the following interim result:

Lemma 5.1. $(F, c, e/n, T(L))$ is a CTC for MAX, where $T(L)$ is a bound on the convergence time to the halting region.

In the following subsection we conclude the analysis of the algorithm with a derivation of a bound $T(L)$.

5.2 The computation time

Because of the constraint $\sum_{i=1}^{n} x_i = 1$, the flow has $n - 1$ independent variables, which we choose as $x_2, \ldots, x_n$. The asymptotic behavior of the solution for the independent variables is $x_i(t) \sim \exp(-(c_1 - c_i)t)$, $i = 2, \ldots, n$. Therefore the time scale of F is

$$\tau_{ch} = \frac{1}{c_1 - c_2}. \tag{17}$$

This can also be obtained from a linearization of F in the vicinity of e^1.

Lemma 5.2. The problem precision for MAX instances with a unique solution satisfies $\epsilon_p = 1/2$ and

$$t_c(\epsilon_p) \leq \tau_{ch} \log n.$$

Proof. $\epsilon_p < 1/2$ since the possible solutions are the vertices of the simplex, which have integer components. t_c is obtained by plugging the analytical solution into the inequality $||x(t) - x^*|| < \epsilon_p$. $\qquad\square$

Proposition 5.1. Let $c \in \mathbb{N}^n$ be an instance of MAX with a unique maximum then

$$t_c(H(c)) \leq \tau_{ch}(\log \tau_{ch} + \log n + \log c_2) . \tag{18}$$

Proof. The attracting region of the problem is the set in which $\dot{x}_i < 0$ for $i > 1$. By the constraint $\sum_{i=1}^n x_i = 1$, x_1 is then guaranteed to increase. The convergence time to the attracting region is a time t such that for all $t' > t$ $\dot{x}_i(t') < 0$ for $i > 1$. From the flow equations and the non-negativity of the x_i's we have that $\dot{x}_i < 0$ for $i > 1$ iff

$$\sum_{j=1}^n c_j x_j > c_i , \; i = 2, \ldots, n . \tag{19}$$

Since by assumption $c_2 \geq c_j$ for $j > 2$, this is equivalent to:

$$\sum_{j=1}^n c_j x_j > c_2 . \tag{20}$$

The result follows by plugging in the analytical solution and solving for t. $\qquad\square$

Remark 5.1. The condition which defines the attracting region equation (20) can be expressed as $h(x) > h(e^2)$. When this is satisfied, it is satisfied for all subsequent times, since the cost function of a gradient flow is increasing along a trajectory. Or in other words, the set $\{x \in \Delta_{n-1} : h(x) > h(e^2)\}$ is a trapping set (positively invariant set in the language of dynamical systems) of the flow. This condition is appropriate for any gradient flow. Also, the condition on proximity to the attractor can be substituted here for proximity of the cost function to its value on the attractor.

Remark 5.2. In the case when the maximum c_i is not unique any combination of the maximal vertices is a maximum of h. The bound we obtained remains essentially unchanged in that case as well [19].

5.3 Complexity of the algorithm

We now proceed to analyze the problem size dependence of the above bound on $t_c(H)$, Equation (18). This dependence varies according to the set from which the input is taken through the problem size dependence of the characteristic time scale. We recall that the bit-size complexity of a problem instance, L, is the length of the binary encoding of the input. This is appropriate for models over the integers or rationals. When the inputs are integers, $L = \sum_{i=1}^n (1 + \log(c_i + 1))$. As in the BSS model of computation over the real numbers [16], for real inputs the size of a problem is the number of inputs. The complexity for different input sets is summarized in Table 1, and is easily derived from expressions (17) and (18).

We now discuss the results of table 1. The second row of the table considers the case of inputs which are integer or rationals with bounded denominators (rational numbers which can be specified with fixed precision). In these two cases we obtain sub-linear (logarithmic)

Input space	problem size	bound on τ_{ch}	T
bounded integers or bounded rationals with bounded denominators	$L = O(n)$	$O(1)$	$\log n$
integers or rationals with bounded denominators	L	$O(1)$	$\log L$
rationals	L	L	$L \log L$
reals	n	unbounded	poly in condition number logarithmic in n

Table 1: Bounds on τ_{ch} and T as a function of the input set.

complexity, which may seem surprising. However notice that the variables of a CTC can be considered as processing units. Therefore when the number of variables is an increasing function of the size of the input, as in the CTC we presented for MAX, the model becomes inherently parallel. There are various models of parallel computation, and the complexity of MAX is different in each of them: in the PRAM model its complexity is $O(\log \log n)$ [40]; in the circuit model its complexity is constant or logarithmic depending on the fan-in (unbounded or constant, respectively). It is not clear to which model ours is most closely related to.

For general rational inputs (third row of the table) the complexity is again comparable to that obtained by a naive algorithm in the Turing model: for a problem of size L, the comparison of two numbers requires $O(L)$ bit operations. This is multiplied by by the number of comparisons required between numbers.

For real inputs there is no bound on τ_{ch}, and hence on the computation time. In such cases we consider complexity as a function of a "condition number". Note that in the BSS model the MAX problem with real inputs can be solved efficiently because comparisons between real numbers are allowed.

In the numerical analysis literature it is common to consider the condition number of a problem instance as a measure of its difficulty [18]. The condition number is defined as the norm of the condition operator which measures the effects of infinitesimal perturbations in the input on the result of a computation [17]. In many settings the condition number is shown to be the reciprocal of the distance to the set of ill-posed problem, where a problem instance is said to be ill-posed if its solution is not unique. Such results are called "condition number theorems". In combinatorial optimization the output does not depend continuously on the input so the condition operator cannot be defined in this manner. In the context of the linear programming problem, Renegar [41] postulates the condition number as the inverse of the distance to the set of ill-posed problems. Such a definition is motivated by these condition number theorems. A condition number theorem can be proven in for the flow for MAX, and argued in the general case [19].

6   Linear Programming and MAXFLOW

In this section we present a CTC for the maximum network flow problem (MAXFLOW) which is based on a flow for linear programming. The flow does not yield an algorithm which is efficient in a worst case analysis for general linear programming instances. However, it turns out to be efficient for MAXFLOW and other related problems which can be expressed as linear programming problems. A probabilistic analysis that shows that given a Gaussian distribution of problem instance the flow is highly efficient on average or "with high probability".

6.1 A flow for linear programming

We begin with the definition of the linear programming problem (LP) and a vector field for solving it introduced in [8]. The *standard form* of LP is to find

$$\max\{c^T x \; : \; x \in \mathbb{R}^n, Ax = b, x \geq 0\} \tag{21}$$

where $c \in \mathbb{R}^n, b \in \mathbb{R}^m, A \in \mathbb{R}^{m \times n}$ and $m \leq n$. The set generated by the constraints in (21) is a polyhedron, and if a bounded optimal solution exists, it is obtained at one of its vertices. Let $B \subset \{1, \ldots, n\}, |B| = m$, and $N = \{1, \ldots, n\} \setminus B$, and denote by x_B the coordinates with indices from B, and A_B, the $m \times m$ matrix whose columns are the columns of A with indices from B. A vertex of the LP problem is defined by a set of indices B that is called a *basic set* if

$$x_B = A_B^{-1} b \geq 0 \;. \tag{22}$$

The components of a vertex are x_B that satisfy (22), and $x_N = 0$. If a vertex has more than one basic set that defines it then the polyhedron is said to be degenerate.

The Faybusovich vector field is a projection of the gradient of the linear cost function onto the constraint set, relative to a Riemannian metric which enforces the positivity constraints (see Appendix B). Let $h(x) = c^T x$ and denote its gradient by $\mathrm{grad}\, h$. The explicit form of the gradient is:

$$\mathrm{grad} h(x) = [D(x) - D(x)A^T (AD(x)A^T)^{-1} AD(x)]\, c \;, \tag{23}$$

where $D(x)$ is the diagonal matrix $\mathrm{Diag}(x_1 \ldots x_n)$. A complete characterization of the dynamics of this vector field is as follows:

Theorem 6.1. *[8] Let (A, b, c) be the data for a nondegenerate linear program with a unique bounded solution then:*

1. *The faces of the polyheder are invariant sets of the dynamics induced by $\mathrm{grad} f$.*

2. *The set of fixed points of $\mathrm{grad} f$ coincides with the vertices of the polyheder.*

3. *On an interior initial condition, the dynamics converges exponentially to the maximal vertex of the LP problem.*

Since the formal solution of the Faybusovich vector field is the basis of our analysis we give its derivation in Appendix B. The formal solution shown below describes how the components x_N of a maximum vertex x^* go to zero. Denote by $e^1, \ldots, e^n$ the standard basis of $\mathbb{R}^n$, and define $n - m$ vectors

$$\mu^i = e^i + \sum_{j=1}^{m} \alpha_{ji} e^j \;, \tag{24}$$

where

$$\alpha_{ji} = -(A_B^{-1} A_N)_{ji} \tag{25}$$

is an $(n - m) \times m$ matrix. The vectors μ^i are perpendicular to the rows of A and are parallel to the faces of the polyheder defined by the constraints. In this notation the analytical solution is:

$$x_i(t) = x_i(0) \exp(-\Delta_i t - \sum_{j \in B} \alpha_{ji} \ln \frac{x_j(t)}{x_j(0)}) \, , i \in N, \tag{26}$$

where $x_i(0)$ are the components of the initial condition, and

$$\Delta_i = - < c, \mu^i > \, , \, i \in N \tag{27}$$

$$= -c_i + \sum_{j \in B} \alpha_{ji} c_j.$$

Here $< \cdot, \cdot >$ denotes the standard inner product.

Remark 6.1. If the basic set B in equation (26) is chosen to be a basic set corresponding to a maximum vertex then all the Δ_i are positive. Thus it is evident that the analytical solution is only a formal one, and does not provide an answer to the LP problem.

Remark 6.2. If c is perpendicular to a face of the polyheder then the maximum vertex of the LP problem is not unique, and some of the Δ_i are 0. In such a case the flow converges to the optimal *face* of the polyheder, i.e., to a convex combination of the optimal vertices.

The computation time of the system is determined by the system size dependence of the constants Δ_i and α_{ij}. If for example the Δ_i are small then long computation times will be required. For general instances of LP these constants can be exponentially small, for a worst case exponential computation time. Exponentially small Δ_i are possible since Δ_i are defined by a matrix inverse that can yield exponentially small quantities [42]. In the next chapter we show that under a probability distribution on LP instances such "bad" instances happen with vanishing probability as n tends to infinity. In this chapter we take a different approach. Many problems in combinatorial optimization are expressible as linear programming problems that are often simpler to solve than general linear programming problems. Examples include maximum network flow (MAXFLOW) and bipartite matching [43, 44]. Thus, to make the Faybusovich vector field the basis of an algorithm which is efficient even in the worst case, we apply it to LP formulations of MAXFLOW and other related problems, and show that these have polynomially convergent Faybusovich flows. Polynomial convergence occurs in these cases since the constants Δ_i and α_{ji} are small integers. Integrality of the Δ_i will be guaranteed when the constraint matrix is totally unimodular:

Definition 6.1. An integer matrix A is called *totally unimodular* (TUM) if every square non-singular submatrix B of A satisfies $\det B = \pm 1, 0$.

For a problem defined by a totally unimodular matrix, the solution polyheder is integral when b is integer, as can be seen from equation (22). The next theorem gives conditions for TUM:

Theorem 6.2. *[43, 44] Let A be a matrix which is either*

1. The node edge incidence matrix of a directed graph

2. The node edge incidence of an undirected bipartite graph,

then A is TUM. This includes the LP formulations of MAXFLOW, maximum weighted bipartite matching, and shortest path problems.

More general conditions for unimodularity are also known [44, 43]. Total unimodularity yields the following:

Lemma 6.1. Let A be a constraint matrix which is TUM, such that each column has at the most k nonzero entries, and let B and N be basic and non-basic sets respectively, then:

1. $|\alpha_{ji}| = |(A_B^{-1} A_N)_{ji}| \leq k$ for every $i \in B$, $j \in N$;

2. Δ_i is integer for every $i \in N$.

Definition 6.2. A network $\mathcal{N} = (s, s', V, E, b)$ is a directed graph (V, E) with a source $s \in V$ with no incoming edges, a sink $s' \in V$ with no outgoing edges and an integer nonzero capacity b_i for edge i. Each edge is assigned a variable x_i, which is the flow through it. For convenience we add an additional edge with unlimited capacity from s' to s. Let (V, E) be the resulting graph, denote $q = |V|, p = |E|$, and assign the variable x_p to the flow on the edge from s' to s. An assignment of values $x \in \mathbb{R}^p$ is a valid flow for a network $\mathcal{N}$ if

$$0 \leq x \leq b \tag{28}$$

and it satisfies conservation of flow at each vertex $k \in V$:

$$\sum_{i \in \text{in}(k)} x_i - \sum_{i \in \text{out}(k)} x_i = 0 , \tag{29}$$

where $\text{in}(k)$ and $\text{out}(k)$ are the sets of incoming and outgoing edges, respectively, of vertex k. The flow through the network is given by the value of the variable x_p. The objective is to maximize x_p subject to the constraints (28) and (29).

The polyhedron defined by the constraints (28,29) is highly degenerate. Thus in order to use the Faybusovich vector field the degeneracy has to be lifted [19]. Details of the computation of the halting region are also found in [19] for the overall result:

Theorem 6.3. *The CTC for MAXFLOW has complexity $T = 7(m^2 + L)$*

Remark 6.3. The above analysis was carried out specifically for the LP formulation of the MAXFLOW problem. Similar complexity bounds will hold for other problems defined by TUM constraint matrices.

Remark 6.4. If we consider MAXFLOW problems where the in-degree of each vertex is bounded then $|E| = O(|V|)$, in which case $n = O(m)$. Parallel algorithms for the MAXFLOW problem are discussed for example in [45]. The parallel algorithms for the MAXFLOW problem have time complexity $O(|V|^2 \log |V|)$ and use $O(\sqrt{|E|})$ processors. This is comparable to the performance of our algorithm in the case of bounded in/out degree graphs.

6.2 *Solving general LP instance*

We have noted that the Faybusovich vector field has exponential worst case performance for general LP instances due to the possibility of exponentially small Δ_i. This is however, a rare event, and as in the case of the simplex algorithm – exponential worst case behavior does not prevent the algorithm from performing well in practice. Showing this entails assuming a probabilistic model over LP instances, and computing the *average* computation time under that model. As in several other studies, we assumed a Gaussian distribution of inputs ([46] and references therein). Monte-Carlo simulations [47] show that under this distribution of inputs

$$T(n) = n \log n \,, \tag{30}$$

on average, where we took n/m as constant. We are currently working to establish this bound analytically.

7 Conclusion: P and Continuous P

We have defined time complexity for a class of continuous time systems[2]. In the following we compare complexity in our model with the classical theory, so we consider integer or rational inputs. The operations which define a formula makes it computable in NC. However, for the definition of logarithmic time complexity class, a stricter form of uniformity is required, e.g. to allow only those operations which are computable in AC_0 [10].

Definition 7.1. A problem is said to be in CLOG (continuous log) if it has a CTC with a polynomial number of variables and logarithmic time complexity.

This is a counterpart of the classical NC_1 [10]. We have shown that MAX (for integer inputs) is in CLOG. The counterpart of the classical P is CP:

Definition 7.2. A problem is said to be in CP (continuous P) if it has a CTC with a polynomial number of variables and polynomial time complexity.

In Section 6 we have shown a CTC for the maximum network flow problem which places it in CP. The maximum network flow problem is P-complete relative to logspace Turing reductions [48]. Relying on this result we argue that P$\subseteq$CP: If we use the Turing reductions from a P problem to maximum network flow then all efficient Turing computations can be performed polynomially in our framework if we allow the pre-processing required for the reduction. Using Turing reductions which are outside our model might be considered unsatisfactory, but at the moment we know how to solve only specific problems in our framework if we do not use a pre-processing stage. In this context we mention the related result that approximating the fixed point of an NC contracting mapping is P-complete [49], and note that contracting maps converge exponentially to fixed points. This means that that an NC vector field is sufficient to obtain the classical P. The dynamical system used to solve the maximum network flow problem is a gradient flow, so the subclass of CP which consists of analytically solvable gradient flows can be considered as computationally powerful as P.

As of yet we have no argument for the inclusion CP$\subseteq$P. The analytical solution is no help in computing the the attractor of the system, as exemplified in the examples of the MAX and

---

[2]There seems no obvious counterpart for the space resource in these systems. One can consider the variables as memory units, but they also play the part of processing units.

MAXFLOW problems. However, we believe that a polynomial time simulation of the ODE with some numerical integration scheme should be possible for the class of vector fields considered here.

Developement and analysis of algorithms in our framework is different than in the Turing model. It consists of the following stages:

- Finding a dynamical system with an attracting fixed point that corresponds to the solution to the computational problem. This corresponds to the stage of design and verification in classic algorithmics.

- Establishing bounds on the computation time: using an analytical solution or a Lyapunov functional, bound the convergence time to the halting region of the system, and find the input size dependence of the bound. This is sometimes reduced to finding input size dependent bounds on variables such as the Δ_i of Equation (27).

A   Dynamical Systems: Definitions

In this section we give the relevant background in dynamical systems. For a detailed introduction the reader is referred to [38, 50, 12]. The flows we consider in this chapter are defined by autonomous systems of first order ODEs:

$$\frac{dx}{dt} = F(x), \tag{31}$$

where $x(t)$ is a d-dimensional vector and F is a d-dimensional vector function of x with components $(F_1, \ldots F_d)$, called a *vector field*. We will assume that F satisfies a Lipschitz condition to guarantee that a unique solution of (31) exists. A *fixed point*, also called an equilibrium point, of (31) is a point x^* such that $F(x^*) = 0$. The local stability of x^* under the flow (31) is determined by the linear ODE

$$\frac{dx}{dt} = Mx, \tag{32}$$

where M is the stability operator $DF|_{x^*}$, which is the derivative of F at a point x^*. An eigenvalue λ of M is called *attracting*, *repelling*, or *neutral* according to whether the real part of λ is less than zero, greater than zero, or zero, respectively. A fixed point x^* is called *attracting*, *unstable*, or a *saddle* if the eigenvalues of M are respectively all attracting, all repelling, or some attracting and others repelling [50]. A fixed point is called *hyperbolic* if all eigenvalues are not neutral. The fixed points of the dynamical systems considered in this chapter are all hyperbolic. The *basin of attraction* of an attracting fixed point x^* is the set of points that reach x^* in the infinite time limit. A hyperbolic attracting fixed point x^* has the property of *exponential convergence*: for every trajectory $x(t)$ in the basin of attraction of x^* there exists strictly positive constants t_0, c and λ such that for all $t > t_0$, $||x(t) - x^*|| < ce^{-\lambda t}$. This is a result of the solution of equation (32). In fact, convergence to an attracting fixed point is exponential if and only if it is hyperbolic.

An important class of dissipative systems are *gradient flows*. A gradient flow is a flow to a local minimum or maximum of a function $E(x)$, and is defined by the equation

$$\dot{x} = \pm\mathrm{grad}\, E \,, \tag{33}$$

where the sign of the right hand side determines whether the flow is to a local minimum or a local maximum (negative sign for minimization). For unconstrained minimization on $\mathbb{R}^d$, grad E is the usual vector of partial derivatives $\frac{\partial E}{\partial x_i}$. For the definition of gradient flows on Riemannian manifolds the reader is referred to [38, 9]. Such a manifold can take into account for example, the constraint equations of an optimization problem.

B The Faybuosvich Vector Field

The Faybusovich vector field is a gradient flow relative to the inner product $< \xi, \eta >_{D(x)^{-1}} = \xi^T D(x)^{-1} \eta$, This inner product is defined on the positive orthant $\mathbb{R}^n_+ = \{x \in \mathbb{R}^n : x_i > 0, \ i = 1, \ldots, n\}$, where it defines a Riemannian metric. In the following we denote by $a^i, \ i = 1, \ldots, m$ the rows of A. The Faybusovich vector field is the gradient of $h(x) = c^T x$ relative to this metric projected to the constraint set [8]. It can be expressed as:

$$\operatorname{grad} h = D(x)c - \sum_{i=1}^{m} \zeta_i(x)D(x)a^i, \tag{34}$$

where $\zeta_1(x), \ldots, \zeta_m(x)$ make the gradient perpendicular to the constraint vectors, i.e. $A \operatorname{grad} h = 0$, so that $Ax = b$ is maintained by the dynamics.

Let B, N be index sets that define a basic feasible solution of an LP instance and consider the functions

$$\Psi_i(x) = \ln(x_i) + \sum_{j \in B} \alpha_{ji} \ln(x_j) \ \ i \in N. \tag{35}$$

where

$$\alpha_{ji} = -(A_B^{-1} A_N)_{ji} \ \ , i \in N, j \in B. \tag{36}$$

The Ψ_i are defined such that their equations of motion are easily integrated. This gives $n - m$ equations which correspond to the $n - m$ independent variables of the LP problem. To compute the time derivative of Ψ_i we first find:

$$\nabla \Psi_i = \frac{1}{x_i} e^i + \sum_{j \in B} \frac{\alpha_{ij}}{x_j} e^j . \tag{37}$$

We recall the definition

$$\mu^i = e^i + \sum_{j=1}^{m} \alpha_{ji} e^j , \tag{38}$$

and note that the vectors μ^i defined in equation (24) have the following property:

$$< \mu^i, a^j > = 0, \ \ i \in N, \ j \in B ,$$

where $< \cdot, \cdot >$ is the standard inner product. Therefore:

$$\begin{aligned}
\dot{\Psi}_i(x) &= \ < \nabla \Psi_i(x), \dot{x} > \ = \ < \nabla \Psi_i(x), \operatorname{grad} h > \\
&= \ < \mu^i, c - \sum_{j=1}^{m} \zeta_j(x) a^j > \\
&= \ < \mu^i, c > \ \equiv \ -\Delta_i .
\end{aligned} \tag{39}$$

This equation is integrated to yield:

$$x_i(t) = x_i(0) \exp\left(-\Delta_i t - \sum_{j \in B} \alpha_{ij} \ln \frac{x_j(t)}{x_j(0)}\right). \tag{40}$$

References

[1] J. Hertz, A. Krogh, and R. Palmer. *Introduction to the Theory of Neural Computation.* Addison-Wesley, Redwood City, 1991.

[2] A. Cichocki and R. Unbehauen. *Neural networks for optimization and signal processing.* John Wiley, 1993.

[3] X.B. Liang and J. Wang. A recurrent neural network for nonlinear optimization with a continuously differentiable objective function and bound constraints. *IEEE transaction on neural networks*, 2000.

[4] C. Mead. *Analog VLSI and Neural Systems.* Addison-Wesley, 1989.

[5] C. Koch and H. Li. *Vision Chips: Implementation of Vision Algorithms with Analog VLSI Circuits.* IEEE Computer Society, 1994.

[6] J. Indiveri. Winner-take-all networks with lateral excitation. *Analog Integrated Circuits and Signal Processing*, 13:185–193, 1997.

[7] R. W. Brockett. Dynamical systems that sort lists, diagonalize matrices and solve linear programming problems. *Linear Algebra and Its Applications*, 146:79–91, 1991.

[8] L. Faybusovich. Dynamical systems which solve optimization problems with linear constraints. *IMA Journal of Mathematical Control and Information*, 8:135–149, 1991.

[9] U. Helmke and J.B. Moore. *Optimization and Dynamical Systems.* Springer Verlag, London, 1994.

[10] C. Papadimitriou. *Computational Complexity.* Addison-Wesley, Reading, Mass., 1995.

[11] L.O. Chua and G.N. Lin. Nonlinear programming without computation. *IEEE transaction on circuits and systems*, 31(2), 1984.

[12] E. Ott. *Chaos in Dynamical Systems.* Cambridge University Press, Cambridge, 1993.

[13] Olivier Bournez. Achilles and the Tortoise climbing up the hyper-arithmetical hierarchy. *Theoretical Computer Science*, 210(1):21–71, 6 January 1999.

[14] J. von Neumann. In A.H. Taub, editor, *Collected works*, volume A. Pergamon, 1961.

[15] L. Blum, M. Shub, and S. Smale. On a theory of computation and complexity over the real numbers: NP completeness, recursive functions, and universal machines. *Bull. A.M.S.*, 21:1–46, 1989.

[16] L. Blum, F. Cucker, M. Shub, and S. Smale. *Complexity and real Computation.* Springer-Verlag, 1999.

[17] J.P. Dedieu. Approximate solutions of numerical problems, condition number analysis and condition number theorem. In J. Renegar, M. Shub, and S. Smale, editors, *The mathematics of numerical analysis*, pages 263–283, Utah, July 1995. American mathematical society.

[18] S. Smale. Some remarks on the foundations of numerical analysis. *SIAM Review*, 32:211–220, 1990.

[19] A. Ben-Hur, H.T. Siegelmann, and S. Fishman. A theory of complexity for continuous time dynamics. Accepted, Journal of Complexity.

[20] C. Moore. Unpredictability and undecidability in dynamical systems. *Physical Review Letters*, 64:2354–2357, 1990.

[21] P. Koiran, M. Cosnard, and M. Garzon. Computability with low-dimensional dynamical systems. *Theoretical Computer Science*, 132:113–128, 1994.

[22] P. Koiran and C. Moore. Closed-form analytic maps in one and two dimensions can simulate universal Turing machines. *Theoretical Computer Science*, 210:217–223, 1999.

[23] R.W. Brockett. Hybrid models for motion control systems. In H.L. Trentelman and J.C. Willems, editors, *Essays in Control: Perspectives in the Theory and its Applications*, pages 29–53. Birkhauser, Boston, 1993.

[24] M.S. Branicky. Analog computation with continuous ODEs. In *Proceedings of the IEEE Workshop on Physics and Computation*, pages 265–274, Dallas, TX, 1994.

[25] E. Asarin, O. Maler, and A. Pnueli. Reachability analysis of dynamical systems with piecewise-constant derivatives. *Theoretical Computer Science*, 138:35–66, 1995.

[26] P. Orponen. A survey of continuous time computation theory. In *Advances in Algorithms, Languages and Complexity*, Dordrecht, 1997. Kluwer Academic Publishers.

[27] C.E. Shannon. Mathematical theory of the differential analyzer. *Journal of Mathematics and Physics of the Massachusetts Institute of Technology*, 20:337–354, 1941.

[28] M.B. Pour-El. Abstract computability and its relation to the general purpose analog computer (some connections between logic, differential equations and analog computers). *Transactions of the American Mathematical Society*, 199:1–29, 1974.

[29] M.L. Campagnolo, C. Moore, and J.F. Costa. Iteration, inequalities and differentiability in analog computers. To appear, Journal of Complexity.

[30] C. Moore. Recursion theory on the reals and continuous-time computation. *Theoretical Computer Science*, 162:23–44, 1996.

[31] R. Feynman. Quantum mechanical computers. *Foundations of Physics*, 16(6):507–531, 1986. Originally appeared in Optics News, Feb 1985.

[32] H.T. Siegelmann and E.D. Sontag. Analog computation via neural networks. *Theoretical Computer Science*, 131, 1994. 331-360.

[33] H.T. Siegelmann. Computation beyond the Turing limit. *Science*, 268(5210):545–548, April 28 1995.

[34] M. Zak. Terminal attractors in neural networks. *Neural Networks*, 2:259–274, 1989.

[35] J.J. Hopfield. Neurons with graded responses have collective computational properties like those of two-state neurons. In *Proc. of the Natl. Acad. of Sciences*, volume 81, pages 3088–3092, USA, 1984.

[36] J. Sima and P. Orponen. A continuous-time hopfield net simulation of discrete neural networks. Technical Report 773, Academy of Sciences of the Czech Republic, 1999.

[37] B.R. Hunt, T. Sauer, and J.A. Yorke. Prevalence: A translational-invariant "almost every" on infinite dimensional spaces. *Bulletin Of the American Mathematical Society*, 27(2):217–238, 1992.

[38] M. Hirsch and S. Smale. *Differential Equations, Dynamical Systems and Linear Algebra*. Academic Press, New York, 1974.

[39] H.T. Siegelmann and S. Fishman. Computation by dynamical systems. *Physica D*, 120:214–235, 1998.

[40] Y. Shiloach and U. Vishkin. Finding the maximum, merging and sorting in a parallel computation model. *Journal of Algorithms*, 2:88–102, 1981.

[41] J. Renegar. Incorporating condition measures into the complexity theory of linear programming. *SIAM J. Optimization*, 5(3):506–524, 1995.

[42] F.R. Gantmacher. *The Theory of Matrices*. Chelsea Publishing Company, New York, N.Y., 1960.

[43] C.H. Papadimitriou and K. Steiglitz. *Combinatorial Optimization*. Prentice Hall, Inc., Englewood Cliffs, NJ, 1982.

[44] G.L. Nemhauser and L.A. Wolsey. *Integer and Combinatorial Optimization*. John Wiley and Sons, 1988.

[45] A.V. Goldberg. Parallel algorithms for network flow problems. In J.H. Reif, editor, *Synthesis of parallel algorithms*. Morgan Kaufmann Publishers, San Mateo, California, 1993.

[46] Y. Ye. *Interior Point Algorithms: Theory and Analysis*. John Wiley and Sons Inc., 1997.

[47] A. Ben-Hur. *Computation, a dynamical systems approach*. PhD thesis, Technion, IIT, 2001.

[48] L.M. Goldschlager, R.A. Shaw, and J. Staples. The maximum flow problem is log space complete for P. *Theoretical Computer Science*, 21:105–111, 1982.

[49] H.J. Hoover. Real functions, contraction mappings and P-completeness. *Information and Computation*, 93(2):333–349, 1991.

[50] J. Guckenheimer and P. Holmes. *Nonlinear Oscillations, Dynamical Systems, and Bifurcations of Vector Fields*. Springer Verlag, New York, 1983.

Limitations and Future Trends in Neural Computation
S. Ablameyko et al. (Eds.)
IOS Press, 2003

Energy-Based Computation with Symmetric Hopfield Nets

Jiří Šíma*
Department of Theoretical Computer Science,
Institute of Computer Science, Academy of Sciences of the Czech Republic,
P.O. Box 5, 182 07 Prague 8, Czech Republic, sima@cs.cas.cz

Abstract. We propose a unifying approach to the analysis of computational aspects of symmetric Hopfield nets which is based on the concept of "energy source". Within this framework we present different results concerning the computational power of various Hopfield model classes. It is shown that polynomial-time computations by nondeterministic Turing machines can be reduced to the process of minimizing the energy in Hopfield nets (the MIN ENERGY problem). Furthermore, external and internal sources of energy are distinguished. The external sources include e.g. energizing inputs from so-called Hopfield languages, and also certain external oscillators that prove finite analog Hopfield nets to be computationally Turing universal. On the other hand, the internal source of energy can be implemented by a symmetric clock subnetwork producing an exponential number of oscillations which are used to energize the simulation of convergent asymmetric networks by Hopfield nets. This shows that infinite families of polynomial-size Hopfield nets compute the complexity class PSPACE/poly. A special attention is paid to generalizing these results for analog states and continuous time to point out alternative sources of efficient computation.

1 Introduction

The computational potential and limits of neural networks have been studied for more than a decade in order to understand what is, either ultimately or efficiently, computable by particular models [15, 28, 48, 50, 53, 54, 55, 56, 58, 61, 67, 72]. This interest is motivated partly by the quest to formally justify heuristics used in practical neurocomputing, and partly by the realization that despite their formal simplicity, neural networks are computationally quite powerful, and thus may serve as a useful reference model for investigating new sources of efficient computation such as energy, analog states, continuous time, etc.

We will mainly focus on the *symmetric*, so-called *Hopfield nets* that represent one of the fundamental models of neural networks. This model was popularized by John Hopfield in his very influential 1982 and 1984 papers [30, 31] although the dynamics of Hopfield nets had actually already been analyzed earlier by several authors [2, 10, 42]. It is well known that the computational dynamics of this model is governed by a bounded *energy (Liapunov) function* whose values are properly decreasing along any nonconstant state trajectory. Hence, a Hopfield network converges from any initial state towards some stable equilibrium state which is

---

*Research partially supported by grants GA AS CR B2030007, GA ČR No. 201/01/1192.

not usually the case of arbitrary *asymmetric* networks. Because of their well-constrained convergence behavior Hopfield nets have traditionally been used as associative memories, e.g. for removing noise from large patterns [30], but they are also widely applied to the fast approximate solution of combinatorial optimization problems [32]. Part of the appeal of Hopfield nets also stems from their connection to the much-studied *Ising spin glass model* in statistical physics [5] and their natural hardware implementations using analog electrical networks [30] or optical computers [11].

In this paper, we explore the capability of Hopfield nets for general-purpose computation. We propose a unifying approach to their analysis based on the concept of "energy source". This approach provides a common framework within which different results concerning the computational aspects of Hopfield nets can be integrated. In particular, we inspect how the energy consumption constrains the computational power of various Hopfield model classes with different characteristics including feedforward vs. recurrent architectures, binary vs. analog states, discrete vs. continuous time, finite nets vs. infinite families, etc. We compare new sources of efficient computation in Hopfield nets such as energy, analog states and continuous time with the classical Turing complexity measures represented by discrete time and space. Therefore a special attention is also paid to generalizing the results that were originally established for discrete domains to those for analog-state and/or continuous time Hopfield nets although only the main ideas of these rather technical and relatively new results can be sketched here. It turns out that Hopfield nets enrich the traditional repertoire of computational means and even point out new sources of efficient computation.

The present paper is organized as follows. A brief review of the basic definitions and results concerning the computational properties of Hopfield nets is presented in Section 2. Section 3 deals with the important *MIN ENERGY* problem of finding a network state with minimal energy for a given symmetric network which is shown to be NP-hard for both binary and analog Hopfield nets. It follows that polynomial-time computations by nondeterministic Turing machines can be implemented by the process of minimizing the energy in these networks which is the fact often exploited in combinatorial optimization applications.

In Section 4, the computational power of *finite* Hopfield nets that are used as language acceptors is analyzed which is strictly less than that of asymmetric networks because of the energy constraints. Therefore, *external* sources of "computational energy" are considered such as energizing inputs that form a fully characterized subclass of the regular languages, so-called Hopfield languages. Or an external oscillator of certain type is supplied to achieve Turing universality for finite analog Hopfield nets.

In Section 5, on the other hand, a symmetric *clock* network—a simulated binary counter which produces an exponential number of oscillations before it converges, is built and then used as an *internal* source of computational energy. In particular, this clock is exploited to energize the simulation of *convergent* asymmetric networks by Hopfield nets, which implies that *infinite* families of polynomial-size symmetric networks can simulate (nonuniform) polynomial-space Turing machines (more precisely, they compute the complexity class PSPACE/poly). The simulation also provides evidence that the *convergence* in binary neural networks is, in a quite strong sense, "equivalent" to the *symmetry* of their weights. Moreover, an analog implementation of the clock represents an interesting example of the analog Hopfield net whose computation terminates later than that of any other binary symmetric network of the same representation length. This result suggests that analog models of computation may be worth investigating more for their gains in representational efficiency than for their theoretical capability for arbitrary-precision real number computation.

In Section 6, the results from Section 5 are generalized for *continuous-time* analog Hopfield nets. Section 7 concludes with some open problems. Note that only the main ideas of proofs are sketched in this paper since, besides lack of space, the aim of this work is to present a unifying view on energy-based computation with Hopfield nets rather than to deal with technicalities. The underlying details can be found in [51, 65, 68, 69, 70, 71].

2 Computational Properties of Hopfield Nets

In this section we will recall the basic definitions and results regarding the Hopfield networks.

2.1 Computational Dynamics

A *finite recurrent neural network* consists of s simple computational *units* or *neurons*, indexed as $V = \{1, \ldots, s\}$ where $s = |V|$ is called the network *size*. Some of these units can serve as external inputs or outputs, and hence we assume that the network has n *input* and m *output* neurons, respectively. The remaining ones are called *hidden* neurons. The units are densely connected into an oriented graph representing the *architecture* of the network, in which each edge (i, j) leading from neuron i to j is labeled with a real *(synaptic) weight* $w(i, j) = w_{ji} \in \Re$. The absence of a connection within the architecture corresponds to a zero weight between the respective neurons and vice versa. Special attention has been paid to *symmetric* or *Hopfield* networks whose weights satisfy

$$w(i, j) = w(j, i) \tag{1}$$

for every $i, j \in V$, and consequently the underlying architecture is an undirected graph.

The *computational dynamics* of a neural network determines for each neuron $j \in V$ the evolution of its real *state (output)* $y_j^{(t)} \in \Re$ as a function of time $t \geq 0$. This establishes the global *network state* $\mathbf{y}^{(t)} = (y_1^{(t)}, \ldots, y_s^{(t)}) \in \Re^s$ at each time instant $t \geq 0$. At the beginning of a computation, the neural network is placed in an *initial state* $\mathbf{y}^{(0)}$ which may also include an external input. A *discrete-time* neural network then updates its state only at time instants $t = 1, 2, \ldots$. An *excitation*

$$\xi_j^{(t)} = \sum_{i=0}^{s} w_{ji} y_i^{(t)} \tag{2}$$

is assigned to each neuron $j \in V$ at time $t \geq 0$ as the respective weighted sum of its inputs. This includes a *bias* value $w_{j0} \in \Re$, which can be viewed as the weight from a formal constant unit input $y_0^{(t)} \equiv 1$. At the next instant $t + 1$, the neurons $j \in \alpha_{t+1}$ from a selected subset $\alpha_{t+1} \subseteq V$ compute their new outputs $y_j^{(t+1)}$ by applying an *activation function* $\sigma : \Re \longrightarrow \Re$ to $\xi_j^{(t)}$ as follows:

$$y_j^{(t+1)} = \sigma\left(\xi_j^{(t)}\right), \quad j \in \alpha_{t+1}, \tag{3}$$

while the remaining units $j \notin \alpha_{t+1}$ do not change their states, that is $y_j^{(t+1)} = y_j^{(t)}$ for $j \notin \alpha_{t+1}$. In this way the new network state $\mathbf{y}^{(t+1)}$ at time $t + 1$ is determined.

Neural networks with *binary states* $y_j \in \{0, 1\}$ usually employ the *Heaviside* or *hard limiter* activation function

$$\sigma(\xi) = \begin{cases} 1 & \text{for } \xi \geq 0 \\ 0 & \text{for } \xi < 0. \end{cases} \tag{4}$$

In this case, *integer* weights can be assumed without loss of generality [47], and the number of bits that are necessary [29] and sufficient [49] for representing a single integer weight parameter is $\Theta(s \log s)$. Sometimes, when more appropriate, bipolar values $\{-1, 1\}$ (or even more general discrete domains) can be substituted for binary values $\{0, 1\}$ without any substantial change in the size of weights [55, 56].

On the other hand, *analog-state* networks usually approximate discrete activation function (4) with some continuous sigmoid function. For simplicity, we will mostly fix the activation function σ to be the *saturated-linear* map:

$$\sigma(\xi) = \begin{cases} 1 & \text{for } \xi \geq 1 \\ \xi & \text{for } 0 < \xi < 1 \\ 0 & \text{for } \xi \leq 0 \end{cases} \tag{5}$$

Hence, the states of analog neurons are real numbers within interval $[0, 1]$.

2.2 Computational Modes

Various computational modes are possible for recurrent networks, depending on the choice of sets α_t of the updated units in rule (3). A recurrent network is said to operate in a *sequential* mode if at every time instant $t \geq 1$ at most one unit updates its state according to (3), that is $|\alpha_t| \leq 1$. In order to formally avoid long constant intermediate computations when only those units are updated that effectively do not change their outputs, the notion of a *productive* computation of length $t^\star$ discrete updates is introduced, meaning that for every $1 \leq t \leq t^\star$ there exists a unit $j \in \alpha_t$ updated at time t such that $y_j^{(t)} \neq y_j^{(t-1)}$. A productive computation of a recurrent network *terminates, converges* or *reaches a stable state* $\mathbf{y}^{(t^\star)}$ at time $t^\star \geq 0$ if $\mathbf{y}^{(t^\star)} = \mathbf{y}^{(t^\star+k)}$ for all $k \geq 1$ (or for converging analog networks, at least $\|\mathbf{y}^{(t^\star)} - \mathbf{y}^{(t^\star+k)}\| \leq \varepsilon$ holds for some small constant $0 \leq \varepsilon < 1$). Usually, a *systematic* choice of α_t is employed, e.g. $\alpha_{\tau s+j} = \{j\}$ for $j = 1, \dots, s$ where a discrete *macroscopic time* $\tau = 0, 1, 2, \dots$ is introduced, during which all the units in the network are updated (in general some of them may update their outputs even several times). For a *parallel* mode, in contrast, there exists a time instant $t \geq 1$ when at least two neurons re-compute their new outputs simultaneously, i.e. with $|\alpha_t| \geq 2$. Typically, a *fully parallel* mode is considered in which all the units are updated at each time instant, that is $\alpha_t = V$ for every $t \geq 1$.

In *asynchronous* computations the choice of the update set α_t is arbitrary, and each unit in the network may in fact decide independently at which time instant its state is updated. In contrast, in *synchronous* computations the sets α_t are predestined deterministically for each time instant t. The seemingly less powerful asynchronous models have proved for binary states to have the same computational power as their systematic synchronous counterparts, at the cost of only a small overhead in the size and time of the (simulating) asynchronous network for both sequential and parallel modes and even for Hopfield nets [52]. Hence, a synchronous model will be assumed in the sequel.

2.3 Input Protocols

For the purpose of universal computations over inputs of arbitrary lengths, different input protocols have been introduced. Thus in the following both recurrent networks with a finite number of units and infinite families of networks, one for each input length, are considered.

The computational power of recurrent networks has been studied analogously to the traditional models of computations so that the networks are exploited as acceptors of languages $L \subseteq \{0,1\}^*$ over the binary alphabet. In the case of *finite networks*, or so called *neural acceptors* working under fully parallel updates, an input string $\mathbf{x} = x_1 \ldots x_n \in \{0,1\}^n$ of arbitrary length $n \geq 0$ is sequentially presented to the network bit by bit via an input neuron $inp \in V$. The state of this unit is externally set to the respective input bits at prescribed time instants, regardless of any influence from the remaining units in the network. The output neuron $out \in V$ subsequently signals whether the input string $\mathbf{x}$ belongs to the underlying language L. Especially in the case of *binary-state* neural acceptors, these input bits x_i ($i = 1, \ldots, n$) are presented with a given *period* of $p \geq 1$ discrete steps, i.e. $y_{inp}^{(p(i-1))} = x_i$, and the output neuron recognizes each prefix of the input string online, possibly with some time delay $k \geq 1$, that is $y_{out}^{(p(i-1)+k+1)} = 1$ iff $x_1 \ldots x_i \in L$. In the case of *analog-state* networks usually $p = 1$, and an additional *validation* input unit $ival \in V$ is employed to indicate the end of the input string, i.e. $y_{ival}^{(t)} = 1$ for $t = 0, \ldots, n-1$ and $y_{ival}^{(t)} = 0$ for $t \geq n$. Correspondingly, the output neuron after some time $T(n) \geq n$ that depends on the input length n provides the result of recognition, which is again announced by a validation output unit $oval \in V$, i.e. $y_{oval}^{(T(n))} = 1$, and $y_{out}^{(T(n))} = 1$ iff $\mathbf{x} \in L$, whereas $y_{out}^{(t)} = y_{oval}^{(t)} = 0$ for $t \neq T(n)$. In analog networks, another input protocol is also possible, namely by encoding an input string $\mathbf{x}$ of arbitrary length n into a real initial state of the input neuron, e.g. as $y_{inp}^{(0)} = \sum_{i=1}^{n} (2x_i + 1)/4^i$ [64].

In an alternative input protocol, *infinite families* $\{N_n\}$ of recurrent networks, one N_n for each input length $n \geq 0$, are exploited for universal computations analogously as in circuit complexity [75]. Thus, for n-bit binary inputs $\mathbf{x} \in \{0,1\}^n$, network N_n is used whose n input neurons are initialized accordingly within the initial network state. For recognizing a language $L \subseteq \{0,1\}^*$, the respective network N_n is employed for input strings $\mathbf{x} \in \{0,1\}^n$ and, after it converges in time t^*, its single output neuron out is read which indicates whether $\mathbf{x}$ belongs to L, that is $y_{out}^{(t^*)} = 1$ iff $\mathbf{x} \in L$. Within this context the *size* $S(n)$ can be defined as the number of units in N_n.

2.4 Energy Function

The well-known fundamental property of (symmetric) Hopfield nets is that their dynamics is constrained by an *energy*, or *Liapunov* function E which is a bounded function defined on their state space decreasing along any productive computation. From the existence of such a function it follows that the network state converges towards some stable state corresponding to a local minimum of E. In binary symmetric nets, sequential computations starting from any initial state terminate provided that $w(j,j) \geq 0$ for every $j \in V$ (such networks are sometimes called *semisimple* networks) [30]. This result can be proved by using e.g. the energy function

$$E(\mathbf{y}) = -\sum_{j=1}^{s} y_j \left(w_{j0} + \frac{1}{2} \sum_{i=1; i \neq j}^{s} w_{ji} y_i + w_{jj} y_j \right). \tag{6}$$

It can be shown that parallel computations of binary Hopfield nets either reach a stable state (e.g. when the quadratic form (6) is negative definite [21, 22]), or eventually alternate between two different states [9, 21, 57, 74]. These convergence results were further generalized for analog symmetric networks, which can be proved under mild hypotheses to converge to a fixed point or to a limit cycle of length at most two for parallel updates [17, 38] by applying an energy function of the form (6) extended with additive term $\sum_{j=1}^{s} \int_{0}^{y_j} \sigma^{-1}(y)dy$ (cf. equation (8)).

2.5   Stable States

As the Hopfield networks were originally proposed for use as associative memories, it is of interest to determine the number of their stable states corresponding to the stored patterns. It has been shown that there are on the average asymptotically $1.05 \times 2^{0.2874s}$ many stable states in a binary Hopfield net of size s whose feedbacks and biases are zero ($w_{jj} = w_{j0} = 0$ for $j \in V$), and whose other weights are independent, identically distributed zero-mean Gaussian random variables [46, 73]. For a particular binary symmetric network, however, the issue of deciding whether there are e.g. at least one (when negative feedback weights are allowed) [13], two [41], or three [13] stable states, is NP-complete. Indeed, the problem of determining the exact number of stable states for a given binary Hopfield net is #P-complete [13, 41] (see [18] for the definition of the complexity class #P). Also the problem of finding a stable state in a binary symmetric network is known to be complete (by LOGSPACE reductions) for the complexity class of polynomial-time local search problems PLS [59] (see [35] for a precise definition of this class). Furthermore, the problem of computing the *attraction radius* of a stable state, i.e. how many binary outputs can be flipped in a given stable network state so that the respective sequential or fully parallel Hopfield net still converges back to it, is NP-hard [14]. There is even no polynomial-time algorithm approximating the attraction radius in a sequential or fully parallel binary Hopfield net to within a factor of $s^{1-\varepsilon}$ for any fixed $0 < \varepsilon \leq 1$, unless $P = NP$ [14].

2.6   Continuous Time

In continuous-time neural networks the dynamics of the analog network state $\mathbf{y}(t) \in \Re^s$ is defined for every real $t > 0$ usually as the solution of a system of s differential equations, one for each continuous-time unit. The corresponding boundary conditions are given by an initial network state $\mathbf{y}(0)$. For example, consider the system:

$$\frac{dy_j}{dt}(t) = -y_j(t) + \sigma(\xi_j(t)) = -y_j(t) + \sigma\left(\sum_{i=0}^{s} w_{ji}y_i(t)\right) \qquad j = 1, \ldots, s, \qquad (7)$$

where the excitation $\xi_j(t)$ of unit j is defined as in (2) and the saturated-linear activation function (5) is employed, implying that $\mathbf{y}(t) \in [0, 1]^s$. Using the energy function

$$E(\mathbf{y}) = -\sum_{j=1}^{s} y_j \left(w_{j0} + \frac{1}{2}\sum_{i=1}^{s} w_{ji}y_i\right) + \sum_{j=1}^{s}\int_{0}^{y_j} \sigma^{-1}(y)dy \qquad (8)$$

it can be shown that a continuous-time symmetric network (with $w_{ji} = w_{ij}$) conforming to this model converges from any initial state $\mathbf{y}(0)$ to some stable state satisfying $dy_j/dt = 0$ for all $j = 1, \ldots, s$ [10, 31].

3 The Minimum Energy Problem

In this section we will deal with the *MIN ENERGY* or *GROUND STATE problem* of finding a network state with *minimal energy E* (see equations (6), (8)) for a given Hopfield network. This problem is of special interest because besides its importance for the Ising spin glass model in statistical physics [5] minimizing the energy in Hopfield networks has often been exploited for the fast approximate solution of hard combinatorial optimization problems such as the traveling salesman problem [32]. The cost function of an optimization problem is here encoded into the energy function of a Hopfield network which is then minimized in the course of computation. After the Hopfield net converges to a stable state corresponding to a local minimum of the energy function, an optimal or semi-optimal solution of the original combinatorial problem can be read from this state. Intuitively, from such heuristic reductions of the NP-hard optimization problems to MIN ENERGY it follows that this problem must also be computationally hard. In other words, the process of minimizing the energy in Hopfield nets has a potential to implement polynomial-time nondeterministic Turing computations.

3.1 Bipolar States

In particular, for *binary* Hopfield networks the decision version of MIN ENERGY, i.e. the question whether there exists a network state having energy (6) less than a prescribed value, can formally be proved to be NP-complete [5] although it is known that MIN ENERGY has polynomial time algorithms for binary Hopfield nets whose architectures are planar lattices [8] or planar graphs [5]. Perhaps the most straightforward reduction to MIN ENERGY is from the MAX CUT problem (see e.g. [6]). In *MAX CUT* we are given an undirected graph $G = (V, A)$ with an integer edge cost function $c : A \longrightarrow \mathcal{Z}$, and we want to find a *cut $V_1 \subseteq V$* which maximizes the *cut size*

$$c(V_1) = \sum_{\{i,j\} \in A;\, i \in V_1,\, j \notin V_1} c(\{i,j\}) - \sum_{\{i,j\} \in A;\, c(\{i,j\}) < 0} c(\{i,j\}). \tag{9}$$

Note that the standard MAX CUT problem is here generalized by allowing also the negative edge costs, which is used for the opposite reduction from MIN ENERGY to MAX CUT [19].

Now, we will shortly recall the well-known simple correspondence between MIN ENERGY and MAX CUT problems. For simplicity, we consider here the Hopfield nets with zero biases and feedback weights, that is $w_{j0} = 0$ and $w_{jj} = 0$ for $j = 1, \ldots, s$. In addition, without loss of generality (see Paragraph 2.1), we will work with bipolar states $\{-1, 1\}$ of neurons instead of binary ones $\{0, 1\}$ and assume integer weights. The architecture $G = (V, A)$ of a bipolar Hopfield net from a MIN ENERGY instance then corresponds to an undirected graph in MAX CUT whose edge costs coincide with the opposite weights in this network, i.e.

$$c(\{i,j\}) = -w(i,j) \tag{10}$$

for all $\{i, j\} \in A$. We will show that any cut $V_1 \subseteq V$ of G corresponds to a Hopfield net state $\mathbf{y} \in \{-1, 1\}^s$ where

$$y_j = \begin{cases} 1 & \text{for } j \in V_1 \\ -1 & \text{for } j \in V \setminus V_1, \end{cases} \tag{11}$$

so that the cut size $c(V_1)$ and energy $E(\mathbf{y})$ are related as follows:

$$
\begin{aligned}
E(\mathbf{y}) &= -\frac{1}{2} \sum_{i,j \in V} w(i,j) y_i y_j \\
&= -\frac{1}{2} \sum_{y_i = y_j} w(i,j) + \frac{1}{2} \sum_{y_i \neq y_j} w(i,j) + \frac{1}{2} \sum_{y_i \neq y_j} w(i,j) - \frac{1}{2} \sum_{y_i \neq y_j} w(i,j) \\
&= -\frac{1}{2} \sum_{i,j \in V} w(i,j) + \sum_{y_i \neq y_j} w(i,j) = -\frac{1}{2} \sum_{w(i,j)<0} w(i,j) - \frac{1}{2} \sum_{w(i,j)>0} w(i,j) \\
&\quad + \sum_{y_i \neq y_j} w(i,j) + \frac{1}{2} \sum_{w(i,j)>0} w(i,j) - \frac{1}{2} \sum_{w(i,j)>0} w(i,j) \\
&= -\frac{1}{2} \sum_{w(i,j)<0} w(i,j) + \frac{1}{2} \sum_{w(i,j)>0} w(i,j) - \sum_{w(i,j)>0} w(i,j) + \sum_{y_i \neq y_j} w(i,j) \\
&= W + 2 \sum_{\{i,j\} \in A; c(\{i,j\})<0} c(\{i,j\}) - 2 \sum_{\{i,j\} \in A; i \in V_1, j \notin V_1} c(\{i,j\}) \\
&= W - 2c(V_1) \tag{12}
\end{aligned}
$$

where

$$
W = \frac{1}{2} \sum_{i,j \in V} |w(i,j)| \tag{13}
$$

is the total *weight* of the Hopfield net. Clearly, it follows from equation (12) that the minimum energy state corresponds to the maximum cut. Thus, we can conclude that the MIN ENERGY problem is NP-complete since the MAX CUT problem is one of the famous NP-complete problems [36].

On the other hand, the correspondence (12) between MIN ENERGY and MAX CUT problems can be also used to design an approximation algorithm for the MIN ENERGY problem. Recently, a randomized approximation algorithm with a high performance guarantee $\alpha = 0.87856$ for the MAX CUT formulation (9) has been proposed [19] and later de-randomized [45], which can straightforwardly be exploited for approximating the MIN ENERGY problem. Namely, for bipolar Hopfield nets it can be observed that MIN ENERGY can be approximated in a polynomial time within absolute error less than $0.243W$ [70] where W is the network weight (13). For $W = O(s^2)$, e.g. for Hopfield nets with s binary neurons and constant weights, this result matches the lower bound $\Omega(s^{2-\varepsilon})$ [6] which cannot be guaranteed by any approximate polynomial-time MIN ENERGY algorithm for every $\varepsilon > 0$, unless $P = NP$. In addition, the MIN ENERGY problem can be approximately solved to within absolute error $O(s/\log s)$ in polynomial time for special binary Hopfield nets whose architectures are two-level grids [7].

3.2   Analog States

In practical optimization, however, the Hopfield nets with the *analog* states rather than those with the binary ones have usually been used. Surprisingly, the complexity of the MIN EN- ERGY problem for analog Hopfield nets has been resolved only recently [70]. This is possibly because there is a slight technical complication to the issue, related to the fact that unlike binary networks, analog Hopfield nets can also converge to an interior point of their state space. Nevertheless, the MIN ENERGY problem is NP-hard also for analog Hopfield nets with the energy function (8). To prove this NP-hardness result by using the reduction from MAX CUT we need to ensure that the minimum energy values of the underlying analog Hopfield net are actually reached close to extremum points of its state space. In this paragraph we will sketch the main idea of this proof.

The following argument is valid for any activation function σ that is continuous and strictly increasing on an interval $[\alpha, \beta]$ ($\alpha < \beta$, with possibly $\alpha = -\infty$ or $\beta + \infty$), and constant outside:

$$\sigma(\xi) = \begin{cases} a & \text{for } \xi \leq \alpha \\ b & \text{for } \xi \geq \beta . \end{cases} \tag{14}$$

For $\alpha = -\infty$ or $\beta = +\infty$, we require that $\lim_{\xi \to -\infty} \sigma(\xi) = a$ or $\lim_{\xi \to +\infty} \sigma(\xi) = b$, respectively. We will also assume that σ is differentiable on (α, β) (thus we know that $\sigma'(\xi) > 0$ for $\xi \in (\alpha, \beta)$), and that the respective integrals in (8) are bounded, i.e.

$$\sup_{y_j \in [a,b]} \left| \int_0^{y_j} \sigma^{-1}(y) dy \right| < I_\sigma , \tag{15}$$

where $0 < I_\sigma < +\infty$. These conditions are satisfied by all the commonly used continuous sigmoid activation functions (e.g. the saturated-linear map (5) or the hyperbolic tangent).

The decision version of the *MIN ENERGY(σ)* problem for the analog Hopfield nets with activation function σ is the question whether a given analog symmetric network possesses a state $\mathbf{y} \in [a, b]^s$ for which the energy $E(\mathbf{y})$ defined in (8) has value less than a prescribed constant. This problem can be shown to be NP-hard by using the connection with the MAX CUT problem introduced in Paragraph 3.1. In fact, the SIMPLE MAX CUT problem, which is also known to be NP-complete [18], is sufficient for the reduction to the MIN ENERGY(σ). In *SIMPLE MAX CUT*, we are given an undirected graph $G = (V, A)$ and we want to find a cut $V_1 \subseteq V$ with the maximal size

$$c(V_1) = |\{e \in A; \ e \cap V_1 \neq \emptyset\}| . \tag{16}$$

Note that this is a special case of the MAX CUT problem that is restricted to the unit costs.

Thus the reduction from SIMPLE MAX CUT to MIN ENERGY(σ) is similar to the bipolar case (cf. equation (10)):

$$w(i, j) = \begin{cases} -C & \text{for } \{i, j\} \in A \\ 0 & \text{for } \{i, j\} \notin A, \ i \neq j \end{cases} \tag{17}$$

for some suitable positive constant $C > 0$ that maps linearly the general range $[a, b]$ of σ to $[-1, 1]$ (see [70] for technical details). However, we need to force the analog energy (8) to achieve its minimum at a state sufficiently close to one of the extremal points $\{a, b\}^s$ corresponding to possible cuts V_1: $j \in V_1$ if $y_j = b$ whereas $y_j = a$ for $j \in V \setminus V_1$ (cf. equation (11)). The SIMPLE MAX CUT solution can be then decoded from such a minimum energy state $\mathbf{y}^\star \in ([a, \sigma(\eta)] \cup [\sigma(\vartheta), b])^s$ as follows:

$$V_1 = \{j \in V; \ y_j^\star \in [\sigma(\vartheta), b]\} \tag{18}$$

when a sufficiently large interval $(\sigma(\eta), \sigma(\vartheta)) \subset [a, b]$ of the state space is excluded. This is achieved by introducing large positive feedbacks

$$w_{jj} > \frac{1}{\delta} \tag{19}$$

for every $j \in V$ where

$$\delta = \inf_{\xi \in (\eta, \vartheta)} \sigma'(\xi) > 0. \tag{20}$$

For such feedbacks it will be proved that if $\mathbf{y}^\star = (y_1^\star, \dots, y_s^\star) \in [a, b]^s$ is a local minimum of energy function (8) then $y_j^\star \notin (\sigma(\eta), \sigma(\vartheta))$ for every $j \in V$.

Suppose that $\mathbf{y}^\star \in [a, b]^s$ is a local minimum of energy function (8). Clearly, $y_j^\star \notin (\sigma(\eta), \sigma(\vartheta))$ for $y_j^\star \in \{a, b\}$. On the other hand, for $y_j^\star \in (a, b)$ consider function

$$E_j(y) = E\left(y_1^\star, \dots, y_{j-1}^\star, y, y_{j+1}^\star, \dots, y_s^\star\right) \tag{21}$$

of one variable y. Thus, the derivative $E_j'(y_j^\star) = 0$ and

$$E_j''(y_j^\star) = \frac{\partial^2 E}{\partial y_j^2}(\mathbf{y}^\star) = -w_{jj} + \frac{1}{\sigma'(y_j^\star)} \geq 0 \tag{22}$$

since $\mathbf{y}^\star$ is a local minimum of E. It follows from (22) that $w_{jj} \leq 1/\sigma'(y_j^\star)$, and hence $y_j^\star \notin (\sigma(\eta), \sigma(\vartheta))$ according to (19), (20).

By showing that the MIN ENERGY problem is NP-hard for both binary and analog Hopfield nets we know that the polynomial-time computations by nondeterministic Turing machines can be reduced to the process of minimizing the energy in these networks.

4 External Sources of Computational Energy

In this section, we will analyze the computational power of *finite symmetric* neural acceptors as compared to that of general asymmetric networks. As we know, the computational dynamics of Hopfield nets is severely constrained since these networks consume the energy in the course of computation and eventually converge to a limit cycle of length at most two. Therefore their capability to recognize the inputs of unbounded length is limited and depends on external sources of energy. To be able to classify the computational characteristics of Hopfield nets within a more general framework we will first shortly review the results concerning the finite asymmetric neural networks.

4.1 The Power of Asymmetric Weights

The computational power of finite recurrent neural networks, with in general *asymmetric* weights employing the saturated-linear activation function (5), is known to increase with the Kolmogorov complexity (information contents) of their weights [4]. For *integer* weights these models coincide with finite *binary-state* networks with activation function (4) which have only a finite number of global network states. Thus, their computational power corresponds to that of finite automata [37], and they can shortly be called *neuromata*. Also finer descriptive measures have been studied [1] to find out how efficient such neural implementations of finite automata can be. It has been shown that a neuromaton of size $O(\sqrt{q})$ can be constructed which, for a constant period $p = 4$ of presenting the input bits, simulates a given deterministic finite automaton with q states [33, 34] and in the worst case, this size $\Omega(\sqrt{q})$ cannot be reduced if either the period is at most $p = O(\log q)$ [33] or polynomial weights are assumed [34]. Moreover, the size of neuromata can also be compared to the length of regular expressions whose descriptional efficiency may exceed that of deterministic finite automata. In this case, an optimal-size neuromaton with $\Theta(\ell)$ units and period $p = 1$ can be constructed for recognizing a regular language described by a given regular expression of length ℓ [71].

Furthermore, with *rational* weights such *analog* networks can simulate arbitrary Turing machines step per step [64]. Hence, by implementing a universal Turing machine, any function computable by a Turing machine in time $T(n)$ can be computed by a fixed analog network with only 886 units in time $O(T(n))$ [64]. The size of this universal network can further be reduced even to 25 neurons at the cost of increasing the simulation time to $O(n^2 T(n))$ [34]. With arbitrary *real* weights the analog networks can have 'super-Turing' computational capabilities [63]. For example, polynomial time computations by such networks correspond to the nonuniform complexity class P/poly (see [3] for a definition), and within exponential time any input-output mapping can be computed. On the other hand, these results assume arbitrary-precision real number calculations while any amount of *analog noise* reduces the computational power of this model to that of neuromata [43] or even more [44, 62].

4.2 Hopfield Languages: Energizing Inputs

Now, consider a binary Hopfield acceptor with *symmetric* weights (and e.g. with period $p = 1$ of presenting the input bits) to be used for recognizing a given regular language similarly as the general asymmetric neuromaton was exploited for this purpose in Paragraph 4.1. In fact, such a symmetric neuromaton represents a Hopfield net that under fully parallel updates either converges or alternates between two states within a finite number of steps provided that its input unit inp is ignored. This input neuron inp whose state is externally set to input bits independently of any influence from the remaining units can, on the other hand, break the symmetry of weights and serve as an external source of energy to prevent the symmetric neural acceptor from converging. However, not all the inputs from a regular language are able to "energize" their own recognition. For example, consider a regular language $(000)^*$ that contains all the strings of 0s whose lengths are divisible by 3. Clearly, for a sufficiently long input string of 0s the symmetric neuromaton converges to a limit cycle of length at most two states. Therefore, the output unit out can then distinguish only between even and odd lengths of input strings, which is not sufficient for correct recognition of $(000)^*$. Thus, not all the regular languages can be recognized by Hopfield neuromata [28].

A language that is recognized by a symmetric neuromaton is called a *Hopfield language*. We already know that the class of Hopfield languages is strictly contained within the class of regular languages. Intuitively, a Hopfield language includes only those strings that possess an "energy charge" sufficient for their recognition. We will now formulate a so-called *Hopfield condition* that completely characterizes the class of Hopfield languages [65]: A regular language $L \subseteq \{0, 1\}^*$ is a Hopfield language iff for every prefix and suffix $\mathbf{v}_1, \mathbf{v}_2 \in \{0, 1\}^*$ and for any two-bit string $\mathbf{x} \in \{0, 1\}^2$ there exists k_0 such that either $\mathbf{v}_1\mathbf{x}^k\mathbf{v}_2 \in L$ for every $k \geq k_0$ or $\mathbf{v}_1\mathbf{x}^k\mathbf{v}_2 \notin L$ for every $k \geq k_0$. Clearly, every Hopfield language must satisfy the Hopfield condition since input strings $\mathbf{v}_1\mathbf{x}^{k_1}\mathbf{v}_2$ and $\mathbf{v}_1\mathbf{x}^{k_2}\mathbf{v}_2$ ($k_1 \neq k_2$) cannot be distinguished by a finite Hopfield neuromaton for sufficiently large $k_1, k_2 > k_0$ (e.g. k_0 is the number of all possible neuromaton states) because the symmetric acceptor converges to a limit cycle of length at most two when a sequence $\mathbf{x}^{k_0}$ of input bits is presented to the network.

On the other hand, for a regular language satisfying the Hopfield condition a symmetric neuromaton of linear size with respect to the length of a corresponding regular expression can be constructed for its recognition [65]. We will now outline the main ideas of this construction (see [65] for technical details). Observe first that a *finite language* that contains only a finite number of strings clearly meets the Hopfield condition. At the same time this language can be recognized by an asymmetric neuromaton whose architecture is an acyclic graph, that is, by a *feedforward* neural acceptor that can easily be constructed from the regular expression which does not contain iterations [71]. The feedforward neural acceptor can then be implemented by using only symmetric weights within the same architecture [55]. This is achieved by modifying the asymmetric weights (the input weights to each unit including its bias are multiplied by a suitable large positive constant) so that all the oriented paths in the acyclic network are labeled with decreasing sequences of weights while the network operation is preserved. Now the oriented edges are replaced by undirected ones with modified symmetric weights which ensure that any computation proceeds only along the direction of the original oriented paths. Hence, the finite languages can be recognized by Hopfield neuromata.

The result is generalized to regular expressions with iterations as follows. The iteration of one bit can be implemented by a feedback weight whereas the two-bit iterations are implicitly realized by symmetric weights. The problem lies in constructing general iterations of length greater than two bits by using only symmetric weights. It is because the computation follows the decreasing sequences of symmetric weights while in the iteration a signal should be propagated backwards from a unit with small weights to that with a large bias around a cycle. Nevertheless, the iterations comply with the Hopfield condition which implies that the underlying iterated sequence of bits contains a three-bit substring of form $b x \bar{b} \in \{0, 1\}^3$ where $b \neq \bar{b}$, which is used to "energize" the respective backward signal propagation. For example, for $b = 1$ an auxiliary unit inp_1 is introduced into the Hopfield neuromaton whose output copies the input bits from inp. This neuron is further connected via a large positive weight to each cycle in the network implementing an iteration with $b = 1$ at a unit c_1 whose small input weight needs a support to exceed its large bias for propagating the signal around the cycle. Note that this support is suppressed by $\bar{b} = 0$ later in the next second time step when subsequent unit c_2 in the cycle has received the signal from c_1 so that this signal cannot reversely influence neuron c_1 being supported by inp_1. This completes the construction of the Hopfield neuromaton that recognizes a given regular language satisfying the Hopfield condition.

4.3   *Turing Universality of analog Hopfield Nets with an External Oscillator*

The Hopfield languages can also be faithfully recognized by *analog-state* symmetric neural networks that can simulate binary Hopfield nets for a general class of activation functions [43, 60, 66]. This provides a lower bound on the computational power of analog Hopfield nets. A natural question then concerns improvements of this lower bound: could this model too be Turing universal, i.e. can a Turing machine simulation be achieved with finite symmetric networks and rational weights similarly as in the asymmetric case discussed in

Paragraph 4.1? The main obstacle here is that under fully parallel updates any analog Hopfield net with rational weights converges to a limit cycle of length at most two [38]. Thus the only possibility of simulating Turing machines would be to exploit finer and finer distinctions among a sequence of rational network states converging to a limit cycle. Such a simulation seems to be tricky at best, if possible at all.

A more reasonable approach is to augment the analog symmetric network with an *external oscillator* that produces an appropriately sequenced infinite stream of binary pulses, thus providing it with an external energy source similarly as the Hopfield neuromata were energized by their ordinary inputs in Paragraph 4.2. In particular, the analog Hopfield net receives as an additional external input any infinite binary sequence that contains infinitely many three-bit substrings of the form $bx\bar{b} \in \{0,1\}^3$ where $b \neq \bar{b}$, and, as we already know, this condition must be satisfied to prevent the network from converging. By using this gadget a Hopfield net with size $3s + 8$ units can simulate a given *asymmetric* analog network of size s neurons within the same maximum Kolmogorov complexity of weights where each occurance of substring $bx\bar{b}$ is exploited for the simulation of one computational step [70]. Indeed, the computational power of analog Hopfield nets with an external clock is the same as that of asymmetric analog networks. Especially for rational weights, this implies that such networks are Turing universal (see Paragraph 4.1). Thus we obtain a full characterization of the computational power of finite analog-state discrete-time networks in the form of

"Turing universality $\equiv$ asymmetric network $\equiv$ symmetric network + oscillator"

together with the necessary and sufficient condition that the external oscillator needs to satisfy in order to qualify for this equivalence.

5 A Symmetric Clock as an Internal Source of Energy

In Section 4, external sources of computational energy have been studied such as oscillators that prevent Hopfield nets from converging. A natural question arises whether a symmetric *clock* network that produces a sequence of binary pulses can be built and integrated within the Hopfield net to energize its computation internally without a need for an external support. However, this energizing symmetric network is also governed by the Liapunov function and thus it converges in a finite number of updates. Nevertheless, a binary counter can be implemented by using only symmetric weights, which traverses most of the network state space before it converges, and thus produces an exponential number of oscillations in terms of its size. These binary pulses can then be used to energize the computation for a sufficiently long time.

5.1 A Simulated Binary Counter

By induction on n we will now shortly sketch the construction of a binary-state symmetric clock network $\mathcal{C}_n$ of size $s_n = 3n + 1$ units, which simulates an $(n + 1)$-bit *binary counter* under fully parallel updates [23, 24]. Assume that all the states in the clock are initially zero. The induction starts with a network $\mathcal{C}_0$ of "order 0" containing only a single unit c_0 with zero bias $w(0, c_0) = 0$, which represents the least significant counter bit. As assumed, neuron c_0 is initially *passive* (its state is 0). However, at the next time instant c_0 will *fire* or be *active* (its state is 1) according to (4) since its excitation is nonnegative including only the zero bias. Hence, c_0 simply implements counting from 0 to 1.

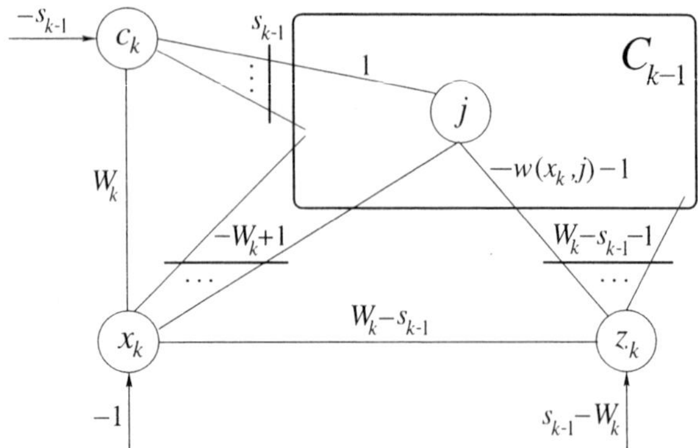

Figure 1: Inductive construction of discrete-time counter network $\mathcal{C}_k$

For the induction step depicted in Figure 1 (the edges in this graph drawn without an originating unit correspond to the biases), assume that an "order $(k-1)$" counter network $\mathcal{C}_{k-1}$ ($1 \leq k \leq n$) has been constructed, containing the first k counter units $c_0, \ldots, c_{k-1}$, together with auxiliary neurons x_ℓ, z_ℓ for $\ell = 1, \ldots, k-1$, for a total of $s_{k-1} = 3(k-1)+1$ units. Then the next counter unit c_k is connected to all the s_{k-1} neurons $j \in \mathcal{C}_{k-1}$ via unit weights $w(j, c_k) = 1$, which, together with its bias $w(0, c_k) = -s_{k-1}$, make c_k to fire shortly after all these units are active. This includes the first k active counter bits $c_0, \ldots, c_{k-1}$ which means that the simulated counting from 0 to $2^k - 1$ has been accomplished and hence, the next counter bit c_k must fire. In addition, unit c_k is connected to x_k which is further linked to z_k so that these auxiliary neurons are, one by one, activated after c_k fires. This is implemented by the following weights $w(c_k, x_k) = W_k$, $w(x_k, z_k) = W_k - s_{k-1}$, and biases $w(0, x_k) = -1$, $w(0, z_k) = s_{k-1} - W_k$ where

$$W_k = 1 - \sum_{j \in \mathcal{C}_{k-1}} w(j, x_k) > 0 \tag{23}$$

is a sufficiently large positive parameter determined by formula (24) below, ensuring that neurons x_k, z_k are not directly influenced by a computation of units from $\mathcal{C}_{k-1}$ except via c_k.

Neuron x_k is used to reset all the lower-order units in $\mathcal{C}_{k-1}$ back to their initial zero states which is consistent with the correct counter computation when c_k fires. To achieve this effect, x_k is linked with each $j \in \mathcal{C}_{k-1}$ via a large negative weight

$$w(x_k, j) = -1 - w(c_k, j) - \sum_{i \in \mathcal{C}_{k-1}; \, w(i,j)>0} w(i, j) \tag{24}$$

which exceeds the positive influence of units from $\mathcal{C}_{k-1} \cup \{c_k\}$ on j.

Finally, unit z_k balances the negative influence of x_k on $\mathcal{C}_{k-1}$ so that the first k counter bits can again count from 0 to $2^k - 1$ but now with c_k being active. This is achieved by the exact weights $w(z_k, j) = -w(x_k, j) - 1$ for each $j \in \mathcal{C}_{k-1}$ in which the -1 compensates for $w(c_k, j) = 1$. Clearly, units $j \in \mathcal{C}_{k-1}$ cannot reversely affect z_k since their maximal contribution

$$\sum_{j \in \mathcal{C}_{k-1}} w(j, z_k) = -s_{k-1} - \sum_{j \in \mathcal{C}_{k-1}} w(x_k, j) = W_k - s_{k-1} - 1 \tag{25}$$

to the excitation of z_k computed by (23) cannot overcome its bias. This completes the induction step of the counter network construction.

It follows that before the clock network C_n converges the least significant counter bit c_0 outputs a binary sequence composed of 2^n substrings 0111, which will be exploited as an internal oscillator for energizing the computation by Hopfield nets in Paragraph 5.3.

5.2 Convergence Time

The clock network C_n described in Paragraph 5.1 also provides an explicit example of a Hopfield net whose convergence time, i.e. the number of discrete-time updates before the network converges, is exponential [25]. In particular, this yields a $\Omega(2^{s/3})$ lower bound on the convergence time of binary Hopfield nets with s neurons working in a fully parallel mode [23, 24]. An asynchronous implementation of the binary counter by a symmetric network was designed [26] witnessing a corresponding exponential convergence-time lower bound $\Omega(2^{s/8})$ also for sequential updates [27]. On the other hand, in Hopfield nets of s binary neurons a trivial 2^s upper bound holds since there are only 2^s different network states. Nevertheless, a very fast average-case convergence of only $O(\log \log s)$ parallel update steps can be shown for binary Hopfield nets under reasonable assumptions [39].

However, the previous bounds do not take into account the size of the *weights*. An upper bound of $O(W)$ on the convergence time of binary sequential [16, 20, 22, 24] and parallel [21] Hopfield nets, where W is the total weight (13) of the network, follows from the characteristics of the energy function (6). For integer weights (for real weights see [16, 22]), this upper bound can be expressed more precisely as $(\sum_{j=1}^{s} \sum_{i=1;i\neq j}^{s} |w_{ji}| + \sum_{j=1}^{s} |w_{j0} + e_j|)/(2 + 2\min_{j\in V} w_{jj})$ for sequential mode, or $(\sum_{j=1}^{s} \sum_{i=1}^{s} |w_{ji}| + 3\sum_{j=1}^{s} |w_{j0} + e_j| - s)/2$ for parallel updates where $e_j = 1$ if $\sum_{i=0}^{s} w_{ji}$ is even, and $e_j = 0$ otherwise [12]. This yields polynomial-time convergence for binary symmetric networks with polynomial weights.

Moreover, these results can further be translated into convergence time bounds with respect to the full descriptional complexity of Hopfield nets, i.e. the number of bits in their representations of weights. For binary symmetric networks which are described within M bits, convergence-time lower and upper bounds $2^{\Omega(M^{1/3})}$ and $2^{O(M^{1/2})}$, respectively, have been shown [70]. This can be compared to the convergence-time result for analog Hopfield nets in which the precision of real weight parameters plays an important role. In particular, the corresponding lower bound $2^{\Omega(g(M))}$ updates have been obtained, where $g(M)$ is an arbitrary continuous function such that $g(M) = \Omega(M^{2/3})$, $g(M) = o(M)$, and $M/g(M)$ is increasing, which provides an example of the analog Hopfield net whose computation terminates later than that of any other binary symmetric network of the same representation size [70]. This result suggests that analog models may be worth investigating more for their efficiency gains than for their theoretical capability for arbitrary-precision real number computation.

5.3 Simulating the Asymmetric Networks

The computational power of Hopfield nets is properly less than that of asymmetric networks due to their different asymptotic behavior [28]. Because of the Liapunov property, Hopfield nets always converge to a limit cycle of length at most two, while the asymmetric networks can have arbitrarily complicated limit behavior. However, it was shown first in [51] that this is the *only* feature that cannot be reproduced in Hopfield nets, in the sense that any fully parallel

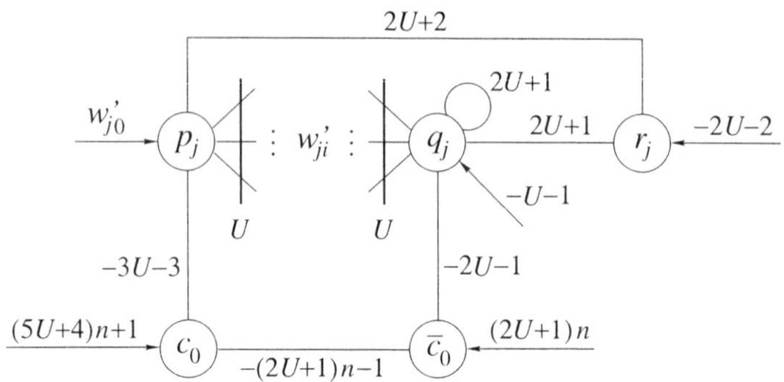

Figure 2: Symmetric simulation of neuron j

computation by a recurrent neural network of n binary neurons with asymmetric weights, *converging* within $t^\star$ discrete-time update steps, can be simulated by a Hopfield net with $6n + 2$ neurons, converging within $4t^\star$ steps [70]. The idea behind this simulation is that each neuron from the asymmetric network to be simulated is implemented by a small symmetric subnetwork of three units whose computation is energized by the symmetric clock subnetwork $\mathcal{C}_n$ introduced in Paragraph 5.1. Observe that any converging computation by an asymmetric network of n binary neurons must terminate within $t^\star \leq 2^n$ steps. Hence, 2^n binary pulses produced by clock $\mathcal{C}_n$ are sufficient to support this simulation when each sequenced substring 0111 generated by unit c_0 is exploited for the simulation of one computational step.

We will now shortly describe the simulating Hopfield net. For the purpose of simulation, the weights in $\mathcal{C}_n$ are modified so that the clock is not influenced by the simulating subnetwork it drives. This effect is achieved when the inductive construction of $\mathcal{C}_n$ starts with unit c_0 that has a sufficiently large bias $w(0, c_0) = (5U + 4)n + 1$ where

$$U = \max_{j=1,\dots,n} \sum_{i=0}^{n} |w'_{ji}| \tag{26}$$

and w'_{ji} for $j = 1,\dots n$, $i = 0,\dots,n$ denote the weights and biases in an asymmetric network to be simulated. Furthermore, an auxiliary neuron $\bar{c}_0$ is added, which computes the negation of the c_0 output. Then for each neuron j from the asymmetric network, three units p_j, q_j, r_j are introduced in the Hopfield net so that p_j represents the new (current) state $y_j^{(t)}$ of j at time $t \geq 1$ while q_j stores the old state $y_j^{(t-1)}$ of j from the preceding time instant $t - 1$, and r_j is an auxiliary neuron realizing the update of the old state. The corresponding symmetric subnetwork simulating one neuron j is depicted in Figure 2. At the beginning of the simulation all the neurons in the Hopfield net are passive, except for those units q_j that correspond to the original initially active neurons j, i.e. $y_j^{(0)} = 1$. Then an asymmetric network update at time $t \geq 1$ is simulated by a cycle of four steps in the Hopfield net as follows.

In the first step, unit c_0 fires and remains active until its state is changed by the clock, since its large positive bias makes it independent of all the n neurons p_j. Also unit $\bar{c}_0$ fires because it computes the negation of c_0 that was initially passive. At the same time, each neuron p_j computes its new state $y_j^{(t)}$ from the old states $y_i^{(t-1)}$, which are stored in the corresponding units q_i. Thus, each neuron p_j is connected with units q_i via the original weights $w(q_i, p_j) =$

$w'(i, j)$, and also its bias $w(0, p_j) = w'(0, j)$ is preserved. So far, unit q_j keeps the old state $y_j^{(t-1)}$ due to its feedback. In the second step, the new state $y_j^{(t)}$ is copied from p_j to r_j, and the active neuron c_0 makes each neuron p_j passive by means of a large negative weight, which exceeds the positive influence from units q_i ($i = 1, \dots, n$) including its bias $w(0, p_j)$ according to (26). Similarly, the active neuron $\bar{c}_0$ erases the old state $y_j^{(t-1)}$ from each neuron q_j by making it passive with the help of a large negative weight which, together with the negative bias, exceeds its feedback and the positive influence from units p_i ($i = 1, \dots, n$). Finally, also neuron $\bar{c}_0$ becomes passive since c_0 was active. In the third step, the current state $y_j^{(t)}$ is copied from r_j to q_j since all the remaining incident neurons p_i and $\bar{c}_0$ are and remain passive due to c_0 being active. Therefore also unit r_j becomes passive. In the fourth step, c_0 becomes passive and the state $y_j^{(t)}$, being called old from now on, is stored in q_j. Thus the Hopfield net finds itself at the starting condition of the time $t + 1$ asymmetric network simulation step, which proceeds in the same way. Altogether, the whole simulation is achieved within $4t^\star$ discrete-time steps.

5.4   The Computational Power of Families of Hopfield Nets

The simulation from Paragraph 5.3 actually provides a tight converse to Hopfield's convergence theorem [30] for binary symmetric networks, that is, it holds in a quite strong sense that

$$\text{"convergence} \equiv \text{symmetry"}$$

within linear size and time. Thus, not only do all Hopfield nets converge, but also all convergent computations by asymmetric networks can be implemented efficiently in symmetric networks [51, 70]. This also has some practical implications because recurrent networks with arbitrary asymmetric interconnections can always be replaced, without much overhead in network size or computation time, by symmetric networks with their guaranteed convergence properties, and in some technologies more efficient implementations.

In the context of infinite families of neural networks, it is known that polynomial-size families of binary asymmetric networks are computationally equivalent to (nonuniform) polynomially space-bounded Turing machines [40]. Thus, the equivalence between the convergent asymmetric and the symmetric networks gives the same result for the families of binary Hopfield nets with a polynomially increasing number of binary neurons. Stated in standard complexity theoretic notation [3], such sequences of Hopfield nets compute exactly the functions from the complexity class PSPACE/poly [51]. In addition, if the Hopfield nets in these families are restricted to have *polynomial* symmetric weights in terms of the input length, then their computational power reduces to P/poly [51].

6   The Continuous-Time Simulation

We will now outline how the simulation and related results from Section 5 can be generalized for *continuous-time* analog symmetric Hopfield nets with the saturated-linear activation (5) whose computational dynamics complies with the system of differential equations (7).

6.1   Simulating a Discrete Neuron

It was shown in [68] that a continuous-time analog unit with the dynamics equation (7) can simulate a discrete neuron employing the Heaviside activation (4). The binary output values 0 and 1 of a discrete neuron are represented by excitations (2) of a corresponding continuous-time unit which are below the lower saturation threshold of 0 or above the upper saturation threshold of 1, respectively, for the activation function (5). For brevity, we will simply say that a unit j is *saturated* at 0 or 1 at time t if its excitation satisfies $\xi_j(t) \leq 0$ or $\xi_j(t) \geq 1$, respectively. We also say that neuron j is *unsaturated* when $0 < \xi_j(t) < 1$. Note that we use the *excitations* $\xi_j(t)$, not the actual *states* $y_j(t)$ of unit j to represent the binary values since the states in continuous-time networks evolve smoothly in time, and exhibit no abrupt "firing" transitions. Thus, a *defect* $\delta_j(t)$ of unit j saturated at $b \in \{0, 1\}$ at time t can be defined as a distance from limit value b in its state:

$$\delta_j(t) = |b - y_j(t)| . \tag{27}$$

The dynamics equation of such a saturated unit j is independent of the equations for other neurons in the network and can be isolated from system (7):

$$\frac{dy_j}{dt}(t) = -y_j(t) + b , \tag{28}$$

and solved explicitly as follows:

$$y_j(t) = \left| b - \delta_j e^{-(t-t_0)} \right| \tag{29}$$

where $\delta_j = \delta_j(t_0)$ is an *initial defect* measured at some time instant $t_0 \geq 0$. It follows that the states of saturated units converge rapidly to their saturation values.

Furthermore, assume that $I \subseteq V$ is a subset of continuous-time units which are saturated for the duration of a sufficiently long time interval $[t_0, t_f]$ such that $t_f > t_0 + t_1$ where

$$t_1 = \frac{\ln 2}{\varepsilon} \tag{30}$$

for some small positive parameter ε (e.g. $0 < \varepsilon < 1/400$). Clearly, units in I may correspond to discrete neurons whose binary states are represented by their saturations as described above. In addition, suppose that these binary states are among the inputs for a discrete neuron to be simulated by a continuous-time unit j, and that they already decide about its next binary output (3) according to (4). For example, this happens when either

$$w_{j0} + \sum_{i \in I; \xi_i(t_0) \geq 1} w_{ji} + \sum_{i \in V \setminus I; w_{ji} > 0} w_{ji} < -\varepsilon \tag{31}$$

or

$$w_{j0} + \sum_{i \in I; \xi_i(t_0) \geq 1} w_{ji} + \sum_{i \in V \setminus I; w_{ji} < 0} w_{ji} > 1 + \varepsilon . \tag{32}$$

In this case one can prove [68] that after transient time t_1 the defects in the states of neurons from I decrease sufficiently according to (29) so that the continuous-time unit j is then saturated at either 0 or 1, respectively, for the duration of time interval $[t_0 + t_1, t_f]$. This means that the continuous-time units actually implement the discrete update rule (2)–(4) of corresponding binary neurons after transient time t_1, provided that the incident saturated units remain saturated.

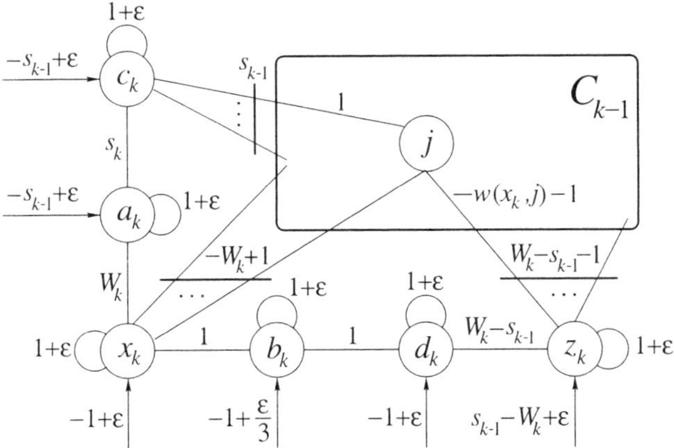

Figure 3: Inductive construction of continuous-time counter network $\mathcal{C}_k$

6.2 A Continuous-Time Clock

The inductive construction of a continuous-time Hopfield net simulating a binary counter [69] which is depicted in Figure 3 is similar to the corresponding discrete-time version presented in Figure 1 and discussed in greater detail in Paragraph 5.1. This is because the continuous-time units approximate the dynamics of discrete neurons as has been shown in Paragraph 6.1. The main difference is that the continuous-time clock $\mathcal{C}_n$ contains additional auxiliary units a_k, b_k, d_k for $k = 1, \ldots, n$ as compared to its discrete-time counterpart. The purpose of these units is only to slow down the continuous-time state flow in order to synchronize the binary counter simulation. Furthermore, each continuous-time unit $j \in \mathcal{C}_n$ has an activating feedback weight $w_{jj} = 1 + \varepsilon$ and its bias w_{j0} is increased by fraction ε (or $\varepsilon/3$ for technical reasons [69] that are not discussed in this paper) where $\varepsilon > 0$ is a small positive parameter introduced already in Paragraph 6.1. Such a feedback and bias are used to activate a typical continuous-time unit in the clock implementing the transition from its saturation at 0 to that at 1 which simulates the update of binary state 0 by its new value 1.

Consider a typical unit $j \in \mathcal{C}_n \setminus \{x_k; k = 1, \ldots, n\}$ to be activated whose excitation reaches the lower saturation threshold of 0 from below at a time instant t_0, that is $\xi_j(t_0) = 0$. In addition, let the remaining units from $\mathcal{C}_n \setminus \{j\}$ incident on j be saturated for a sufficiently long period. This happens when a positive weighted feedback defect $(1 + \varepsilon)\delta_j > 0$ $(y_j(t_0) = \delta_j)$ together with a "clean" contribution

$$w_{j0} + \sum_{i \in \mathcal{C}_n; \xi_i(t_0) \geq 1} w_{ji} = \varepsilon \tag{33}$$

from the incident activated neurons to excitation $\xi_j(t_0)$ of unit j are balanced by a negative *total weighted defect*

$$\Delta_j = \sum_{i \in \mathcal{C}_n \setminus \{j\}; \xi_i(t_0) \leq 0} w_{ji}\delta_i - \sum_{i \in \mathcal{C}_n; \xi_i(t_0) \geq 1} w_{ji}\delta_i \tag{34}$$

in states of units from $C_n \setminus \{j\}$, that is

$$\xi_j(t_0) = \varepsilon + (1 + \varepsilon)\delta_j + \Delta_j = 0. \tag{35}$$

Since the time instant t_0, excitation of unit j is described by equation

$$\xi_j(t) = \varepsilon + (1 + \varepsilon)y_j(t) + \Delta_j e^{-(t-t_0)} \tag{36}$$

as far as the incident units are saturated and controlled by (29), which determines the dynamics equation (7) for *unsaturated* j (i.e. $\sigma(\xi_j(t)) = \xi_j(t)$) as follows:

$$\frac{dy_j}{dt}(t) = -y_j(t) + \xi_j(t) = -y_j(t) + \varepsilon + (1 + \varepsilon)y_j(t) + \Delta_j e^{-(t-t_0)}. \tag{37}$$

From formula (35) a boundary condition

$$y_j(t_0) = \delta_j = \frac{-\varepsilon - \Delta_j}{1 + \varepsilon} \tag{38}$$

is obtained for differential equation (37) whose explicit solution can then be derived:

$$y_j(t) = \frac{e^{\varepsilon(t-t_0)} - \Delta_j e^{-(t-t_0)}}{1 + \varepsilon} - 1, \tag{39}$$

and plugged in equation (36) to get an explicit formula also for j's excitation:

$$\xi_j(t) = e^{\varepsilon(t-t_0)} - 1. \tag{40}$$

Clearly, $\xi_j(t) > 0$ for $t > t_0$ witnessing that j is unsaturated, which justifies the dynamics equation (37). The preceding analysis of activating a continuous-time unit can partially be generalized also for x_k ($k = 1, \dots, n$) whose incident neurons become unsaturated (for details see [69]).

An important fact is that the influence of total defect Δ_j on j's excitation (36) is canceled in equation (40), which makes also the length of time interval $(t_0, t_0 + t_1)$ during which j is unsaturated, constant and independent of initial defects. Thus unit j saturates at 1 exactly at time instant $t_0 + t_1$, that is $\xi_j(t_0 + t_1) = 1$ where t_1 is determined explicitly in formula (30) from equation (40). This fact is exploited for synchronizing the counter simulation. In particular, the same transient time t_1 that is sufficient for the continuous-time simulation of a discrete neuron (see Paragraph 6.1) is, on the other hand, necessary for activating a typical unit j in the clock. In other words, correct timing can be achieved during the simulation so that the activity is properly propagated in one part of the clock while at the same time the defects in the states of units in the remaining part are guaranteed to decrease below the level that could corrupt the computation.

A full formal verification of the simulation, which has the form of a rather tedious case analysis, can be found in [69]. In Figure 4 we present only a numerical simulation example of clock C_3 (with $\varepsilon = 0.1$) which shows the evolution of the states of counter units c_0, c_1, c_2, c_3 for a period of $2^3 - 1 = 7$ simulated discrete steps witnessing the validity of the construction.

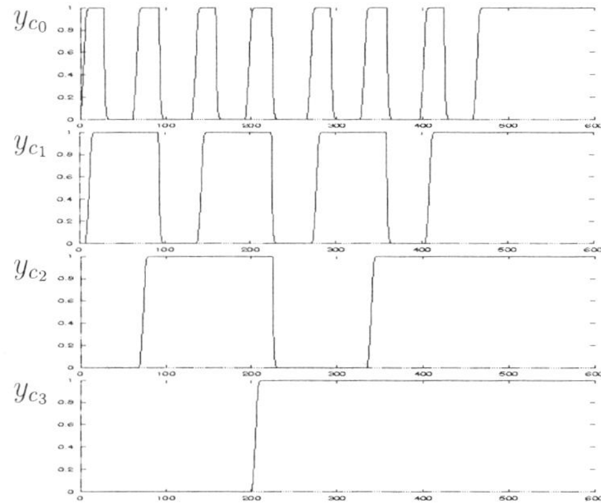

Figure 4: Continuous-time simulation of clock C_3 for $\varepsilon = 0.1$

6.3 The Computational Power of Continuous-Time Hopfield Nets

The clock network C_n introduced in Paragraph 6.2 provides an example of a continuous-time Liapunov-function controlled dynamical system with an exponential transient period, and thus generalizes the convergence-time results from Paragraph 5.2 for continuous-time Hopfield nets. Such an exponential-transient oscillator can also be used for supporting a general Turing machine simulation by infinite families of continuous-time Hopfield nets as follows. Similarly as the clock construction from Paragraph 5.1 has been generalized for continuous time in Paragraph 6.2, the simulation of a convergent binary-state asymmetric network introduced in Paragraph 5.3 can also be achieved with *continuous-time* Hopfield nets by using techniques from Paragraph 6.1 when the continuous-time clock C_n is exploited to energize the computation. In particular, it was proved in [68] that any computation by a discrete recurrent network of n binary neurons with asymmetric weights of maximum absolute size $w_{\max}$, converging within t^* discrete update steps, can be simulated by a continuous-time symmetric Hopfield net of size $18n + 7$ units, within continuous time $\Theta(t^*/\varepsilon)$ for any positive real $0 < \varepsilon < 1/400$ such that $w_{\max}2^{3n} \leq \varepsilon 2^{1/\varepsilon}$. This result shows that the continuous-time symmetric Hopfield nets are at least as powerful as their discrete counterparts. Thus, it follows from Paragraph 5.4 that given any polynomially space-bounded Turing machine, we can construct a family of polynomial-size continuous-time symmetric Hopfield nets for simulating it. This means that such families compute faithfully at least the functions from the complexity class PSPACE/poly. An open question remains whether this is also an upper bound on their computational power.

7 Conclusions and Open Problems

We have presented the known results concerning the computational capabilities of Hopfield nets within a unifying framework based on the concept of "energy source". It turns out that the Hopfield nets that lose the energy in the course of computation are computationally less powerful than the asymmetric networks and need an energy support to perform the computation desired. We have classified the underlying results according to the type of the support that is provided to Hopfield nets whose computational power then ranks from the subregular language acceptors to Turing universality. It would be interesting to introduce a new general complexity measure based on the energy that would be robust for both the classical and the alternative models of computation.

A special attention has also been paid to analog-state and/or continuous-time models that may, in some cases, gain in representational efficiency as compared to their discrete counterparts. It has been proved that these models can, in fact, faithfully simulate their discrete versions, which provides a lower bound on their computational power. Thus another challenge for further research is to prove the upper bounds on the computational power and convergence time of these networks in order to exploit the full potential of analog computation.

However, from the point of view of understanding analog computation in general the developed techniques are somewhat unsatisfying, since we are still basically discretizing the continuous-time computation. It would be most interesting to develop some theoretical tools (e.g. complexity measures, reductions, universal computation) for "naturally" continuous-time computations excluding the use of discretizing oscillations.

Our understanding of the general computational power of recurrent neural network models is now rather satisfactory. Profitable work could be done, however, on developing some analysis and synthesis techniques for more special-purpose analog recurrent networks, in view of their applications in e.g. associative memory, trajectory following, or time series analysis.

References

[1] N. Alon, A.K. Dewdney, and T.J. Ott, Efficient simulation of finite automata by neural nets, *Journal of the ACM* **38** (2) (1991) 495–514.

[2] S.-I. Amari, Neural theory of association and concept formation, *Biological Cybernetics* **26** (1977) 175–185.

[3] J.L. Balcázar, J. Díaz, and J. Gabarró, *Structural Complexity I*, 2nd edition, Springer–Verlag, Berlin (1995).

[4] J.L. Balcázar, R. Gavaldà, and H.T. Siegelmann, Computational power of neural networks: A characterization in terms of Kolmogorov complexity, *IEEE Transactions of Information Theory* **43** (4) (1997) 1175–1183.

[5] F. Barahona, On the computational complexity of Ising spin glass models, *Journal of Physics A: Mathematical and General* **15** (10) (1982) 3241–3253.

[6] A. Bertoni and P. Campadelli, On the approximability of the energy function, in: *Proceedings of the 4th International Conference on Artificial Neural Networks ICANN'94, Sorrento, Italy*, Springer–Verlag, Berlin (1994) 1157–1160.

[7] A. Bertoni, P. Campadelli, C. Gangai, and R. Posenato, Approximability of the ground state problem for certain Ising spin glasses, *Journal of Complexity* **13** (3) (1997) 323–339.

[8] I. Bieche, R. Maynard, R. Rammal, and J.P. Uhry, On the ground states of the frustration model of a spin glass by a matching method of graph theory, *Journal of Physics A: Mathematical and General* **13** (8) (1980) 2553–2576.

[9] J. Bruck and J.W. Goodman, A generalized convergence theorem for neural networks, *IEEE Transactions of Information Theory* **34** (5) (1988) 1089–1092.

[10] M.A. Cohen and S. Grossberg, Absolute stability of global pattern formation and parallel memory storage by competitive neural networks, *IEEE Transactions on Systems, Man, and Cybernetics* **13** (5) (1983) 815–826.

[11] N.H. Farhat, D. Psaltis, A. Prata, and E. Paek, Optical implementation of the Hopfield model, *Applied Optics* **24** (1985) 1469–1475.

[12] P. Floréen, Worst-case convergence times for Hopfield memories, *IEEE Transactions of Neural Networks* **2** (5) (1991) 533–535.

[13] P. Floréen and P. Orponen, On the computational complexity of analyzing Hopfield nets, *Complex Systems* **3** (6) (1989) 577–587.

[14] P. Floréen and P. Orponen, Attraction radii in Hopfield nets are hard to compute, *Neural Computation* **5** (5) (1993) 812–821.

[15] P. Floréen and P. Orponen, Complexity issues in discrete Hopfield networks, Research Report A–1994–4, Department of Computer Science, University of Helsinki (1994).

[16] F. Fogelman-Soulié, E. Goles-Chacc, and G. Weisbuch, Transient length in sequential iterations of threshold functions, *Discrete Applied Mathematics* **6** (1) (1983) 95–98.

[17] F. Fogelman-Soulié, C. Mejia, E. Goles-Chacc, and S. Martínez, Energy function in neural networks with continuous local functions, *Complex Systems* **3** (3) (1989) 269–293.

[18] M.R. Garey and D.S. Johnson. *Computers and Intractability: A Guide to the Theory of NP-completeness*, W.H. Freeman & Co., New York (1979).

[19] M.X. Goemans and D.P. Williamson, Improved approximate algorithms for maximum cut and satisfiability problems using semidefinite programming, *Journal of the ACM* **42** (6) (1995) 1115–1145.

[20] E. Goles-Chacc, Dynamics of positive automata networks, *Theoretical Computer Science* **41** (1985) 19–32.

[21] E. Goles-Chacc, Lyapunov functions associated to automata networks, in: F. Fogelman-Soulié, Y. Robert, and M. Tchuente, eds., *Automata networks in Computer Science—Theory and Applications*, Manchester University Press (1987) 58–81.

[22] E. Goles-Chacc, F. Fogelman-Soulié, and D. Pellegrin, Decreasing energy functions as a tool for studying threshold networks, *Discrete Applied Mathematics* **12** (3) (1985) 261–277.

[23] E. Goles-Chacc and S. Martínez, Exponential transient classes of symmetric neural networks for synchronous and sequential updating, *Complex Systems* **3** (6) (1989) 589–597.

[24] E. Goles-Chacc and S. Martínez, *Neural and Automata Networks: Dynamical Behavior and Applications*, Kluwer Academic Publishers, Dordrecht (1990).

[25] E. Goles-Chacc and J. Olivos A., The convergence of symmetric threshold automata, *Information and Control* **51** (2) (1981) 98–104.

[26] A. Haken, Connectionist networks that need exponential time to stabilize, Unpublished manuscript, Department of Computer Science, University of Toronto (1989).

[27] A. Haken and M. Luby, Steepest descent can take exponential time for symmetric connectionist networks, *Complex Systems* **2** (2) (1988) 191–196.

[28] R. Hartley and H. Szu, A comparison of the computational power of neural network models, in: *Proceedings of the IEEE First International Conference on Neural Networks, San Diego*, IEEE Press, New York (1987) 15–22.

[29] J. Håstad, On the size of weights for threshold gates, *SIAM Journal on Discrete Mathematics* **7** (3) (1994) 484–492.

[30] J.J. Hopfield, Neural networks and physical systems with emergent collective computational abilities, in: *Proceedings of the National Academy of Sciences USA*, **79** (1982) 2554–2558.

[31] J.J. Hopfield, Neurons with graded response have collective computational properties like those of two-state neurons, in: *Proceedings of the National Academy of Sciences USA*, **81** (1984) 3088–3092.

[32] J.J. Hopfield and D.W. Tank "Neural" computation of decision in optimization problems, *Biological Cybernetics* **52** (3) (1985) 141–152.

[33] B.G. Horne and D.R. Hush, Bounds on the complexity of recurrent neural network implementations of finite state machines, *Neural Networks* **9** (2) (1996) 243–252.

[34] P. Indyk, Optimal simulation of automata by neural nets, in: *Proceedings of the 12th Annual Symposium on Theoretical Aspects of Computer Science STACS'95*, LNCS **900**, Springer–Verlag, Berlin (1995) 337–348.

[35] D.S. Johnson, C.H. Papadimitriou, and M. Yannakakis, How easy is local search?, *Journal of Computer and System Sciences* **37** (1) (1988) 79–100.

[36] R.M. Karp, Reducibility among combinatorial problems, in: R.E. Miller and J.W. Thatcher, eds., *Complexity of Computer Computations*, Plenum Press, New York (1972) 85–103.

[37] S.C. Kleene, Representation of events in nerve nets and finite automata, in: C.E. Shannon and J. McCarthy, eds., *Automata Studies*, Vol. **34** of Annals of Mathematics Studies, Princeton University Press, NJ (1956) 3–41.

[38] P. Koiran, Dynamics of discrete time, continuous state Hopfield networks, *Neural Computation* **6** (3) (1994) 459–468.

[39] J. Komlós and R. Paturi, Convergence results in an associative memory model, *Neural Networks* **1** (3) (1988) 239–250.

[40] M. Lepley and G. Miller, Computational power for networks of threshold devices in asynchronous environment, Technical Report, Department of Mathematics, MIT (1983).

[41] J. Lipscomb, On the computational complexity of finding a connectionist model's stable state vectors, M.Sc. thesis, Department of Computer Science, University of Toronto (1987).

[42] W.A. Little and G.L. Shaw, Analytical study of the memory storage capacity of a neural network, *Mathematical Biosciences* **39** (1978) 281–290.

[43] W. Maass and P. Orponen, On the effect of analog noise in discrete-time analog computations, *Neural Computation* **10** (5) (1998) 1071–1095.

[44] W. Maass and E.D. Sontag, Analog neural nets with Gaussian or other common noise distribution cannot recognize arbitrary regular languages, *Neural Computation* **11** (3) (1999) 771–782.

[45] S. Mahajan and H. Ramesh, Derandomizing approximation algorithms based on semidefinite programming, *SIAM Journal on Computing* **28** (5) (1999) 1641–1663.

[46] R.J. McEliece, E.C. Posner, E.R. Rodemich, and S.S. Venkatesh, The capacity of the Hopfield associative memory, *IEEE Transactions on Information Theory* **33** (4) (1987) 461–482.

[47] M.L. Minsky and S.A. Papert, *Perceptrons*, The MIT Press, Cambridge, MA (1969).

[48] S. Muroga, *Threshold Logic and its Applications*, Wiley–Interscience, New York (1971).

[49] S. Muroga, I. Toda, and S. Takasu, Theory of majority decision elements, *Journal of the Franklin Institute* **271** (1961) 376–418.

[50] P. Orponen, Computational complexity of neural networks: A survey, *Nordic Journal of Computing* **1** (1) (1994) 94–110.

[51] P. Orponen, The computational power of discrete Hopfield nets with hidden units, *Neural Computation* **8** (2) (1996) 403–415.

[52] P. Orponen, Computing with truly asynchronous threshold logic networks, *Theoretical Computer Science* **174** (1-2) (1997) 123–136.

[53] P. Orponen, The computational power of continuous time neural networks, in: *Proceedings of the 24th Seminar on Current Trends in Theory and Practice of Informatics SOFSEM'97, Milovy, Czech Republic*, LNCS **1338**, Springer–Verlag, Berlin (1997) 86–103.

[54] P. Orponen, An overview of the computational power of recurrent neural networks, in: H. Hyötyniemi, ed., *Proceedings of the 9th Finnish AI Conference STeP 2000–Millennium of AI, Espoo, Finland*, Vol. **3**: "AI of Tomorrow": Symposium on Theory, Finnish AI Society, Vaasa, Finland (2000) 89–96.

[55] I. Parberry, A primer on the complexity theory of neural networks, in: R.B. Banerji, ed., *Formal Techniques in Artificial Intelligence: A Sourcebook*, Vol. **6**: Studies in Computer Science and Artificial Intelligence, Elsevier, North–Holland, Amsterdam (1990) 217–268.

[56] I. Parberry, *Circuit Complexity and Neural Networks*, The MIT Press, Cambridge, MA (1994).

[57] S. Poljak and M. Sůra, On periodical behaviour in societies with symmetric influences, *Combinatorica* **3** (1) (1983) 119–121.

[58] V.P. Roychowdhury, K.-Y. Siu, and A. Orlitsky, eds., *Theoretical Advances in Neural Computation and Learning*, Kluwer Academic Publishers, Boston (1994).

[59] A.A. Schäffer and M. Yannakakis, Simple local search problems that are hard to solve, *SIAM Journal on Computing* **20** (1) (1991) 56–87.

[60] H.T. Siegelmann, Recurrent neural networks and finite automata, *Journal of Computational Intelligence* **12** (4) (1996) 567–574.

[61] H.T. Siegelmann, *Neural Networks and Analog Computation: Beyond the Turing Limit*, Birkhäuser, Boston (1999).

[62] H.T. Siegelmann, A. Roitershtein, and A. Ben-Hur, Noisy neural networks and generalizations, in: S.A. Solla, T.K. Leen, and K.-R. Müller, eds., *Advances in Neural Information Processing Systems* **12**, *NIPS'99*, The MIT Press (2000) 335–341.

[63] H.T. Siegelmann and E.D. Sontag, Analog computation via neural networks, *Theoretical Computer Science* **131** (2) (1994) 331–360.

[64] H.T. Siegelmann and E.D. Sontag, Computational power of neural networks, *Journal of Computer System Science* **50** (1) (1995) 132–150.

[65] J. Šíma, Hopfield languages, in: *Proceedings of the 22nd Seminar on Current Trends in Theory and Practice of Informatics SOFSEM'95, Milovy, Czech Republic*, LNCS **1012**, Springer–Verlag, Berlin (1995) 461–468.

[66] J. Šíma, Analog stable simulation of discrete neural networks, *Neural Network World* **7** (6) (1997) 679–686.

[67] J. Šíma, The computational capabilities of neural networks (extended abstract), in: *Proceedings of the 5th International Conference on Artificial Neural Networks and Genetic Algorithms ICANNGA'2001, Prague, Czech Republic*, Springer–Verlag, Vienna (2001) 22–26.

[68] J. Šíma and P. Orponen, Computing with continuous-time Liapunov systems, in: *Proceedings of the 33rd Annual ACM Symposium on Theory of Computing STOC'2001, Crete, Greece*, ACM Press, New York (2001) 722-731.

[69] J. Šíma and P. Orponen, Exponential transients in continuous-time Hopfield Nets, in: *Proceedings of the 11th International Conference on Artificial Neural Networks ICANN'2001, Vienna, Austria*, LNCS **2130**, Springer–Verlag, Berlin (2001) 806–813.

[70] J. Šíma, P. Orponen, and T. Antti-Poika, On the computational complexity of binary and analog symmetric Hopfield nets, *Neural Computation* **12** (12) (2000) 2965–2989.

[71] J. Šíma and J. Wiedermann, Theory of neuromata, *Journal of the ACM* **45** (1) (1998) 155–178.

[72] K.-Y. Siu, V.P. Roychowdhury, and T. Kailath, *Discrete Neural Computation: A Theoretical Foundation*, Prentice Hall, Englewood Cliffs, NJ (1995).

[73] F. Tanaka and S.F. Edwards, Analytic theory of the ground state properties of a spin glass: I. Ising spin glass, *Journal of Physics F: Metal Physics* **10** (1980) 2769–2778.

[74] M. Tchuente, Sequential simulation of parallel iterations and applications. *Theoretical Computer Science* **48** (2-3) (1986) 135–144.

[75] I. Wegener, *The Complexity of Boolean Functions*, Wiley/Teubner, Chichester (1987).

Computational Complexity and the Elusiveness of Global Optima

Marcello Pelillo

Dipartimento di Informatica
Università Ca' Foscari di Venezia
Via Torino 155, 30172 Venezia Mestre, Italy
E-mail: pelillo@dsi.unive.it

Abstract. We present a continuous optimization framework for various combinatorial problems of increasing computational complexity, namely: rooted and unrooted subtree isomorphism (both belonging to the P class), graph isomorphism (which very likely is neither NP-complete nor solvable in polynomial-time), and subgraph isomorphism (which is NP-complete). The approach is based on an equivalent maximum clique formulation of these problems, and it is centered around a fundamental result proved by Motzkin and Straus in the mid-1960s, and recently expanded in various ways, which allows us to formulate the maximum clique problem in terms of a standard quadratic program. The attractive feature of this formulation is that a clear one-to-one correspondence exists between the solutions of the quadratic programs and those in the original combinatorial problems. To approximately solve the program we use the so-called "replicator" equations, a class of straightforward continuous- and discrete-time dynamical systems developed in various branches of theoretical biology. Extensive experimental results obtained over both randomly generated graphs as well as graphs arising from computer vision problems are presented. As it turns out, they exhibit a seemingly non-accidental regularity which raises some intriguing questions concerning the connections between standard notions of computational complexity and the "elusiveness" of global optima in a continuous setting.

1 Introduction

The relationships between discrete and continuous mathematics have always been a subject of intensive study since the discovery of the irrationals by the Pythagorean school. Apart from the underlying philosophical implications, the interaction between the two domains can provide new insights into old problems and often allows techniques from one side to be profitably imported into the other. Entire branches of modern mathematics have been created with the specific motivation of exploring such connections, examples of which are singularity theory, combinatorial topology, and spectral graph theory. In more recent years, with the introduction of the ellipsoid and the interior point methods for linear programming, there has also been a tremendous interest in computer science and operations research in solving combinatorial optimization problems using continuous methods [17, 35].

Following the seminal works of Hopfield and Tank [22], and Durbin and Willshaw [11], the neural network community also became interested in using continuous approaches for combinatorial optimization. The basic idea consists in deriving a continuous "energy" function whose minimizers are in correspondence with the solutions of the discrete problem, and then minimizing it using continuous- or discrete-time dynamical systems, typically embedded in a parallel network of locally interacting processing elements. Almost invariably, the minimization algorithms developed so far incorporate techniques borrowed from statistical mechanics, in particular mean field theory, which allow one to escape from poor local solutions. Examples of problems attacked within this framework include the traveling salesman problem [11, 22], graph bipartitioning [12], the maximum clique problem [23, 37], the linear assignment problem [26], the knapsack problem [33] and graph/subgraph isomorphism problems [16, 43].

This paper provides a summary of recent work done within this framework [38, 41, 39]. We consider various combinatorial problems of increasing computational complexity, namely: rooted and unrooted subtree isomorphism (both belonging to the P class [31, 44]), graph isomorphism (which very likely is neither NP-complete nor solvable in polynomial-time [13, 24]), and subgraph isomorphism (which is NP-complete [13]). We present a common continuous framework for these problems which is based on the idea of reducing them to the maximum clique problem, another well-known combinatorial optimization problem [6]. Central to our approach is a powerful result originally proved by Motzkin and Straus [32], and recently extended in various ways [5, 14, 15, 40], which allows us to formulate the maximum clique problem in terms of an indefinite quadratic program. In the proposed formulation an elegant one-to-one correspondence exists between the solutions of the (continuous) quadratic program and those of the original (discrete) problem. We also present a class of straight-forward continuous- and discrete-time dynamical systems known in mathematical biology as *replicator equations*, and show how, owing to their properties, they provide a natural and useful heuristic for solving the Motzkin-Straus program, and hence graph and tree isomorphism problems.

It may be argued that trying to solve the "simple" problems by reducing them to the maximum clique problem is an altogether inappropriate choice. In fact, finding just the cardinality of the maximum clique in a graph is known to be NP-hard and, according to recent theoretical results, so is the problem of approximating it within a certain tolerance [19].[1] The experimental results presented in this paper, however, seem to contradict this claim. By using simple relaxation equations which are inherently unable to avoid local optima, we get results which compare favorably with those obtained using state-of-the-art sophisticated neural network algorithms which, by contrast, are explicitly designed to escape from local solutions. This suggests therefore that the proposed Motzkin-Straus formulation is a promising framework within which to develop powerful graph and tree matching heuristics.

As it turns out, the results obtained also exhibit a seemingly non-accidental regularity which raises some intriguing questions concerning the connections between standard notions of computational complexity and the "elusiveness" of global optima in a continuous setting.

---

[1] It should be pointed out, however, that these are worst-case results, and there are certain classes of graphs for which the problem is solvable in polynomial time [17, 6].

2 Graph and tree matching as clique search

2.1 Notations and definitions

Before going into the details of the proposed framework, we need to introduce some graph-theoretical notations and definitions. More details can be found in standard textbooks of graph theory, such as [18]. Let $G = (V, E)$ be a graph, where V is the set of nodes and E is the set of (undirected) edges. The *order* of G is the number of nodes in V, while its *size* is the number of edges. Two nodes $u, v \in V$ are said to be *adjacent* (denoted $u \sim v$) if they are connected by an edge. The *degree* of a vertex is the number of vertices adjacent to it. A *path* is any sequence of distinct nodes $u_0 u_1 \ldots u_n$ such that for all $i = 1 \ldots n$, $u_{i-1} \sim u_i$; in this case, the *length* of the path is n. If $u_0 \sim u_n$ the path is called a *cycle*. A graph is said to be *connected* if any pair of nodes is joined by a path. The *distance* between two nodes u and v, denoted by $d(u, v)$, is the length of the shortest path joining them (by convention $d(u, v) = \infty$, if there is no such path). Given a subset of nodes $C \subseteq V$, the *induced subgraph* $G[C]$ is the graph having C as its node set, and two nodes are adjacent in $G[C]$ if and only if they are adjacent in G.

A connected graph with no cycles is called a *free tree*, or simply a *tree*. A *rooted tree* is one which has a distinguished node, called the *root*. The *level* of a node u in a rooted tree, denoted by $\text{lev}(u)$, is the length of the path connecting the root to u. Note that there is an obvious equivalence between rooted trees and directed trees, where the edges are assumed to be oriented. We shall therefore use the same terminology typically used for directed trees to define the relation between two adjacent nodes. In particular, if $u \sim v$ and $\text{lev}(v) - \text{lev}(u) = +1$, we say that u is the *parent* of v and, conversely, v is a *child* of u. Trees have a number of interesting properties. One which turns out to be very useful for our characterization is that in a tree any two nodes are connected by a *unique* path.

Given a graph $G = (V, E)$, a subset of vertices C is called a *clique* if all its vertices are mutually adjacent, i.e., for all $u, v \in C$ we have $u \sim v$. A clique is said to be *maximal* if it is not contained in any larger clique, and *maximum* if it is the largest clique in the graph. The *clique number*, denoted by $\omega(G)$, is defined as the cardinality of the maximum clique.

2.2 Matching arbitrary graphs

Given two graphs $G_1 = (V_1, E_1)$ and $G_2 = (V_2, E_2)$, an *isomorphism* between them is any bijection $\phi : V_1 \to V_2$ such that $u \sim v \Leftrightarrow \phi(u) \sim \phi(v)$, for all $u, v \in V_1$. Two graphs are said to be *isomorphic* if there exists an isomorphism between them. The graph isomorphism problem is therefore to decide whether two graphs are isomorphic and, in the affirmative, to find an isomorphism. The subgraph isomorphism problem is to check whether a given graph is isomorphic to a subgraph of another one. The maximum common subgraph problem is more general and difficult [13], and includes the graph and the subgraph isomorphism problems as special cases. It consists of finding the largest isomorphic subgraphs of G_1 and G_2. A simpler version of this problem is to find a maximal common subgraph, i.e., an isomorphism between subgraphs which is not included in any larger subgraph isomorphism.

Barrow and Burstall [3], and also Kozen [27], introduced the notion of an *association graph* as a useful auxiliary graph structure for solving general graph/subgraph isomorphism problems. The association graph derived from graphs $G_1 = (V_1, E_1)$ and $G_2 = (V_2, E_2)$ is the undirected graph $G = (V, E)$, where

$$V = V_1 \times V_2$$

and, for any two nodes (u, w) and (v, z) in V, we have

$$(u, w) \sim (v, z) \quad \text{iff} \quad u \neq v, \; w \neq z, \; \text{and} \; u \sim v \Leftrightarrow w \sim z$$

The following result, whose proof is obvious from the definition just given, establishes an equivalence between the graph matching problem and the maximum clique problem.

Theorem 1. *Let $G_1 = (V_1, E_1)$ and $G_2 = (V_2, E_2)$ be two graphs of order n, and let G be the corresponding association graph. Then, G_1 and G_2 are isomorphic if and only if $\omega(G) = n$. In this case, any maximum clique of G induces an isomorphism between G_1 and G_2, and vice versa. In general, maximal/maximum cliques in G are in one-to-one correspondence with maximal/maximum common subgraph isomorphisms between G_1 and G_2, respectively.*

2.3   Matching rooted trees

In many practical problems graphs are organized in a hierarchical manner, i.e., are rooted trees. Since in the standard association graph formulation the solutions are not constrained to preserve the required partial order, it is not clear how to apply the association graph framework in these cases. To illustrate the difficulties with the standard formulation, consider the problem of finding the largest subtree in the left tree of Figure 1 which is isomorphic to a subtree in the right tree. Up to permutations, the correct solution is clearly given by $3 \rightarrow a$, $4 \rightarrow b$, $5 \rightarrow c$, $6 \rightarrow d$, $7 \rightarrow f$, and $8 \rightarrow g$. In other words, the subtree rooted at node 3 is matched against that rooted at node a in the tree on the right. However, using the standard association graph formulation given before, it is easily verified that the solutions induced by the maximum cliques correspond (up to permutations) to the following: $2 \rightarrow h$, $3 \rightarrow a$, $4 \rightarrow b$, $5 \rightarrow c$, $6 \rightarrow d$, $7 \rightarrow f$, and $8 \rightarrow g$, which, while perfectly in accordance with the usual subgraph isomorphism constraints, *does* violate the requirement that the matched subgraphs be trees (note, in fact, that nodes 2 and h are isolated from the rest of the matched subtrees).

We provide a solution to this problem by providing a novel way of deriving an association graph from two rooted trees, based on the graph-theoretic notions of connectivity and the distance matrix.

Let $T_1 = (V_1, E_1)$ and $T_2 = (V_2, E_2)$ be two rooted trees. Any bijection $\phi : H_1 \rightarrow H_2$, with $H_1 \subseteq V_1$ and $H_2 \subseteq V_2$, is called a *subtree isomorphism* if it preserves the adjacency and hierarchical relationships between the nodes and, in addition, the induced subgraphs $T_1[H_1]$ and $T_2[H_2]$ are trees. The former condition amounts to stating that, given $u, v \in H_1$, we have $u \sim v$ if and only if $\phi(u) \sim \phi(v)$, and u is the parent of v if and only if $\phi(u)$ is the parent of $\phi(v)$. A subtree isomorphism is *maximal* if there is no other subtree isomorphism $\phi' : H_1' \rightarrow H_2'$ with H_1 a strict subset of H_1', and *maximum* if H_1 has largest cardinality. The maximal (maximum) subtree isomorphism problem is to find a maximal (maximum) subtree isomorphism between two rooted trees. A word of caution about terminology is in order here. Despite name similarity, we are not addressing the so-called subtree isomorphism problem, which consists of determining whether a given tree is isomorphic to a subtree of a larger one. In fact, we are dealing with a generalization thereof, the maximum common subtree problem, which consists of determining the largest isomorphic subtrees of two given trees. We shall

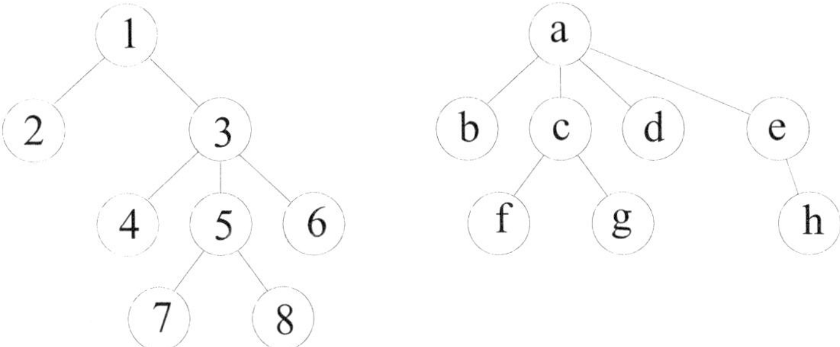

Figure 1: An example of matching two trees. In the standard formulation of the association graph, the maximum cliques do not preserve the hierarchical structure of the two trees (see text for details).

continue to use our own terminology, however, as it emphasizes the role of the isomorphism ϕ.

We now introduce the notion of a *path-string*, which will be central to the subsequent development. Let u and v be two distinct nodes of a rooted tree T, and let $u = x_0 x_1 \ldots x_n = v$ be the (unique) path joining them. The *path-string* of u and v, denoted by $\mathrm{str}(u, v)$, is the string $s_1 s_2 \ldots s_n$ on the alphabet $\{-1, +1\}$ where, for all $i = 1 \ldots n$, $s_i = \mathrm{lev}(x_i) - \mathrm{lev}(x_{i-1})$. By convention, when $u = v$ we define $\mathrm{str}(u, v) = \varepsilon$, where ε is the null string (i.e., the string having zero length).

The path-string concept has a very intuitive meaning. Suppose that you stand on a particular node in a rooted tree and want to move to another adjacent node. Because of the orientation induced by the root, only two types of moves can be done, i.e., going down to one of the children (if one exists) or going up to the parent (if you are not on the root). Let us assign to the first move the label $+1$, and to the second the label -1. Now, suppose that you want to move from node u to v, following the unique path joining them. Then, the path-string of u and v is simply the string of elementary moves required to reach v, starting from u. It may be thought of as the degree of relationship between two relatives in a "family" tree. As an illustrative example, referring to Figure 1, we have $\mathrm{str}(2, 8) = -1 + 1 + 1 + 1$.

The *tree association graph* (TAG) of two rooted trees $T_1 = (V_1, E_1)$ and $T_2 = (V_2, E_2)$ is the graph $G = (V, E)$ where

$$V = V_1 \times V_2$$

and, for any two nodes (u, w) and (v, z) in V, we have

$$(u, w) \sim (v, z) \ \text{ iff } \ \mathrm{str}(u, v) = \mathrm{str}(w, z) \ .$$

Intuitively, two nodes (u, w) and (v, z) are adjacent in the TAG, if and only if the hierarchical relationship between u and v in T_1 is the same as that between w and z in T_2.

The following theorem establishes a one-to-one correspondence between the maximum subtree isomorphism problem and the maximum clique problem.

Theorem 2. *Any maximal (maximum) subtree isomorphism between two rooted trees induces a maximal (maximum) clique in the corresponding TAG, and vice versa.*

Proof (outline). Let $\phi : H_1 \to H_2$ be a maximal subtree isomorphism between rooted trees T_1 and T_2, and let $G = (V, E)$ denote the corresponding tree association graph. Let

$C_\phi \subseteq V$ be defined as:

$$C_\phi = \{(u, \phi(u)) : u \in H_1\}.$$

From the definition of a subtree isomorphism it follows that ϕ maps the path between any two nodes $u, v \in H_1$ onto the path joining $\phi(u)$ and $\phi(v)$. This clearly implies that $\mathrm{str}(u, v) = \mathrm{str}(\phi(u), \phi(v))$ for all $u \in H_1$, and therefore C_ϕ is a clique. Trivially, C_ϕ is a maximal clique because ϕ is maximal, and this proves the first part of the theorem.

Suppose now that $C = \{(u_1, w_1), \cdots, (u_n, w_n)\}$ is a maximal clique of G, and let $H_1 = \{u_1, \cdots, u_n\} \subseteq V_1$ and $H_2 = \{w_1, \cdots, w_n\} \subseteq V_2$. Define $\phi : H_1 \to H_2$ as $\phi(u_i) = w_i$, for all $i = 1 \ldots n$. From the definition of a tree association graph and the hypothesis that C is a clique, it is simple to see that ϕ is a one-to-one and onto correspondence between H_1 and H_2, which trivially preserves both the adjacency and the hierarchical relationships between nodes. The fact that ϕ is a maximal isomorphism is a straightforward consequence of the maximality of C.

To conclude the proof we have to show that the induced subgraphs $T_1[H_1]$ and $T_2[H_2]$ are trees, and this is equivalent to showing that they are connected. Suppose by contradiction that this is not the case, and let $u_i, u_j \in H_1$ be two nodes which are not joined by a path in $T_1[H_1]$. Since both u_i and u_j are nodes of T_1, however, there must exist a path $u_i = x_0 x_1 \ldots x_m = u_j$ joining them in T_1. Let $x^* = x_k$, for some $k = 1 \ldots m$, be a node on this path which is not in H_1. Moreover, let $y^* = y_k$ be the k-th node on the path $w_i = y_0 y_1 \ldots y_m = w_j$ which joins w_i and w_j in T_2 (remember that $\mathrm{str}(u_i, u_j) = \mathrm{str}(w_i, w_j)$, and hence $d(w_i, w_j) = m$).

It is easy to show that the set $\{(x^*, y^*)\} \cup C \subseteq V$ is a clique, and this contradicts the hypothesis that C is a maximal clique. This can be proved by exploiting the obvious fact that if x is a node on the path joining any two nodes u and v, then $\mathrm{str}(u, v)$ can be obtained by concatenating $\mathrm{str}(u, x)$ and $\mathrm{str}(x, v)$.

The "maximum" part of the statement is proved similarly. $\qquad\square$

The next proposition provides us with a straightforward criterion to construct the TAG.

Proposition 1. *Let $T_1 = (V_1, E_1)$ and $T_2 = (V_2, E_2)$ be two rooted trees, $u, v \in V_1$, and $w, z \in V_2$. Then, $\mathrm{str}(u, v) = \mathrm{str}(w, z)$ if and only if the following two conditions hold:*

(a) $d(u, v) = d(w, z)$

(b) $\mathrm{lev}(u) - \mathrm{lev}(v) = \mathrm{lev}(w) - \mathrm{lev}(z)$

This property allows us to efficiently derive the TAG by using a classical representation for graphs, i.e., the so-called *distance matrix* (see, e.g., [18]) which, for an arbitrary graph $G = (V, E)$ of order n, is the $n \times n$ matrix $D = (d_{ij})$ where $d_{ij} = d(u_i, u_j)$, the distance between nodes u_i and u_j. Efficient, classical algorithms are available for obtaining such a matrix [9].

2.4 Matching free trees

We now show how the very same framework described before can be adapted in a straightforward way to the case of matching free (i.e. unrooted) trees, a type of structure which arises frequently in a variety of application domains ranging from pattern recognition [10] to biochemistry [1].

Let $T_1 = (V_1, E_1)$ and $T_2 = (V_2, E_2)$ be two free trees. As before, any bijection $\phi : H_1 \rightarrow H_2$, with $H_1 \subseteq V_1$ and $H_2 \subseteq V_2$, is called a *subtree isomorphism* if it preserves both the adjacency relationships between the nodes and the connectedness of the matched subgraphs. Formally, this means that, given $u, v \in H_1$, we have $u \sim v$ if and only if $\phi(u) \sim \phi(v)$ and, in addition, the induced subgraphs $T_1[H_1]$ and $T_2[H_2]$ are connected. The notions of maximal and maximum subtree isomorphisms are defined as in the rooted case.

The *free tree association graph* (FTAG) of two trees $T_1 = (V_1, E_1)$ and $T_2 = (V_2, E_2)$ is the graph $G = (V, E)$ where

$$V = V_1 \times V_2$$

and, for any two nodes (u, w) and (v, z) in V, we have

$$(u, w) \sim (v, z) \Leftrightarrow d(u, v) = d(w, z) \ .$$

Again, we can establish a one-to-one correspondence between the problem of matching free trees and the maximum clique problem (the proof proceeds along the same line as the one of Theorem 2—see [39] for details).

Theorem 3. *Any maximal (maximum) subtree isomorphism between two free trees induces a maximal (maximum) clique in the corresponding FTAG, and vice versa.*

3   Continuous formulation of the maximum clique problem

Let $G = (V, E)$ be an arbitrary undirected graph of order n, and let S_n denote the standard simplex of $\mathbb{R}^n$:

$$S_n = \left\{ \mathbf{x} \in \mathbb{R}^n \ : \ x_i \geq 0 \ \text{for all } i = 1 \ldots n, \ \text{and} \ \sum_{i=1}^{n} x_i = 1 \right\} \ .$$

Given a subset of vertices C of G we shall denote by $\mathbf{x}^c$ its *characteristic vector*, which is the point in S_n defined as

$$x_i^c = \begin{cases} 1/|C|, & \text{if } i \in C \\ 0, & \text{otherwise} \end{cases}$$

where $|C|$ denotes the cardinality of C.

Now, consider the following quadratic function

$$f(\mathbf{x}) = \mathbf{x}^T A \mathbf{x} \tag{1}$$

where $A = (a_{ij})$ is the adjacency matrix of G, i.e., the $n \times n$ symmetric matrix $A = (a_{ij})$ defined as

$$a_{ij} = \begin{cases} 1, & \text{if } u_i \sim u_j \\ 0, & \text{otherwise} \end{cases} \ .$$

and "T" denotes transposition. A point $\mathbf{x}^* \in S_n$ is said to be a *global* maximizer of f in S_n if $f(\mathbf{x}^*) \geq f(\mathbf{x})$, for all $\mathbf{x} \in S_n$. It is said to be a *local* maximizer if there exists an $\epsilon > 0$ such that $f(\mathbf{x}^*) \geq f(\mathbf{x})$ for all $\mathbf{x} \in S_n$ whose distance from $\mathbf{x}^*$ is less than ϵ, and if $f(\mathbf{x}^*) = f(\mathbf{x})$ implies $\mathbf{x}^* = \mathbf{x}$, then $\mathbf{x}^*$ is said to be a *strict* local maximizer.

The Motzkin-Straus theorem [32] establishes a remarkable connection between global (local) maximizers of the function f in S_n and maximum (maximal) cliques of G. Specifically, it states that a subset of vertices C of a graph G is a maximum clique if and only if its characteristic vector $\mathbf{x}^c$ is a global maximizer of f on S_n. A similar relationship holds between (strict) local maximizers and maximal cliques [15, 40]. This result has an intriguing computational significance in that it allows us to shift from the discrete to the continuous domain in an elegant manner. The Motzkin-Straus theorem has served as the basis of many clique-finding procedures [8, 7, 14, 36, 37, 30], and has also been used to determine theoretical bounds on the clique number [36, 49].

One drawback associated with the original Motzkin-Straus formulation relates to the existence of spurious solutions, i.e., maximizers of f which are not in the form of characteristic vectors. This was observed empirically by Pardalos and Phillips [36] and has more recently been formalized by Pelillo and Jagota [40]. In principle, spurious solutions represent a problem since, while providing information about the cardinality of the maximum clique, do not allow us to easily extract its vertices. Fortunately, there is straightforward solution to this problem which has recently been introduced and studied by Bomze [5]. Consider the following regularized version of function f:

$$\hat{f}(\mathbf{x}) = \mathbf{x}^T A \mathbf{x} + \frac{1}{2}\mathbf{x}^T \mathbf{x} \tag{2}$$

which is obtained from (1) by substituting the adjacency matrix A of G with

$$\hat{A} = A + \frac{1}{2}I_n$$

where I_n is the $n \times n$ identity matrix.

The following is the spurious-free counterpart of the original Motzkin-Straus theorem (see [5] for proof).

Theorem 4. *Let C be a subset of vertices of a graph G, and let $\mathbf{x}^c$ be its characteristic vector. Then the following statements hold:*

(a) C is a maximum clique of G if and only if $\mathbf{x}^c$ is a global maximizer of the function $\hat{f}$ over the simplex S_n. In this case, $\omega(G) = 1/2(1 - \hat{f}(\mathbf{x}^c))$.

(b) C is a maximal clique of G if and only if $\mathbf{x}^c$ is a local maximizer of $\hat{f}$ in S_n.

(c) All local (and hence global) maximizers of $\hat{f}$ over S_n are strict and are characteristic vectors of maximal cliques of G.

In an exact sense, therefore, a one-to-one correspondence exists between maximal cliques and local maximizers of $\hat{f}$ in S_n on the one hand, and maximum cliques and global maximizers on the other hand. This solves the spurious solution problem in a definitive manner.

4 Replicator equations for graph and tree matching

Let W be a non-negative $n \times n$ matrix, and consider the following dynamical system:

$$\frac{d}{dt}x_i(t) = x_i(t)\left(\pi_i(t) - \sum_{j=1}^{n} x_j(t)\pi_j(t)\right) , \quad i = 1 \ldots n \tag{3}$$

where $\pi_i(t) = \sum_{j=1}^{n} w_{ij} x_j(t)$, $i = 1 \ldots n$, and its discrete-time counterpart:

$$x_i(t+1) = \frac{x_i(t)\pi_i(t)}{\sum_{j=1}^{n} x_j(t)\pi_j(t)} , \quad i = 1 \ldots n . \tag{4}$$

It is readily seen that the simplex S_n is invariant under these dynamics, which means that every trajectory starting in S_n will remain in S_n for all future times.

Both (3) and (4) are called *replicator equations* in theoretical biology, since they are used to model evolution over time of relative frequencies of interacting, self-replicating entities [21]. The discrete-time dynamical equations turn also out to be a special case of a general class of dynamical systems introduced by Baum and Eagon [4] in the context of Markov chain theory.

Theorem 5. *If W is symmetric, then the quadratic polynomial $F(\mathbf{x}) = \mathbf{x}^T W \mathbf{x}$ is strictly increasing along any non-constant trajectory of both continuous-time (3) and discrete-time (4) replicator equations. Furthermore, any such trajectory converges to a (unique) stationary point. Finally, a vector $\mathbf{x} \in S_n$ is asymptotically stable under (3) and (4) if and only if $\mathbf{x}$ is a strict local maximizer of F on S_n.*

The previous result is known in mathematical biology as the Fundamental Theorem of Natural Selection [21, 47]. As far as the discrete-time model is concerned, it can be regarded as a straightforward implication of the more general Baum-Eagon theorem [4]. The fact that all trajectories of the replicator dynamics converge to a stationary point is proven in [28].

Recently, there has been much interest in evolutionary game theory around the following exponential version of replicator equations, which arises as a model of evolution guided by imitation [20, 47]:

$$\frac{d}{dt} x_i(t) = x_i(t) \left(e^{\kappa \pi_i(t)} - \sum_{j=1}^{n} x_j(t) e^{\kappa \pi_j(t)} \right) , \quad i = 1 \ldots n \tag{5}$$

where κ is a positive constant. As κ tends to 0, the orbits of this dynamics approach those of the standard, first-order replicator model (3), slowed down by the factor κ. Hofbauer [20] has recently proven that when the matrix W is symmetric, the quadratic polynomial F defined in Theorem 5 is also strictly increasing, as in the first-order case. After discussing various properties of this, and more general dynamics, he concluded that the model behaves essentially in the same way as the standard replicator equations, the only difference being the size of the basins of attraction around stable equilibria. A customary way of discretizating equation (5) is given by the following difference equations:

$$x_i(t+1) = \frac{x_i(t) e^{\kappa \pi_i(t)}}{\sum_{j=1}^{n} x_j(t) e^{\kappa \pi_j(t)}} , \quad i = 1 \ldots n \tag{6}$$

which enjoys many of the properties of the first-order system (4), e.g., they have the same set of equilibria. From our computational perspective, exponential replicator dynamics are particularly attractive because, as demonstrated by the extensive numerical results reported in the next section, they turn out to be considerably faster and sometimes more accurate than the standard, first-order models.

The properties discussed above naturally suggest using replicator equations as a useful heuristic for graph and tree matching problems. Considering arbitrary graph matching, let G_1

and G_2 be two graphs of order n, and let A denote the adjacency matrix of the corresponding N-vertex association graph G. By letting

$$W = A + \frac{1}{2}I_N$$

we know that the replicator dynamical systems, starting from an arbitrary initial state, will iteratively maximize the function $\hat{f}(\mathbf{x}) = \mathbf{x}^T(A + \frac{1}{2}I_N)\mathbf{x}$ in S_N, and will eventually converge to a strict local maximizer which, by virtue of Theorem 4 will then correspond to the characteristic vector of a maximal clique in the association graph. This will in turn induce an isomorphism between two subgraphs of G_1 and G_2 which is "maximal," in the sense that there is no other isomorphism between subgraphs of G_1 and G_2 which includes the one found. For subtree isomorphism, we proceed in the same way, that is by making replicator equations search for a maximal clique in the corresponding TAG/FTAG. The converged solutions will induce a maximal subtree isomorphism.

Clearly, in theory there is no guarantee that the converged solution will be a *global* maximizer of $\hat{f}$, and therefore that it will induce a "maximum" isomorphism between the two original graphs.

5　Experiments and results

5.1　Graph isomorphism

In order to assess the effectiveness of the proposed approach, extensive simulations were performed over randomly generated graphs of various connectivities. Random graphs represent a useful benchmark not only because they are not constrained to any particular application, but also because it is simple to replicate experiments and hence to make comparisons with other algorithms. Before going into the details of the experiments, however, we need to enter a preliminary caveat.

It is often said that random graph isomorphism is trivial. Essentially, this claim is based on a result due to Babai, Erdös and Selkow [2] which shows that a straightforward, linear-time graph isomorphism algorithm does work for *almost all* random graphs.[2] It should be pointed out, however, that there are various probability models for random graphs [34]. The one adopted by Babai considers random graphs as uniformly distributed random variables, i.e., they assume that the probability of generating any n-vertex graph equals $2^{-\binom{n}{2}}$. By contrast, the customary way in which random graphs are generated leads to a distribution which only in a special case is uniform. Specifically, given a parameter p $(0 < p < 1)$ which represents the expected connectivity, a graph of order n is generated by randomly entering edges between the vertices with probability p. Note that p is related to the expected size of the resulting graph, which indeed is $\binom{n}{2}p$. It is straightforward to see that in so doing the probability that a graph of order n and size s be generated is given by $p^s(1-p)^{\binom{n}{2}-s}$, which only in the case $p = \frac{1}{2}$ equals Babai's uniform distribution. Now, the results presented in [2] are based on the observation that, using a uniform probability model, the degrees of the vertices have large variability and this is in fact the key to their algorithm. In the non-uniform probability model, the degree random variable has variance $(n-1)p(1-p)$ and it is no accident that attains

---

[2] A property is said to hold for *almost all* graphs, if the probability that the property holds tends to 1 as the order of the graph approaches infinity.

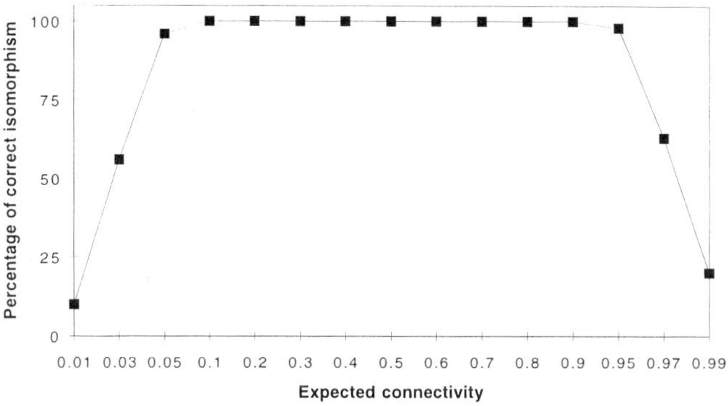

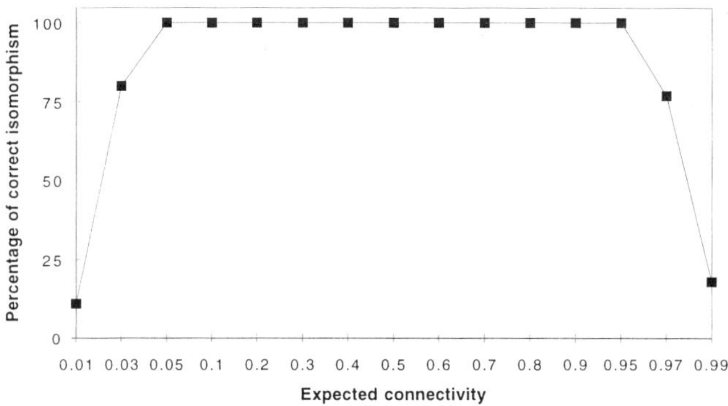

Figure 2: Percentage of correct isomorphisms obtained using the first-order (TOP) and the exponential (BOT-TOM) replicator equations, as a function of the expected connectivity.

its largest value exactly at $p = \frac{1}{2}$. However, as p moves away from $\frac{1}{2}$ the variance becomes smaller and smaller, tending to 0 as p approaches 0 or 1. As a result, Babai's arguments are no longer applicable. It seems therefore that, using the customary graph generation model, random graph isomorphism is not as trivial as is generally believed, especially for very sparse and very dense graphs. As a matter of fact, the experience reported in [42, 43, 46] and also the results presented below, provide support to this claim.

In the experiments reported here, the discrete-time replicator equation (4) and its exponential counterpart (6) with $\kappa = 10$ were used. The algorithms were started from the barycenter of the simplex and they were stopped when either a maximal clique was found or the distance between two successive points was smaller than a fixed threshold, which was set to 10^{-17}. In the latter case the converged vector was randomly perturbed, and the algorithm restarted from the perturbed point. Because of the one-to-one correspondence between local maximizers and maximal cliques, this situation corresponds to convergence to a saddle point. All the experiments were run on a Sparc20.

Undirected 100-vertex random graphs were generated with expected connectivities ranging from 1% to 99%. For each connectivity value, 100 graphs were produced and each of them had its vertices randomly permuted so as to obtain a pair of isomorphic graphs. Over-

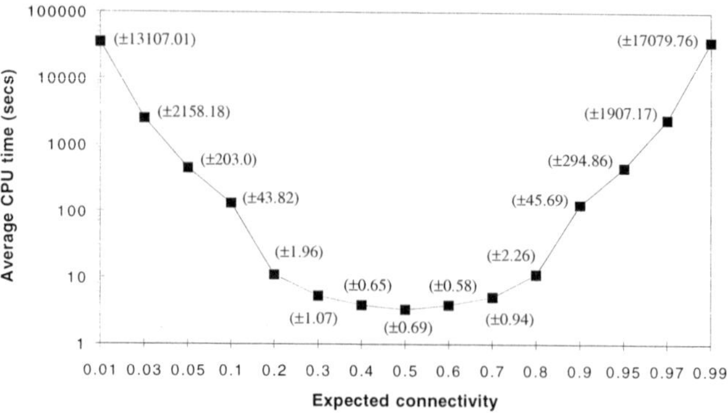

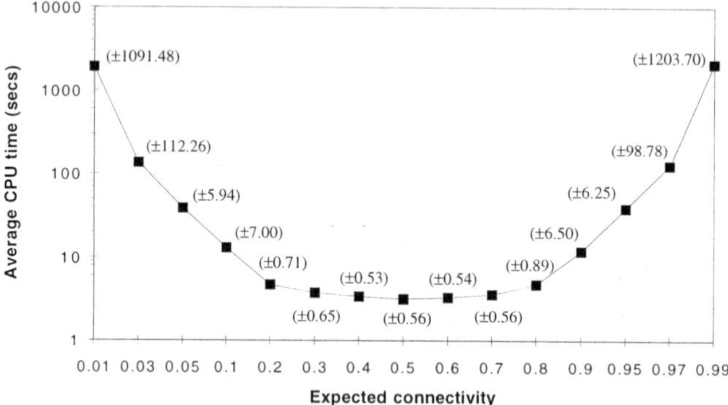

Figure 3: Average computational time taken by the first-order (TOP) and the exponential (BOTTOM) replicator equations, as a function of the expected connectivity. The vertical axes are in logarithmic scale, and the numbers in parentheses represent the standard deviation.

all, therefore, 1500 pairs of isomorphic graphs were used. Each pair was given as input to the replicator models and, after convergence, a success was recorded when the cardinality of the returned clique was equal to the order of the graphs given as input (i.e., 100).[3] Because of the stopping criterion employed, this guarantees that a maximum clique, and therefore a correct isomorphism, was found. The proportion of successes as a function of the expected connectivities for both replicator models is plotted in Figure 2, whereas Figure 3 shows the average CPU time taken by the two algorithms to converge (in logarithmic scale). Notice how the exponential replicator system (6) is dramatically faster and also performs better than the first-order model (4).

These results are significantly superior to those reported by Simić [46] who obtained poor results at connectivities less than 40% even on smaller graphs (i.e., up to 75 vertices). They also compare favorably with the results obtained more recently by Rangarajan *et al.* [42] on 100-vertex random graphs for connectivities up to 50%. Specifically, at 1% and 3% connec-

---

[3]Due to the high computational time required, in the 1% and 99% cases the first-order replicator algorithm (4) was tested only on 10 pairs, instead of 100.

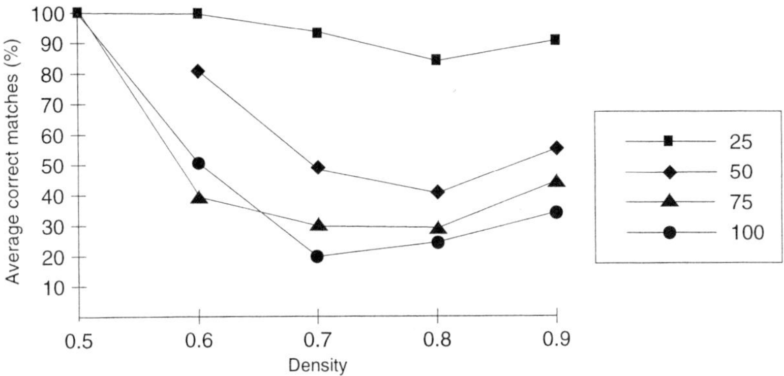

Figure 4: Average correct matches obtained using the (first-order) replicator dynamics for the subgraph isomorphism problem, as a function of the expected connectivity (density).

tivities they report a percentage of correct isomorphisms of about 30% and 0%, respectively. Using our approach we obtained, on the same kind of graphs, a percentage of success of 80% and 11%, respectively. Rangarajan and Mjolsness [43] also ran experiments on 100-vertex random graphs with various connectivities, using a powerful Lagrangian relaxation network. Except for a few instances, they always obtained a correct solution. The computational time required by their model, however, turns out to largely exceed ours. As an example, the average time taken by their algorithm to match two 100-vertex 50%-connectivity graphs was about 30 minutes on an SGI workstation. As shown in Figure 3, we obtained identical results in about 3 seconds.

It should be emphasized that all the algorithms mentioned above do incorporate sophisticated annealing mechanisms to escape from poor local minima. By contrast, in the presented work no attempt was made to prevent the algorithm from converging to such solutions. It seems that, as far as the graph isomorphism problem is concerned, global maximizers of the Motzkin-Straus objective have large basins of attraction. A similar observation was also made in connection to earlier experiments concerning the maximum clique problem [8, 37].

5.2　Subgraph isomorphism

We performed a few experiments aimed at studying the performance of the replicator dynamics on the subgraph isomorphism problem, which is NP-complete. To this end, we generated random graphs using the same procedure described before. Specifically, graphs of order 25, 50, 75, and 100 were generated with edge connectivities ranging from 50% to 90%, in steps of 10%. For each order/connectivity value 30 graphs were obtained. Each of the 600 graphs thus produced was randomly corrupted by deleting 10% of its vertices, and the remaining vertices were permuted randomly.

At the end of the replicator processes, we counted the number of vertices in the maximal clique found (i.e., the number of correct matches) and divided by the order of the smaller graph, which coincides with the size of the maximum clique in the association graph. Figure 4 shows the behavior of the percentage of correct matches, averaged over the 30 graphs, as a function of edge connectivity (density) for all graph orders. As can be seen (and as it might be expected due to the computational complexity of the subgraph isomorphism problem) the results are quite poor. Only at 50% connectivity value we obtained good results, but the quality of the solutions found degrades substantially as the density and the order of the graphs being matched increase.

It is clear that in this case more sophisticated optimization techniques are required to avoid poor local optima. Algorithms based on pivoting [30, 29] or annealing [7] seem good alternatives to the simple replicator dynamics.

5.3 Matching "shock" trees for visual shape recognition

We now illustrate our framework for matching hierarchical structures with numerical examples of shape matching. Our representation for shape is based on an abstraction of the *shocks* (or singularities) of a curve evolution process, acting on a simple closed curve in the plane, into a shock tree. We begin by providing some background on the representation (for details see [25, 45]) and then present experimental results on matching shock trees.

In [25] the following evolution equation was proposed for visual shape analysis:

$$\begin{aligned} \mathcal{C}_t &= (1 + \alpha\kappa)\mathcal{N} \\ \mathcal{C}(p,0) &= \mathcal{C}_0(p). \end{aligned} \tag{7}$$

Here $\mathcal{C}(p,t)$ is the vector of curve coordinates, $\mathcal{N}(p,t)$ is the inward normal, p is the curve parameter, and t is the evolutionary time of the deformation. The constant $\alpha \geq 0$ controls the regularizing effects of curvature κ. When α is large, the equation becomes a geometric heat equation; when $\alpha = 0$, the equation is hyperbolic and *shocks*, or entropy-satisfying singularities, can form. In the latter case the locus of points through which the shocks migrate is related to Blum's grassfire transformation [25], although significantly more information is available via a "coloring" of these positions. Four types can arise, according to the local variation of the radius function along the medial axis (Figure 5). Intuitively, the radius function varies monotonically at a type 1, reaches a strict local minimum at a type 2, is constant at a type 3 and reaches a strict local maximum at a type 4. The classification of shock positions according to their colors, and an enumeration of the possible local neighborhoods around each shock type is at the heart of the representation.

Shocks of the same type that form a connected component are grouped together to comprise the nodes of a *shock graph*, with the 1-shock groups separated at branch-points of the skeleton. Directed edges in the graph are placed between shock groups that touch one another, such that each parent node contains no shocks that formed prior to any shocks in a child node. This corresponds to a "reversal" in time of the curve evolution process to obtain a hierarchy of connected components. The graph is rooted at a unique vertex #, the children of which are the last shock groups to form, e.g., the palm of the hand shape in Figure 6, with associated nodes 3-004a and 3-004b in the graph. (The letters 'a' and 'b' denote different sides of the same shock group). A key property of the shock graph is that its topological structure is highly constrained because the events that govern the birth, combination and death of shock groups are completely characterized by a shock grammar, with a small number of rewrite rules [45]. In particular, each shock graph can be reduced to a unique rooted shock tree.

We now illustrate the power of the hierarchical structure matching algorithm on shock trees. Whereas each node has geometric attributes, related to properties of the shocks in each group, here we shall consider only the shock tree topologies (but see [41] for more sophisticated models). We selected 25 silhouettes representing eight different object classes (Table 1,

Query Shape	Top 8 Topological Matches							
	1	2	3	4	5	6	7	8
[shape]	1.00	1.00	.916	.900	.825	.771	.750	.750
[shape]	1.00	1.00	.916	.900	.825	.771	.750	.750
[shape]	1.00	.900	.900	.833	.833	.833	.833	.807
[shape]	1.00	.958	.875	.825	.729	.666	.641	.641
[shape]	1.00	.909	.875	.826	.738	.738	.738	.711
[shape]	1.00	.958	.909	.859	.755	.668	.668	.609
[shape]	1.00	1.00	.966	.966	.900	.800	.784	.771
[shape]	1.00	.937	.937	.904	.875	.750	.731	.731
[shape]	1.00	1.00	.966	.966	.937	.928	.773	.771
[shape]	1.00	.928	.928	.900	.900	.875	.833	.825
[shape]	1.00	1.00	.966	.966	.937	.928	.773	.771
[shape]	1.00	1.00	.966	.966	.904	.900	.800	.784
[shape]	1.00	1.00	.801	.750	.733	.733	.720	.708
[shape]	1.00	1.00	.801	.750	.733	.733	.720	.708
[shape]	1.00	.807	.801	.801	.801	.801	.722	.721
[shape]	1.00	.900	.826	.755	.750	.729	.675	.675
[shape]	1.00	.900	.859	.825	.738	.675	.600	.600
[shape]	1.00	.977	.956	.800	.800	.785	.785	.773
[shape]	1.00	.977	.933	.784	.784	.772	.772	.759
[shape]	1.00	.956	.933	.771	.771	.760	.760	.746
[shape]	1.00	.916	.916	.833	.833	.833	.785	.772
[shape]	1.00	1.00	.833	.833	.801	.733	.733	.720
[shape]	1.00	1.00	.833	.833	.801	.733	.733	.720
[shape]	1.00	.687	.675	.675	.656	.612	.600	.600
[shape]	1.00	.693	.692	.692	.687	.673	.673	.661

Table 1: A tabulation of the top 8 topological matches for each query. The scores indicate the average of the fraction of nodes matched in each of the two trees (see text). Note that *only* the topology of the shock trees was used; the addition of geometric information permits finer discrimination (see [41]).

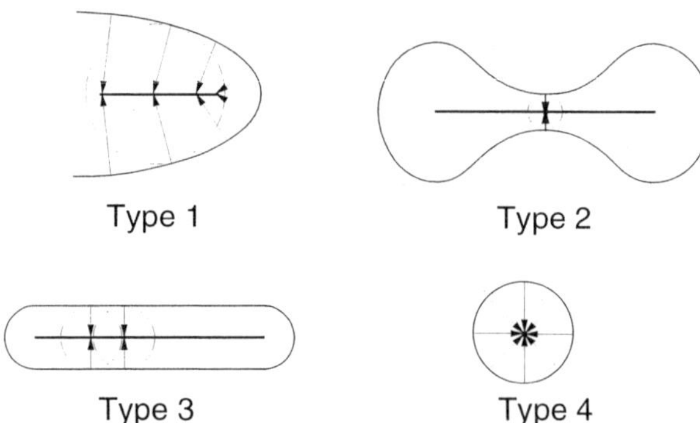

Figure 5: A coloring of shocks into four types [25]. A 1-shock derives from a *protrusion*, and traces out a curve segment of adjacent 1-shocks, along which the radius function varies monotonically. A 2-shock arises at a *neck*, where the radius function attains a strict local minimum, and is immediately followed by two 1-shocks flowing away from it in opposite directions. 3-shocks correspond to an annihilation into a curve segment due to a *bend*, along which the radius function is constant, and a 4-shock an annihilation into a point or a *seed*, where the radius function attains a strict local maximum. The loci of these shocks gives Blum's medial axis.

first column); the tool shapes were taken from the Rutgers Tools database. Each shape was then matched against *all* entries in the database. Figure 7 shows the maximal subtree isomorphisms found by the algorithm for three examples. The top 8 matches for each query shape, along with the associated scores, are shown in Table 1. The scores indicate the average of n/n_1 and n/n_2, where n is the size of the maximal clique found, and n_1 and n_2 are the number of nodes in each tree. We observed that in *all* our experiments the maximal cliques found were also maximum cliques, thereby confirming previous observations concerning the basins of attraction of the Motzkin-Straus quadratic program for maximum clique [37, 8]. The matching algorithm generally takes only two to three seconds to converge on a Sparc 10.

Note that despite the fact that metric/label information associated with nodes in the shock trees was discounted altogether, all exemplars in the same class as the query shape are typically within the top 5 matches, illustrating the potential of a topological matching process for indexing into a database of shapes. Nevertheless, there are shapes with similar shock tree topologies but dissimilar geometries, e.g., the profile and the brushes in the first two rows. In [41] we extended our framework to incorporate geometric information contained in each shock sequence (the location, time of formation, speed and direction of each shock) as attributes on the nodes. This leads to better discrimination between shapes than that provided by shock tree topologies alone.

5.4 Matching free trees

In this series of experiments, the following protocol was used. A hundred 100-node free trees were generated uniformly at random using a procedure described by Wilf in [48]. Then, each such tree was subject to a corruption process which consisted of randomly deleting a fraction of its terminal nodes, thereby obtaining a tree isomorphic to a proper subtree of the original one. Various levels of corruption (i.e., percentage of node deletion) were used, namely 2%,

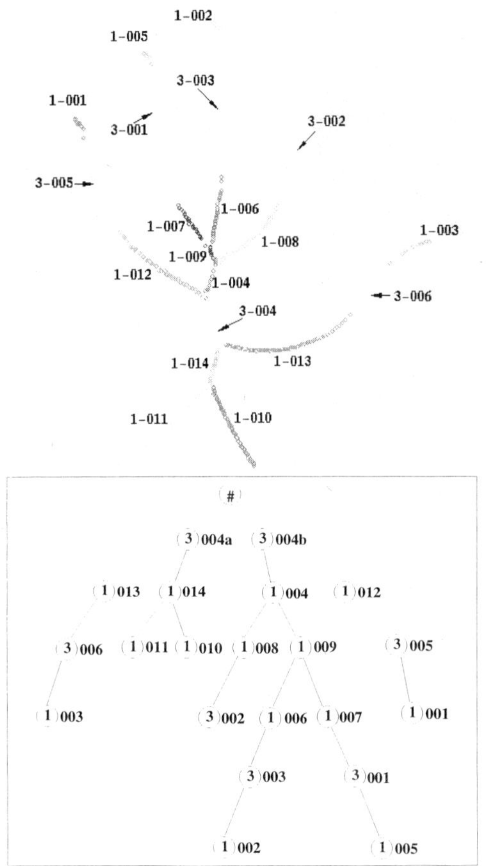

Figure 6: An illustrative example of the shocks obtained from curve evolution (from [45]). TOP: The notation associated with the locus of shock points is of the form shock_type-identifier. BOTTOM: The tree has the shock_type on each node, and the identifier is adjacent. The last shocks to form during the curve evolution process appear under the root node labeled #.

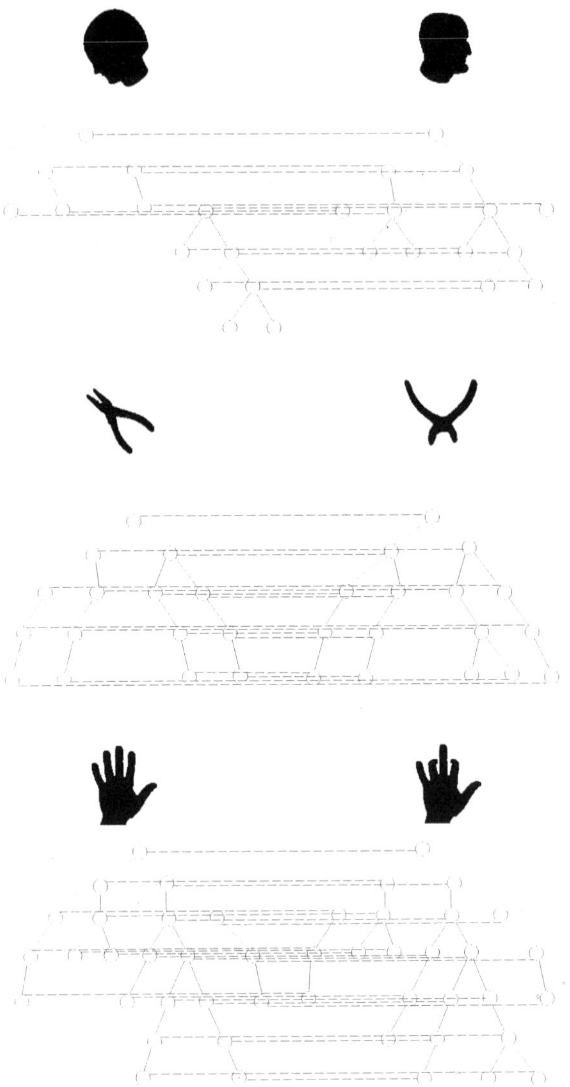

Figure 7: Maximal subtree isomorphisms found for three illustrative examples.

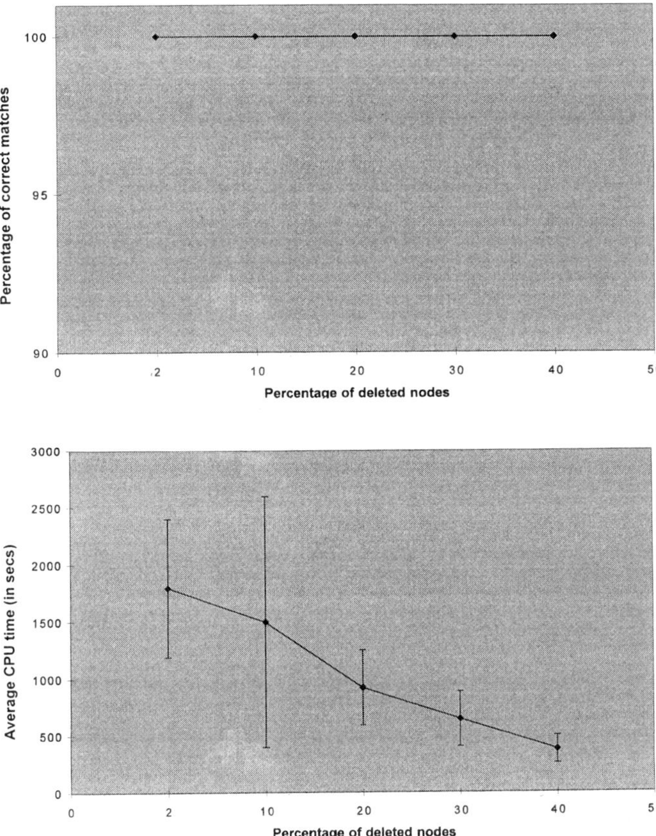

Figure 8: Results obtained over 100-node random free trees with various levels of corruption, using the first-order dynamics (4). Top: Percentage of correct matches. Bottom: Average computational time taken by the replicator equations.

10%, 20%, 30% and 40%. This means that the order of the pruned trees ranged from 98 to 60. Overall, therefore, 500 pairs of trees were obtained, for each of which the corresponding FTAG was constructed.

As in the previous series of experiments, both the linear and the exponential dynamics were used, with identical parameters and stopping criterion. After convergence, we calculated the proportion of matched nodes, i.e., the ratio between the cardinality of the clique found and the order of the smaller subtree, and then we averaged. Figure 8(a) shows the results obtained using the linear dynamics (4) as a function of the corruption level. As can be seen, the algorithm was *always* able to find a correct maximum isomorphism, i.e. a maximum clique in the FTAG. Figure 8(b) plots the corresponding (average) CPU time taken by the processes, with corresponding error bars (simulations were performed on a 350MHz AMDK6-2 processor).

In Figure 9, the results pertaining to the exponential dynamics (6) are shown. In terms of solution's quality the algorithm performed exactly as its linear counterpart, but this time it was dramatically faster.

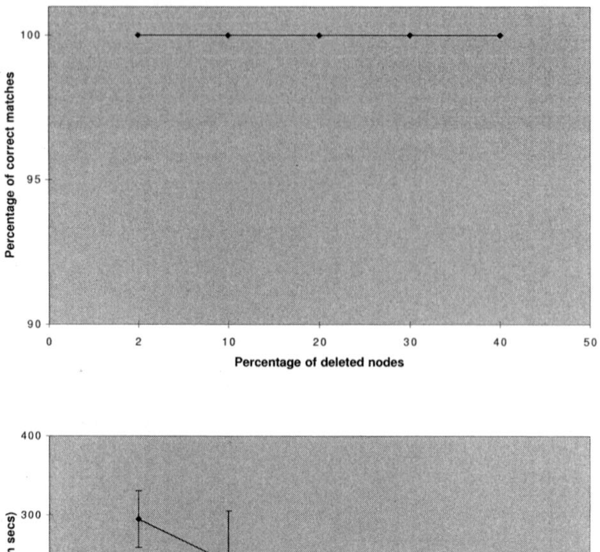

Figure 9: Results obtained over 100-node random free trees with various levels of corruption, using the exponential dynamics (6). Top: Percentage of correct matches. Bottom: Average computational time taken by the replicator equations.

6   Summary and conclusions

We have considered various combinatorial optimization problems of increasing computational complexity, namely rooted/unrooted subtree isomorphism, graph isomorphism and subgraph isomorphism, using a common continuous optimization framework. The approach is based on an equivalent maximum clique formulation of these problems, and it is centered around a fundamental result proved by Motzkin and Straus in the mid-1960s, and recently expanded in various ways, which allows us to formulate the maximum clique problem in terms of an indefinite quadratic program. The attractive feature of this formulation is that a clear one-to-one correspondence exists between the solutions of the quadratic programs and those in the original combinatorial problems. To approximately solve the program we use the so-called "replicator" equations, a class of straightforward continuous- and discrete-time dynamical systems developed in various branches of theoretical biology.

From the extensive experiments conducted on both random graphs and graphs arising from real-world computer vision problems, an intriguing picture does emerge. For "simple" problems (rooted and unrooted tree matching) the replicator dynamics, which are essentially gradient-following procedures, were *always* able to find the globally optimal solution; for the "intermediate" problem (graph isomorphism) this happened *almost always*, more precisely it did not happen on very sparse and very dense graphs. Finally, as expected, for the "difficult" problem (subgraph isomorphism) this *hardly ever* happened. In other words, the hierarchical relationship among the problems imposed by their computational complexity is preserved in a quite unexpected way: it seems that, as far as our problems are concerned, their complexity is somehow related to the landscape of the corresponding energy function or, more formally, to the volume of the basins of attraction around global optima: the simpler the problem the better-behaved the energy, and it is not obvious at all why this should happen.

These results naturally suggest the following intriguing questions: Is there any relationship between standard notions of computational complexity and the "elusiveness" of global optima in a continuous setting? In other words: given a "simple" problem (i.e., one that can be solved in polynomial time), is it possible to write down a corresponding "well-behaved" energy function? namely, one where straightforward gradient-based optimization techniques work well? And, if so, is there a systematic way to do it? Conversely, given a well-behaved objective function for a problem (whose computational complexity is perhaps unknown) is this a sign that a polynomial-time algorithm for it exists?

It is not clear whether there is a crisp answer to these questions, but the work described in this paper seems at least to suggest that such connections might indeed be possible.

References

[1] J. E. Ash, P. A. Chubb, S. E. Ward, S. M. Welford, and P. Willett. *Communication, Storage and Retrieval of Chemical Information*. Ellis Horwood, Chichester, UK, 1985.

[2] L. Babai, P. Erdös, and S. M. Selkow. Random graph isomorphism. *SIAM J. Comput.*, 9(3):628–635, 1980.

[3] H. G. Barrow and R. M. Burstall. Subgraph isomorphism, matching relational structures and maximal cliques. *Inform. Process. Lett.*, 4(4):83–84, 1976.

[4] L. E. Baum and J. A. Eagon. An inequality with applications to statistical estimation for probabilistic functions of Markov processes and to a model for ecology. *Bull. Amer. Math. Soc.*, 73:360–363, 1967.

[5] I. M. Bomze. Evolution towards the maximum clique. *J. Glob. Optim.*, 10:143–164, 1997.

[6] I. M. Bomze, M. Budinich, P. M. Pardalos, and M. Pelillo. The maximum clique problem. In D.-Z. Du and P. M. Pardalos, editors, *Handbook of Combinatorial Optimization—Suppl. Vol. A*, pages 1–74. Kluwer Academic Publishers, Boston, MA, 1999.

[7] I. M. Bomze, M. Budinich, M. Pelillo, and C. Rossi. Annealed replication: A new heuristic for the maximum clique problem. *Discr. Appl. Math.*, 121(1–3):27–49, 2002.

[8] I. M. Bomze, M. Pelillo, and R. Giacomini. Evolutionary approach to the maximum clique problem: Empirical evidence on a larger scale. In I. M. Bomze, T. Csendes, R. Horst, and P. M. Pardalos, editors, *Developments in Global Optimization*, pages 95–108. Kluwer, Dordrecht, The Netherlands, 1997.

[9] T. H. Cormen, C. E. Leiserson, and R. L. Rivest. *Introduction to Algorithms*. MIT Press, Cambridge, MA, 1990.

[10] R. O. Duda, P. E. Hart, and D. G. Stork. *Pattern Classification*. Wiley, New York, 2nd edition, 2001.

[11] R. Durbin and D. Willshaw. An analog approach to the travelling salesman problem using an elastic net method. *Nature*, 326:689–691, 1987.

[12] Y. Fu and P. W. Anderson. Application of statistical mechanics to NP-complete problems in combinatorial optimization. *J. Phys. A*, 19:1605–1620, 1986.

[13] M. R. Garey and D. S. Johnson. *Computers and Intractability: A Guide to the Theory of NP-Completeness.* W. H. Freeman, San Francisco, CA, 1979.

[14] L. E. Gibbons, D. W. Hearn, and P. M. Pardalos. A continuous based heuristic for the maximum clique problem. In D. S. Johnson and M. Trick, editors, *Cliques, Coloring, and Satisfiability—Second DIMACS Implementation Challenge,* pages 103–124. American Mathematical Society, 1996.

[15] L. E. Gibbons, D. W. Hearn, P. M. Pardalos, and M. V. Ramana. Continuous characterizations of the maximum clique problem. *Math. Oper. Res.,* 22:754–768, 1997.

[16] S. Gold and A. Rangarajan. A graduated assignment algorithm for graph matching. *IEEE Trans. Pattern Anal. Machine Intell.,* 18(4):377–388, 1996.

[17] M. Grötschel, L. Lovász, and A. Schrijver. *Geometric Algorithms and Combinatorial Optimization.* Springer-Verlag, Berlin, 1988.

[18] F. Harary. *Graph Theory.* Addison-Wesley, Reading, MA, 1969.

[19] J. Hastad. Clique is hard to approximate within $n^{1-\varepsilon}$. In *Proc. 37th Ann. Symp. Found. Comput. Sci.,* pages 627–636, 1996.

[20] J. Hofbauer. Imitation dynamics for games. Collegium Budapest, preprint, 1995.

[21] J. Hofbauer and K. Sigmund. *Evolutionary Games and Population Dynamics.* Cambridge University Press, Cambridge, UK, 1998.

[22] J. J. Hopfield and D. W. Tank. "Neural" computation of decisions in optimization problems. *Biol. Cybern.,* 52:141–152, 1985.

[23] A. Jagota. Approximating maximum clique with a Hopfield neural network. *IEEE Trans. Neural Networks,* 6:724–735, 1995.

[24] D. S. Johnson. The NP-completeness column: An ongoing guide. *J. Algorithms,* 9:426–444, 1988.

[25] B. B. Kimia, A. Tannenbaum, and S. W. Zucker. Shape, shocks, and deformations I: The components of two-dimensional shape and the reaction-diffusion space. *Int. J. Computer Vision,* 15:189–224, 1995.

[26] J. J. Kosowsky and A. L. Yuille. The invisible hand algorithm: Solving the assignment problem with statistical physics. *Neural Networks,* 7:477–490, 1994.

[27] D. Kozen. A clique problem equivalent to graph isomorphism. *SIGACT News,* pages 50–52, 1978.

[28] V. Losert and E. Akin. Dynamics of games and genes: Discrete versus continuous time. *J. Math. Biol.,* 17:241–251, 1983.

[29] A. Massaro and M. Pelillo. Matching graphs by pivoting. *Pattern Recognition Lett.* (in press).

[30] A. Massaro, M. Pelillo, and I. M. Bomze. A complementary pivoting approach to the maximum weight clique problem. *SIAM J. Optim.,* 12(4):928–948, 2002.

[31] D. W. Matula. An algorith for subtree identification. *SIAM Rev.,* 10:273–274, 1968.

[32] T. S. Motzkin and E. G. Straus. Maxima for graphs and a new proof of a theorem of Turán. *Canad. J. Math.,* 17:533–540, 1965.

[33] M. Ohlsson, C. Peterson, and B. Söderberg. Neural networks for optimization problems with inequality constraints: The knapsack problem. *Neural Computation,* 5:331–339, 1993.

[34] E. M. Palmer. *Graphical Evolution: An Introduction to the Theory of Random Graphs.* John Wiley & Sons, New York, 1985.

[35] P. M. Pardalos. Continuous approaches to discrete optimization problems. In G. D. Pillo and F. Giannessi, editors, *Nonlinear Optimization and Applications,* pages 313–328. Plenum Press, 1996.

[36] P. M. Pardalos and A. T. Phillips. A global optimization approach for solving the maximum clique problem. *Int. J. Computer Math.,* 33:209–216, 1990.

[37] M. Pelillo. Relaxation labeling networks for the maximum clique problem. *J. Artif. Neural Networks,* 2:313–328, 1995.

[38] M. Pelillo. Replicator equations, maximal cliques, and graph isomorphism. *Neural Computation*, 11(8):2023–2045, 1999.

[39] M. Pelillo. Matching free trees, maximal cliques, and monotone game dynamics. *IEEE Trans. Pattern Anal. Machine Intell.*, 24(9), 2002.

[40] M. Pelillo and A. Jagota. Feasible and infeasible maxima in a quadratic program for maximum clique. *J. Artif. Neural Networks*, 2:411–420, 1995.

[41] M. Pelillo, K. Siddiqi, and S. W. Zucker. Matching hierarchical structures using association graphs. *IEEE Trans. Pattern Anal. Machince Intell.*, 21(11):1105–1120, 1999.

[42] A. Rangarajan, S. Gold, and E. Mjolsness. A novel optimizing network architecture with applications. *Neural Computation*, 8:1041–1060, 1996.

[43] A. Rangarajan and E. Mjolsness. A Lagrangian relaxation network for graph matching. *IEEE Trans. Neural Networks*, 7(6):1365–1381, 1996.

[44] S. W. Reyner. An analysis of a good algorithm for the subtree problem. *SIAM J. Comput.*, 6:730–732, 1977.

[45] K. Siddiqi, A. Shokoufandeh, S. Dickinson, and S. W. Zucker. Shock graphs and shape matching. *Int. J. Computer Vision*, 35(1):13–32, 1999.

[46] P. D. Simić. Constrained nets for graph matching and other quadratic assignment problems. *Neural Computation*, 3:268–281, 1991.

[47] J. W. Weibull. *Evolutionary Game Theory*. MIT Press, Cambridge, MA, 1995.

[48] H. Wilf. The uniform selection of free trees. *J. Algorithms*, 2:204–207, 1981.

[49] H. Wilf. Spectral bounds for the clique and independence numbers of graphs. *J. Combin. Theory, Ser. B*, 40:113–117, 1986.

Impact of Neural Networks on Signal Processing and Communications

Simon HAYKIN
McMaster University, Hamilton, Ontario, Canada

Abstract

Signal-processing and communication environments are characterized by two common characteristics: nonstationarity and non-Gaussianity, which make adaptive and learning systems a natural tool for dealing with these environments. In this chapter, we first discuss performance ingredients that are basic to the operation of adaptive and learning systems
This discussion sets the stage for the following topics:
- Linear adaptive filters configured around a single computational unit.
- Autoregressive models for data parameterization and spectral analysis.
- Target tracking in an environment dominated by clutter (e.g., radar backscatter from an ocean environment)
- Learning the dynamics of a nonstationary environment, with particular emphasis given to recurrent multilayer perceptrons and related open research problems.

1. Introduction

Signal-processing environments and communication channels are stochastic in that their characterizations involve probabilistic laws. Moreover, these environments and channels (exemplified by radar and sonar on the one hand, and wireless and underwater communications on the other) share the following common characteristics:
- Nonstationarity
- Non-Gaussianity

These two characteristics have profound implications for the design of radar, sonar, and communication systems, a task that is further complicated by the fact that their underlying statistical parameters are typically unknown. To improve system performance, we naturally resort to the use of an adaptive system, in one form or another.

A critical examination of the signal-processing and communications literature reveals that neural networks have not received the attention they deserve. Rather, we find that the most commonly used adaptive solutions are based on the least-mean-square (LMS) and recursive least-squares (RLS) algorithms, largely because of their simplicity. In this chapter, we will address the reasons for why these two adaptive filtering algorithms and their variants are so highly popular, and how they can be incorporated with neural networks to provide solutions to difficult signal-processing problems. We will also discuss how recurrent neural networks have the potential for solving equally difficult signal-processing problems.

We begin the discussion by identifying a list of performance ingredients that are considered to be essential for successfully dealing with the uncertainties posed by having to operate in a nonstationary stochastic environment with unknown statistics.

2. Important Performance Ingredients

The primary motivation for using an adaptive system is two-fold: (1) to learn from data representing a stochastic environment of interest so as to account for the unknown statistical structure of the environment, and (2) to track slowly varying statistics (probably density functions) of the environment. Regardless of how the design of the adaptive system is accomplished, we may identify a number of performance ingredients, each of which is important in its own way as briefly described here [1]; the terms estimator and system are used interchangeably in what follows.

Prior Information

In adjusting the free parameters of an adaptive system, be it in a supervised or unsupervised manner, the task at hand is basically to transfer information contained in the input data and store it in those parameters. Clearly, if prior information about the environment is available, then it should be incorporated into the design of the system. This is indeed the sensible thing to do as it saves the effort that would be expended in having the system discover that prior information, if at all.

The prior information may be in the form of hints; learning from *hints* may be viewed as a generalization of learning from examples, allowing for a variety of prior information about the unknown function to be used in the learning process [2]. Alternatively, we may gather prior information relevant to the task at hand by understanding the physical laws that govern the generation of the input data. However the prior information is obtained, there is the problem of how to incorporate it into the design of the adaptive system.

Regularization

Two related problems are said to be the *inverse* of each other if the formulation of either one requires partial or full knowledge of the other. Ordinarily, we find that one of these two problems has been studied in greater detail than the other, in which case we refer to that particular problem as the *direct problem* and to the other (with less knowledge) as the *inverse problem* [3]. From a mathematical perspective, there is another important difference between a direct problem and the associated inverse problem. Specifically, a problem may be well-posed or ill-posed. A problem is said to be *well-posed* if three conditions are satisfied [4]:

(i)   **Existence**. For every input, there does exist a corresponding output.
(ii)   **Uniqueness**. For every pair of inputs, the respective outputs are equal if and only if the inputs themselves are equal.
(iii) **Continuity**. The input-output mapping that defines the output in terms of the input is continuous.

If any of these three conditions is violated, the problem is said to be *ill-posed*. In basic terms, an ill-posed problem means that large data sets may contain a surprisingly small amount of information about the desired solution. With these definitions at hand, we find that a direct problem is often well-posed, whereas the corresponding inverse problem is ill-posed.

We may further clarify the distinction between direct and inverse problems by invoking the notion of a function. By definition, a function is a mapping from an input to an output space in such a way that each input has a unique corresponding output. If the direct problem has the characteristics of a function, then the inverse problem does not have such characteristics unless the direct problem belongs to the special class of invertible functions.

Many of the signal-processing and communication problems encountered in practice are ill-posed problems; examples include dynamic reconstruction, probability density estimation, and communication channel equalization. These problems are ill-posed inverse problems for the following reasons. First, there may not be as much information in the input data as we really need to reconstruct the input-output mapping uniquely; for example, sometimes an input *A* produces output *B*, but at some other times the same input produces a different output *C*. Secondly, the unavoidable presence of noise or numerical imprecision in the input data adds uncertainty to the reconstructed solution, possibly causing it to violate the continuity criterion. Thus, given an ill-posed inverse problem, the reconstructed input-output mapping may have little or nothing to do with the true solution. There is no way to overcome this difficulty unless some prior information about the input-output mapping is available. Stated in another way, a lack of prior information about the learning task of interest cannot be remedied by mathematical trickery [5].

The principled approach to make an ill-posed problem into a well-posed one is to invoke the use of regularization theory [6]. The basic idea of regularization is to *stabilize* the solution by means of some auxiliary nonnegative functional that embeds prior information about the solution into its formulation [7]. In its most basic form, the embedded information is defined by the squared norm $\|\mathbf{D}F\|^2$, where $\mathbf{D}$ is a linear differential operator and F is the proposed input-output mapping. The primary purpose of the differential operator $\mathbf{D}$ is to *stabilize* the solution by making it smooth and thereby satisfy the property of continuity.

Robustness

The robustness of an estimator can be assessed in deterministic or stochastic terms, depending on the approach taken. In a deterministic sense, an estimator is said to be robust if unavoidable disturbances (e.g., errors due to the wrong choice of initial conditions, model mismatch, and use of finite-precision arithmetic) are not magnified by the estimator. To be more precise, let F denote the transfer operator that maps these disturbances at the input of the estimator to estimation errors at the output as depicted in Fig. 1. We may then define the *energy gain* of the estimator as the ratio of the error energy at the output to the total energy of the disturbances applied to the input. Clearly, this ratio depends on the particular choice of input disturbances. To remove this dependence, we consider the largest energy gain over all possible conceivable disturbances. In so doing, we will have defined the H^∞ *norm* of the transfer operator F. The objective here is to design a causal system (estimator) that minimizes the H^∞ norm [8]. The H^∞ optimal estimation problem may be viewed as a game-theoretic problem in the following sense. Nature, acting as the opponent, has access to the unknown disturbances, thereby having the potential to maximize the energy gain. On the other hand, the designer has the choice of finding a causal estimator (system) that minimizes the energy gain. Since no assumptions are made about the disturbances, an H^∞ estimator has to account for all possible disturbances. Accordingly, an H^∞ estimator may be "over-conservative"; that is, it is a "mini-max" estimator.

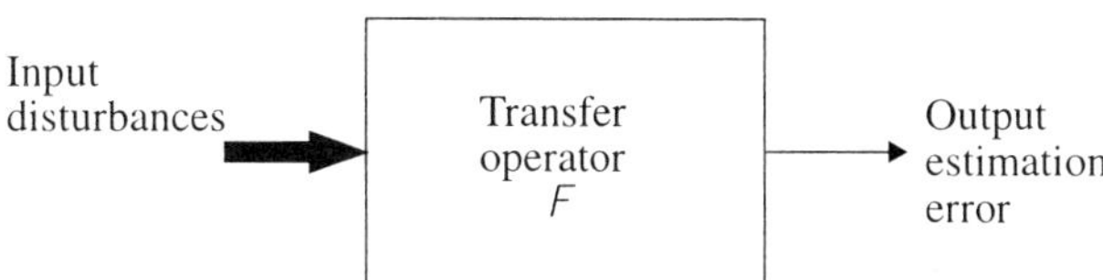

Figure 1: Setting the picture for robustness

Turning next to robustness in stochastic terms, an estimator is said to be *robust* when its performance is not impaired by small deviations in the probability density function of the error produced by the estimator from the probability density function of the assumed model [9]. For example, the design of an estimator based on the method of least squares is equivalent to maximum-likelihood estimation (which, in a sense, is the best that one can do) provided that the estimation error is white and Gaussian [10]. Moreover, under this assumption the least-squares estimator is a *minimum-variance unbiased (MVU) estimator*, which is a desirable property. Unfortunately, however, an estimator optimized for a Gaussian noise (estimation error) model does not perform satisfactorily when the unexpected occurrences of large noise values are likely to arise. To mitigate this problem and thereby robustify the solution, we need to start with a cost function whose formulation uses an appropriate probability density function: superGaussian or subGaussian, depending on the estimation problem at hand.

Feedback

Feedback is a powerful engineering principle, the proper application of which has many beneficial effects (e.g., an improved rate of convergence, reduced sensitivity to parameter variations, and improved robustness to unavoidable disturbances). For example, in solving the least-squares problem using a lattice structure, we may reduce numerical precision effects by incorporating a form of error feedback over the update formula for computing the reflection coefficients (i.e., free parameters) of the lattice structure [10]. For another example, to solve a dynamic estimation problem involving a multilayer perceptron as the basic structure, we may account for *time* by incorporating *memory* (e.g., tapped-delay-line) in the input layer of the network, and thereby retain its feedforward nature. Alternatively, we may build feedback around the multilayer perceptron by feeding the output signals of hidden layers back to the input of preceding layer(s) [11]. The application of feedback configured in this manner not only turns a static multilayer perceptron into a dynamic one (namely, recurrent multilayer perceptron) but also offers the potential for improving system performance.

3. Linear Adaptive Filters

Linear adaptive filters, based on the least-mean-square (LMS) and recursive least-squares (RLS) algorithms, as well as their respective variants, are built around a single linear neuron. These filters are linear in that when their adjustable weights are fixed, they satisfy the principle of superposition, and only then. In reality, however, they are nonlinear because the adjustable parameters are dependent on the input signal, hence violating the principle of superposition. Moreover, the filtering adjustments are performed in an on-line manner, thereby making it possible to track the slowly varying statistics of a nonstationary environment.

LMS Algorithm

The LMS algorithm, developed by Widrow and Hoff [12], is simple to design, yet highly effective and robust in performance. Indeed, it is these qualities that have maintained its popular use for over four decades. For temporal processing, the algorithm is built around a tapped-delay-line filter. Let

$$\mathbf{u}(n) = [u(n), u(n-1), \cdots, u(n-M)]^{T}$$

denote the vector of tap-inputs, where n denotes discrete time and M is the filter order (i.e., number of storage elements). Let

$$\hat{\mathbf{w}}(n) = [\hat{w}_0(n), \hat{w}_1(n), \cdots, \hat{w}_M(n)]^{T}$$

denote the corresponding vector of tap-weights (i.e., free parameters) of the filter. Let $d(n)$ denote the desired response of the filter. Then, assuming that the input data are all real valued, the adjustment to the weight vector $\hat{\mathbf{w}}(n)$ is made in accordance with the following recursive rule [10,13]:

$$\hat{\mathbf{w}}(n+1) = \hat{\mathbf{w}}(n) + \mu\mathbf{u}(n)[d(n) - y(n)] \tag{1}$$

where $y(n)$ is the filter's output defined by

$$y(n) \doteq \hat{\mathbf{w}}^T(n)\mathbf{u}(n) \tag{2}$$

An important property of the LMS algorithm is that it is robust in the sense that it minimizes the H^∞ norm [8].

Affine Projection Adaptive Algorithm

A serious limitation of the LMS algorithm is that it is slow to converge. The affine projection adaptive (APA) algorithm provides a practical means for overcoming this limitation, but at the expense of increased computational complexity [10,13].

The APA algorithm follows from the *principle of minimal disturbance*: From one iteration to the next, the weight vector of an adaptive filter should be changed in a minimal manner, subject to a constraint imposed on the updated filter's output. Based on this principle, the criterion for deriving the APA algorithm is as follows: Minimize the squared Euclidean norm of the change in the weight vector

$$\delta\hat{\mathbf{w}}(n+1) = \hat{\mathbf{w}}(n+1) - \hat{\mathbf{w}}(n)$$

subject to a set of N constraints

$$d(n-k) = \hat{\mathbf{w}}^T(n+1)\mathbf{u}(n-k) \quad \text{for } k = 0, 1, \cdots, N\text{-}1$$

The solution to this constraint optimization problem is given by [10,13]

$$\delta\hat{\mathbf{w}}(n+1) = \tilde{\mu}\mathbf{A}^T(n)(\mathbf{A}(n)\mathbf{A}^T(n))^{-1}\mathbf{e}(n) \tag{3}$$

where the step-size parameter $\tilde{\mu}$ is introduced to exercise control over the change in the weight vector, and the N-by-M data matrix $\mathbf{A}(n)$ is defined by

$$\mathbf{A}^T(n) = [\mathbf{u}(n), \mathbf{u}(n-1), \cdots, \mathbf{u}(n-N+1)]$$

The error vector $\mathbf{e}(n)$ is correspondingly defined by

$$\mathbf{e}(n) = \mathbf{d}(n) - \mathbf{A}(n)\hat{\mathbf{w}}(n)$$

where

$$\mathbf{d}^T(n) = [d(n), d(n-1), ..., d(n-N+1)]$$

For $N=1$, the APA algorithm reduces to the normalized version of the LMS algorithm. Thus, the APA algorithm is an intermediate algorithm that lies between the normalized LMS algorithm and the RLS algorithm discussed next.

RLS Algorithm

The RLS algorithm is a special form of the celebrated Kalman filter. Whereas the computational complexity of the LMS algorithm is linear in the filter order M, the computational complexity of the RLS algorithm is of order M^2. However, it offers the advantage of a faster rate of convergence than the LMS algorithm. The H^∞ norm of the RLS algorithm is dependent on the input data, which, in general, makes it less robust than the LMS algorithm [14].

The adjustment to the weight vector in the RLS algorithm follows the following recursive rule [10]:

$$\mathbf{k}(n) = \frac{\mathbf{P}(n-1)\mathbf{u}(n)}{\lambda + \mathbf{u}^T(n)\mathbf{P}(n-1)\mathbf{u}(n)} \qquad (4)$$

$$\xi(n) = d(n) - \hat{\mathbf{w}}(n-1)\mathbf{u}(n) \qquad (5)$$

$$\hat{\mathbf{w}}(n) = \hat{\mathbf{w}}(n-1) + \mathbf{k}(n)\xi(n) \qquad (6)$$

$$\mathbf{P}(n) = \mathbf{P}(n-1) - \lambda^{-1}\mathbf{k}(n)\mathbf{u}^T(n)\mathbf{P}(n-1) \qquad (7)$$

where λ is an exponential weighting (forgetting) factor that lies in the range $0 < \lambda \leq 1$. The vector $\mathbf{k}(n)$ is the gain vector, and $\mathbf{P}(n)$ is the covariance matrix of the weight vector $\hat{\mathbf{w}}(n)$ except for a scaling factor.

Square-root RLS Filter

A serious limitation of the RLS filter is that it is potentially numerically unstable. Examination of Eq. (7) reveals that since the updated term $\mathbf{P}(n)$ involves the difference between two quantities, it is possible for $\mathbf{P}(n)$ to assume a negative value. However, $\mathbf{P}(n)$ represents a covariance matrix, which, by definition, must be nonnegative definite -- hence, the possibility for the RLS algorithm to experience numerical divergence when the precision used to perform the computation is not fine enough.

The divergence phenomenon in RLS filters may be overcome by using numerically stable orthogonal transformation at every iteration of the computation [10]. Specifically, the matrix $\mathbf{P}(n)$ is propagated in a square-root form by using the Cholesky factorization:

$$\mathbf{P}(n) = \mathbf{P}^{1/2}(n)\mathbf{P}^{T/2}(n)$$

where $\mathbf{P}^{1/2}(n)$ is reserved for a lower triangular matrix, and $\mathbf{P}^{T/2}$ is its matrix transpose. In matrix algebra, the Cholesky factor $\mathbf{P}^{1/2}(n)$ is commonly referred to as the square root of the matrix $\mathbf{P}(n)$. Accordingly, any variant of the RLS filter based on the Cholesky factorization is referred to as square-root filtering. The important thing to note here is that the matrix product $\mathbf{P}^{1/2}(n)\ \mathbf{P}^{T/2}(n)$ is unlikely to become indefinite, because the product of any square matrix and its transpose is always nonnegative definite. Indeed, even in the presence of roundoff errors, the numerical conditioning of the Cholesky factor $\mathbf{P}^{1/2}(n)$ is generally much better than that of $\mathbf{P}(n)$ itself.

There are various ways of implementing a square-root RLS filter. However, when the objective is to compute the weight vector $\hat{\mathbf{w}}(n)$ in a numerically robust manner, then the recommended procedure is to use the inverse *QR-RLS filter* [10,15]. This filter derives its name from the following facts:

- The filter uses a form of decomposition known in matrix algebra as the QR-decomposition, the use of which is motivated by its good numerical properties.
- The covariance matrix $\mathbf{P}(n)$ is, by definition, the inverse of the correlation matrix of the tap-inputs applied to the filter.

As with the conventional RLS algorithm, the computational complexity of the inverse QR-RLS algorithm is on the order of M^2, where M is the filter order. However, an attractive feature of the inverse QR-RLS filter is that it lends itself to parallel implementation.

Order-recursive Adaptive Filtering Algorithms

The computational complexity of recursive least-squares estimators can be made to increase linearly with the filter order M by exploiting the time-shifting property that is inherent to temporal processing. This highly desirable design objective manifests itself in order recursiveness, which gives the adaptive filter a *computationally efficient, modular, latticelike structure*. In particular, as the filter order is increased from M to $M+1$, the lattice structure permits us to carry over certain information gathered from previous computations to filter order $M+1$.

There are various ways of building order-recursive least-squares lattice (LSL) algorithms [10]. Figure 2 shows the structure of one such algorithm configured to perform one-step prediction in the forward as well as backward direction. The blocks labeled z^{-1} represent unit delays. Each stage of the lattice filter is characterized by two adjustable parameters: $\kappa_{f,m}$ and $\kappa_{b,m}$ where $m = 1, 2, \cdots, M$. In response to the input $u(n)$, the outputs of the mth stage are the forward prediction error $\eta_m(n)$ and backward prediction error $\beta_m(n)$, both of which are of the *a priori* kind. For $m = 0$, we have

$$\eta_0(n) = \beta_0(n) = u(n)$$

An important property of the least-squares lattice filter is that the backward prediction errors $\beta_0(n), \beta_1(n), \cdots, \beta_M(n)$ produced at the various stages of the predictor are uncorrelated (orthogonal) with each other in a time-averaged sense at all instants of time. In other words, the least-squares lattice predictor transforms a correlated input data sequence $\{u(n), u(n-1), ..., u(n-M)\}$ into a new sequence of uncorrelated backward prediction errors, as shown by

$$\{u(n), u(n-1), ..., u(n-M)\} \rightleftharpoons \{\beta_0(n), \beta_1(n), \cdots, \beta_M(n)\}$$

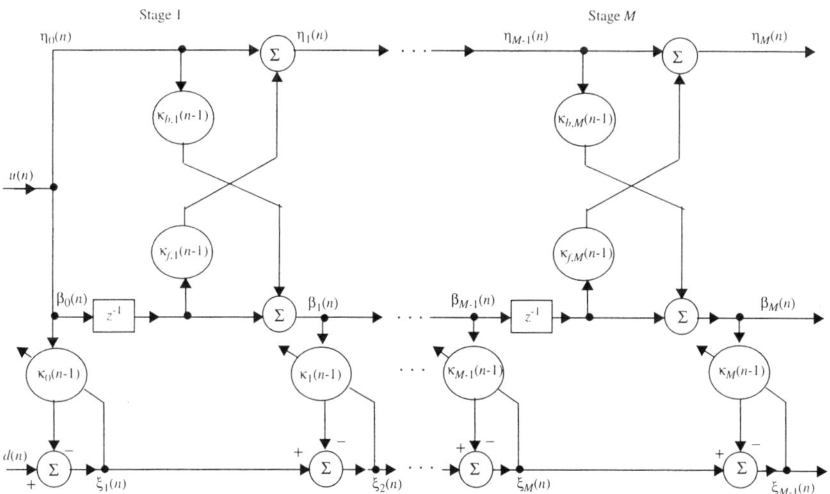

Figure 2: Joint process estimator using the recursive LSL algorithm based on *a priori* estimation errors

The transformation is reciprocal, which means that the least-squares lattice filter preserves the full information content of the input data. A side benefit of the decoupling property is the relative ease with which it may be possible to find the optimal filter order.

An algorithm used to compute the reflection coefficients of the predictor (for real-valued data) is described by the recursions [10]

$$F_{m-1}(n) = \lambda F_{m-1}(n-1) + \gamma_{m-1}(n-1)|\eta_{m-1}(n-1)|^2$$

$$B_{m-1}(n-1) = \lambda B_{m-1}(n-2) + \gamma_{m-1}(n-1)|\beta_{m-1}(n-1)|^2$$

$$\eta_m(n) = \eta_{m-1}(n) + \kappa_{f,m}(n-1)\beta_{m-1}(n-1)$$

$$\beta_m(n) = \beta_{m-1}(n-1) + \kappa_{b,m}(n-1)\eta_{m-1}(n)$$

$$\kappa_{f,m}(n) = \kappa_{f,m}(n-1) - \frac{\gamma_{m-1}(n-1)\beta_{m-1}(n-1)}{B_{m-1}(n-1)}\eta_m(n)$$

$$\kappa_{b,m}(n) = b(n-1) - \frac{\gamma_{m-1}(n-1)\eta_{m-1}(n-1)}{F_{m-1}(n-1)}\beta_m(n)$$

$$\gamma_m(n-1) = \gamma_{m-1}(n-1) - \frac{\gamma_{m-1}^2(n-1)|\beta_{m-1}(n-1)|}{B_{m-1}(n-1)}$$

The algorithm described herein is built around the use of error feedback, which means that the reflection coefficients are computed in a recursive manner. The corrections applied to these parameters are of an *a priori* nature in that they all depend on old values of the reflection coefficients. Most importantly, the use of feedback is invoked in these computations so as to improve the robustness of the algorithm to numerical imprecision that arises in the course of implementation, be it in software or hardware form.

Robustness of the least-squares lattice predictor to numerical imprecision can be further improved through the use of QR-decomposition [10]. However, the price paid for this improvement is a significant increase in the coding of the algorithm.

4. Autoregressive Models

Among the different models developed for describing a stochastic process, the *autoregressive (AR) model* is perhaps the most popular. For a stationary process, applicability of an AR model is justified by virtue of *Wold's decomposition theorem*, which states that any stationary discrete-time stochastic process can be decomposed into the sum of a generalized linear process and a predictable process, with these two processes being uncorrelated with each other [10]. The component represented by the generalized linear process can itself be realized using an AR model, provided that the model order is high enough.

Figure 3 shows the block diagram of an AR model of order M, with the input $v(n)$ defined by a white process of zero mean and variance σ_v^2. The AR parameters are denoted by the tap-weights $w_1, w_2, \ldots, w_M$. As before, the blocks labeled z^{-1} represent unit delays. In mathematical terms, we write

$$u(n) = \sum_{k=1}^{M} w_k u(n-k) + v(n) \tag{8}$$

Clearly, stability considerations dictate that all the poles of the filter in Fig. 3 lie inside the unit circle in the z-plane.

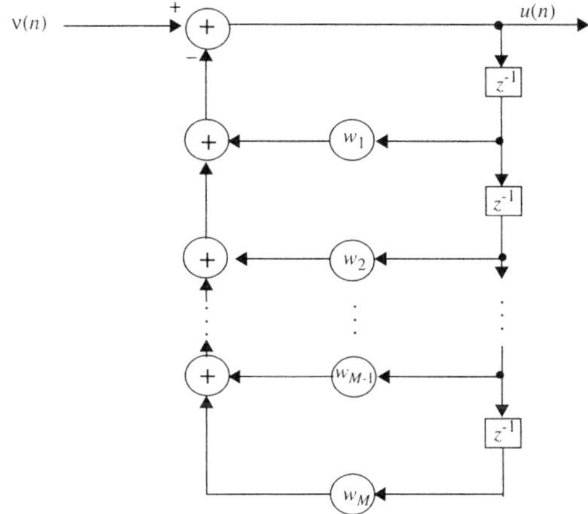

Figure 3: All-pole model

The practical utility of an autoregressive model becomes all the more compelling when the stochastic process of interest is nonstationary. In this kind of situation, we rewrite Eq. (8) in the time-varying form

$$u(n) = \sum_{k-1}^{M} \hat{w}_k(n)u(n-k) + v(n) \tag{9}$$

where $\hat{w}_k(n)$ is an estimate of the kth AR parameter w_k at time n. Such an estimate can be derived using the LMS, APA, RLS, or inverse QR-RLS algorithm. Furthermore, the variance of the driving force represented by the zero-mean noise term $v(n)$ is now time-varying, being denoted by $\sigma_v^2(n)$.

For the time-varying AR model of Eq. (9) to function properly, some upper limit on the adaptation rate must be invoked. In particular, the AR parameters can only change slowly in time, such that the changes in the AR parameters within one iteration of the algorithm are small compared to the estimation error, defined as the difference between the actual value of the AR parameter and its estimate. If this condition is not satisfied, then the process is highly nonstationary, giving rise to transients that cannot be captured by the adaptive AR model.

Putting $z = e^{j\omega}$ for an assumed sampling period of unity, we readily find from Fig. 3 that the process $\{u(n)\}$ is represented by the *AR power spectrum*

$$S_u(\omega, n) = \frac{\sigma_v^2(n)}{\left| 1 - \sum_{k=1}^{M} \hat{w}_k(n)e^{-jk\omega} \right|^2} \tag{10}$$

The AR power spectrum is commonly referred to as a super-resolution or high-resolution spectrum in the sense that it exhibits a sub-Rayleigh resolution as power spectrum estimator [16]. More specifically, the AR power spectrum of Eq. (10) exhibits the following properties [17]:

- It is *evolutionary* in that, unlike an ordinary power spectrum, it varies with time n; stated in another way, the spectrum of Eq. (10) is an estimate of the time-frequency spectrum of the process $\{u(n)\}$.

- According to Priestley [18], the *principle of uncertainty* states that, given an evolutionary power spectrum, the more accurately we determine that spectrum as a function of frequency, the less accurately we determine it as a function of time, and vice versa. In other words, it is impossible to simultaneously obtain a high degree of resolution in both time and frequency. In the context of AR models, the problem of selecting the model order and the update coefficient may be viewed as a reformulation of the principle of uncertainty; for RLS algorithms, the update coefficient is defined as $1-\lambda$ where λ is the forgetting factor. The model order corresponds to frequency resolution and the update coefficient determines the time resolution, which means that for a given update parameter an optimal model order exists, and vice versa.

- Compared to other methods, the evolutionary AR spectrum is most significant when it is not feasible to compute the average of an ensemble of different realizations of the process $\{u(n)\}$. However, a problem with an AR power spectrum is its sensitivity to the choice of model order M. We may get around this problem by focusing on the set of AR parameter estimates $\{\hat{\mathbf{w}}(n), \sigma_v^2(n)\}$ as the signature of the stochastic process $\{u(n)\}$. This compact set of estimates is a causal set in the sense that it lends itself to computation in real-time for on-line applications.

5. Target Tracking

From a signal detection viewpoint, the set of AR estimates $\{\hat{\mathbf{w}}(n), \sigma_v^2(n)\}$ also defines *sufficient statistics* for the input data. Specifically, given this set of parameters, we may use the all-pole structure of Fig. 3 to reconstruct the original input data $\{u(n)\}$ in the second-order sense. Moreover, the adaptive AR model is a *nonparametric estimator* in that it does not require knowledge of the underlying probability distributions. These nice properties of adaptive AR model can be put to practical use for radar target tracking in a clutter background. The approach taken for target tracking builds on the treatment of this problem as a pattern classification problem. (In [19], the related problem of target detection is successfully treated as an adaptive pattern classification problem). Recognizing the nature of target tracking, what we need is a nonparametric approach to pattern classification. With that in mind, Fig. 4 shows the block diagram of the proposed target tracking scheme.

Data Parameterization: Feature Extraction
To be specific, consider the difficult problem of tracking a radar target in a background of sea clutter; the target may be a fishing boat navigating the ocean or a small piece of ice floating in the ocean. In [20], it has been demonstrated that the nonlinear dynamics of sea clutter can be described closely using an AR model, which provides further justification for the use of an adaptive AR model as a "feature extractor".

Pattern Classification
The next major task in the proposed target tracking scheme of Fig. 4 is that of pattern classification, which is to be performed in a self-organized manner. Two popular methods of implementing such a classifier are described here.

(i) <u>Nearest neighbor classifier</u>
Let $\mathbf{x}_{\text{test}}$ denote a test vector, namely, the current estimate of cepstral coefficients $\{c_1(n), c_2(n), ..., c_M(n)\}$. Let

$$\mathbf{x}'_N \in \{\mathbf{x}_1, \mathbf{x}_2, \cdots, \mathbf{x}_N\}$$

The vector $\mathbf{x}'_N$ is said to be a neighbor of $\mathbf{x}_{\text{test}}$ if

$$\min_i d(\mathbf{x}_i, \mathbf{x}_{\text{test}}) = (\mathbf{x}'_N, \mathbf{x}_{\text{test}}), \qquad i = 1, 2, \cdots, K$$

where $d(\mathbf{x}_i, \mathbf{x}_{\text{test}})$ is the Euclidean distance between the labeled vector $\mathbf{x}_i$ and the test vector $\mathbf{x}_{\text{test}}$. This learning rule is conceptually simple, and leads to a fast and efficient procedure from the viewpoint of hardware implementation. Just as importantly, in [21] it is shown that under certain mild assumptions the probability of classification error incurred by the nearest neighbor rule is bounded above by twice the Bayes probability of error, which is the minimum probability of error over all possible decision rules.

The nearest neighbor classifier can be generalized to the *k-nearest neighbor* classifier by proceeding as follows:
- Identify the k-classified patterns that lie nearest to the test vector $\mathbf{x}_{\text{test}}$ for some integer k.
- Assign $\mathbf{x}_{\text{test}}$ to the class (hypothesis) that is most frequently represented in the k nearest neighbors to $\mathbf{x}_{\text{test}}$ (i.e., use a majority rule to make the classification).

Thus the k-nearest neighbor classifier acts like an averaging system, which makes it capable of discriminating against a single outlier; an outlier is an observation that is probably large for a nominal model of interest.

(ii) <u>Self-organizing map</u>
In this self-organized clustering algorithm, the neurons are placed at the nodes of a lattice that are usually two-dimensional in form. The neurons become selectively tuned to various input patterns in the course of a competitive learning process [10,22]. A nice feature of the self-organizing map is the formation of a topographic map of the input patterns, in which the spatial locations (i.e., coordinates) of the neurons in the lattice are indicative of intrinsic statistical features contained in the input patterns, hence the name "self-organizing map". Because of the inherently nonlinear nature of the map, it may be viewed as a nonlinear generalization of principal components analysis. In any event, after the self-organized learning process is completed, class labels are assigned to the neurons in the two-dimensional lattice by stimulating it with ground-truthed data. As a result of this second stage of stimulation, the neurons in the lattice are partitioned into a number of coherent regions, coherent in the sense that each sub-group of neurons may represent a distinct set of contiguous labels.

From this discussion, it is apparent that the self-organizing map is computationally more demanding than the nearest-neighbor classifier, but it is more revealing in the way it displays the clustered nature of the input data.

Probabilistic Reasoning
The last operation indicated in Fig. 4 is that of probabilistic reasoning, the purpose of which is first to determine a set of possible target tracks and then solve the target detection problem through track selection in accordance with a Bayesian-based hypothesis-testing procedure within the traditional framework of probability theory [23]. The inclusion of probabilistic reasoning in Fig. 4 makes up for a major deficiency of classical neural networks: the inability to query test points at different instances.

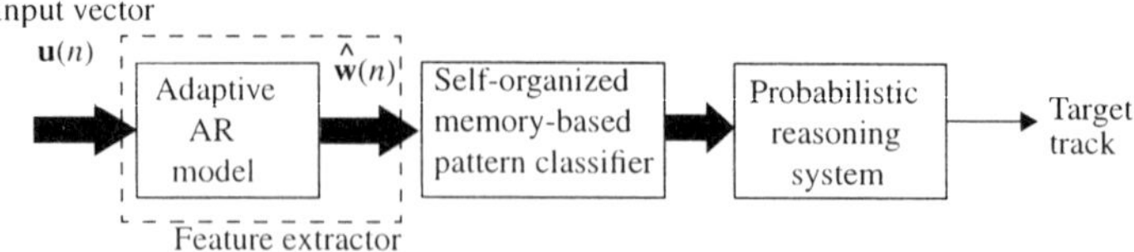

Figure 4: Block diagram of a target tracker based on pattern classification

6. Recurrent Neural Networks

In this section, we switch gear and focus attention on nonlinear dynamical problems whose solutions may benefit from the use of *dynamically driven* recurrent neural networks whose construction involves some form of global feedback.

In a dynamically driven recurrent multilayer perceptron, the application of feedback enables the recurrent network to acquire *state* representation, which makes it a suitable system for such applications as nonlinear prediction and modeling, adaptive equalization of a communication channel, speech processing, plant control, and automobile engine diagnostics. Potential benefits of global feedback include the possibility of a significant reduction in memory requirement compared to dynamically driven feedforward networks.

State-space Model
Figure 5 shows the block diagram of a state-space model built around a multilayer perceptron with a single hidden layer. The hidden neurons of the network define the state, a delayed version of which is fed back to the input via a bank of unit delays. Thus the input layer consists of a concatenation of feedback nodes and external source nodes.

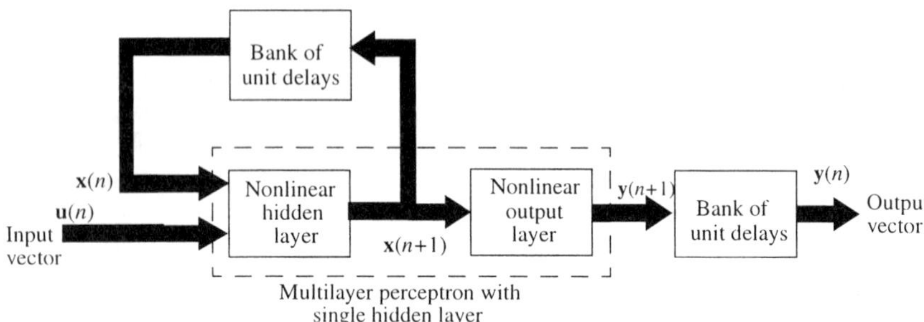

Figure 5: State-space model

Let $\mathbf{u}(n)$ denote the externally applied input vector, and let $\mathbf{x}(n)$ denote the current state of the network. We may then describe the dynamic behavior of the state-space model of Fig. 5 as follows:

$$\mathbf{x}(n+1) = \mathbf{f}(\mathbf{x}(n), \mathbf{u}(n))$$

$$\mathbf{y}(n) = \mathbf{g}(\mathbf{x}(n))$$

where $\mathbf{f}(\cdot,\cdot)$ is a nonlinear function characterizing the input layer, and $\mathbf{g}(\cdot)$ is another nonlinear function characterizing the output layer.

In a generic sense, the state of a dynamical system defines a set of quantities that summarizes all the information about the past behavior of the system that is needed to uniquely describe its future behavior, except for the purely external effects arising from the applied input. Recognizing the way in which the input $\mathbf{u}(n)$ and the state $\mathbf{x}(n)$ are concatenated in the input layer, we may redefine the state-space model as

$$\mathbf{x}(n+1) = \varphi(\mathbf{W}_a\mathbf{x}(n) + \mathbf{W}_b\mathbf{u}(n)) \tag{11}$$

$$\mathbf{y}(n) = \theta(\mathbf{W}_c\mathbf{x}(n)) \tag{12}$$

The matrices $\mathbf{W}_a$, $\mathbf{W}_b$, and $\mathbf{W}_c$ represent three different sets of weights. The issue of interest is how to compute these weights for a learning task of interest. Note that in the model described herein, only those hidden neurons that feed back their outputs to the input layer via delays are responsible for defining the state of the recurrent network. This statement therefore excludes the neurons in the output layer from the definition of the state.

The state-space model of Fig. 5 is naturally rooted in modern control theory, which makes it highly elegant from a theoretical perspective and highly suited for the design of nonlinear dynamical systems. The practical utility of this learning model would be significantly enhanced if we could find some means of building prior knowledge into its design.

Design Algorithms

The design objective is to determine suitable values for the weight matrices $\mathbf{W}_a$, $\mathbf{W}_b$, and $\mathbf{W}_c$, given a set of input-output data representative of the nonlinear dynamical environment of interest. A popular design algorithm is the *real-time recurrent learning (RTRL) algorithm*, which derives its name from the fact that adjustments are made to the synaptic weights of a fully connected recurrent network in real time, that is, while the network continues to perform its signal processing function [11,24]. Derivation of the RTRL algorithm follows a procedure similar to that used for the LMS algorithm. However, a much more profound algorithm is the one devised by Puskorious, Feldkamp and collaborators [11,25], which is based on the extended Kalman filter. A critical issue here is, given the architectural complexity of a recurrent multilayer perceptron, how to proceed with this approach in a computationally feasible manner without compromising the application of Kalman filter theory. The answer is found in using a *decoupled* form of the extended Kalman filter (EKF), in which the computational complexity is made to suit the requirements of a particular application and available computational resources. Although, indeed, the decoupled EKF is always computationally less demanding than the global EKF, current computer speeds and memory sizes have now made the global EKF feasible for some practical problems, especially in the off-line training of recurrent multilayer perceptrons.

The EKF is an approximate algorithm that allows us to extend the Kalman filtering idea to nonlinear state-space models. In the context of the nonlinear dynamical system described by Eqs. (11) and (12), the basic idea of the EKF is to locally linearize the state-space model described therein at each time instant around the most recent estimate of the state. This is achieved by invoking a first-order Taylor approximation of the nonlinear factionals φ and θ around estimates of $\mathbf{x}(n)$, given all the input data up to times n and n-1, respectively.

The EKF, be it used in the decoupled or global form, uses second-order information, which, in turn, makes it possible for the algorithm to overcome the vanishing gradients problem. This problem arises in the case of learning algorithms (e.g., RTRL algorithm), which are gradient-based; the learning of long-term dependencies in such algorithms is made difficult, if not virtually impossible, by having to rely solely on first-order information in the form of gradients.

As already mentioned, the EKF is a first-order approximation to the solution of a nonlinear dynamical problem. The performance of the basic EKF may be improved by using the *iterated EKF*, where improved reference trajectories are incorporated into the estimates. The fundamental idea of the iterated filter is that once the filtered state estimate is generated, that value would serve as a better state estimate than the predicted state for evaluating the measurement equation. Nevertheless, appreciable errors for highly nonlinear state-space models are often introduced into the computation, which could limit the practical utility of the EKF or its iterated version in the training of nonlinear state-space models.

To overcome this difficulty, we may use a nonlinear filtering algorithm called the *unscented Kalman filter* [26,27]. Unlike the EKF, the unscented Kalman filter does *not* require the computation of Jacobians needed for linearizing the state-space model; hence the unscented Kalman filter is a *derivative-free state estimator.* This important property means that differentiable nonlinear functions are no longer a necessary requirement for application of the unscented Kalman filter.

Another procedure for derivative-free state estimation is described in [28]. In this second approach, hereafter referred to as the *NPR-Kalman filter* in recognition of its originators, the linearized Taylor series expansion in the vicinity of the current state estimate (which is basic to the derivation of the EKF) is replaced by the use of Stirling's interpolation formula for approximating a nonlinear function over an interval of selected length. Thereby, a straightforward interpretation of the quantities that must be chosen as part of the design procedure is achieved. Stirling's interpolation formula computes the average of two other interpolations: forward and backward Newton-Gauss interpolations. In [29], the application of a simplified version of the NPR-Kalman filter to the supervised training of a recurrent multilayer perceptron is explored. Therein, the following advantages over the EKF for a similar test case are reported:

- Much faster training on a per-epoch basis.
- Frequent attainment of a more refined solution.

The important point to note here is that the availability of the unscented Kalman filter and NPR-Kalman filter provides the designer of neural networks a powerful new tools for the study of nonlinear dynamical systems built around recurrent multilayer perceptrons.

7. Learning the Dynamics of Nonstationary Environments: Open Research Problems

The issue of learning, or else accounting for, the underlying physical laws that govern the nonstationary behavior of a dynamical environment is of immense practical importance. The need for this learning process arises in such applications as predictive modeling, system identification, and channel equalization (i.e., inverse system identification) to name just a few. With these applications in mind, we find that among the many known neural networks, the recurrent multilayer perceptron embodied in the basic state-space model of Fig. 5 is perhaps the most well suited for performing the requisite learning process. In a limited sense, the validity of this statement has been demonstrated by different computer experiments reported independently in [30-32]. Unfortunately, the approximations realizable by the model are valid on compact subsets of the state space and only for finite time intervals with the result that, in general, interesting dynamical characteristics of the environment may not be reflected in the model [33].

To set the stage for a more detailed discussion of the learning problem posed herein, there are two requisites for training of the state-space model of Fig. 5:
- The input-output data available for training are representative of the environment.

- The network is trained with an algorithm capable of reliably transferring information contained in the input-output data and storing it in the adjustable weights of the network.

Once the training is completed, the weights of the network are fixed.

The stage is now set for raising the following two related questions:

Question 1. Once the training session is completed, is it possible for the state-space model of Fig. 5 to adapt to an unknown environment without any further adjustments to the weights of the model?

Question 2. If the answer to Question 1 is an emphatic yes, how does the fixed-weight state-space model of Fig. 5 acquire this extraordinary capability?

Unfortunately, at the present we do not have a rigorous answer to Question 1. Rather, what we do have is some experimental evidence that provides support for the notion that a properly trained recurrent multilayer perceptron with fixed weights does have the potential to adapt to an unknown environment, once the training is completed. What is also highly remarkable is the fact that the network acquires the adaptive capability with a relatively small number of fixed weights. In this context, we may mention the following two different types of training data experimented on in the literature:

- The training data for a predictive modeling experiment was created from instances of different input-output mappings; the parameters of those mappings did not change with time [30]. The network's task to adapt to changes in the input data was made particularly difficult by scaling data derived from a logistic map to occupy approximately the same dynamic range as that of a randomly generated sequence. In this sense, first-order statistics of the two different sequences constituting the input data were probably equalized.

- The training data consisted of a sequence of images, with each image represented in a vector format, thereby making the predictive modeling problem into a high-dimensional one [32]. In this situation, many difficulties may arise in the image sequence prediction that are not present in one-dimensional time-series prediction problems. First, the object of interest may be clustered with background objects, or may even be occluded by foreground objects. Second, the network may have to predict the motion of numerous types of objects located at different places in the scene of interest.

In both of these entirely different predictive modeling experiments, the recurrent multilayer perceptron was trained using the decoupled extended Kalman filtering algorithm. Most importantly, in both cases, the fixed-weight network was found to exhibit an adaptive capability.

Turning next to Question 2, in [30] it is hypothesized that, as a result of training, the fixed, weight recurrent multilayer perceptron develops internal behavioral states that can distinguish among the various subtasks on which it has been trained. The network is hereby enabled to choose among the corresponding input-output forms of behavior stored in the network.

Stated in another way, we may say the following:

- The outputs of the hidden neurons in the fixed-weight network play the role of a *state* vector, which is fed back to the preceding input layer after an appropriate delay. This statement should be interpreted in the following sense: The signal applied to each hidden neuron is made up of all current inputs from the preceding layer and from previous time steps of the same hidden layer; the latter contributions constitute the feedback signal.

- Distinct patterns contained in the signal applied to the input layer of the network tend to produce changes in the feedback signal, which, in turn, result in corresponding changes in the state vector.

The resulting evolution of the state vector is thus influenced by the distinct patterns contained in the input data and reinforced by the feedback signals, thereby prompting the network to choose the particular orbital attractor most suited for adapting to the task at hand.

Tracking of Slowly Varying Statistics

From the discussion just presented, it is apparent that a properly trained recurrent multilayer perceptron with fixed weights has the potential to *adapt* to an unknown environment. When the environment is nonstationary, we have the added task of *tracking* slowly varying statistics in the input data, which prompts us to raise our last question:

> ***Question 3. By the very nature of it, tracking requires the use of on-line training. With no desired response no longer available, how can this additional requirement be mechanized?***

As a possible answer to this fundamental question, we may look to the literature on blind deconvolution based on the Bussgang algorithm [10]. The block diagram of Fig. 6 shows the basic idea behind this algorithm. The output of the adaptive tapped-delay-line filter is applied to a memoryless nonlinear estimator, the resulting output of which is utilized as the desired response. In the context of adaptive equalization of a communication channel, for example, it is presumed that the decisions made by the receiver are correct with high probability, which means that the estimate of the desired response is correct most of the time [34]. Under the assumption that distortion is largely dominated by intersymbol interference due to the dispersive nature of the channel. In [10,35] it is shown that the choice of a minimum mean-square error criterion yields a conditional mean estimator. Moreover, the memoryless nonlinear estimator of Fig. 6 is closely approximated by a hyperbolic target function [10].

Thus, building on what we know about the Bussgang algorithm, we may extend the state-space model of Fig. 5 to account for nonstationarity by incorporating on-line adaptation around the output layer, as depicted in Fig. 7. (To simplify matters, the output signal is assumed to be scalar here.) The resulting scheme represents a *semi-blind optive system*, whose function is two-fold:

- To adapt to an unknown environment through off-line training applied to the weights in both the hidden and output layers of the network.
- To track statistical variations in the environment through on-line adaptation applied to the weights in the output layer alone.

In this section, we have identified open research problems related to these two issues. We have sketched ways of explaining or accounting for them. To proceed further, we need more detailed theoretical and experimental investigations into them, and explore their implications for practical applications.

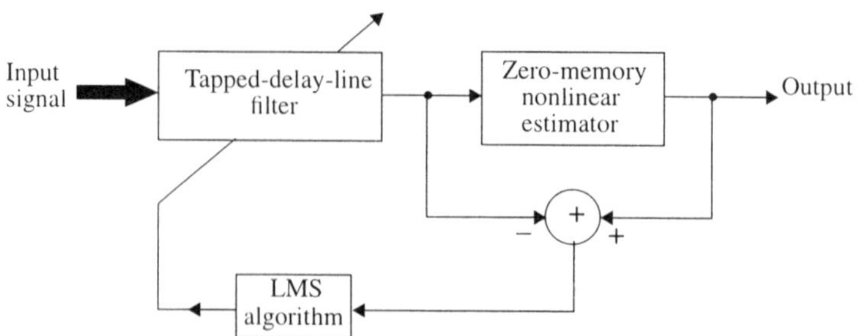

Figure 6: Basic structure for implementing the Bussgang algorithm
for blind adaptation

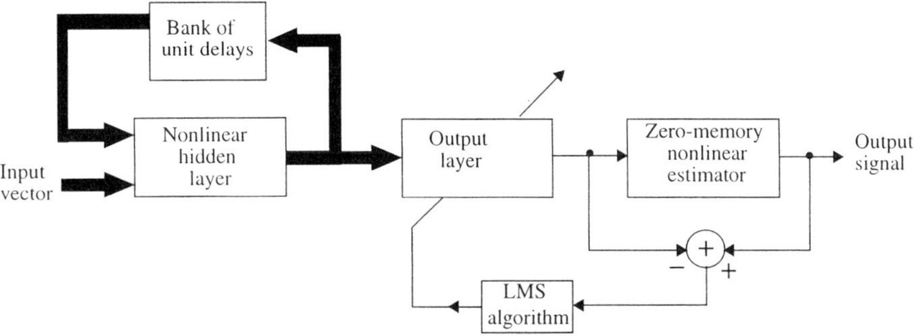

Figure 7: State-space model with a tracking capability

8. Discussion

In this chapter, we have emphasized the continued importance of linear adaptive filters as basic functional blocks. Linear adaptive filtering algorithms, exemplified by the LMS and RLS algorithms, lend themselves to the design of adaptive autoregressive models, which provide a powerful approach for time-frequency analysis and data parameterization.

An example application of autoregressive modeling is in the parameterization of radar clutter data. In a coherent radar setting, the received radar signal consists of an in-phase and a quadrature component. Correspondingly, the autoregressive model takes on a complex-valued nature of its own. Such a model provides the first stage as feature extractor for the tracking of a radar target in the presence of clutter.

In the remainder of the chapter, we discussed recurrent multilayer perceptrons that provide a powerful tool for uncovering the nonlinear dynamics of an unknown environment. The extended Kalman filter is a method of choice for the supervised training of recurrent multilayer perceptrons, offering the following virtues:

- First-order approximations are employed to yield second-order information exemplified by the state-error covariance matrix, which, in turn, overcomes the vanishing gradient problem.
- The amount of second-order information used in the training process can be controlled through the use of a decoupled version of the extended Kalman filter.
- The sequential nature of the extended Kalman filter makes it possible to compute the updates to the weights of the recurrent multilayer perceptron on a sample-by-sample basis.
- Through the simple approach of adding artificial noise to the process equation that describes the time evolution of the weights, a stochastic approach to the evolution of the weight space is developed, and with it the likelihood of an improved solution is enhanced.

Acknowledgements

The author expresses his gratitude to the Natural Sciences and Engineering Research Council (NSERC) of Canada for supporting the research described herein. He is deeply indebted to his colleagues, Rembrandt Bakker, Brian Currie, Behnam Shahrrava, and Zhe (Sage) Chen for many useful discussions and helpful inputs.

References

[1]   S. Haykin, "Signal processing: Where physics and mathematics meet", IEEE Signal Processing Magazine, vol. 18, No. 4, pp. 6-7, July 2001.

[2]   Y.S. Abu-Mostafa, "Hints", Neural Computation, vol. 7, pp. 639-671, 1995.

[3]   J.B. Keller, "Inverse problems", American Mathematical Monthly, vol. 83, pp. 107-118, 1976.

[4]   A. Kirsch, An Introduction to the Mathematical Theory of Inverse Problems, Springer-Verlag, 1996.

[5]   C. Lanczos, Linear Differential Equations, Van Nostrand, 1964.

[6]   A.N. Tikhonov and V.Y. Arsenin, Solutions of Ill-posed Problems, W.H. Winston, 1977.

[7]   T. Poggio and F. Girosi, "Networks for approximation and learning", Proc. IEEE, pp. 1481-1497, 1990.

[8]   B. Hassibi, A.H. Sayed, and T. Kailath, "H^∞ optimality of the LMS algorithm", IEEE Trans. Signal Processing, vol. 44, pp. 267-280, 1996.

[9]   P.S. Huber, Robust Statistics, Wiley, 1981.

[10]   S. Haykin, Adaptive Filter Theory, 4th Edition, Prentice-Hall, 2001.

[11]   S. Haykin, Neural Networks: A Comprehensive Foundation, Second Edition, Prentice-Hall, 1999.

[12]   B. Widrow and M.E. Hoff, Jr., "Adaptive Switching Circuits", IRE WESCON Convention Record, Pt. 4, pp. 96-104, 1960.

[13]   J. Benesty, T. Gänsler, D.R. Morgan, M.M. Sondhi, and S.L. Gay, Advances in Network and Acoustic Echo Cancellation, Springer, 2001.

[14]   B. Hassibi and T. Kailath, H-infinity bounds on least-squares estimators", IEEE Trans. Automatic Control, vol. 46, pp. 309-314, 2001.

[15]   S.T. Alexander and A.L. Ghirnikar, "A method for recursive least-squares filtering based upon an inverse WR decomposition", IEEE Trans. Signal Processing, vol. 41, pp. 20-30, 1993.

[16]   S.M. Kay, Modern Spectral Estimation: Theory and Application, Prentice-Hall, 1988.

[17]   A. Schlögl, The Electroencephalogram and the Adaptive Autoregressive Model: Theory and Applications, Springer-Verlag, 2000.

[18]   M.B. Priestley, Spectral Analysis and Time Series, Academic Press, 1981.

[19]　S. Haykin and D.J. Thomson, "Signal detection in a nonstationary environment reformulated as an adaptive pattern classification problem", Proc. IEEE, vol. 86, pp. 2325-2345, 1998.

[20]　S. Haykin, R. Bakker, and B. Currie, "Uncovering nonlinear dynamics: The Case Study of Sea Clutter", Proc. IEEE, under review.

[21]　T.M. Cover and P.C. Hart, "Nearest neighbor pattern classification", IEEE Trans. Information Theory, vol. IT-13, pp. 21-27, 1967.

[22]　T. Kohenen, Self-organizing Maps, Second Edition, Springer-Verlay, 1997.

[23]　J. Pearl, Probabilistic Reasoning in Intelligent Systems, Morgan Kaufmann, 1988.

[24]　R.J. Williams and D. Zipser, "Gradient-based learning algorithms for recurrent networks and their computational complexity", Neural Computation, vol. 1, pp. 270-280, 1989.

[25]　G.V. Puskorius and L.A. Feldkamp, "Neurocontrol of nonlinear dynamical systems with Kalman filter-trained recurrent networks", IEEE Trans. Neural Networks, vol. 5, pp. 279-297, 1994.

[26]　S.J. Julier and J.K. Uhlmann, "A new extension of the Kalman filter to nonlinear systems", The 11th Symposium on Aerospace/Defence Sensing, Simulation and Control, Orlando, Florida, 1997.

[27]　E.A. Wan and R. van der Merwe, The Unscented Kalman filter, In S. Haykin, Editor, Kalman Filtering and Neural Networks, Chapter 7, Wiley, 2001.

[28]　M. Norgard, N. Paulsen, and O. Raw, Advances in Derivative-free state Estimation for Nonlinear Systems, TR, Technical University of Denmark, 2000.

[29]　L.A. Feldkamp, T.M. Feldkamp, and D.V. Prokhorov, "Neural network training with nprKF", International Joint Conference on Neural Networks, Washington, DC, July 15-19, 2001.

[30]　L.A. Feldkamp, D. Prokhorov and T.M. Feldkamp, "Conditional Adaptive Behavior from a Fixed Neural Network", Proceedings of the Eleventh Yale Workshop on Adaptive and Learning Systems, pp. 78-83, 2001.

[31]　J.T. Lo and D. Bassu, "Adaptive vs. Accommodative Neural Networks for Adaptive System Identification", pp. 1279-1283, 2001.

[32]　G. Patel, S. Becker and R. Racine, Learning Shape and Motion from Image Sequences, in S. Haykin, Editor, Kalman Filtering and Neural Networks, Chapter 3, Wiley, 2001.

[33]　E.D. Sontag, "Recurrent neural networks: Some learning and systems-theoretic aspects", Department of Mathematics, Rutgers University, NJ, 1996.

[34]   R.W. Lucky, "Techniques for adaptive equalization of digital communication systems", Bell Syst. Tech. J., vol. 45, pp. 255-286, 1966.

[35]   S. Bellini, "Bussgang techniques for blind deconvolution and equalization". In S. Haykin, editor, Blind Deconvolution, Chapter 2, Prentice-Hall, 1994.

Limitations and Future Trends in Neural Computation
S. Ablameyko et al. (Eds.)
IOS Press, 2003

From Clustering Data to Traveling as a Salesman: Empirical Risk Approximation as a Learning Theory

Joachim M. Buhmann

Rheinische Friedrich–Wilhelms–Universität

Institut für Informatik III, Römerstr. 164, D-53117 Bonn, Germany

jb@cs.uni-bonn.de, http://www-dbv.informatik.uni-bonn.de

Abstract

Data Clustering is one of the fundamental techniques in pattern recognition to extract structure from data. Dependent on the data representation as vectors, proximity relations or histograms the clustering problem can mathematically be formulated as density estimation or as a combinatorial optimization problem. Learning algorithms for these problems have to demonstrate robustness to data fluctuations and efficiency in the same way as in supervised learning of classification or regression solutions. Another problem from the class of stochastically perturbed combinatorial optimization problems is the **T**raveling **S**alesman **P**roblem with uncertain travel times or distances. As in clustering, robust TSP solutions should generalize from one instance to a second one.

In all these cases, the fundamental limitations of learning are determined by large deviations of costs from a training sample instance to a test instance. Techniques from large deviation theory can be employed to determine bounds on the complexity of clustering solutions with small generalization error. The inference principle of *Empirical Risk Approximation* allows us to relate the robustness requirements in unsupervised learning to temperature based regularization concepts in Markov Chain Monte Carlo algorithms.

1 Introduction

Intelligent data analysis extracts symbolic information and relations between objects from quantitative or qualitative data. A prominent class of methods are clustering or grouping principles which are designed to discover and extract structures hidden in data sets [19]. The parameters which represent the clusters are estimated on the basis of quality criteria or cost functions. Clustering as a fundamental pattern recognition problem can be characterized by the following four design steps: (i) *Data Representation*, (ii) *Cluster Modeling*, (iii) *Cluster Optimization/Estimation* , (iv) *Cluster Validation*. It is important to note that the data representation predetermines what kind of cluster structures can be discovered in the data. Vectorial data, proximity or similarity data and histogram data are three examples of a wide variety of data types which are analyzed in the clustering literature.

Many clustering algorithms for these data types are based on quality criteria which measure compactness or connectedness. Compactness favors the partitioning of objects into subsets such that mutual similarities of objects in the same subset are maximized. Connectedness refers to the graph-theoretical approach to clustering where a pair of objects are assigned to the same cluster if they can be connected by a chain of mediating objects with high similarity. Data clustering methods which use the minimum spanning tree of the data (see [19]) are representatives of this category. We will give precise meaning to these two criteria in Sect 2. These criteria fall in the category of combinatorial optimization cost functions and resemble the well-known traveling salesman problem. To stress the commonalities for these problems we will discuss the issue of robust optimization algorithms and the validation of their results in Sects.5 and 6, respectively.

2   Modeling of Cluster Structure

Various data types have been introduced in the pattern recognition literature. Mathematically, a datum is defined as a relation between a design space $\mathfrak{O}$ and a measurement space $\mathfrak{F}$. The pair $(\mathbf{o}, \mathbf{x}) \in \mathfrak{O} \times \mathfrak{F}$ of an object configuration $\mathbf{o} \in \mathfrak{O}$ and a measurement $\mathbf{x} \in \mathfrak{F}$ can represent a functional dependency $\mathbf{x} : \mathbf{o} \mapsto \mathbf{x}(\mathbf{o})$ between objects and measurements or a stochastic dependency $\mathbf{P}\{\mathbf{x}|\mathbf{o}\}$. This categorization yields the following data types which are most common in data analysis problems:

Vectorial data characterize an object $\mathbf{o}$ by a number of attributes which are combined to a d-dimensional feature vector $\mathbf{x}(\mathbf{o}) \in \mathfrak{F} \subset \mathbb{R}^d$.

Distributional data of an object $\mathbf{o}$ are described by an empirical probability distribution or histogram $\mathbf{P}\{\mathbf{x}|\mathbf{o}\}$ over features $\mathbf{x} \in \mathfrak{F}$.

Proximity data are characterized by pairwise comparisons between objects according to a proximity measure, e.g., $\mathbf{x}(\mathbf{o}_i) := \{\mathcal{D}(\mathbf{o}_i, \mathbf{o}_j) \in \mathbb{R} : 1 \leq j \leq n\}$.

Various polyadic data types like co-occurrence data (word bigrams in linguistics, consumer behavior data in economics, ...) or even more complex data types (trigrams) are occasionally considered in the empirical sciences.

The goal of data clustering is to determine a partitioning of object space $\mathfrak{O}$ into subsets $\mathcal{G}_\alpha$, $1 \leq \alpha \leq k$. Mathematically, assignments of objects to clusters are represented by an assignment function $m : \mathfrak{O} \to \{1, 2, \ldots, k\}$ which yields the clusters $\mathcal{G}_\alpha := \{\mathbf{o} \in \mathfrak{O} : m(\mathbf{o}) = \alpha\}$. The space of all clustering solutions is the set of all assignment functions $\mathfrak{M} = \{m : \mathfrak{O} \to \{1, 2, \ldots, k\}\}$. The quality of these partitions are evaluated by an appropriate homogeneity measure for the respective data type. The most commonly used clustering costs are invariant under permutations of the cluster indices. Hierarchical and topological clustering methods impose additional structure on the partitions.

2.1   Central Clustering or Vector Quantization

Clustering objects, which are represented as vectorial data, induces a partition of the feature space $\mathfrak{F} \subset \mathbb{R}^d$. A set of n objects is represented by a set of data points $\mathcal{X} := \{(\mathbf{x}_i)_{i=1}^n, \mathbf{x}_i \in \mathfrak{F}\}$.

Each subset of the partition is represented by a cluster center, also called centroid $\mathbf{y}_\nu \in \mathcal{Y} = \{\mathbf{y}_\nu \in \mathfrak{F} : 1 \leq \nu \leq k\}$. The set of objects is partitioned in such a way that the average distance of data points to their cluster centers is minimized. The representation of data $\mathbf{x}_i$ by the centroid $\mathbf{y}_{m(i)}$ induces distortion/quantization costs $\mathcal{D}_{i,m(i)}$ due to information loss. The functional form of $\mathcal{D}_{i,m(i)}$ depends on the weighting of data distortions, in which quadratic costs $\mathcal{D}_{i,m(i)} = \left|\mathbf{x}_i - \mathbf{y}_{m(i)}\right|^2$ and k means $\mathbf{y}_\alpha = \sum_{\mathbf{o}_i \in \mathcal{G}_\alpha} \mathbf{x}_i / |\mathcal{G}_\alpha|$ are the most common choices. More general distortion measures like l_p-norms are occasionally considered. The cost function for k-means clustering is defined as

$$\mathcal{R}^{\mathrm{cc}}(m, \mathcal{Y}; \mathcal{X}) = \sum_{i \leq n} \mathcal{D}_{i,m(i)} = \sum_{i \leq n} \left|\mathbf{x}_i - \mathbf{y}_{m(i)}\right|^2. \tag{1}$$

The size k of the cluster set, i.e., the complexity of the clustering solution, has to be determined a priori or by a problem-dependent complexity measure [8]. A minimum of the cost function (1) can be found by two closely related strategies: (i) we vary the assignments $m(i)$ and the centroids $\mathbf{y}_{m(i)}$ independently; or (ii) we vary the assignments $m(i)$ and we strictly enforce the centroid constraints $\mathbf{y}_\alpha = \sum_{\mathbf{o}_i \in \mathcal{G}_\alpha} \mathbf{x}_i / |\mathcal{G}_\alpha|$. This procedure is a search in a discrete space with exponentially many states.

2.2 Distributional Clustering

Distributional data represent the co-occurrence of objects and features by histograms [28]. The histogram clustering model was developed on the basis of the distributional clustering model [23] for the analysis resp. grouping of objects characterized by co–occurrence of objects and certain feature values [16]. Application domains for this explorative data analysis approach can be found for example in texture segmentation [24], in statistical language modeling [23] or in document retrieval [17].

Denote by $\mathfrak{O} \times \mathfrak{F}$ the data space, i.e., the product space of objects $\mathbf{o}_i \in \mathfrak{O}, 1 \leq i \leq n$ and features $\mathbf{x}_j \in \mathfrak{F}, 1 \leq j \leq f$. In information retrieval, objects might be documents and features might be keywords. The $\mathbf{o}_i \in \mathfrak{O}$ are characterized by the set of l observations $\mathcal{Z} = \left\{(\mathbf{o}_{i(r)}, \mathbf{x}_{j(r)}) : 1 \leq r \leq l\right\} \subseteq (\mathfrak{O} \times \mathfrak{F})^l$. The sufficient statistics [15] of how often the object–feature pair $(\mathbf{o}_i, \mathbf{x}_j)$ occurs in $\mathcal{Z}$ is measured by the frequencies $\tilde{\mathcal{Z}} = \{n_{ij} :$ number of observations $(\mathbf{o}_i, \mathbf{x}_j)/l\}$.

These distributional data can be generated/explained by a mixture of data sources: (i) select an object $\mathbf{o}_i \in \mathfrak{O}$ with probability n_i; (ii) choose the cluster ν according to the cluster membership of $\nu = m(i)$; (iii) select $\mathbf{x}_j \in \mathfrak{F}$ according to the class–conditional distribution $q_{j|\nu}$. The different values ν of the data assignments denote the mixture components. The negative log-likelihood of the data yields the clustering cost function

$$\mathcal{R}^{\mathrm{hc}}(m, q; \mathcal{Z}) = \sum_{i \leq n} \mathcal{D}_{i,m(i)} = -\sum_{i \leq n} \sum_{j \leq f} n_{ij} \log q_{j|m(i)} \tag{2}$$

The negative logarithm of the cluster probabilities $q_{j|m(i)}$ weighted with the frequency n_{ij} is the loss $\mathcal{D}_{i,m(i)}$ of observing $(\mathbf{o}_i, \mathbf{x}_j)$. An insightful information theoretic interpretation [27] of the costs (2) relates histogram clustering to rate distortion theory [12], which stresses the importance of context information.

2.3 Pairwise Clustering

Clustering non-metric data which are characterized by proximity information and not by explicit Euclidean coordinates can be formulated as a graph optimization problem. Given is a graph $(\mathcal{V}, \mathcal{E})$ with weights $\mathcal{D} := \{\mathcal{D}_{ij}\}$ on the edges (i, j), the weights $\mathcal{D} \subseteq \mathfrak{F}$ being a subset of the feature space. The vertices denote the objects to be grouped and the edge weights encode dissimilarity information. Compact clusters are represented by a partition of the vertex set with small dissimilarities between all objects which belong to the same cluster. To simplify the notation, the subset of edges with both vertices in cluster α is denoted by $\mathcal{E}_\alpha = \{(i, j) \in \mathcal{E} : o_i, o_j \in \mathcal{G}_\alpha\}$. A meaningful cost function for pairwise clustering which primarily avoids grouping dissimilar objects into one cluster is defined by

$$\mathcal{R}^{\mathrm{pc}}(m; \mathcal{D}) = \sum_{i \leq n} \mathcal{D}_{i,m(i)} = \sum_{i \leq n} \frac{|\mathcal{G}_{m(i)}|}{|\mathcal{E}_{m(i)}|} \sum_{j:(i,j)\in\mathcal{E}_{m(i)}} \mathcal{D}_{ij}. \tag{3}$$

Preferred clusters according to this cost function are those subsets of objects with minimal average intra cluster dissimilarities, weighted by the cluster size $|\mathcal{G}_\nu|$. This cost function has the remarkable and for applications extremely valuable invariance that the assignments do not change if all dissimilarities are shifted by the same offset $\mathcal{D}_0$, i.e., $\mathcal{D}_{ij} \to \mathcal{D}_{ij} + \mathcal{D}_0$. $\mathcal{R}^{\mathrm{pc}}(m; \mathcal{D})$ is identical to the k-means clustering criterion for Euclidean distances $\mathcal{D}_{ij} = |\mathbf{x}_i - \mathbf{x}_j|^2$.

2.4 Path-based Clustering

A connection to graph theoretic clustering methods is provided by a concept of path-based clustering. This idea replaces direct dissimilarity measurements $\mathcal{D}_{ij}$ by an effective dissimilarity D_{ij}^{eff} between two objects o_i and o_j which reflects the degree of smoothness in the transition from o_i to o_j. The effective dissimilarity D_{ij}^{eff} is defined as the maximal inter object distance on the minimal connecting path:

$$\mathcal{D}_{ij}^{\mathrm{eff}}(m, \mathcal{D}) = \min_{\mathbf{p}\in\mathcal{P}_{ij}(m)} \left\{ \max_{1 \leq h < |\mathbf{p}|} \left\{ \mathcal{D}_{p_h,p_{h+1}} \right\} \right\}, \tag{4}$$

where the tuple $\mathbf{p} = (p_1, \ldots, p_{|\mathbf{p}|-1})$ denotes a path from o_i to o_j and $\mathcal{P}_{ij}(m)$ is the set of all paths connecting o_i with o_j, all vertices being in cluster $\mathcal{G}_{m(i)}$. If both objects belong to different clusters, $\mathcal{P}_{ij}(m)$ is the empty set and the effective dissimilarity is not defined.

3   The Traveling Salesman Problem

The probably most well-known combinatorial optimization problem is the traveling salesman problem. A salesman has to solve the problem how to visit n cities in the most economic way. The cities are usually characterized by pairwise travel costs which depend either on city distances or on travel times between the cities. Several classes of TSP problems have been distinguished on the basis of restrictions which are fulfilled by the distances. Of particular interest in practice are *metric* TSP problems where the cities correspond to points in some metric space. Metric TSP problems can in the worst case be efficiently approximated up to an approximation factor $\frac{3}{2}$ of the length of the optimal tour by Christophides' algorithm [3]. A special case of the class of metric TSP problems are the *Euclidean* TSP problems with cities located in the two-dimensional plane and Euclidean distances as costs. *Euclidean* TSP instances can be approximated arbitrarily well [2] in polynomial time.

These approximation results characterize the complexity of the optimization problem in the deterministic case — meaning that we neglect any noise perturbation of the travel times. It is certainly worth debating if real world optimization problems with all the uncertainty in parameter identification are appropriately modeled by deterministic combinatorial or continuous optimization problems. The deterministic abstraction of an optimization problem with noise fluctuations might renders questions meaningful which are computationally hard to solve and, at the same time, would make little or no sense in the fully stochastic setting. For example it might be hard to find the best solution of an optimization with a particular realization of the noise but it might be easy to stochastically approximate the solution with an approximation error comparable to the noise fluctuations. In such a situations the stochastic approximation might be preferable since (i) it can be efficiently computed and (ii) it averages over the noise due to its stochastic behavior and, therefore, yields a robust solution.

This section introduces a version of the traveling salesman problem which we call the NOISY TRAVELING SALESMAN PROBLEM. Take a TSP instance and perturb all the distance values by noise of fixed variance. This setting converts the TSP problem into a learning problem since we now have to search for solutions which are robust to noise. A solution which has been selected on a training instance of the combinatorial optimization problem also has to yield a good result on a test instance with a different noise perturbation. Complexity control as used in classification and regression might be necessary to avoid overfitting. The connection to learning problems becomes even more apparent if we compare the graph theoretic formulation of pairwise clustering (3) with the TSP problem, both being $\mathcal{NP}$–hard optimization problems. In the following we will concentrate on the Euclidean TSP problem.

A simple model which shows the same essential characteristics of a noisy TSP problem is defined as follows: Fix a number of cities $n \in \mathbb{N}$ with the parameters $c_1, \ldots, c_n \in \mathbb{R}^2$ and $\sigma \in \mathbb{R}_+$. Then, the locations for all cities are drawn randomly as samples from the probability distribution ($i \in \{1, \ldots, n\}$)

$$C_i \sim \Pr\{c_i | \sigma^2\}. \tag{5}$$

In order to adhere to standard notation, we will denote the cities by their locations C_i. The task consists in finding a closed tour of minimal length through all cities which also generalizes well to a new TSP instance. The tours can be represented by permutations $\pi \in \mathfrak{S}_n$ which minimizes

$$\mathcal{R}^{\mathrm{TSP}}(\pi; \mathcal{D}) = \mathcal{D}_{\pi(n)\pi(1)} + \sum_{i=1}^{n-1} \mathcal{D}_{\pi(i)\pi(i+1)} \tag{6}$$

$$\mathcal{D}_{ij} = |C_i - C_j|^2. \tag{7}$$

We call this problem "noisy" instead of "random" to stress the fact that there is some underlying structure common to all instances, in contrast to the random traveling salesman problem, as discussed in [4], where the cities are uniformly drawn from the unit square.

It is apparent in data clustering but also in the noisy TSP problem that we are interested in robust solutions which are as little as possible effected by the fluctuations in the problem instance. This property of optimization solutions is mathematically modeled by tools of statistical learning theory and we will now present this relation in the following sections 4, 5 and 6 on generalization, maximum entropy optimization and validation, respectively.

4 Generalization in clustering and traveling salesman problems

The key issue in learning focusses on the question how well does a solution which has been inferred on a *training* instance generalize to a second *test* instance. In classification, for example, we train a classifier on a training sample set of labelled data and, after the training phase, we measure the classification error on test samples. The quality of a classifier is determined by his performance on test data rather than minimizing training errors only. We consider this two sample set scenario as fundamental and the discussion of generalization issues in this paper is based on it. The notation refers to training data or variables by the upper index [1], whereas all quantities related to the test instance are denoted by the upper index [2].

What should be learned in clustering and traveling salesman problems? Let us approach this question in two steps by first discussing the k-means case and then the general clustering and TSP issues. A situation which is similar to the well understood case of classification and regression exists for k-means clustering [22]. Given are two sets of n objects represented by d-dimensional Euclidean data $\mathcal{X}^{(1,2)} := \{\mathbf{x}_i^{(1,2)} \in \mathfrak{F} \subset \mathbb{R}^d : 1 \leq i \leq n\}$. Both data sets which are denoted by training data $\mathcal{X}^{(1)}$ and test data $\mathcal{X}^{(2)}$ are generated by the same data source. Learning a clustering solution means that we use a search method to find a data partition which minimizes or approximates the k-means clustering costs (1) for the training data. This search algorithm returns a set of centroids $\mathcal{Y}^{(1)}$ and a set of assignments $m^{(1)}$. To generate a clustering solution for the test data set we minimize the cross validated costs

$$\mathcal{R}^{\mathrm{cc}}(m; \mathcal{X}^{(2)}, \mathcal{Y}^{(1)}) = \sum_{i \leq n} \left| \mathbf{x}_i^{(2)} - \mathbf{y}_{m(i)}^{(1)} \right|^2, \tag{8}$$

which mixes the test data with the statistics of the training instance. A minimum of (8) is achieved by the nearest neighbor rule $m(i) = \arg\min_\nu \left| \mathbf{x}_i^{(2)} - \mathbf{y}_\nu^{(1)} \right|$, i.e., the assignments are chosen according to the Voronoi partition of the feature space $\mathfrak{F}$ by the centroids $\mathbf{y}_1^{(1)}, \ldots, \mathbf{y}_k^{(1)}$ derived from the training set. (Alternatively to the nearest neighbor rule, Markov chain Monte Carlo algorithms [7] could be used to sample assignments according to the Gibbs distribution for k-means clustering costs which would approximate rather than minimize the costs (8).)

The learning problem in central clustering is conceptually simple from a mathematical point of view since the centroids are known to be a sufficient statistics of mixture models for fixed covariance matrices. Given the centroids the assignment $m(i)$ of object $\mathbf{o}_i$ is independent from the data $\mathcal{X}\backslash\{\mathbf{x}_i\}$ and, therefore, is also independent of assignments of other objects. The problem of jointly optimizing n assignment variables decomposes in n optimization problems with a single variable.

This strategy to statistically decouple optimization variables can be used for combinatorial optimization problems as well. In section 5 we introduce the maximum entropy method for optimization with the well-known technique of mean-field approximation which allows us to capture the notion of statistical decoupling in a quantitative way. Learning in the general case of clustering or TSP would then follow the four steps:

Decoupling Statistics: Calculate a statistics which decouples the optimization variables as completely as possible. Perfect decoupling as in k-means clustering is only possible in cases where a sufficient statistics is known. In all other cases we have to resort to approximative solutions for the decoupling.

Instance Mapping: Determine a mapping of optimization variables which are used in the training instance to variables of the test instance. In pairwise clustering it is not at all obvious how we should find an object $\mathbf{o}_{i'}$ of the test instance which corresponds to an object $\mathbf{o}_i$ of the training instance.

Cross-validation Costs: Evaluate the effective decoupling costs on the test instance given the training solution.

Optimization of Test Solution: Find a solution for the test instance which optimizes the effective decoupling costs for the test instance.

Step 1, the *decoupling statistics* is achieved by the technique of mean-field approximation which is frequently used in pattern recognition, neural computation and computer vision (see Sect. 5.3). The *instance mapping* of training solutions to test solutions is strongly dependent on the problem formulation. For example, when grouping proteins based on alignment dissimilarity data we might know that the same set of proteins has been used to generate the training and the test dissimilarity matrix. In this case fluctuations might have been caused by biologically motivated alignment parameters which are stochastic in nature. This setting would imply the identity mapping of training solutions to test solutions. On the other hand, two different sets of proteins might be used to robustly estimate protein families and in this case we have to find a statistically sensible mapping of training solutions to test solutions which is far from the identity. Given the decoupling costs and the instance mapping, the *cross-validation costs* are computationally straight forward to calculate and the final optimization step to generate a test solution poses no additional conceptual problem.

5 Stochastic Optimization by Markov Chain Monte Carlo Methods

The clustering cost functions for the training data $\mathcal{X}^{(1)}$ can be minimized in principle by various deterministic or stochastic methods from combinatorial and continuous optimization. The class of stochastic Markov Chain Monte Carlo (MCMC) optimization algorithms with *Simulated Annealing* as a prominent technique plays an eminent role in pattern recognition and we will focus on this method here. To simplify notation we will omit the upper indices which distinguish between training and test data and refer to the optimization step on the training data. In MCMC optimization methods, the variables of the optimization problem, e.g., the assignments in clustering or the city permutation in TSP, are treated as random variables of a stochastic (Markovian) process. Robust clustering methods are derived from the maximum entropy principle [26, 25] which states that assignments are distributed according to the Gibbs distribution

$$\mathbf{P}(m; \mathcal{D}) \;=\; \exp\!\big(-(\mathcal{R}(m; \mathfrak{D}) - \mathcal{F})/T\big), \tag{9}$$

$$\mathcal{F} \;=\; -T \log \sum_{m \in \mathfrak{M}} \exp\left(-\mathcal{R}(m; \mathcal{D})/T\right). \tag{10}$$

The "computational temperature" T serves as a Lagrange parameter to control the expected costs. The free energy $\mathcal{F}$ in Eq. (10) normalizes the Boltzmann factor $\exp(-\mathcal{R}(m; \mathcal{D})/T)$ and serves as a generating function for moments of the random optimization variables. We will first discuss MCMC based optimization for the simple cases of k-means and histogram clustering and then, we introduce the mean field approximation technique for pairwise clustering.

5.1 Stochastic Optimization of Central Clustering

Clustering vectorial data is modeled by the k-means clustering cost function $\mathcal{R}^{\text{cc}}$ which is linear in the assignments. This fact is the mathematical reason why the free energy can be calculated in close form:

$$\frac{\mathcal{F}}{T} \;=\; -\log \sum_{m \in \mathfrak{M}} \exp\left(-\sum_{i \le n} \mathcal{D}_{i,m(i)}/T\right) \;=\; -\log \sum_{m \in \mathfrak{M}} \prod_{i \le n} \exp\left(-\mathcal{D}_{i,m(i)}/T\right) \tag{11}$$

$$\;=\; -\log \prod_{i \le n} \sum_{m(i) \in \{1,\dots,k\}} \exp\left(-\mathcal{D}_{i,m(i)}/T\right) \;=\; -\sum_{i \le n} \log \sum_{\nu \le k} \exp\left(-\mathcal{D}_{i,\nu}/T\right). \tag{12}$$

The interchange of the sum and the product going from (11) to (12) is exact since there exist no interaction between $m(i)$ and $m(j)$, $j \ne i$ for given $\mathcal{Y}$. Inserting the normalization (12) into (9) yields the factorized Gibbs distribution

$$\mathbf{P}(m; \mathcal{D}) \;=\; \prod_{i \le n} \mathbf{P}_{i,m(i)} \quad \text{with} \quad \mathbf{P}_{i,\nu} := \frac{\exp(-\mathcal{D}_{i,\nu}/T)}{\sum_{\mu \le k} \exp(-\mathcal{D}_{i,\mu}/T)} \quad 1 \le \nu \le k. \tag{13}$$

$\mathbf{P}_{i,\nu}$ denote expectation values of assignments.

The optimized parameter set $\mathcal{Y}$ can be derived from the maximum entropy principle. We maximize the entropy w.r.t. $\mathcal{Y}$ assuming that the assignments $m(.)$ are distributed according to the Gibbs distribution, i.e.,

$$\hat{\mathbf{y}}_\alpha = \arg\max_{\mathbf{y}_\nu}\left(-\sum_{m\in\mathfrak{M}}\mathbf{P}_{i,\nu}\log\mathbf{P}_{i,\nu}\right)$$

$$= \arg\max_{\mathbf{y}_\nu}\left(\frac{1}{T}\sum_{m\in\mathfrak{M}}\mathcal{R}^{\mathrm{cc}}(m,\mathcal{Y};\mathcal{X})\mathbf{P}_{i,\nu} + \sum_{i\leq n}\log\sum_{\nu\leq k}\exp\left(-\mathcal{D}_{i,\nu}/T\right)\right) \tag{14}$$

The first term in the sum $\sum_{m\in\mathfrak{M}}\mathcal{R}^{\mathrm{cc}}(m,\mathcal{Y};\mathcal{X})\mathbf{P}_{i,\nu}$ is constant since the temperature plays the role of a Lagrange multiplier to keep the expected costs fixed. Differentiating the second term yields the necessary extreme value condition

$$0 = \sum_{i\leq n}\mathbf{P}_{i,\nu}\frac{\partial}{\partial\mathbf{y}_\nu}\mathcal{D}_{i,\nu}, \quad \forall\nu\in\{1,\ldots,k\}. \tag{15}$$

The centroid equation (15) can be solved for $\mathbf{y}_\alpha$ in the k-means case with $\mathcal{D}_{i,\nu} := \left|\mathbf{x}_i - \mathbf{y}_{m(i)}\right|^2$ which yields the means

$$\mathbf{y}_\alpha = \frac{\sum_{i\leq n}\mathbf{P}_{i,\alpha}\mathbf{x}_i}{\sum_{i\leq n}\mathbf{P}_{i,\alpha}}, \quad \forall\alpha\in\{1,\ldots,k\}. \tag{16}$$

The equations (15,13) form a system of kn coupled transcendental equations which are usually solved by fixed point iteration. First, the assignment probabilities are randomly initialized in the range $[0,1]$ observing the constraint $\sum_{\nu\leq k}\mathbf{P}_{i,\nu} = 1, \forall i$. Then, the centroids are estimated for fixed assignments. Given these new assignments, the centroids are re-estimated synchronously until no more changes are measurable during an update step. Often an asynchronous update of the re-estimation equations is preferable over the synchronous mode to avoid oscillatory behavior of the discrete dynamics. For the asynchronous update dynamics we randomly select an object $\mathbf{o}_i$ and choose the assignments to the centroids according to (13) and (15). Then, another object is selected and updated in the same manner. A compromise between fully asynchronous and parallel update are variants like updating objects in a random order and selecting a new order after n updates or selecting small groups of objects and updating them in parallel. To optimize complex cost functions like the clustering costs or the travel costs in TSP, a search heuristics of simulated cooling has been introduced [21, 11]. Starting at a high temperature the search algorithm systematically decreases the temperature according to a predefined schedule down to zero temperature. A deterministic variant called deterministic annealing has been successfully used in many applications in computer vision, speech processing and information retrieval. See for a review of the method e.g. [9, 10].

The Gibbs distribution (13) can also be interpreted as the complete data likelihood for mixture models with parameters $\mathcal{Y}$. Basically, the Gibbs distribution of the k clusters describes a mixture model with equal priors for each component and equal, isotropic covariances of size T. The assignments $m(i)$ and their expectations $\mathbf{P}_{i,\nu}$ correspond to the unobservable variables in mixture models and the component densities, respectively. The parallel iterative algorithm of assignments and centroids correspond to the expectation and maximization step in the EM procedure and it converges to a local maximum of the likelihood [14].

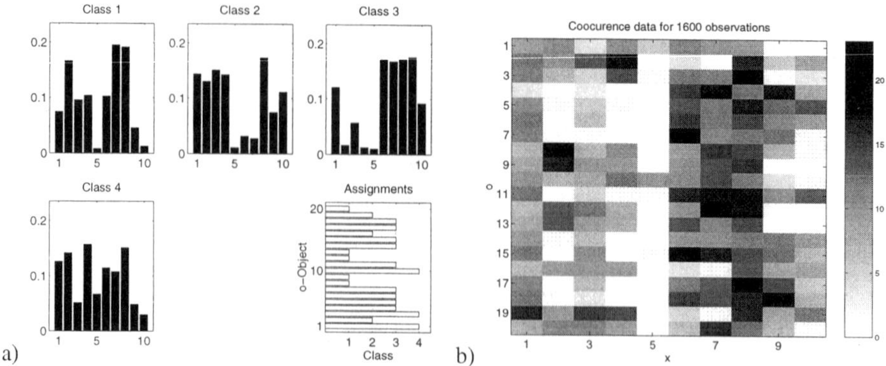

Figure 1: A simple example of a generative model for co–occurrence data. Depicted are the class–conditional distributions $q_{j|\nu}$, $\nu = 1, \ldots 4$, the assignments of the objects $\mathbf{o}_i$, $i = 1, \ldots, 20$ to classes (part a) and an example of co–occurrence data (part b) which is the only information the data analyst has at hand. Here the absolute frequencies are shown.

The temperature parameter T controls the uncertainty in the clustering problem, i.e., it coarsens the approximation precision by raising the expected costs above the global costs minimum. In the limit $T \to 0$, e.g., no approximation error, the solution of (13) corresponds to hard clustering with Boolean assignments $\mathbf{P}_{i,\nu} \in \{0, 1\}$ of a data vector $\mathbf{x}_i$ to the closest cluster center $\mathbf{y}_\nu$. Large temperature, e.g., coarse approximation precision, represents the fuzzy limit with partial assignments of data vectors to several clusters ($0 \leq \mathbf{P}_{i,\nu} \leq 1$).

5.2 Stochastic Optimization of Histogram Clustering

The cost function for histogram clustering falls in the same class of linear assignment problems as k-means clustering and the MCMC optimization is treated in an analogous fashion.

A toy example for the generative model of histogram clustering is given in figure 1. The modeling idea behind the histogram clustering is best contrasted by comparing it to k–means clustering where each object, i. e. data point $\mathbf{x}_i$, should be assigned to a prototypical centroid. In the histogram clustering the objects $\mathbf{x}_i$ should be uniquely assigned to a cluster which is characterized by a specific feature histogram $q_{j|\nu}$. These prototypical feature histograms are not defined as points in a Euclidean space but as generators for cluster–specific feature distributions in the space of discrete distributions.

In addition to the cluster conditional distributions $\vec{q} = \left(q_{j|\nu}\right)$ we introduce an assignment function $m : \mathfrak{O} \to \{1, \ldots, k\}$ to denote the cluster membership of object $\mathbf{x}_i$. Using these variables the observed data $\mathcal{Z}$ is distributed according to the generative model over $\mathfrak{O} \times \mathfrak{F}$:

$$\mathbf{P}\left(\mathbf{o}_i, \mathbf{x}_j | m, \vec{q}\right) = \frac{1}{n}\, q_{j|m(i)}. \tag{17}$$

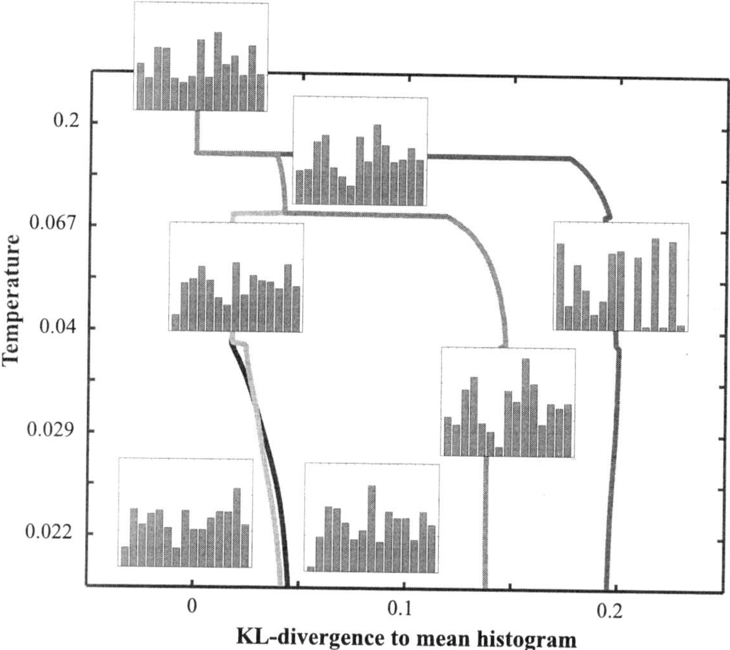

Figure 2: Solutions of the histogram clustering model for different temperatures. The KL divergence of the cluster histograms to the mean histogram is plotted to depict phase transitions.

For the analysis of the unknown data source — characterized (at least approximatively) by the empirical data $\mathcal{Z}$ — a structure $(m, \vec{q})$ has to be inferred. The aim of a histogram clustering analysis is to estimate for each cluster a prototypical feature distribution $q_{j|\nu}$. The log–likelihood function is given by

$$L \;=\; \sum_{r \le l} \log\left(\mathbf{P}\left(\mathbf{o}_{i(r)}, \mathbf{x}_{j(r)}\middle| (m, \vec{q})\right)\right) = \sum_{r \le l} \log q_{j(r)|m(i(r))} - l \log n. \tag{18}$$

The maximization of the log–likelihood is equivalent to the minimization of the KL–divergence between the empirical distribution of $(\mathbf{o}, \mathbf{x})$ and the model distribution $\mathbf{P}\left(\mathbf{o}_i, \mathbf{x}_j \middle| (m, \vec{q})\right)$. A good approximation for the empirical distribution, therefore, should in principle yield a good approximation for the true distribution of the unknown data source. The conditions for this property to generalize with respect to unknown observations are formulated in the context of uniform convergence results from statistical learning theory and will be examined in Sect. [6].

Using the sufficient statistics $\tilde{\mathcal{Z}} = (n_{ij})$ and the *loss function* $\mathbf{h}(\mathbf{o}_i, \mathbf{x}_j) = \log n - \log q_{j|m(i)}$

the maximization of the likelihood can be formulated as minimization of the *empirical risk*:

$$\mathcal{R}^{(1)}(m; \tilde{\mathcal{Z}}) = \sum_{i \leq n} \sum_{j \leq f} n_{ij} \mathbf{h}(\mathbf{o}_i, \mathbf{x}_j), \tag{19}$$

where the essential quantity to be minimized is the *expected risk*:

$$\mathcal{R}(m) = \sum_{i \leq n} \sum_{j \leq f} \mathbf{P}^{\mathrm{true}}(\mathbf{o}_i, \mathbf{x}_j) \, \mathbf{h}(\mathbf{o}_i, \mathbf{x}_j). \tag{20}$$

Minimization of (19) using differentiation and the method of Lagrange parameters to ensure proper normalization of the model parameters yields the stationary equations for the empirical estimates of $\vec{q}$ resp. $m(.)$:

$$\hat{q}_{j|\nu} = \frac{1}{|\mathcal{G}_\nu|} \sum_{i \in \mathcal{G}_\nu} n_{ij} = \sum_{i \in \mathcal{G}_\nu} \frac{n_i}{|\mathcal{G}_\nu|} n_{j|i}, \tag{21}$$

$$\hat{m}(i) = \arg\min_\mu \left\{ -\sum_{j \leq f} n_{j|i} \log \hat{q}_{j|\mu} \right\}. \tag{22}$$

A local minimum for the minimization of (19) (local maximum of 18) is obtained by alternating these equations until a fixed point is found. It is worth mentioning, that (21) generalizes the centroid condition of the k–means algorithm since it averages the conditional histograms of objects assigned to a specific cluster (compared to the vectors in k-means clustering). Furthermore, (22) is the histogram clustering version of a nearest neighbor rule, i. e. it assigns each object $\mathbf{o}_i$ to the cluster ν such that the empirically estimated distribution $n_{j|i}$ has minimal KL–divergence to the cluster–conditional distribution $q_{j|\nu}$.

As in classical k–means the deterministic annealing version of histogram clustering is obtained by replacing the assignments variables $m(.)$ by their probabilistic counterparts:

$$\mathbf{P}\{m(i) = \nu\} := \mathbf{P}_{i,\nu} = \frac{\exp\left(\frac{1}{T} \sum_{j \leq f} n_{j|i} \log q_{j|\nu}\right)}{\sum_{\mu \leq k} \exp\left(\frac{1}{T} \sum_{j \leq f} n_{j|i} \log q_{j|\mu}\right)}. \tag{23}$$

Empirically there exists evidence [16] that stopping at a finite temperature ($T > 0$) avoids overfitting., i. e. the inferred structure α generalizes with respect to the unknown distribution. The dynamics of the cooling process is depicted in Fig. 2. At high temperatures all feature distributions $q_{j|\nu}$ are the same. At a critical temperature $T \approx 0.15$ the feature distributions differentiate into two clusters and at still lower temperatures into three and four clusters. The phase transition plot (Fig. 2) depicts the distance of the inferred cluster distributions $q_{j|\nu}$ from the mean feature histogram. At zero temperature, all $k = 4$ clusters are distinct.

5.3 Mean Fields for Pairwise Clustering

It is substantially more complicated to calculate the Gibbs distribution for pairwise clustering [18]. Minimization of the rational cost function (3) turns out to be algorithmically complicated due to pairwise, potentially conflicting dependencies between assignments. There is no algebraic transformation known which allows us to decouple the interactions between assignments $m(i)$ and $m(j), j \neq i$. Therefore, we follow the strategy of the linear case (k-means clustering) and approximate as tight as possible the Gibbs distribution of the interacting assignments with a system of statistically decoupled assignment variables, governed by the costs

$$\mathcal{R}^{\mathrm{mf}}(m; \mathcal{D}_{i,\nu}) = \sum_{i \leq n} \mathcal{D}_{i,m(i)}. \tag{24}$$

The decoupling parameters $\mathcal{D}_{i,\nu}, 1 \leq \nu \leq n$ which denote the effective clustering costs for object o_i should sum up the cost contributions of all other objects $o_j, j \neq i$ when interacting with o_i in a particular clustering solution. Since we are interested in stochastic optimization we should choose the parameters $\mathcal{D}_{i,\nu}$ such that the Gibbs distribution for pairwise clustering is optimally approximated by the factorial Gibbs distribution for $\mathcal{R}^{\mathrm{mf}}(m; \mathcal{D}_{i,\nu})$. A "distance" measure for probability distributions with a solid foundation in information theory [12] and mathematical statistics, e.g., differential geometry of statistical manifolds [20], is the Kullback-Leibler divergence. To determine optimal $\mathcal{D}_{i,\nu}$ parameters we minimize the Kullback-Leibler divergence of the mean field distribution w.r.t. the pairwise Gibbs distribution, i.e.,

$$\hat{\mathcal{D}}_{i,\nu} = \arg\min_{\mathcal{D}_{i,\nu}} \sum_{m \in \mathfrak{M}} \exp\left(-(\mathcal{R}^{\mathrm{mf}} - \mathcal{F}^{\mathrm{mf}})/T\right) \log \frac{\exp\left(-(\mathcal{R}^{\mathrm{mf}} - \mathcal{F}^{\mathrm{mf}})/T\right)}{\exp\left(-(\mathcal{R}^{\mathrm{pc}} - \mathcal{F}^{\mathrm{pc}})/T\right)}. \tag{25}$$

It is worth noticing that the stochastic combinatorial search through the discrete space of assignments $\mathfrak{M}$ in clustering or the space of permutation in TSP is replace by a deterministic continuous optimization problem over a subset $\{\mathcal{D}_{i,\nu}\} \subset \mathbb{R}^{n \cdot k}$. This extension of the search problem from a discrete to a continuous space is known as a continuation method in mathematical optimization [1].

The minimization of (25) yields for pairwise clustering the set of equations[1]

$$\mathbf{P}_{i,\nu} = \frac{\exp(-\mathcal{D}_{i,\nu}/T)}{\sum_{\mu \leq k} \exp(-\mathcal{D}_{i,\mu}/T)}, \tag{26}$$

$$\mathcal{D}_{i,\nu} = \frac{1}{\pi_{\nu \backslash i} + 1} \sum_{(i,j) \in \mathcal{E}} \mathbf{P}_{j,\nu} \left(\mathcal{D}_{ij} - \frac{1}{2\pi_{\nu \backslash i}} \sum_{(j,r) \in \mathcal{E}} \mathbf{P}_{r,\nu} \mathcal{D}_{jr} \right). \tag{27}$$

The variables $\mathcal{D}_{i,\nu}$ depend on the given distance matrix $\mathcal{D}_{ik}$, the average assignment variables $\{\mathbf{P}_{i,\nu}\}$ and the cluster weights $\pi_{\nu \backslash i} := \sum_{j \leq n : j \neq i} \mathbf{P}_{j,\nu}$. Equation (27) suggests an algorithm for learning the optimized cluster assignments which resembles the EM algorithm: In the E-step, the assignments $\{\mathbf{P}_{i,\nu}\}$ are estimates for given $\{\mathcal{D}_{i,\nu}\}$. In the M-step the $\{\mathcal{D}_{i,\nu}\}$ are reestimated on the basis of new assignment estimates $\{\mathbf{P}_{i,\nu}\}$. This iterative algorithm converges to a local minimum of the Kullback Leibler divergence between the factorial ansatz and the correct Gibbs distribution which can be interpreted as consistent assignments for the pairwise data.

---

[1]See reference [18] for a detailed derivation.

6   Empirical Risk Approximation and Validation

An indispensable property of data clustering solutions is their stability to sampling noise. A clustering solution with low costs on a *training* instance should yield comparably low costs on a second *test* instance. This robustness requirement limits e.g. the number of clusters which can be reliably inferred from the data. If too many clusters are supposed to be estimated then instance noise will strongly influence the values of the cluster parameters.

The field of *Statistical Learning Theory* addresses robustness questions and model complexity issues in the context of supervised learning, in particular for classification and regression. The same tradeoff between the complexity of the hypothesis class and the size of the data set limits the inference precision in data clustering. A theoretical analysis has to estimate the probability of large deviations between solutions found on two different sample sets.

The space of clustering solutions is composed of the product space $\mathfrak{M} \times \mathfrak{S}$ of assignments and continuous parameters, e.g., the means $\mathfrak{S} = \mathcal{Y}$ in k-means clustering or the conditional probabilities $\mathfrak{S} = \{q_{j|\nu}\}$ in distributional clustering. Assume that the cluster solution is quantified by the costs $\mathcal{R}(m; \mathcal{D})$ and that we have two data sets $\mathcal{D}^{(1)}, \mathcal{D}^{(2)}$ drawn from the same probability distribution ($\mathcal{R}^{(1,2)}(m) := \mathcal{R}(m; \mathcal{D}^{(1,2)})$). The optimal cluster assignments w.r.t. the two data sets are denoted by $m_j = \arg\min_m \mathcal{R}^{(j)}(m), j \in \{1, 2\}$. It is assumed that an optimization algorithm is able to sample randomly from the set of approximating solutions $m_\gamma \in \mathcal{L}_\gamma := \{m : \mathcal{R}^{(1)}(m) - \mathcal{R}^{(1)}(m_1) \leq \gamma\}$. It is assumed that a problem dependent mapping of the variables of the training solutions to variables of the test solution exists, i.e., $f : \mathfrak{M} \times \mathfrak{F} \to \mathfrak{M}$ maps the product space of solution space times feature space to the solution space. The dependence of this map f on the training data $\mathcal{D}^{(1)}$ is suppressed in our notation. The solution $f(m)$ can be interpreted as an adaptation of a training solution m to a valid test solution. For example in the special case of clustering the same objects $\{o_i : 1 \leq i \leq n\}$ in training and test instance, the identity mapping $f(m(i)) = m(i)$ would be the most natural choice.

The robustness criterion

$$\Delta \mathcal{R}^{(2)}(m_\gamma) := \mathcal{R}^{(2)}(f(m_\gamma)) - \mathcal{R}^{(2)}(m_2) \tag{28}$$

estimates the quality of an approximating training solution m_γ on a test instance should be upper bounded in probability by large deviation arguments, i.e.,

$$\mathbf{P}\left\{\Delta \mathcal{R}^{(2)}(m_\gamma) > \epsilon\right\} \leq \delta. \tag{29}$$

Notice that m_γ depends on the selection algorithms and is a random variable for stochastic sampling from the approximation set $\mathcal{L}_\gamma$.

Statistical learning theory relates this deviation to the complexity of the solution space $\mathfrak{M}$. Since the space of all data partitionings is too large to yield meaningful bounds we coarsen this space by a minimal γ-cover $\mathcal{M}_\gamma$, i.e., every function $m \in \mathfrak{M}$ is at most γ distant from the closest function in $\mathcal{M}_\gamma$. Distances between two functions are measured by the l_1-distance, i.e., $d(m, \hat{m}) := \sum_{i=1}^{n} |\mathcal{D}^{(2)}_{i,m(i)} - \mathcal{D}^{(2)}_{i,\hat{m}(i)}|/n$.

The robustness measure $\Delta\mathcal{R}^{(2)}(m_\gamma)$ can be bound by Vapnik and Chervonenkis type inequalities (1971).

$$
\begin{aligned}
\Delta\mathcal{R}^{(2)}(m_\gamma) &\leq \mathcal{R}^{(2)}(m_\gamma) - \inf_{m\in\mathcal{M}_\gamma} \mathcal{R}^{(2)}(m) + \gamma \\
&\leq \mathcal{R}^{(2)}(m_\gamma) - \mathcal{R}^{(1)}(m_\gamma) + \sup_{m\in\mathcal{M}_\gamma} |\mathcal{R}^{(1)}(m) - \mathcal{R}^{(2)}(m)| + 2\gamma \\
&\leq 2 \sup_{m\in\mathcal{M}_\gamma\cup\mathcal{L}_\gamma} |\mathcal{R}^{(1)}(m) - \mathcal{R}^{(2)}(m)| + 2\gamma.
\end{aligned}
\tag{30}
$$

We now have to find bounds on the probability of large deviations of training costs from test costs $|\mathcal{R}^{(1)}(m) - \mathcal{R}^{(2)}(m)|$ for fixed clustering solution $m(.)$. This probability can be bound by Bernstein's inequality [29] which is sensitive to the scale of cost contributions from single objects.

The expected risk of the empirical minimizer exceeds the global minimum of the expected risk by 2ϵ with a probability bounded by Bernstein's inequality

$$
\begin{aligned}
\mathbf{P}\left\{\Delta\mathcal{R}^{(2)}(m_\gamma) > 2\epsilon\right\} &\leq \mathbf{P}\left\{\sup_{m\in\mathcal{M}_\gamma\cup\mathcal{L}_\gamma} |\mathcal{R}^{(1)}(m) - \mathcal{R}^{(2)}(m)| \geq \epsilon - \gamma\right\} \\
&\leq \sum_{m\in\mathcal{M}_\gamma\cup\mathcal{L}_\gamma} \mathbf{P}\left\{|\mathcal{R}^{(1)}(m) - \mathcal{R}^{(2)}(m)| \geq \epsilon - \gamma\right\} \\
&\leq 2|\mathcal{M}_\gamma\cup\mathcal{L}_\gamma| \sup_{m\in\mathcal{M}_\gamma\cup\mathcal{L}_\gamma} \exp\left(-\frac{n(\epsilon-\gamma)^2}{2\sigma_m^2 + \tau_m\sigma_m(\epsilon-\gamma)}\right) =: \delta.
\end{aligned}
\tag{31}
$$

The parameters σ_m, τ_m which determine the Bernstein inequality are dependent on the specific solution $m \in \mathcal{M}_\gamma$. The complexity of the considered γ-cover $|\mathcal{M}_\gamma\cup\mathcal{L}_\gamma|$ of the hypothesis class $\mathfrak{M}$ has to be small enough to guarantee with high confidence small ϵ–deviations.

This large deviation inequality weighs two competing effects in the learning problem, i. e., the probability of a large deviation exponentially decreases with growing sample size n, whereas a large deviation becomes increasingly likely with growing cardinality of the γ–cover of the hypothesis class.

The sample complexity $n_0(\gamma, \epsilon, \delta)$ describes the dependency of the instance size n on the approximation precision ϵ, the confidence δ and the coarsening γ. It is defined according to eq. (31) by

$$
\log|\mathcal{M}_\gamma\cup\mathcal{L}_\gamma| - \sup_{m\in\mathcal{M}_\gamma\cup\mathcal{L}_\gamma} \frac{n_0(\epsilon-\gamma)^2}{2\sigma_m^2 + \tau_m\sigma_m(\epsilon-\gamma)} + \log\frac{2}{\delta} = 0.
\tag{32}
$$

The optimal coarsening of the hypothesis class according to the bound (31) is achieved if we minimize the bound (32) w.r.t. γ, i.e., if the condition $d\epsilon/d\gamma = 0$ is satisfy. To establish the link between the large deviation bound (32) and **MCMC** algorithms with the computational temperature as a control parameter we interpret the log–cardinality $\log|\mathcal{L}_\gamma|$ of the approximation set $\mathcal{L}_\gamma$ as microcanonical entropy and the approximation parameter γ as energy. This interpretation completely corresponds to the microcanonical approach to statistical physics and respective

Gibbs samplers have been proposed in the literature [13]. The temperature as a Lagrange parameter to enforce the expected cost constraint is defined by the relation

$$\frac{d\,\text{entropy}}{d\,\text{energy}} = T^{-1} \approx \frac{\log|\mathcal{L}_{\gamma+\Delta\gamma}| - \log|\mathcal{L}_\gamma|}{\Delta\gamma}. \tag{33}$$

The entropy is related to the cardinality $|\mathcal{M}_\gamma \cup \mathcal{L}_\gamma|$ by the inequalities

$$|\mathcal{M}_\gamma \cup \mathcal{L}_\gamma| \le |\mathcal{M}_\gamma| + |\mathcal{L}_\gamma| \le c\frac{|\mathfrak{M}|}{|\mathcal{L}_\gamma|} + |\mathcal{L}_\gamma|, \tag{34}$$

which yields the equation for the temperature

$$\frac{d}{d\gamma}\log\left(c\frac{|\mathfrak{M}|}{|\mathcal{L}_\gamma|} + |\mathcal{L}_\gamma|\right) = -\frac{1 - c|\mathcal{L}_\gamma|^2/|\mathfrak{M}|}{1 + c|\mathcal{L}_\gamma|^2/|\mathfrak{M}|}\frac{d}{d\gamma}\log|\mathcal{L}_\gamma| \approx -T^{-1} \tag{35}$$

c is a constant which depends on the hypothesis class and the metric but not on γ. Since the approximation set $\mathcal{L}_\gamma$ is expected to be much smaller than the solution space $\mathfrak{M}$ ($\mathcal{L}_\gamma \ll \mathfrak{M}$) we neglect the small correction term $c|\mathcal{L}_\gamma|^2/|\mathfrak{M}|$. Then the minimal temperature to guarantee generalization is given by

$$\frac{1}{T^{\text{stop}}} \le -\frac{d}{d\gamma}\sup_{m\in\mathcal{M}_\gamma\cup\mathcal{L}_\gamma}\frac{n_0\left(\epsilon - \gamma\right)^2}{2\sigma_m^2 + \tau_m\sigma_m\left(\epsilon - \gamma\right)}\Bigg|_{\frac{d\epsilon}{d\gamma}=0}. \tag{36}$$

The bound (32) relates the precision ϵ and the coarsening of the hypothesis class γ to the sample size n_0 with $\epsilon^{\text{opt}} := \min_\gamma \epsilon(\gamma, n_0, \delta)$ and $\gamma^{\text{opt}} := \arg\min_\gamma \epsilon(\gamma, n_0, \delta)$. With probability $1 - \delta$ the deviation of the training costs $\mathcal{R}(m_\gamma; \mathcal{D}^{(1)})$ from the test costs $\mathcal{R}(m_\gamma; \mathcal{D}^{(2)})$ is bounded by $(\epsilon^{\text{opt}} - \gamma^{\text{opt}})$. Given the precision ϵ the equation (36) bounds the control parameter for MCMC algorithms, the computational temperature, from below. This bound guarantees that optimization results by annealing algorithms do not deviate more than 2ϵ from the best test result if we keep a minimal uncertainty in the search process.

The existence of such a minimal non-zero stop temperature also reflects the fact that we are not able to single out one robust solution which generalizes from a training to a test instance but we can only identify a set of solutions. Averaging over a function sphere with radius γ^{opt} around the minimizer of the training instance yields a hypothesis corresponding to a statistically significant structure in the data. The main technical task in the following remains to calculate an upper bound for the cardinality $|\mathcal{M}_\gamma \cup \mathcal{L}_\gamma|$ of the γ–cover which can be achieved by Markov Chain Monte Carlo methods (see Sinclair (1993)).

7   Results

The bound (36) provides a guarantee against overfitting, which means that we do not suffer from too large cost deviations (28) between training and test solution. It is by no means necessarily tight and we have to test the quality of the chain of inequalities (31) in controlled experiments with preferably computer generated data. This section summarizes two series of experiments for histogram clustering and synthetic TSP instances. In the case of histogram clustering MCMC experiments allowed us to measure the quality of the predicted stop temperatures.

i	$m(i)$	i	$m(i)$	i	$m(i)$
1	5	11	2	21	2
2	3	12	4	22	3
3	2	13	1	23	1
4	5	14	5	24	1
5	2	15	3	25	2
6	2	16	5	26	5
7	5	17	3	27	5
8	4	18	4	28	2
9	2	19	1	29	2
10	2	20	2	30	1

ν	$q_{j|\nu}$
1	$\{0.11, 0.01, 0.11, 0.07, 0.08, 0.04, 0.06, 0,$ $0.13, 0.07, 0.08, 0.1, 0, 0.11, 0.03\}$
2	$\{0.18, 0.1, 0.09, 0.02, 0.05, 0.09, 0.08, 0.03,$ $0.06, 0.07, 0.03, 0.02, 0.07, 0.06, 0.05\}$
3	$\{0.17, 0.05, 0.05, 0.06, 0.06, 0.05, 0.03, 0.11,$ $0.09, 0, 0.02, 0.1, 0.03, 0.07, 0.11\}$
4	$\{0.15, 0.07, 0.1, 0.03, 0.09, 0.03, 0.04, 0.05,$ $0.06, 0.05, 0.08, 0.04, 0.08, 0.09, 0.04\}$
5	$\{0.09, 0.09, 0.07, 0.1, 0.07, 0.06, 0.06, 0.11,$ $0.07, 0.07, 0.1, 0.02, 0.07, 0.02, 0\}$

Figure 3: Generative model used in the Monte–Carlo experiments for the evaluation of the theoretical results for histogram clustering. The left table shows the assignments of the objects to classes, while the right table lists the used class–conditional distributions $q_{j|\nu}$.

7.1 Learning in Histogram Clustering

For the evaluation of the derived theoretical result (36) a series of Monte–Carlo experiments on artificial data has been performed for histogram clustering. Given are the number of objects $n = 30$, the number of groups $k = 5$ and the size of the histograms $f = 15$; then the generative model for this experiments was created randomly and is summarized in figure 3. From this generative model sample sets of arbitrary size can be generated and the true distributions $\mathbf{P}^{\text{true}}\{\mathbf{x}_j|\mathbf{o}_i\}$ can be calculated.

In figure 4a,b the predicted temperatures (vertical lines) are compared to the empirically observed critical temperatures (minima of the expected risk), which have been estimated on the basis of 2000 different samples of randomly generated co–occurrence data for each l_0. The expected risk (solid) and empirical risk (dashed) of these 2000 inferred models are averaged.

Figure 4c indicates that on average the minimal expected risk is assumed when the effective number is smaller than or equal five, i. e. the number of clusters of the true generative model. Therefore predicting the right computational temperature also enables the data analyst to solve the cluster validation problem for the histogram clustering model. Especially for $l_0 = 800$ these results suggest that in the light of such a small training set five clusters normally can not be estimated in a reliable way. On the other hand for $l_0 = 1600$ and $l_0 = 2000$ the right temperature prevents the algorithm to infer too many clusters, which would be an instance of overfitting. As an interesting point one should note that for an infinite number of observations the critical inverse temperature diverges, but not more than the five effective clusters are extracted. At this point we conclude, that the Empirical Risk Approximation principle solves the problem of model validation for the case of histogram clustering when the correct model is in the hypothesis class, i. e. it chooses the correct number of clusters.

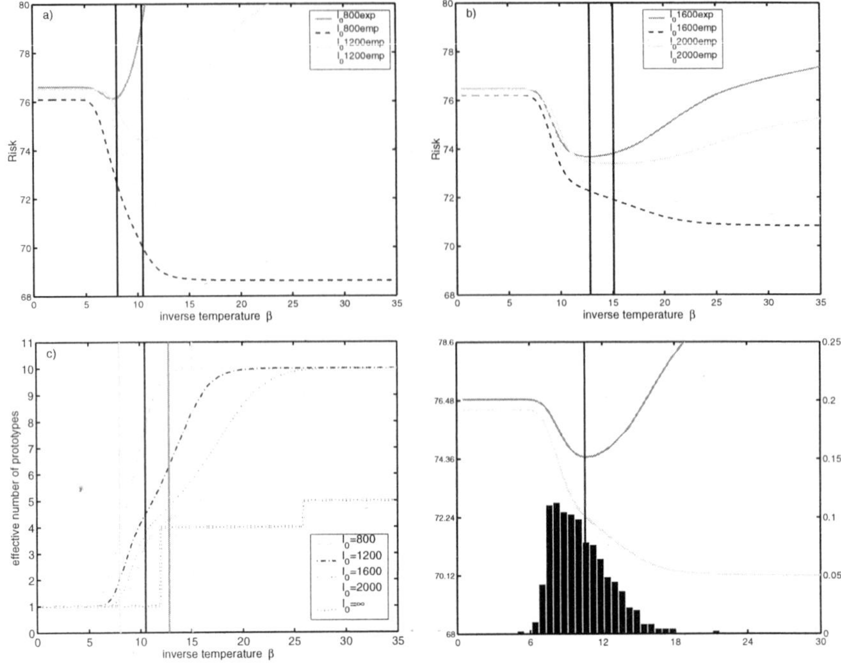

Figure 4: Comparison between theoretically derived upper bound on the optimal temperature and the observed critical temperatures (minimum of the temperature vs. expected risk curve). The bold (dashed) lines denote expected (empirical) risk averaged over 2000 i.i.d. sample sets. Depicted are the plots for $l_0 = 800, 1200, 1600, 2000$. Vertical lines indicate the predicted critical temperatures. In addition the average effective number of clusters is drawn in part c). In part d the distribution of the plug-in estimates for the stop temperatures is shown for $l_0 = 1200$.

7.2 Noisy TSP

The second example of a noisy optimization problem is the traveling salesman problem where the link weights are given by random variables $\mathcal{D}_{ij}$. Let $\ell^{(1)} = \mathcal{R}^{\mathrm{TSP}}(\pi; \mathcal{D}^{(1)})$ and $\ell^{(2)} = \mathcal{R}^{\mathrm{TSP}}(\pi; \mathcal{D}^{(2)})$ be the length functions defined on the set of all permutations $\pi \in \mathfrak{S}_n$ resulting from two samples of weights. We are interested in the performance of the optimal solution computed on $\ell^{(1)}$ plugged into $\ell^{(2)}$. We will call $\ell^{(1)}$ the *training instance* and $\ell^{(2)}$ the *test instance*.

As a basis for our discussion, let $\ell^{(1)}$ and $\ell^{(2)}$ be derived from the following traveling salesman model. Choose two natural numbers k, n. The model consists of n groups with four clusters of k cities each. The traveling costs between the cities within one cluster vanish. Each

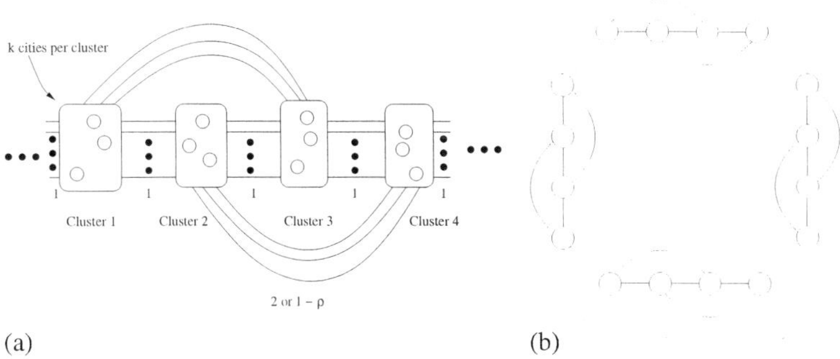

Figure 5: (a) Link weights in one group. Among the k^2 links connecting clusters 1 and 3, one is chosen uniformly and its weight is set to $1 - \rho$. The same applies to the links from cluster 2 to 4. (b) The example for $n = 4$. Each circle represents k cities. Within a cluster, the costs to move from one city to another are 0. Each line represents k^2 links. The links corresponding to the straight lines have costs 1, the curved lines have costs 2, except for one which is drawn uniformly and independently among the k^2 links and has cost $1 - \rho$.

group is linked as depicted in figure 5(a). The groups are arranged in a circular list. The costs to move from one cluster to an adjacent one are 1, and to move to the next but one cluster within one group are 2. Noise is introduced as follows: one link between cluster 1 and 3 and one link between cluster 2 and 4 in each block are chosen at random and their costs are set to $1 - \rho$, where $0 \leq \rho < 1$.

7.3 The Empirical Minimizer

We now study the behavior of the minimizer of $\ell^{(1)}$. Let $\pi^* \in \mathfrak{S}_{4n}$ be the solution which visits the clusters in linear order and has total costs of $4n$. This tour is optimal on average. When $\rho > 0$, then there exists a path which takes the $1 - \rho$ links visiting the clusters within one group in the order 1, 3, 2, 4 having total costs of $2n(1 - \rho) + 2n$, which is smaller than $4n$. But the probability that the same links will cost $1 - \rho$ on $\ell^{(2)}$ is $1/k^4$ per link. With probability $1 - 1/k^{4n}$ at least one of the links will have cost 2 on $\ell^{(2)}$, resulting in total costs of up to $6n$ when none of the $1 - \rho$ links matches in test and training instance.

In this example, the minimal solution $\pi^{(1)} \in \mathfrak{S}_{4n}$ of $\ell^{(1)}$ performs suboptimally on $\ell^{(2)}$, even if ρ is small and $\ell^{(1)}(\pi^{(1)})$ is approximately $\ell^{(1)}(\pi^*)$, i.e. $\pi^{(1)}$ and π^* are solutions of nearly equal quality on $\ell^{(1)}$. Denote by $[\pi]$ the set of permutations with costs equal to π. Then, $\#[\pi^*] = 8n(k!)$, whereas $\#[\pi^{(1)}] = 8n(k-1)!$ (To see this, consider the number of possibilities to move through each of the clusters. In the latter case, the cheap link of cost $1 - \rho$ has to be taken, such that the number of possibilities is $(k-1)!$ per cluster. Each of these possibilities exist in two direction.) This means that most of the nearly optimal solutions of $\ell^{(1)}$ are robust, that is perform well on the test instance $\ell^{(2)}$. The optimal solutions of $\ell^{(1)}$ are results of infrequent

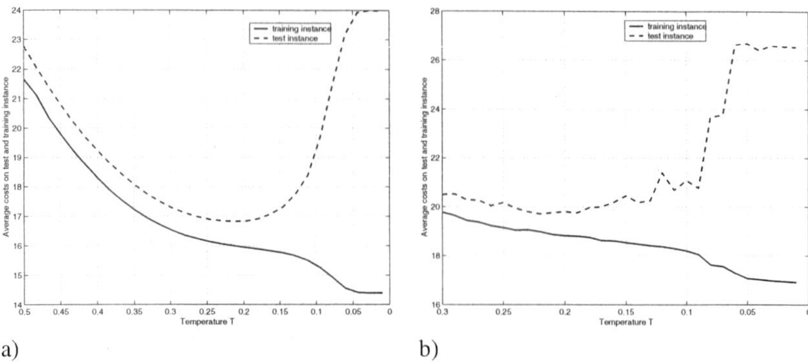

Figure 6: (a) Mean costs with respect to the Gibbs measure at different temperatures. The parameters of the model where $k = 3$ cities per cluster, $4n = 16$ clusters, $\rho = 0.2$. (b) Average costs for an extension of the first example. More lines were introduced and each link was slightly distorted.

random events which are unlikely to be exhibited on the test instance $\ell^{(2)}$. This effect leads to suboptimal performance and it is well-known as *overfitting*.

7.4 Markov Chain Monte Carlo Sampling and Robustness

Instead of computing the minimizer $\pi^{(1)}$ on $\ell^{(1)}$, an alternative strategy is to draw uniformly from a set of solutions nearly equivalent to $\pi^{(1)}$. The term "nearly equivalent" is defined in a mathematically precise way by the approximating set $\mathcal{L}_\gamma := \{\pi : \ell^{(1)}(\pi) - \ell^{(1)}(\pi^{(1)}) \leq \gamma\}$, i.e., all permutations with a length not exceeding the empirical minimizer by more than γ are eligible.

A possible implementation of this technique uses a Markov Chain Monte Carlo algorithm to sample from the Gibbs distribution for $\ell^{(1)}$, given by

$$G_T^{(1)}(\pi) = \frac{\exp(-\ell^{(1)}(\pi)/T)}{\sum_{\tilde{\pi}} \exp(-\ell^{(1)}(\tilde{\pi})/T)}. \tag{37}$$

(See [21] for the application of Gibbs sampling to the TSP and [6] for the general theory) The Gibbs distribution has a parameter $T \geq 0$, the computational temperature. For $T = 0$, the Gibbs measure is concentrated on the minimizers of $\ell^{(1)}$, for $T \to \infty$, the Gibbs measure tends to the uniform distribution. Figure 6a depicts the average costs of permutations drawn with respect to the Gibbs measure at different temperatures. At temperature $T \approx 0.2$, most solutions are drawn from $[\pi^*]$, which means that the solutions are robust on average. For lower temperatures, the ratio shifts such that only solutions with $1 - \rho$ links are drawn. Empirical evidence and classification experiments with noisy training samples indicate that the optimal generalization is achieved for $T \approx \rho$, i.e., it should be not too costly (in terms of T equivalents) to select the far more abundant robust links rather than the noisy links.

The same experiments were conducted on an extension of the problem above (see fig. 6b) and led to basically the same results. Links of cost two, three and four were introduced between all cities which were two, three or four clusters away from each other. Furthermore, each link was a priori distorted by a uniform random value in the interval $[-\rho/2, \rho/2]$ ($\rho = 0.2$). The roughness of the graph is due to fewer iterations in the sampling process than in the first experiment.

The overfitting phenomenon in TSP is by no means specific to the linearly arranged clusters of cities with perturbed links. The same sensitivity to overfitting can be observed in Euclidean TSP with city positions perturbed by Gaussian noise (see eq. 5 and reference [5]). The following scenario has been adopted. Cities are positioned in equal distances on a closed, sufficiently smooth curve in the two dimensional plain. A specific TSP instance is generated by adding Gaussian noise of variance σ to the city position. An example of this process can be seen in fig. 7c where the open circles indicate the city positions. The averaging of Gibbs sampled solutions is performed in the Euclidean plane where the circular symmetry is normalized out (for details see [5]). Averages derived from a Gibbs sampling process at different temperatures are depicted in figure 7a. At high temperature the averages follow closely the empirical risk minimization solution, whereas at high temperature the averaged tour crumbles well inside of the generating circle. Test tours are generated from the averages by traveling along the averaged tour and locally adapting the sequence of test cities in a finite horizon window of w cities. Figure 7b shows clearly that an average at $T \approx 0.15$ generates a tour which is less sensitive to the instance noise that the empirical risk minimizer gained at $T = 0$.

8 Discussion

Data clustering as one of the most fundamental information processing procedures to extract symbolic information from sub-symbolic data follows the four design steps of Pattern Recognition: (i) data representation, (ii) structure definition, (iii) structure optimization and (iv) structure validation. The structure definition for clusters emphasizes homogeneity or connectivity for the different data representations, e.g., vectorial, distributional and dissimilarity data. A natural choice to optimize the cluster parameters are stochastic optimization algorithms with their theoretically supported robustness to noise. Large deviation techniques from statistical learning theory and empirical process theory allow us to understand this insensitivity and to address the model selection problem in clustering. The strict separation of the four design steps greatly facilitates the search for application adapted clustering principles and provides a basis for rational algorithm design in data analysis.

This analysis of different clustering models, i.e., formulations of clustering as combinatorial optimization problems, has motivated the study on the Noisy Traveling Salesman Problem where the same questions of robustness and generalization emerge. Statistical learning theory together with stochastic optimization and its temperature controlled MCMC methods provide a mathematical frame to extend the deterministic view on combinatorial and continuous opti-

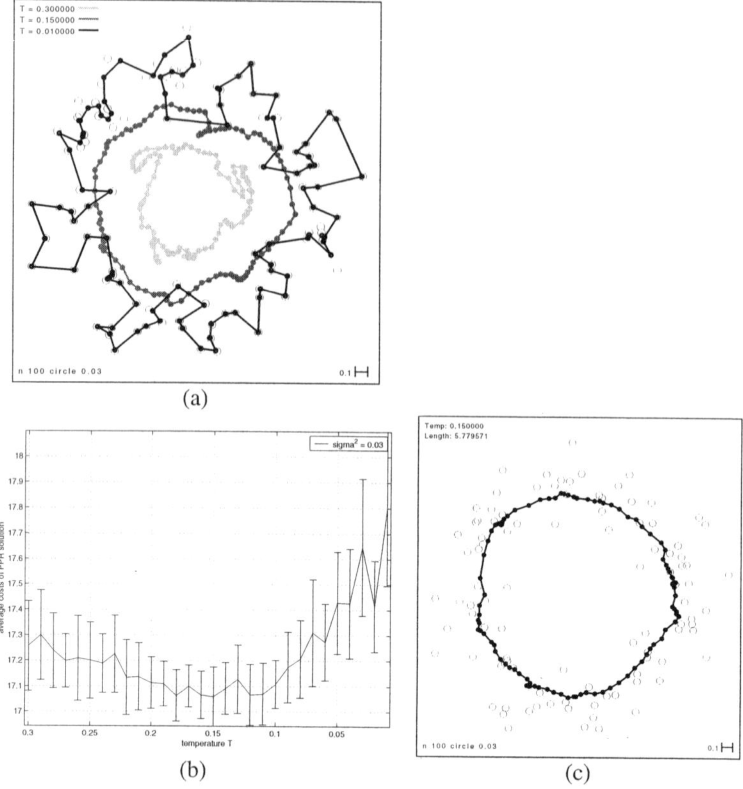

(a)

(b)　　(c)

Figure 7: **(a)** Average trajectories at different temperatures for $n = 100$ cities on a circle with $\sigma^2 = 0.03$. **(b)** Average tour length of finite horizon adapted solutions for the circle instance plotted in (a). The horizon window was $w = 5$. The average fits to noise in the data if the temperature is too low, leading to overfitting phenomena. Note that the average best solution is ≤ 16.5. **(c)** The average trajectory with the smallest average length of its finite horizon adapted solutions in (b).

mization problems.

Acknowledgement: It is a pleasure to acknowledge fruitful collaborations with Marcus Held on histogram clustering and with Mikio Braun on noisy TSP and various discussions with Volker Roth.

References

[1] Eugene Allgower and Kurt Georg. *Numerical Continuation Methods*, volume 13 of *Springer Series in Computational Mathematics*. Springer Verlag, 1990.

[2] Sanjeev Arora. Polynomial time approximation schemes for Euclidean traveling salesman and other geometric problems. *Journal of the ACM*, 45(5):753–782, 1998.

[3] G. Ausiello, P. Crescenzi, G. Gambosi, V. Kann, A. Merchetti-Spaccamela, and M. Protasi. *Complexity and Approximation*. Springer-Verlag, New York, Berlin, Heidelberg, 1999.

[4] J. Beardwood, J. H. Halton, and J. M. Hammersley. The shortest path through many points. *Proceedings of the Cambridge Philosophical Society*, 55:299–327, 1959.

[5] Mikio L. Braun and Joachim M. Buhmann. The Noisy Euclidian Traveling Salesman Problem and learning. In *Advances in Neural Information Processing System 13*, page xxx. MIT Press, 2002. (in press).

[6] Pierre Bremaud. *Markov Chains. Gibbs Fields, Monte Carlo Simulation and Queues*. Springer, New York, 1999.

[7] Joachim M. Buhmann. Data clustering and learning. In M. Arbib, editor, *Handbook of Brain Theory and Neural Networks*, pages 278–282. Bradfort Books/MIT Press, 1995.

[8] Joachim M. Buhmann and Hans Kühnel. Vector quantization with complexity costs. *IEEE Transactions on Information Theory*, 39(4):1133–1145, July 1993.

[9] Joachim M. Buhmann and Jan Puzicha. Annealing: Fast heuristics for large scale non–linear optimization. In Martin Grötschel, Sven O. Krumke, and Jörg Rambau, editors, *Online Optimization of Large Scale Systems*, pages 740–778. Springer Verlag, 2001.

[10] Joachim M. Buhmann and Jan Puzicha. Multiscale annealing and robustness: Fast heuristics for large scale non–linear optimization. In Martin Grötschel, Sven O. Krumke, and Jörg Rambau, editors, *Online Optimization of Large Scale Systems*, pages 779–802. Springer Verlag, 2001.

[11] V. Černy. Thermodynamical approach to the travelling salesman problem: an efficient simulation algorithm. *Journal of Optimization Theory and Applications*, 45:41–51, 1985.

[12] T. M. Cover and J. A. Thomas. *Elements of Information Theory*. John Wiley & Sons, New York, 1991.

[13] M. Creutz. Microcanonical monte carlo simulation. *Physical Review Letters*, 50(19):1411–1414, 1983.

[14] A. P. Dempster, N. M Laird, and D. B. Rubin. Maximum likelihood from incomplete data via the em algorithm. *J. Royal Statist. Soc. Ser. B*, 39:1–38, 1977.

[15] Richard O. Duda, Peter E. Hart, and David G. Stork. *Pattern Classification*. John Wiley & Sons, Inc., New York, 2001.

[16] T. Hofmann and J. Puzicha. Statistical models for co-occurrence data. AI–MEMO 1625, Artifical Intelligence Laboratory, Massachusetts Institute of Technology, 1998.

[17] T. Hofmann, J. Puzicha, and M.I. Jordan. Learning from dyadic data. In M. S. Kearns, S. A. Solla, and D. A. Cohn, editors, *Advances in Neural Information Processing Systems 11*. MIT Press, 1999. to appear.

[18] Thomas Hofmann and Joachim M. Buhmann. Pairwise data clustering by deterministic annealing. *IEEE Transactions on Pattern Analysis and Machine Intelligence*, 19(1):1–14, 1997.

[19] A. Jain and R. Dubes. *Algorithms for Clustering Data*. Prentice Hall, Englewood Cliffs, NJ 07632, 1988.

[20] Robert E. Kass and Paul W. Vos. *Geometric Foundations of asmptotic inference*. Wiley Interscience, New York, 1997.

[21] S. Kirkpatrick, C. Gelatt, and M. Vecchi. Optimization by simulated annealing. *Science*, 220(4598):671–680, 1983.

[22] Tamas Linder, Gabor Lugosi, and Kenneth Zeger. Rates of convergence in the source coding theorem, in empirical quantizer design, and in universal lossy source coding. *IEEE Transactions on Information Theory*, 40(6):1728–1740, 1994.

[23] F.C.N. Pereira, N.Z. Tishby, and L. Lee. Distributional clustering of english words. In *30th Annual Meeting of the Association for Computational Linguistics, Columbus, Ohio*, pages 183–190, 1993.

[24] J. Puzicha, T. Hofmann, and J.M. Buhmann. Discrete mixture models for unsupervised texture segmentation. In *Proceedings of the DAGM-Symposium Mustererkennung 1998*, pages 135–142, 1998.

[25] K. Rose, E. Gurewitz, and G. Fox. A deterministic annealing approach to clustering. *Pattern Recognition Letters*, 11:589–594, 1990.

[26] Y. Tikochinsky, N.Z. Tishby, and R. D. Levine. Alternative approach to maximum–entropy inference. *Physical Review A*, 30:2638–2644, 1984.

[27] N. Tishby, F. Pereira, and W. Bialek. The information bottleneck method. In *Proceedings of the 37-th Allerton Conference on Communication, Control and Computing*, pages 368–377. IEEE Computer Society Press, 1999.

[28] N. Tishby and N. Slonim. Data clustering by markovian relaxation and the information bottleneck method. In *Advances in Neural Information Processing Sytems*, volume 13. NIPS, 2001. to appear.

[29] Aad W. van der Vaart and Jon A. Wellner. *Weak Convergence and Empirical Processes.* Springer-Verlag, New York, Berlin, Heidelberg, 1996.

Learning high-dimensional data

Michel VERLEYSEN
Université catholique de Louvain, Microelectronics laboratory
3 place du Levant, B-1348 Louvain-la-Neuve, Belgium
e-mail: verleysen@dice.ucl.ac.be

Abstract. Observations from real-world problems are often high-dimensional vectors, i.e. made up of many variables. Learning methods, including artificial neural networks, often have difficulties to handle a relatively small number of high-dimensional data. In this paper, we show how concepts gained from our intuition on 2- and 3-dimensional data can be misleading when used in high-dimensional settings. When then show how the "curse of dimensionality" and the "empty space phenomenon" can be taken into account in the design of neural network algorithms, and how non-linear dimension reduction techniques can be used to circumvent the problem. We conclude by an illustrative example of this last method on the forecasting of financial time series.

1. Introduction

In the last few years, data analysis, or data mining, has become a specific discipline, sometimes far from its mathematical and statistical origin. Analyzing data is a real scientific job, where experience and thinking is often more valuable than using mathematical theorems and statistical criteria.

The specificity of modern data mining is that *huge* amounts of data are considered. Compared to just a few years ago, we now use daily huge databases in medical research, imaging, financial analysis, and many other domains. Not only new fields are open to data analysis, but also it becomes easier, and cheaper, to collect large amounts of data.

One of the problems related to this tremendous evolution is the fact that analyzing these data becomes more and more difficult, and requires new, more adapted techniques than those used in the past. A main concern in that direction is the *dimensionality* of data. Think of each measurement of data as one observation, each observation being composed of a set of variables. It is very different to analyze 10000 observations of 3 variables each, than analyzing 100 observations of 50 variables each! One way to get some feeling of this difficulty is to imagine each observation as a point in a space whose dimension is the number of variables. 10000 observations in a 3-dimensional space most probably form a structured shape, one or several clouds, from which it is possible to extract some relevant information, like principal directions, variances of clouds, etc. On the contrary, at first sight 100 observations in a 50-dimensional space do not represent anything specific, because the number of observations is too low. Imagine that one would like to extract information from 4 observations in a 3-dimensional space...

Nevertheless, many modern databases *have* this unpleasant characteristic. Should we conclude that nothing has to be done, and that data mining is just impossible in that situation? Of course not. First because it is the duty of scientists to invent methods adapted to real, existing problems (and not to invent unrealistic problems that "prove" the validity of their results...). Secondly because even in such situation, there *are* ways to analyze the data, to extract information and to draw conclusions from observations. The point is that the methods are different, and sometimes more related to ad-hoc but sounded algorithms than to mathematical theorems not valid in this context.

This paper makes no pretence of presenting generic solutions to this problem; the current state-of-the-art is far from that. However, we will try to convince the reader about the importance of this topic, not only in data mining, but also in function approximation, identification, forecasting, i.e. all domains where the learning abilities of artificial neural networks are exploited. We will show through a few examples how distributions of points in high-dimensional spaces can behave in a drastically different way from our intuition (mostly gained from 2- and 3-dimensional schemes). Finally, we will show how projection tools could be used, not to remove the difficulties related to high-dimensional data, but to circumvent them by working with lower-dimensional representations.

2. High-dimensional data are difficult to use

Many references dealing with the problems and difficulties related to the use of high-dimensional data exist in the scientific literature. Unfortunately, most of them are somewhat hopeless descriptions of the problems, rather than invitations to a new, fascinating challenge for 21st-century data analysts. I recently discovered the "aide-mémoire" written by David Dohonen for his lecture to the "Mathematical Challenges of the 21st Century" conference of the American Mathematical Society. Despite his lecture is not oriented (or biased...) towards artificial neural networks, the accompanying text is one of the most fascinating ones I had the opportunity to read on this topic recently [1]. The following of this section contains several ideas borrowed from Dohonen's paper.

2.1. Data

Modern data analysis deals with considerable amounts of information. Here are a few examples of domains where collecting information on a large scale opens new lines of research or exploitation.

- Medical data are now collected widely. As an example, digital imaging now makes possible the storage, and the analysis, of vast databases of radiology images. This not only helps the patient, whose medical files are better archived and forwarded between hospitals and doctors; it also contributes to a better understanding of pathologies, through the building-up and comparison of large databases of healthy and unhealthy patients. EEG recordings are another example in this context.
- Investors and traders, in the hope of discovering some helpful laws or trends, analyze financial series continuously; databases with high-frequency values of financial indices are now publicly available.

- All purchases made by credit or payment card are now stored in order to analyze the customer's habits; this helps to the detection of credit card fraud, but also to identify the consumers habits and to target commercial campaigns...

Of course, this list is far from being exhaustive. It serves only to make clear that we are now dealing with *huge* databases, and that elements (or *observations*) in these databases may take different form: scalar values (a single financial index), vectors (simultaneous recording of 40 EEG signals), images, etc.

2.2. Size of data

What we mean by "huge databases" is the fact that many observations are collected. But what about the size of these observations? In other words, how many variables are typically gathered in a single observation? The above examples show a wide variety of answers from one or a few to hundreds or thousands: when an observation is an image, each image is a point in a space whose dimension is the number of pixels! In general, a database has n lines and d columns, where n is the number of observations (which can increase over time) and d is the number of observed variables.

What makes modern data analysis different from traditional mathematical statistics is the fact that we are dealing with very different values for n and d. In addition to larger values, it is the relation between n and d that differs the most sensibly. Think for example to PCA (Principal Component Analysis). Most textbooks explain PCA as a technique to find directions in a cloud of points, and illustrate the method on a 2-dimensional figure with several hundreds of points (thus n = several hundreds, and $d = 2$). But PCA is evenly used in face identification tasks [2] where an observation is an image (d = several hundreds) and the database only contains a few observations! Traditional mathematical statistics is clearly oriented towards situations where $n >> d$. Worst, some results and tools are derived from asymptotic situations where $n \rightarrow \infty$ with d fixed, while in reality we could have d increasing with n fixed!

One of the reasons of increasing d can also be the lack of information about the usefulness of variables. Think for example to the prediction of financial data. It is easy to imagine that the fluctuations of a specific share are largely influenced by the recent fluctuations of stock markets. Using current values of several stock markets as exogenous input variables to a forecasting method, whose output is the share value to predict, is then a standard way of working. Unfortunately, we do not know which stock market (or other...) indices to use, so we are tempted to use as many of them as possible! This increases d (for n fixed), which is non-traditional in terms of statistical analysis.

Another reason why modern data analysis differs from traditional statistics is that in the latter, many nice results make the assumption that data are samples from multivariate normal distributions. As a consequence, tools from linear algebra may be used, and strongly simplify some computations. However, except in some specific situations, multivariate normal distributions are far from being natural; when the dimension d of the space is large, this is further reinforced by the fact that even the central limit theorem cannot be used because of a too small number n of samples (with respect to d).

Data analysis, and other tasks performed by neural networks, must be considered on the "engineering" point of view: we must work with the data we have, with their dimensionality, and adapt the methods we use to their characteristics. Even if it seems hard at first glance!

Up to now, we intentionally did not discuss a lot about artificial neural networks. Indeed when speaking about high dimensions, most of the problems do not come from the use of neural networks, nor from any other competing method. The problems are related to the nature itself of the data: using neural networks or other methods does not change anything. The type of task to achieve is not crucial either: whatever we speak about function approximation, clustering, classification, or (self-)organization of data, we always face the same difficulties if we have a rather small number of high-dimensional data available for learning. Nevertheless, we will try to show in the following that we can take advantage from some neural network techniques to fight successfully against the difficulties related to high-dimensional data.

2.3. The curse of dimensionality

According to [1], Richard Bellman probably invented the phrase "the curse of dimensionality" [3]. Bellman discussed the simple problem of optimizing a function of a few dozens of variables, by exhaustive search in the function domain. If we consider a function defined on the unit cube in dimension d, and if ten discrete points are considered in each dimension, we need 10^d evaluations of the function, which is computationally prohibitive even for moderate d; Bellman used this argument to suggest dynamic programming instead of exhaustive search for function optimization.

More specifically, according to [1], the curse of dimensionality may be seen as follows: in function approximation and optimization, without assumption on the function of d variables to approximate or optimize, we need order $(1/\varepsilon)^d$ evaluations of the function on a grid to obtain an approximation (respectively optimization) with error ε.

We will see in the following that a way to circumvent the curse of dimensionality is to make assumptions on the function to approximate (or to optimize). More specifically, let us have a look again to the problem of forecasting the value of a share, using its past values and stock market indexes as exogenous input variables. As we do not know exactly which exogenous variables we have to use, a conservative way is to use many of them, leading to a high-dimensional problem. Nevertheless, all variables used are not independent one from another: there *is* an influence from each stock market index on all other ones. The information contained in the set of exogenous variables if thus redundant, the problem being that we do not know the characteristics of this redundancy. But the consequence of this is that some of the variables of the input space are dependent from other variables; even if we are in a d-dimensional input space, the points could thus be situated on a m-dimensional surface or submanifold, with $m < d$. The real dimensionality of the problem is m, even if a d-dimensional space is used. In the following, we will see that this concept is related to the *intrinsic* dimensionality of the data, and we will extensively use this property in order to circumvent the curse of dimensionality.

For the sake of completeness, we have to mention that other types of assumptions are also possible. For example, a famous result from Barron [4] shows that it is possible to approximate a function with a rate that is independent from the dimension, provided some specific assumptions about the function itself are met. While this and other results are of importance when dealing with the curse of dimensionality, we concentrate in this paper on assumptions made on data rather than on the function to approximate.

Finally, it is also important to mention that high-dimensional spaces also have their advantages. Donoho [1] mentions a few "blessings of dimensionality" that can be exploited when working with high-dimensional data. The blessings include the so-called "concentration of measure" (the variance of any measure –distance, norm– remains fixed while its norm increases with the dimension of the space), and asymptotic results that can be derived when the dimension increases to infinity.

3. Surprising results in high-dimensional spaces

Intuitive comments in the previous section showed that more learning points are needed in higher-dimensional settings. But two questions arise at this stage:
- what is the limit between low- and high-dimensional spaces?
- what is the number of points required for learning in high-dimensional spaces?

The following subsections give some elements of information about these two questions.

3.1. Limit between low- and high-dimensional data

Textbooks and scientific articles illustrate learning methods and other data analysis tools on one-, two- or three-dimensional examples, and measure their performances on higher-dimensional problems for which no representation is possible. It is also widely accepted that most real-world problems are high-dimensional ones. But where is the limit between small and high dimension?

To answer to this question, let us take a few examples of concepts that are both intuitive in dimensions up to 3 and expandable to larger ones. The dimension where our intuitive view is not valid anymore is the answer to our question.

Scott and Thompson [5] first noticed the problems related to data in high dimensions, and called them "empty space phenomenon".

Consider the volume of a sphere in dimension d. This volume is given by

$$V(d) = \frac{\pi^{d/2}}{\Gamma(d/2+1)} r^d \tag{1}$$

where r is the radius, or equivalently by the recurrence equation

$$V(d) = V(d-2)\frac{\pi}{d-2} r^2 \tag{2}$$

with $V(1) = 2$ and $V(2) = \pi$. Looking at the graph of $V(d)$ when $r = 1$ (Figure 1) leads to the surprising observation that the volume rapidly decreases towards 0 when d increases!

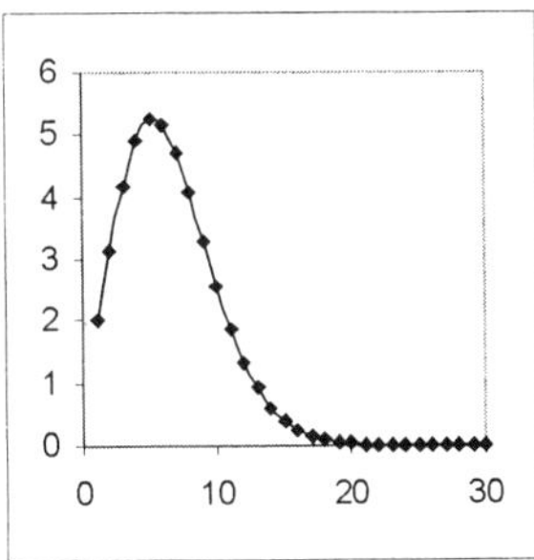

Figure 1: volume of the sphere (radius = 1) versus the dimension of the space.

Figure 1 is the standard graph found in the literature to illustrate the volume of the sphere. Nevertheless, it must be reminded that our intention here is to show that our intuitive view of the volume of a sphere is misleading in high dimension. We should thus compare this volume to a value that seems "natural" to us. One way to do this is to plot the ratio between the volume of a sphere and the volume of a cube (with edge length equal to the diameter of the sphere). Figure 2 shows this ratio.

Having in mind a segment, a circle and a sphere respectively in dimension one, two and three, we understand that the ratio illustrated in Figure 2 will decrease with the dimension of the sphere. What is more surprising is that this ratio is below 10% when the dimension is as low as 6!

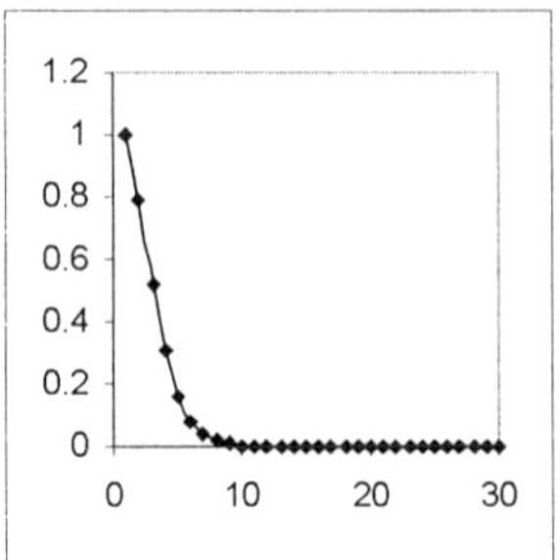

Figure 2: ratio between the volume of a sphere and the volume of a cube (length of an edge equal to the diameter of the sphere) versus the dimension of the space.

Another way to consider this problem is to plot (Figure 3) the ratio between the volume of a sphere with radius 0.9 and a sphere with radius 1, versus the dimension. Obviously, this ratio is equal to 0.9 raised to the power d. The values plotted in Figure 3 mean that 90% of the volume of a sphere in dimension greater than 20 is contained in the spherical shell whose thickness is 10% of the initial radius!

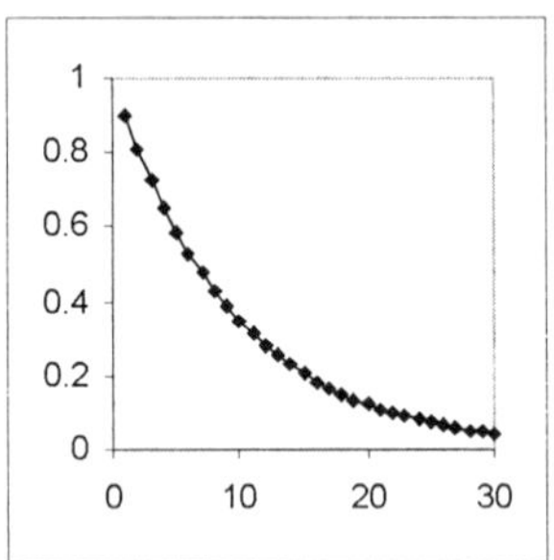

Figure 3: ratio between the volume of a sphere with radius 0.9 and the volume of a sphere with radius 1, versus the dimension of the space.

Another comment concerns Gaussian functions in high dimensions. We will see in the following of this paper that we advocate the use of Gaussian kernels as function approximators (Radial-Basis Function Networks with Gaussian kernels). But what is a Gaussian function in high dimension? Intuitively Gaussian functions are used for their local properties: most of the integral the function is contained in a limited volume around its centre. It is well known that 90% of the samples of a normalized scalar Gaussian distribution fall statistically in the interval [-1.65, 1.65]. What is less obvious is that this percentage rapidly decreases to 0 with the dimension of the space! Figure 4 shows the percentage of samples of a Gaussian distribution falling in the sphere of radius 1.65, versus the dimension of the space. In dimension 10 already this percentage is below 1%!

In other words, when the dimension increases, most of the volume of a Gaussian function is contained in the tails instead of near the centre! This suggests that a Gaussian function could not be appropriate in high dimensions, at least regarding the local character mentioned above. A solution could be to use super-Gaussian functions, as for example the kernels considered in [6].

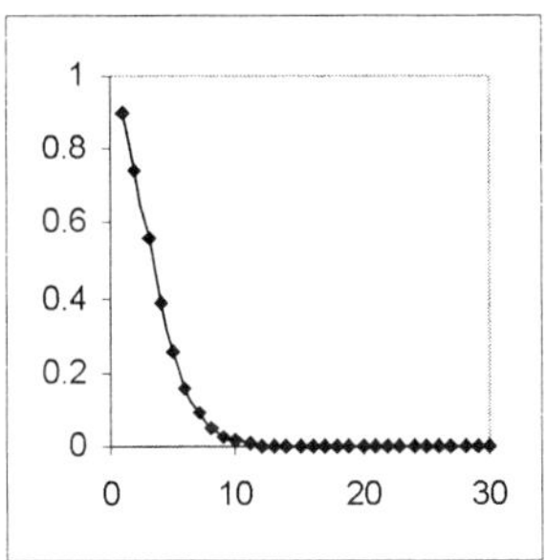

Figure 4: percentage of samples from a Gaussian distribution falling in the sphere of radius 1.65, versus the dimension of the space.

3.2. Number of learning points in high-dimensional settings

Our discussion about the problems related to high dimensions is also intended to point out to the necessity for many samples (and even more...) when the dimension increases. It is difficult to tackle the problem of finding the number of samples required to reach a predefined level of precision in approximation tasks. The reason is that results tackling levels of precision in approximation tasks are usually rather theoretical ones, derived from asymptotic developments where the number of samples tends to infinity.

Intuitively, we understand that this number could increase exponentially with the dimension of the space. Reminding Bellman's argument cited in the previous section, we note that if 10 learning points are necessary to obtain a defined precision in a scalar function approximation problem (i.e. if 10 discrete learning points are considered), the same level of precision would require 10^d learning points in a d-dimensional setting.

As an example, Silverman [7] addressed the problem of finding the required number of samples for a specific problem in the context of the approximation of a Gaussian distribution with fixed Gaussian kernels. Silverman's results are summarized in Figure 5.

Silverman's results can be approximated by [6]

$$\log_{10}N(d) \cong 0.6(d - 0.25).$$

(3)

In practice, any data set that does not grow exponentially with the dimension of the space will be referred to as *small*, or conversely, the dimension will be said to be *large*.

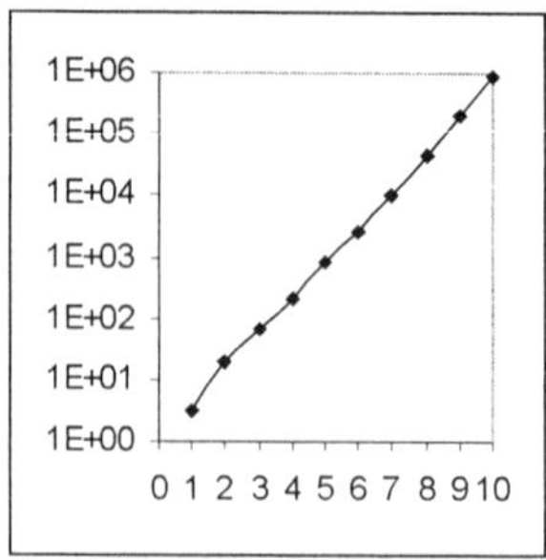

Figure 5: Number of samples required to approximate a Gaussian distribution with fixed Gaussian kernels, with an approximate error of about 10% (according to [6]), versus the dimension of the space.

This section will be concluded by an important comment. The above discussion could make the reader think that one never has enough samples in high dimension. Consider indeed a problem where 10 samples would be required in dimension 1 and 100 in dimension 2 (imagine a segment and a square "filled" by respectively 10 and 100 samples). This would mean that 10^{10} and 10^{20} samples would be required in dimensions 10 and 20 respectively! This is obviously impossible in real-world problems (while dimensions much greater than 20 are common). Having (apparently) too few points for an efficient learning is called the "empty space phenomenon".

Fortunately, as already mentioned in the previous section, it appears that real-world problem do not suffer so severely from the "curse of dimensionality" problem (while its importance should not be neglected tough). This is simply due to the fact that in most situations, data are located near a manifold of dimension m smaller than d. Reducing the dimension of the data to a smaller value than d, in order to decrease the problems related to high dimensions, is a key issue in high-dimensional data learning.

3.3. Concentration of measure phenomenon

While this is not directly related to the two questions introducing this section, the "concentration of measure phenomenon" must be mentioned here, as another surprising result in high-dimensional spaces. Donoho [1] mentions this phenomenon in his list "blessings of dimensionality", meaning that advantage could be gained from it. We prefer to report this phenomenon as something that the data analyst should be aware of, in order to benefit from its advantages but also to take care of its drawbacks.

The "concentration of measure" phenomenon means that, under soft conditions on the distribution of samples (uniform distribution is thus not required), the variance of any measure -distance, norm- remains fixed while its average increases with the dimension of the space. In particular, the standard deviation of the Euclidean norm of samples in a set remains almost constant when the dimension d of the space increases (for large dimensions). Naturally, the average Euclidean norm of the samples increases with the square root of the dimension d; the consequence of this is that, in large dimensions, the samples seem to be normalized (see [8] for a proof of this phenomenon in the case of the Euclidean norm). We will see in the next section that the "concentration of measure phenomenon" must be taken seriously into account when dealing with artificial neural networks.

4. Local artificial neural networks

4.1. Local versus global models

Learning is the way to adapt parameters in a model, in function of known examples. *Learning* is the term used in the neural network community, while researchers in identification speak about *estimation*.

The literature often uses the term *local learning* for methods using combinations of local functions, as opposed to combinations of functions that span the whole input space. For example, RBFN (Radial-Basis Functions) networks use Gaussian functions which are considered as local since they rapidly vanish when the distance from their centres increases; RBFN networks are referred to as local. On the contrary, MLP (Multi-Layer Perceptrons) networks use sigmoid functions or hyperbolic tangents, which never vanish; MLP are referred to as global.

There is a tradition in the literature to consider that local models are less adapted to large-dimensional spaces than global ones. The reason for this is the empty space phenomenon. It has been shown intuitively in the previous section that the number of samples required for learning grows exponentially with the dimension of the space. This corresponds to our intuitive view of "filling" a space with local functions like Gaussian ones: if it is assumed that a Gaussian function corresponds to a fixed volume in the space, "filling" a distribution means to juxtapose a number of Gaussian functions proportional to the volume spanned by the distribution.

On the contrary, there is also a tradition in the literature to consider that global models do not have this limitation. Sigmoids (for example) span the whole input space, so it is assumed that a lower number of sigmoids is needed to fill the volume spanned by a distribution. We are convinced that this view of the problem is not correct; the following paragraphs explain three arguments in this direction.

First, it must be reminded that neural networks are interpolation tools, aimed to generalize information gathered on known data to other locations in the space. Interpolation means that we must have sufficient information in the surroundings of a point in order to interpolate at that point. Look for example at Figure 6. Both the plain and dashed lines are good approximators (interpolators) of the learning data (8 markers on the figure), while they are based on different assumptions (models) on the data. However, despite the fact that learning data range from $x = 0.5$ to $x = 1.7$, the plain and dashed lines give very different approximations around the value $x = 1$; in this case, we speak about extrapolation instead of interpolation. Of course, the example in Figure 6 is obvious, and should not even be commented. Nevertheless, we remind that our point is to show the difficulties of learning in high-dimensional spaces. To imagine how a distribution looks in high dimension, and in particular if the space is "filled" with data or not, is not obvious at all. Filling the space is related both to the density of points in the distribution, and to its convexity. In most situations, it is quite impossible to decide if we have to speak about interpolation or extrapolation.

Having this in mind, it is now clear that interpolation can be achieved only in regions of the space where there are "enough" data to interpolate; the words "richness of data" are sometimes used to define this concept. Even if the approximation function itself spans the whole space (for example in the case of sigmoids), interpolation has no sense in empty regions. The argument that sigmoids span a larger region than Gaussian functions is thus meaningless. Furthermore, the "lack of response" (more precisely outputs near to zero) of combinations of local functions in empty regions of the space could be used to appreciate the fact that there is not enough data to interpolate correctly.

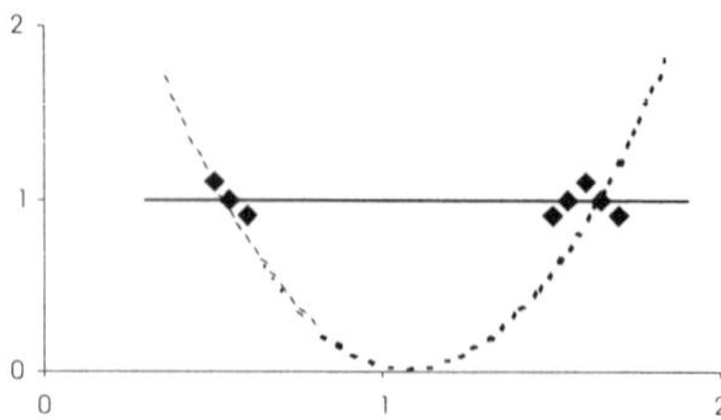

Figure 6: interpolation when the distribution of data is not convex. Plain and dashed lines are good interpolators of learning points, but extrapolate differently around $x = 1$.

The second argument is better explained by simple graphs. It must be reminded that neural network approximators, like MLP and RBFN, work by fitting a combination of sigmoid-like or Gaussian functions to the data to be approximated. Let us consider for simplicity that these combinations are linear. Figure 7 shows that the simple sum of two sigmoids looks like a Gaussian (weights, i.e. multiplying coefficients of the sigmoid in the sum, and thresholds have been chosen appropriately). In most situations when using a MLP, a phenomenon similar to this one will happen. Multiplying coefficients will adjust so that each region of the space is approximated by a weighted sum of a few basis functions (sigmoids). Naturally, since a sigmoid spans the whole space, the sigmoids used in the approximation in a region of the space will influence the approximation function in other regions. Nevertheless, another sigmoid easily cancels this influence, and so on.

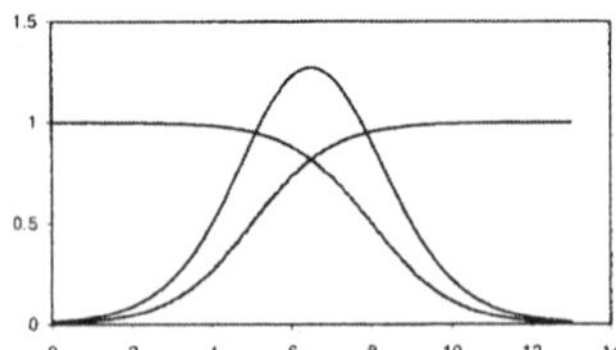

Figure 7: a weighted sum of sigmoids looks like a Gaussian function.

This phenomenon is common in MLPs, and is easily observed in small dimension with a limited number of sigmoids. The verification of this argument in large dimension and in a wide range of applications is a topic for further research.

The third argument is in the same range as the second one. It seems "natural" to think that approximation by a sum of local functions will lead to local functions having approximately identical widths (standard deviation in case of Gaussian functions), and positive weights (multiplying factors); let us just imagine how a set of Gaussian functions could be combined to fill a uniform distribution in a compact region of the space. However, except in some specific situations, it can be shown that this is not the case in practical applications. In particular, we can see that weights are often set to negative values, but also that widths are sometimes set to very large values (compared with the pairwise distance between adjacent kernels), making the contribution of this kernel to the approximation function very flat. Again, this argument reinforces the idea that local and global basis functions are not much different when they are combined to contribute to an approximation function in a high-dimensional space.

4.2. What makes high-dimensional data learning with ANN difficult?

Artificial neural networks compute a function of their input vector; through the weights, this function is adapted to the problem to solve. Most of the functions involved in ANN models begin by computing some *distances* between the input vector and weights vectors. For example:

- Radial-Basis Function Networks (RBFN) compute sums of Gaussian functions whose argument is the *Euclidean norm* of the difference between the input vector and weight vectors;
- Vector quantization (VQ) methods and Kohonen self-organizing maps (SOM) also use the *Euclidean norm* of the difference between the input vector and so-called centroids (weight vectors) to select the winner;
- the first layer of Multi-Layer Perceptrons (MLP) takes the *scalar product* (another distance measure) between the input vector and weight vectors as argument to each non-linear function;
- etc.

It has been shown above that a consequence of the "concentration of measure" phenomenon is that the norm of all vectors seems to be constant in high-dimensional spaces. This result is therefore valid form the Euclidean norm of the difference between any two vectors, and also for the scalar product! Consequently, the input argument to the functions involved in neural networks becomes a constant, and does not depend anymore... from the inputs themselves! Of course, this argument is exaggerated; the consequence of the concentration of measure phenomenon is that all norms *concentrate* around their mean, not *are equal to*. Furthermore, we have no measure on *how much* they concentrate round their mean; we do not know from which dimension this phenomenon must be taken into account. Nevertheless, it is clear that for high-dimensional input vectors, the phenomenon must be taken into account, and appropriate measures taken in the learning itself. The following subsection gives two examples on how the functions involved in artificial neural networks could be modified to take this phenomenon into account.

4.3. Changing distance measures in neural networks

Simple changes in artificial neural network paradigms may help to reduce the problems related to high-dimensional vectors. Again, it is difficult to measure how much such changes help to overcome the problems; but experiences show that they help, sometimes considerably. Assessing the benefits, measuring them in an objective way, and suggesting other modifications in the same spirit is a topic for further research.

Let us take the example of Radial-Basis Function Networks (RBFN), defined by equation (4):

$$f(x) = \sum_{j=1}^{P} w_j \, exp\left(-\frac{\|x - c_j\|^2}{h_j^2} \right), \qquad (4)$$

where x is the input vector to the RBFN, c_j are to so-called centroids, h_j their widths, and w_j multiplying weights. Equation (4) defines a weighted sum of Gaussian functions centered on c_j, with standard deviations proportional to h_j.

The rationale behind the use of Gaussian functions is the fact that they are local, i.e. each function is fitted according to the learning points x that are *close* from c_j, and the function vanishes for inputs *far* from c_j.

It has been shown in the previous section that Gaussian functions in high-dimensional settings do not follow this intuitive view. In dimension as low as five, 75% of the surface beneath the Gaussian function is further away than the traditional 1.65 times standard deviation radius!

In order to overcome this problem (i.e. to make Gaussian functions in high-dimensional spaces *look like* scalar ones), it is suggested to replace the exponent 2 in equation (4) by a larger exponent g:

$$f(x) = \sum_{j=1}^{P} w_j \, exp\left(-\frac{\|x - c_j\|^g}{h_j^g} \right). \tag{5}$$

The descending slope of the local function is now accentuated, so that a larger part of the surface beneath the function is concentrated near its center. The local functions used in (5) are called "super-Gaussian functions"; reference [6] shows an example of how parameter g can be evaluated, in the context of density estimation.

Another possibility to modify equation (4) is to replace the Euclidean norm by a higher-order one, defined by

$$norm_h\left(x - c_j\right) = \sqrt[h]{\sum_{i=1}^{d} \left|x_i - c_{ji}\right|^h} \; ; \tag{6}$$

$h = 2$ gives the standard Euclidean norm. It may be shown on examples that using $h > 2$ diminishes the importance of the "concentration of measure" phenomenon, one of the problems encountered with high-dimensional functions. Intuitively, one understands that larger h should be chosen for higher-dimensional spaces; however, it seems that there is still no theoretical result giving an estimation of the value of h that should be chosen in a specific situation; again this is a topic for further research.

The two suggestions above are only examples of what could be done in high-dimensional settings. Similarly, one could think to replace the scalar product between the input and the weight vectors by another distance measure in Multi-Layer Perceptrons, or to use a higher-order distance in the selection of the winner, in the context of Vector Quantization and Self-Organizing Maps.

5. Intrinsic dimension of data

5.1. Redundancy and intrinsic dimension

Despite all efforts that could be undertaken, learning high-dimensional data remains difficult. For this reason, each learning task should begin by an attempt to *reduce the dimension of the data*. In a previous section, it was argued that data in real problems often lie on or near submanifolds of the input space, because of the redundancy between variables. While redundancy if often a consequence of the lack of information about which type of input variable should be used, it is also helpful in the case where a large amount of noise is unavoidable on the data, coming for example from measures on physical phenomena. To be convinced of this positive remark, let us just imagine that the *same* physical quantity is measured by 100 sensors, each of them adding independent Gaussian noise to the measurement; averaging the 100 measures will strongly decrease the influence of noise on the measure!　The same concept applies if m quantities are measured by n sensors, with $n > m$.

Before thinking to reduce the dimension of the data, one should know how much the variables are redundant.　Let us have a look to Figure 8, which shows the well-known "horseshoe" distribution in a 3-dimensional space.　Looking to the set of data, we are convinced that we should project it on a 2-dimensional surface in order to reduce the dimension.　Two is the number of *degrees of freedom* of the variables in the set, more commonly named the *intrinsic dimension* of the data.

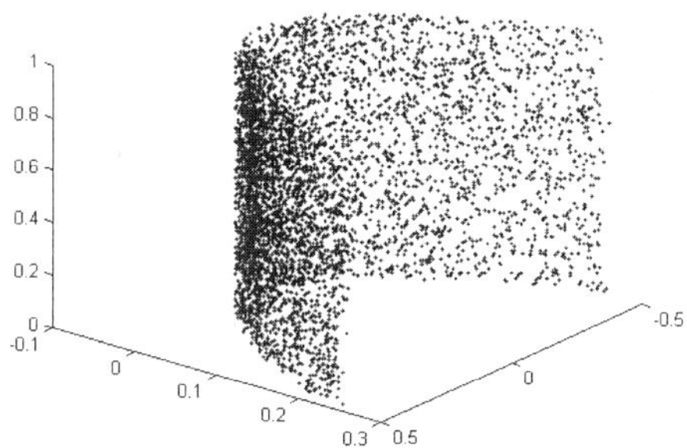

Figure 8. Horseshoe 3-dimensional distribution.

Estimating the intrinsic dimension of data may be a hard task.　First, unlike the distribution in Figure 8, real distributions have varying intrinsic dimensions.　The intrinsic dimension is thus a local concept, and any attempt to project the data should be made on a local basis too.

Secondly, the most used method in statistics to estimate the number of relevant variables is PCA (Principal Component Analysis); note that PCA is a projection method, but that the number of relevant variables may be found by looking to the eigenvalues of the covariance matrix of the data.　Nevertheless, the PCA is a *linear* projection method; this means that PCA will perfectly work when the submanifold is a (hyper-)plane, but that it will fail in all other cases, including the example in Figure 8.

We advocate the use of two types of methods to find the intrinsic dimension of data.

5.2. Box counting methods

Let us recall that the volume of a d-dimensional cube is proportional to r^d, where r is edge of the cube.　If we can make the hypothesis that the local density of points is constant over regions of "sufficient" size, the number of points contained in such a cube will be proportional to r^d if the data "fill" the space.　However, if the intrinsic dimension of the data is m, with $m < d$, this number of points will be proportional to r^m.　Imagine for example a 2-D surface in a 3-D space: any 3-D cube of increasing edge will contain a number of points growing with the square of the edge length, provided that the intersection of the cube with the distribution is approximately plane.　A graph of the logarithm of the number of points contained in such a cube versus the logarithm of its edge length will thus have a slope equal to the local intrinsic dimensionality.

The estimation of the local dimensionality at each sample of the input space obviously requires the computation of the mutual distance between any pair of points, which is computationally cumbersome when the dataset is large. Conversely, when the dataset is small, the condition of constant density over "sufficiently large" regions of the space is seldom achieved.

An easier method to implement is the so-called box-counting method [8], based on the following principle. The d-dimensional input space is divided into d-boxes of decreasing size. When the size of the box will be small compared to distance between neighbouring points in the dataset, the number of non-empty boxes will be proportional to r^{-m} where r is the length of an edge. For example, the number of boxes intersecting a 1-D string in a 3-D space is roughly equal to the length of the string divided by r, while the number of boxes intersecting a 2-D surface in a 3-D space is roughly equal to the area of the surface divided by r^2. A graph of the logarithm of the number of non-empty boxes versus the logarithm of the inverse of r will thus have a slope equal to the intrinsic dimensionality.

The Grassberger-Procaccia method [9] is similar to the box-counting procedure while different in its implementation. In the Grassberger-Procaccia method, all distances between any pair of points are computed. The method then leads to a global intrinsic dimensionality (instead of a local one). However, the advantage is that N points give $N(N-1)/2$ mutual distances, so that the number of points necessary to have an acceptable estimation of the intrinsic dimension is lower than in the box-counting method.

While the box-counting method is probably more convenient to implement than the Grassberger-Procaccia one, it suffers from two drawbacks in practice. First, when the intrinsic dimension is smaller than the dimension of the space (which is usually the case when the goal is to estimate the intrinsic dimension!), the number of empty boxes dramatically increases, leading to an inefficient computational load. Secondly, the local character of the intrinsic dimension is only preserved when the largest of the boxes considered in the method is small enough to keep the constant density hypothesis valid (this makes the first drawback even worse).

Figure 9 shows the box-counting method applied to the intrinsic dimension estimation of a 1-D string in a 2-D space (from [8]).

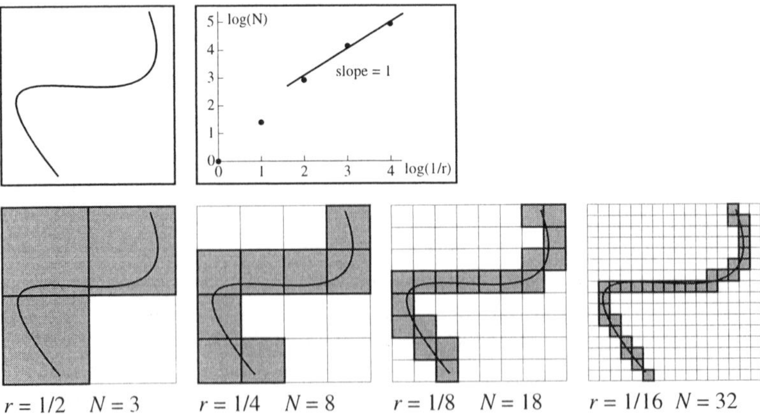

Figure 9: intrinsic dimension estimation of a 1-D string in a 2-D space by the box-counting method (from [8]).

5.3. A posteriori dimension estimation

We consider a second way to estimate the intrinsic dimension of a dataset. In most situations, the information about the intrinsic dimension is required for a further projection of the data space onto a smaller dimensional one. Contrary to PCA, nonlinear projection methods require determining the dimension of the projection space before computing the projection itself.

A simple idea is then to try the projection for several dimensions of the projection space, and to evaluate the results. Projections onto spaces of higher dimension than the intrinsic one will be "good", in the sense that the projection will be nearly bijective. Projections onto space of smaller dimension than the intrinsic one will be "bad", in the sense that points far from each other in the input space will be eventually projected to the same or similar locations in the projection space.

This method presents two major difficulties. First, it is clear that it will be computationally intensive, since the projection method itself must be considered for several dimensions of the projection space, rather than once. Secondly, an appropriate criterion must be defined to evaluate the quality of the projection; furthermore, even with an adequate criterion, the limit between "good" and "bad" projections may be difficult to set in practical situations.

Nevertheless, it has a strong advantage. As written above, the knowledge of the intrinsic dimension is often a prerequisite for a further projection of the data. Linking the measure of the intrinsic dimension to the projection makes sure that the right dimension measure is evaluated. Indeed, the reader noticed that we purposely did not give any clear definition of the concept of intrinsic dimension. The reason is that the definition is related to its measure, so that nothing prevents us to find different results when using the box-counting, Grassberger-Procaccia or any other method!

A further refinement of the *a posteriori* method is to remember that the non-linear projection itself serves as preprocessing to a learning task (function estimation, classification, etc.). Why not then simply try several dimensions for the non-linear projection, then perform the learning task on *each* result (with appropriate cross-validation methods), and finally select the dimension which gives the best result? In fact, this is the ultimate method, since it makes no assumption on any intermediate result (intrinsic dimension, projected distribution, etc.) but directly measures the result of the whole process. Nevertheless, of course, the computational load is dramatically increased. Despite its drawbacks, this last method should be considered in difficult situations, for example when the number of points is low, or when other measures of the intrinsic dimension do not give clear results.

6. Non-linear projection

When the fractal dimension m of the data is known (possibly as a local indicator rather than a global one), it should be possible to project the data from a d-dimensional space to a m-dimensional one: the data in Figure 9 could be projected from a 2-dimensional space to a 1-dimensional one, and those in Figure 8 from a 3-dimensional space to a 2-dimensional one. However, as the data in these figures and in most real situations are concentrated around a submanifold but *not* around a hyperplane, linear techniques like PCA (Principal Component Analysis) cannot be used. This is not good news; PCA is easy to use, gives straightforward and unique results, and does not suffer too much from numerical problems if some precautions are taken. Unfortunately, in our context, PCA is rarely sufficient. This does not mean that PCA is not useful. When handling real data in high-dimensional spaces, it often happens that *some* variables are correlated to others. The use of PCA can be useful to make a first projection, and already reduce sometimes significantly the number of variables. For example, the data from Figure 8 could be the result of the projection to a 3-dimensional space of 4-dimensional data, where the fourth one was a linear combination of the three first ones. But projection to a 2-dimensional space is not possible by PCA in this case.

Non-linear projection is a hot topic. Despite the fact that some methods are known from many years now, the recent needs in data analysis techniques considerably raised the interest towards non-linear projection. A lot of tools or algorithms that can be used for nonlinear dimension reduction exist in the literature. It is not our intention here to make an exhaustive review of these techniques. Some are used in data analysis, some in statistics, some in the neural network community, or in other areas, and it is difficult to compare them objectively in general situations. We have to remind that, unlike linear methods such as PCA, nonlinear methods suffer from two difficulties concerning the evaluation of their performances:

1. nonlinear methods are usually adaptive and/or iterative; this means that parameters (strongly) influence the convergence of the algorithm. Making a method obtaining good results is thus often a question of efforts devoted to parameter tuning. Of course, a primary objective in designing the methods themselves is to make them as insensitive as possible to all parameters. Nevertheless, some sensitivity still remains in most cases.
2. Quality criterions are not so obvious as in linear cases. As described in a previous section, Euclidean distance measures may loose their meaning in high dimensions. Furthermore, most standard correlation criteria are based on second-order relationships; they are thus adapted to measure linear projections, but not non-linear ones.

In the following, we will briefly mention two types of methods used for dimension reduction: Kohonen maps on one side, and Multi-Dimensional Scaling – Sammon's mapping – Curvilinear Component Analysis on the other side. The first type is known in the neural network field, while the second one is mostly known is statistics.

6.1. Kohonen maps

Everybody working with neural networks knows Kohonen Self-Organizing Maps (SOM) [10] as an efficient clustering, quantization, classification and visualization tool; few authors however use it as a dimension reduction tool. Nevertheless the use of the SOM algorithm in that purpose is extremely simple, and may be efficient in some situations. Figure 10 shows a rectangular SOM after convergence on a horseshoe-shaped distribution similar to Figure 8.

The projection consists in using the 2-dimensional index of the centroids on the grid rather than their 3-dimensional coordinates. Of course, this projection is discrete (there is a finite number of centroids); simple (linear or polynomial) interpolation between adjacent centroids however makes this projection continuous.

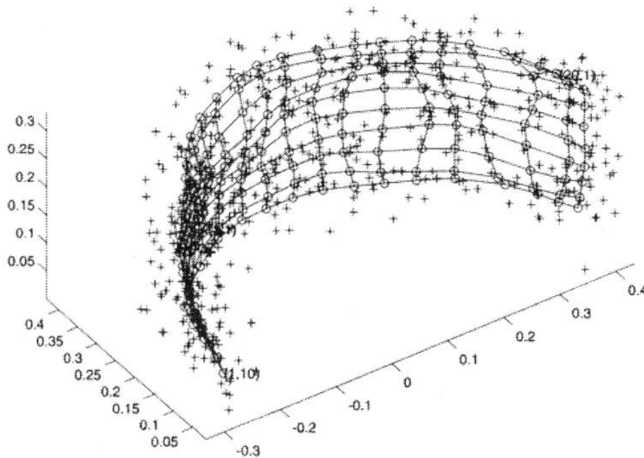

Figure 10: Horseshoe distribution and resulting Kohonen map. From [11].

Two comments must be done about the use of SOM as a non-linear projection method.

- Almost all applications of Kohonen maps in the literature use 2-dimensional grids; only a few ones use 1-dimensional strings, and even less use 3- or more-dimensional meshes. This is clearly a limitation, as it cannot be expected that real data will have an intrinsic dimension less than three… Nevertheless, on a theoretical point of view, nothing prevents us to use 3- or more-dimensional meshes; the convergence of the SOM algorithm faced to the empty space phenomenon in larger-dimensional spaces is however an unanswered question.

- The SOM algorithm is designed to preserve the *topology* between the input and grid spaces; in other words, to input points close one from another will be projected on the same or on close centroids. Nevertheless, the SOM algorithm does not preserve *distances*: there is no relation between the distance between two points in the input space and the distance between the corresponding centroids.

In theory, the last comment is not a limitation. Indeed, what we are looking for with (non-linear) projection, is that discrimination between different data remains possible: two different data in the input space must not be projected to the same location in the output space. In other words, the projection must be bijective. The topology preservation property of the SOM is a way to increase the smoothness of the projection (therefore to facilitate its design). But distance preservation is not strictly necessary!

6.2. Multi-dimensional scaling, Sammon's mapping and Curvilinear Component Analysis

Despite this last comment, many authors prefer to use tools designed to preserve the distances between the input and projection spaces. Our opinion is that the use of these methods is often preferred because of the traditional limitation of Kohonen maps to 2-dimensional grids, rather than the distance-preservation property.

Multi-dimensional scaling [12-13], Sammon's mapping [14] and Curvilinear Component Analysis [15] are methods based on the same principle: if we have n data points in a d-dimensional space, they try to place n points in the m-dimensional projection space, keeping the mutual distances between any pair of points unchanged between the input space and the corresponding pair in the projection space. Of course, having this condition strictly fulfilled is impossible in the generic case (there are $n(n-1)$ conditions to satisfy with nm degrees of freedom); the methods then weight the conditions so that those on shorter distances must be satisfied more strictly than those on large distances. Weighting aims at conserving a local topology (locally, sets of input points will resemble sets of output points).

In the case of nonlinear Multi-Dimensional Scaling (MDS) [12-13], the objective function is simply the ratio of the input distances by the output distances, weighted in such a way that small output distances are more important than large ones.

Sammon's mapping [14] is similar to MDS. However, the objective function is now a mean square error of the differences between distances (between pairs of samples) in the input and output spaces. Contrary to MDS, weighting is done with respect to input distances in Sammon's mapping.

Curvilinear Component Analysis (CCA) [15] also measures the mean square error between distances. But contrary to Sammon's mapping, weighting is done with respect to distances in the projection space.

Dematines claims that this modification enhances the quality of the projection in many situations; our own experience with these algorithms confirms this claim. Another difference is that CCA does not use the n original points, but a smaller number k of centroids obtained after vector quantization of the input space. This decreases the amount of computations, but also facilitates the convergence of the algorithm because the quantization removes the noise on the data to some extend. Nevertheless, the CCA method still suffers from the difficulty to choose the crucial adaptation parameters of the algorithm, and from bad unfolding of difficult databases (for example those where some cutting is necessary to unfold the submanifold). [16] explains how some of these drawbacks can be avoided. Without going into the details of the choice of the adaptation parameters, the CCA method consists in the optimization of criterion

$$E = \sum_{i=1}^{k} \sum_{j=1}^{k} \left(X_{ij} - Y_{ij}\right)^2 F\left(Y_{ij}, \lambda\right), \tag{7}$$

where X_{ij} is the distance between points x_i and x_j in the input space, Y_{ij} the distance between the corresponding points y_i and y_j in the projection space, and F a decreasing function (with parameter λ) of the distances Y_{ij}. A simple step function with threshold λ (decreased during the convergence) may be used.

As the weighting function depends on the distances in the output spaces, a recursive procedure is needed to find the locations of the point y_i in the projection space. Conventional gradient descent on the error function E can be particularly tedious and computationally heavy; Demartines then suggests a simplified procedure where each point y_i is in turn considered as fixed, and all other points around y_i are moved. Under some supplementary assumptions, this lead to the adaptation rule

$$\Delta y_j = \alpha(t) F\left(Y_{ij}, \lambda\right)\left(X_{ij} - Y_{ij}\right)\frac{y_j - y_i}{Y_{ij}}, \quad \forall j \neq i. \tag{8}$$

In order to facilitate the convergence on difficult databases, we suggested in [16] using a kind of "curvilinear distance" instead of the standard Euclidean distance for X_{ij}. This curvilinear distance is measured as the shortest path via links drawn between adjacent centroids. Using this distance increases the possibility for the method to respect criterion (7), and therefore facilitates the convergence of the algorithm. As an example, the distance between any two centroids in Figure 10 is no more the Euclidean distance, but rather the sum of the lengths of all segments drawn in the figure that are necessary to join the two centroids (shortest path).

Figure 11 shows the result of the projection of a sphere on a 2-dimensional space, using the CCA algorithm with curvilinear distances.

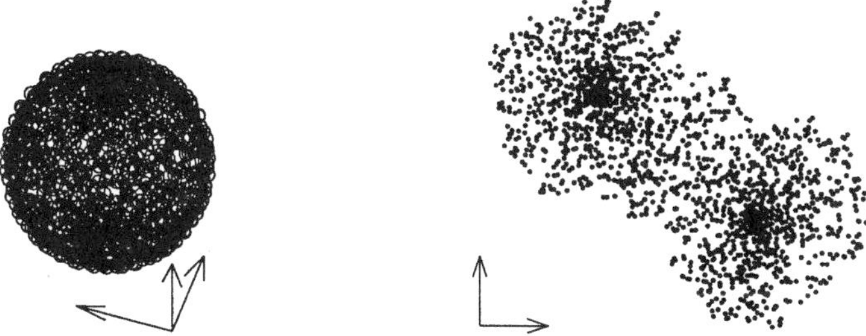

Figure 11: Left: sphere in a 3-dimensional space. Right: its projection on a 2-dimensional plane.

7. An example of dimension reduction

As an illustrative example, we consider the forecasting of the Belgian BEL20 stock market index. The application of time series forecasting to financial market data is a real challenge. The efficient market hypothesis (EMH) remains up to now the most generally admitted one in the academic community, while essentially challenged by the practitioners. Under EMH, one of the classical econometric tools used to model the behaviour of stock market prices is the geometric Brownian motion. If it does represent the true generating process of stock returns, the best prediction that we can obtain of the future value is the actual one (they follow a random walk). Results presented in this section must therefore be analysed with a lot of caution. Analyzing a rather local index as the BEL20 is however facilitated by the fact that local indexes are largely influenced by the evolution of larger ones after a small delay (some hours, one day). As the values of these larger indexes are know, they can be incorporated in the model used to forecast the BEL20. For these exogenous variables, we selected international indices of security prices (SBF 250, S&P500, Topix, FTSE100, etc), exchange rates (Dollar/Mark, Dollar/Yen, etc), and interest rates (T-Bills 3 months, US Treasury Constant Maturity 10 years, etc). We used 42 technical indicators in total [17] (chosen according to [18] and [19]), based on these exogenous variables and of course also on the past values of the series.

We used 2600 daily data of the BEL20 index over 10 years to have a significant data set. The problem considered here is to forecast the sign of the variation of the BEL20 index at time $t+5$, from available data at time t.

If we carry out a Principal Component Analysis (PCA) on these 42 variables, we note that 95% of the original variance is kept with the first 25 principal components: 17 variables can be removed without significant loss of information. The PCA is used to facilitate the subsequent processing by the CCA algorithm (lower computational load and better convergence properties).

The time series of the target variable, x_{t+5}, whose sign has to be predicted, is illustrated in Figure 12.

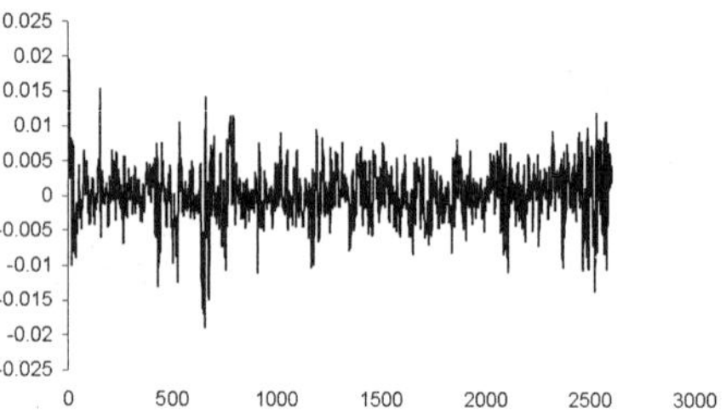

Figure12: Daily values of the BEL20 index.

This variable has to be predicted using the resulting 25 variables selected after PCA. The interpolator we use is a conventional Radial-Basis Function (RBFN) network (RBFN). Our interest goes to the sign of the prediction only, which will be compared to the real sign of the target variable.

The Grassberger-Proccacia method is used to estimate the intrinsic dimension m of the data set; we obtain an approximate value of 9. We then use the CCA algorithm to project the 25-dimensional data (after PCA) on a 9-dimensional space. The RBFN interpolator is used on the resulting 9-dimensional input vectors.

The network is trained with a moving window of 500 data. Each of these data consists in a 9-dimensional input vector (see above) and a scalar target (variation of the BEL20 index). We use 500 data as a compromise between

- a small stationary set but insufficient for a successful training, and
- a large but less stationary training set.

For each window, the 500 input-target pairs form the training set, while the test set consists in the input-target pair right after the training set. This procedure is repeated for 2100 moving windows. On average, we obtain 60,3% correct approximations of the sign of the series on the training sets, and 57.2% on the test sets. These results are encouraging and are far above what can be obtained with RBFN or other interpolators trained on the initial 42-dimensional vectors.

Moreover, it can be seen that better results are obtained during some periods and worse results during others. The first ones correspond to time periods where the series is more stationary than the last ones. Figure 13 represents a moving average on 90 days on the results of the prediction. It clearly shows that that the prediction results themselves do not form a random series: when the forecasting is correct over several consecutive days, the probability that it will be correct at the next time step is high.

To quantify this idea, we filter the results with the following heuristics. We look at the average of sign predictions (correct – not correct) over the last 5 days. If this average increases or remains constant at time t, then we take the forecasting at time $t+1$ into consideration. If it decreases, then we disregard the forecasting at time $t+1$. With this method, we keep 75.4% of the forecasts; the average score of correct prediction rises to 65.3% (about 70% of increases and 60% of decreases). This way of working is a first attempt to use such mathematical procedure in a real-world financial context.

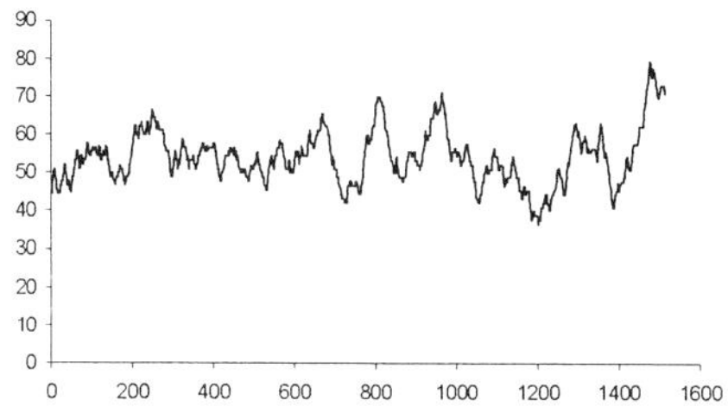

Figure 13: Percentage of correct approximations of the sign on a 90-days moving window.

8. Conclusion

Artificial neural networks are learning methods used in complex problems, where it is difficult to find appropriate physical models, or where most other modeling techniques fail because of their linearity, polynomial character, etc. Most of these complex, real problems, involve observations made of several (many) variables. The observations are thus points in high-dimensional spaces, and unfortunately most adaptive techniques and neural network algorithms are not designed to take this high dimensionality into account. However, the same techniques are effectively used with high-dimension data, and prove to be successful in some cases. But they fail in other situations, because of the "curse of dimensionality" and the "empty space phenomenon".

This paper emphasizes on the problem that can be encountered when high-dimensional data are handled in the same way as low-dimensional ones. It shows that some basic concepts as the interpolation-extrapolation dilemma, the use of Euclidean distances, the local character of Gaussian functions, etc. are misleading when used with high-dimensional data.

We then show through a few examples that even local artificial neural networks can be modified easily to take the curse of dimensionality effect into account. We argue that the difficulties related to the use of high-dimensional data are equivalent with local (RBFN, SOM, etc.) and with global (MLP, etc.) neural networks.

Finally, it is shown how the dimension of data can be reduced, with non-linear techniques, in order to improve the results of a subsequent learning task (classification, approximation, forecasting, etc.), with algorithms like the "Curvilinear Component Analysis". An application of this technique to the forecasting of financial time series concludes the discussion.

Acknowledgements

Michel Verleysen is a Senior Research Associate of the Belgian FNRS (National Fund for Scientific Research).

References

[1] D. L. Donoho, High-Dimensional Data Analysis: The Curses and Blessings of Dimensionality. Lecture on August 8, 2000, to the American Mathematical Society "Math Challenges of the 21st Century". Available from http://www-stat.stanford.edu/~donoho/.

[2] M. Turk, A. Pentland, Eigenfaces for Recognition, *J. Cognitive Neuroscience*, **3**-1 (1991) 71-96.

[3] R. Bellmann, Adaptive Control Processes: A Guided Tour. Princeton University Press, 1961.

[4] A. Barron, Universal Approximation Bounds for Superpositions of a Sigmoidal Function, *IEEE Tr. on Information Theory*, **8**-3 (1993) 930-945.

[5] D. W. Scott, J. R. Thompson, Probability density estimation in higher dimensions. In: J.E. Gentle (ed.), Computer Science and Statistics: Proceedings of the Fifteenth Symposium on the Interface, Amsterdam, New York, Oxford, North Holland-Elsevier Science Publishers, 1983, pp. 173-179.

[6] P. Comon, J.-L. Voz, M. Verleysen, Estimation of performance bounds in supervised classification, *European Symposium on Artificial Neural Networks*, Brussels (Belgium), April 1994, pp. 37-42.

[7] B.W. Silverman, Density estimation for statistics and data analysis. Chapman and Hall, 1986.

[8] P. Demartines, Analyse de données par réseaux de neurones auto-organisés. Ph.D. dissertation (in French), Institut National Polytechnique de Grenoble (France), 1994.

[9] P. Grassberger, I. Procaccia, Measuring the strangeness of strange attractors, *Physica D*, **56** (1983) 189-208.

[10] T. Kohonen, Self-Organizing Maps. Springer Series in Information Sciences, vol. 30, Springer (Berlin), 1995.

[11] A. Choppin, Unsupervised classification of high dimensional data by means of self-organizing neural networks. M.Sc. thesis, Université catholique de Louvain (Belgium), Computer Science Dept., June 1998.

[12] R. N. Shepard, The analysis of proximities: Multidimensional scaling with an unknown distance function, parts I and II, *Psychometrika*, **27** (1962) 125-140 and 219-246.

[13] R.N. Shepard, J.D. Carroll, Parametric representation of nonlinear data structures, *International Symposium on Multivariate Analysis*, P. R. Krishnaiah (ed.) pp. 561-592, Academic Press, 1965.

[14] J.W. Sammon, A nonlinear mapping algorithm for data structure analysis, *IEEE Trans. on Computers*, **C-18** (1969) 401-409.

[15] P. Demartines, J. Hérault, Curvilinear Component Analysis: a self-organizing neural network for nonlinear mapping of data sets, *IEEE Trans. on Neural Networks*,. **8**-1 (1997) 148-154.

[16] J. Lee, A. Lendasse, N. Donckers, M. Verleysen, A robust nonlinear projection method, ESANN'2000 (European Symposium on Artificial Neural Networks), Bruges (Belgium), April 2000, pp. 13-20, D-Facto publications (Brussels).

[17] A. Lendasse, J. Lee, E. de Bodt, V. Wertz, M. Verleysen, Input data reduction for the prediction of financial time series, ESANN'2001 (European Symposium on Artificial Neural Networks), Bruges (Belgium), April 2001, pp. 237-244, D-Facto publications (Brussels).

[18] A.N. Refenes, A.N. Burgess, Y. Bentz, Neural networks in financial engineering: a study in methodology, *IEEE Transactions on Neural Networks*, **8**-6 (1997) 1222-1267.

[19] A.N. Burgess, Nonlinear model identification and statistical significance tests and their application in financial modeling. In *Artificial Neural Networks*, Proceedings of the Inst. Elect. Eng. Conf., 1995.

The curse of dimensionality and the blessing of multiple hybrid networks

Nathan Intrator*
School of Computer Science
Tel-Aviv University
www.cs.tau.ac.il/~nin

Abstract

Multiple networks can reduce the over all error of a system by simple ensemble averaging. I will review some theoretical considerations as well as biological evidence for the increased computation power of such multiple/parallel approach. Hybrid networks have a different purpose, I will review some recently proposed architectures and discuss their applicability.

1 The curse of dimensionality

Some people find it a bit difficult to comprehend the problems that are associated in model estimation from high-dimensional data. While the term "Curse of Dimensionality" has been introduced about 40 years ago by Bellman [2], the implications are still subject for intense investigation. To see why a high dimensional space (HDS) becomes so sparse, lets consider the cube $[0, 1]^n$. We want to study what happens to a neighborhood of a point, say, $(.5, \ldots, .5)$ in this space as a function of the dimensionality n. For the sake of the argument, we consider a neighborhood of that point which consists of half of the total length in each dimension, namely we consider the neighborhood $[.25, .75]^n$. When the distribution of the points in the space is uniform, this neighborhood contains half of the points of the space, in one dimension. However, when the data dimensionality is n, the same neighborhood contains $.5^n$ of the points, namely, the probability to find a point in this neighborhood, or its relative volume, converges to zero exponentially fast. This example suggests that the distance between points in an n dimensional space, grows very rapidly, and thus, inference about structure, clusters etc, becomes highly impractical for finite amounts of data.

One can ask then, how come that many model estimation techniques are performing well in large data dimensions with moderate sample size. One possibility is that models perform well when there is a highly separable data, in which a linear model can achieve the desired separation. In particular, in support vector machines, the Mercer theorem is used for transforming the data to a higher dimensional space so that data in the new representation is linearly separable [11]. However, there might be other reasons for the surprising performance. In this context, the concentration of measures property, has been recently revisited as a relevant feature of HDS [13]. In the next section, we briefly describe a more fundamental property of high dimensional projections which we believe is most relevant to the blessing of high dimensional data sets.

---

*Currently, on leave at the Institute for Brain and Neural Systems, Brown University

1.1   The blessing of the central limit theorem

We argue that a clear and practical blessing of HDS follows from the *central limit theorem*. It suggests that low dimensional projections have nice mathematical properties which can be used for data exploration. The central limit theorem says that when a collection of n independent and identically distributed (iid) random variables (r.v.) is given, each with a mean μ and a variance σ^2, their population average has a mean μ and variance σ^2/n. There is no real need for the different random variables to be identically distributed, the only need is that no single or small number of them is "more important" than the others. The more relaxed conditions are given in the Lindberg-Feller theorem [16]. The connection with projections is clear when the set of r.v.'s $\zeta_i = x_i w_i$, where x_i is the r.v. given by i'th dimension of the data and w_i is the corresponding weight vector of the projection. Thus, when the projection $\mathbf{w} = (w_1, \ldots, w_n)$ is random or irrelevant to the data structure, the r.v. ζ_i are independent and their normalized sum is then Gaussian. This result is related to entropy and the information contents in a collection of variables. The fact that the variables are independent is sufficient to determine the distribution of their mean, no matter what their original distribution is.

It follows that Gaussian distributions are very common and should not come as a surprise. In particular, for any weights-vector that is chosen independently of the data, the projection of the data onto the vector is likely to generate a Gaussian projection. Thus, structure in high dimensional data can be found by searching for weights-vectors for which the projections lead to a non-Gaussian distribution.

2   Non-Gaussian projections: Projection Pursuit

Searching for projections with non-Gaussian distribution is generally discussed in the context of exploratory projection pursuit which is based on seeking *interesting* projections of high-dimensional data [32, 45, 33, 18, 17, 29, 21, 22]. The notion of interesting projections is motivated by an observation discussed above, where for most high-dimensional data clouds, most low-dimensional projections are approximately normal [12]. This finding suggests that the important information in the data is conveyed in those directions whose univariate projected distribution is far from Gaussian. Various projection indices differ in the assumptions about the nature of the deviation from normality, and in their computational efficiency. They can be considered as different priors motivated by specific assumptions on the underlying model.

Since Gaussian distribution maximizes entropy, subject to specified mean and variance, it is possible to test deviation from Gaussianity by the difference between the entropy of a Gaussian, with the same variance, and the given distribution. This measure is non-negative and provides a measure of the information content of the distribution relative to the maximal content of a Gaussian with the same variance. The index is given by

$$
\begin{aligned}
J_I(p) &= H(p_G) - H(p) \\
&= \frac{1}{2}\log(2\pi e) + \log(\sigma) + \int p(x)\log p(x)dx,
\end{aligned} \tag{1}
$$

where p is the probability density function and σ is the standard deviation of the distribution of interest. This index also leads to redundancy reduction and independent component analysis (briefly discussed below.)

As the density $p(x)$ is unknown, it has to be estimated from the data. This is computationally expensive and due to the curse can practically be done only if x is a single dimensional distribution or a distribution of a very small number of projections. A non-parametric estimation of the density, e.g., using the kernel method [47, 46] is not advisable since the uncertainty of the estimation is not uniform and depends on the number of data points in each region. It is therefore, preferred to estimate the integral in (1) by a moment approximation to the density so that integration over all the data is used. When the third and fourth cumulants [30] of the distribution are known,

$$\begin{aligned} \kappa_3 &= \frac{E[(x - \bar{x})^3]}{\sigma^3}, \\ \kappa_4 &= \frac{E[(x - \bar{x})^4]}{\sigma^4} - 3, \end{aligned} \tag{2}$$

the Edgeworth expansion [44] has been proposed for estimation of the entropy in the context of independent components analysis [10]. More recently, the Gram-Charlier expansion [44] has been proposed [1] as it explicitly depends on the third and fourth cumulants of the distribution. The Gram-Charlier approximation has the form

$$p(x) \simeq \alpha(x)\{1 + \frac{\kappa_3}{3!} H_3(x) + \frac{\kappa_4}{4!} H_4(x)\}, \tag{3}$$

where $\alpha(x) = \frac{1}{\sqrt{2\pi}} \exp(-x^2/2)$ and $H_k(x)$ are Chebyshev-Hermite polynomials, given by

$$\begin{aligned} H_3(x) &= 4x^3 - 3x, \\ H_4(x) &= 8x^4 - 8x^2 + 1. \end{aligned} \tag{4}$$

The exact measure of deviation from a Gaussian distribution is clearly expressed in approximation (3) in terms of the skewness and kurtosis of the distribution. If we substitute this approximation into (1) we obtain

$$\hat{J}_I(p) = \sigma - \frac{(\kappa_3)^2}{2 \cdot 3!} - \frac{(\kappa_4)^2}{2 \cdot 4!} + \frac{5}{8}(\kappa_3)^2 \kappa_4 + \frac{1}{16}(\kappa_4)^3. \tag{5}$$

The above two expansions of the entropy are primarily used in the ICA variant of Projection Pursuit [10]. The goal of ICA is to express a set of random variables as linear combinations of statistically independent component variables. We observe k scalar variables $(d_1, d_2, \ldots, d_k)^{\mathrm{T}} \equiv \mathbf{d}$ which are assumed to be linear combinations of n unknown *statistically independent* variables $(s_1, s_2, \ldots, s_n)^{\mathrm{T}}$. We can express this mixing of the sources $\mathbf{s}$ as

$$\mathbf{d} = \mathbf{As} \tag{6}$$

where $\mathbf{A}$ is an unknown $k \times n$ mixing matrix. The problem of ICA is then to estimate both the mixing matrix $\mathbf{A}$ and the sources $\mathbf{s}$ using only the observation of the mixtures d_i. Using the feature extraction properties of ICA, the columns of $\mathbf{A}$ represent features, and s_i represent the amplitude of each feature in the observed mixtures $\mathbf{d}$. These are the features in which we are interested. The key observation here is that a linear combination of independent random variables has a distribution that is more Gaussian than each of the components separately. Thus, the matrix $\mathbf{A}$ makes the independent sources $\mathbf{s}$ appear more Gaussian, and the best way to find an inverse to the unknown matrix $\mathbf{A}$ is to search for linear projections which will make the components of the projections less Gaussian. Different definitions of deviation from Gaussian distribution exist in the ICA literature as well. In particular, deviation is sought in the center of the distribution (sub-kurtotic) or in the tails of the distribution (super-kurtotic) [24].

Friedman [17] suggested to measure the deviation from Gaussian distribution by subjecting first the projections to an inverse Gaussian transformation which maps a Gaussian distribution to a uniform distribution in the finite set $[-1, 1]$ and then simply measure deviation from uniformity of this distribution. While this method is simple and intuitive, it does not scale well to multi-dimensional projections. Intrator and Cooper [27] have shown that a BCM neuron can find structure in the input distribution that exhibits deviation from a Gaussian distribution in the form of multi-modality in the projected distributions. (BCM stands for Bienenstock, Cooper and Munro [4]. It is a learning rule that was constructed to model early visual cortical plasticity. Current versions of this rule, including mathematical properties, statistical motivation and network extensions, are discussed in [27].) Since clusters cannot be found in the data directly, because of its sparsity, this type of deviation, which is measured by the first three moments of the distribution, is particularly useful for finding clusters in high-dimensional data, and is thus useful for classification or recognition tasks. It thus renders this feature extraction technique also appropriate for bias constraints. We present some of the constraints here in a form that exhibits their relation to the BCM feature extraction rule. Connections with independent components analysis and results on natural scene feature extraction are described in [6]. Results on classification of faces are described in [28, 43].

The BCM index does not emphasize deviation in the form of asymmetry, but rather deviations in the tails or in manifestations of multimodality. Sensitivity to outliers is reduced by using a rectified activation function (this rectification has little effect on the ability of kurtosis rules to find interesting projections [6]) denoted by $c = \sigma(\mathbf{d} \cdot \mathbf{m})$ where σ is a smooth monotone sigmoidal function with a positive output, although a slight negative output is also allowed; σ' denotes the derivative of the sigmoid. The rectification is required for all rules that depend on odd moments, because these vanish in a symmetric distribution such as is commonly used in contexts involving natural scenes [6]. The following projection indices where compared on high dimensional data in [6]:

Skewness 1   This measures deviation from symmetry [30] and is of the form

$$S_1 = E[c^3]/(E[c^2])^{3/2}. \tag{7}$$

Maximization of this measure via gradient ascent uses

$$\nabla S_1 = \frac{1}{\Theta_M^{1.5}} E\left[c\left(c - E[c^3]/E[c^2]\right)\sigma'\mathbf{d}\right], \tag{8}$$

where Θ_M is defined as $E[c^2]$.

Skewness 2   A similar measure which requires some stabilization mechanism is given by

$$S_2 = E[c^3] - E^{3/2}[c^2]. \tag{9}$$

This measure has a gradient of the form

$$\nabla S_2 = 3E\left[c\left(c - \sqrt{\Theta_M}\right)\sigma'\mathbf{d}\right], \tag{10}$$

Kurtosis 1   Kurtosis measures deviation from a Gaussian distribution mainly in the tails of the distribution. It has the form

$$K_1 = E[c^4]/E^2[c^2] - 3. \tag{11}$$

This measure has a gradient of the form

$$\nabla K_1 = \frac{1}{\Theta_M^2} E\left[c\left(c^2 - E[c^4]/E[c^2]\right)\sigma'\mathbf{d}\right]. \tag{12}$$

Kurtosis 2 As before, there is a similar form, which requires some stabilization:

$$K_2 = E[c^4] - 3E^2[c^2]. \tag{13}$$

This measure has a gradient of the form

$$\nabla K_2 = 4E\left[c(c^2 - 3\Theta_M)]\sigma'\mathbf{d}\right]. \tag{14}$$

With all the above, maximization of the measure can be used as a goal for projection seeking, so the variable c can be thought of as a (nonlinear) projection of the input distribution on to a certain vector of weights, and the maximization then defines a learning rule for this vector of weights. Under this framework, it is easy to stabilize the above learning rules by requiring for example that the vector of weights, which we denote by m, has a fixed norm, $\| m \| = 1$, say. The multiplicative forms of both kurtosis and skewness do not require this type of stabilization, because of the normalizing factor $1/\Theta_M{}^p$ in each rule.

Quadratic BCM The Quadratic BCM (QBCM) measure as given in [27] is of the form

$$\mathrm{QBCM} = \frac{1}{3}E[c^3] - \frac{1}{4}E^2[c^2]. \tag{15}$$

Maximising this form using gradient ascent uses the gradient function

$$\nabla\mathrm{QBCM} = E[c(c - \Theta_M)\sigma'\mathbf{d}]. \tag{16}$$

The Quadratic BCM rule does not require any additional stabilization. This turns out to be an important property, since additional information can then be transmitted using the resulting norm of the weight vector m [26].

So far we have taken the approach that high dimensional data is not directly applicable to regression and classification and that a specific step of dimensionality reduction/feature extraction has to take place before any attempt for modeling the classification or regression process. In the next part of the paper, we take a different approach where we try to combine the feature extraction and the modeling of the classification problem. We shall then use hybrid and multiple experts.

3 Bias constraints

3.1 Distinction between different bias constraints

Before we discuss bias and variance constraints and their role in modeling, we need to clearly define what are these constraints. In particular, it may sometimes appear difficult to distinguish between bias constraints and variance constraints. For example, how do we treat smoothness constraints? While smoothness reduces the variance, it clearly enforces a bias towards smooth models. Since we are dealing with additive constraints, as will be clear from the way that parameter estimates are calculated (see equation (17)), we can offer a simple distinction. If the update rule leads to no meaningful result when only the additional (bias/variance) constraint is effective, we regard it as a *variance* constraint. When some meaningful result is obtained via this unsupervised constraint only, we regard it as a *bias* constraint. Thus, classical constraints such as smoothness, as well as assumptions about the distribution of the parameters, e.g. favoring small weights via a weight decay or favoring particular distributions such as mixtures of Gaussians [37], are actually variance constraints.

As we shift our attention to the blessing of hybrid and multiple architectures, we start with a brief review of a general framework for hybrid architecture which utilizes bias constraints via projection pursuit [25] or a multi-task architecture [43]. We use the term hybrid when the architecture performs at least two distinct tasks. We present the general framework in the context of feed forward artificial neural network because such networks offer features that simplify training and variance control in HDS; In feed-forward neural nets, the family of ridge functions is limited to sigmoidal functions with variable threshold. This avoids the need for a non-parametric or semi-parametric estimation of the ridge functions, but may require a large number of projections, as in the example in [39]. Moreover, the estimation of several projections is performed concurrently. This allows one to find a low dimensional representation which may not be found when the search is done sequentially [22].

3.2   Hybrid attempts at dimensionality reduction

There have been various attempts to combine unsupervised learning with supervised learning [49, 20, 8]. The formulation discussed below is based on projection pursuit ideas, which generalize many of the classical statistical methods, and, in our case, suggest a well-defined statistical framework that allows formulation and comparison between various methods. Consider the artificial neural network architecture presented in Fig. 1. The only difference from a classical feed-forward architecture [41] is the additional modification term in the hidden units. We consider the hidden unit representation as a new, reduced-dimensionality representation of the data, and add a penalty term to the energy functional minimized by error back-propagation, for the purpose of measuring directly the goodness of the projections sought by the network. This puts the emphasis on choosing the right prior, as a means to improving the bias/variance tradeoff.

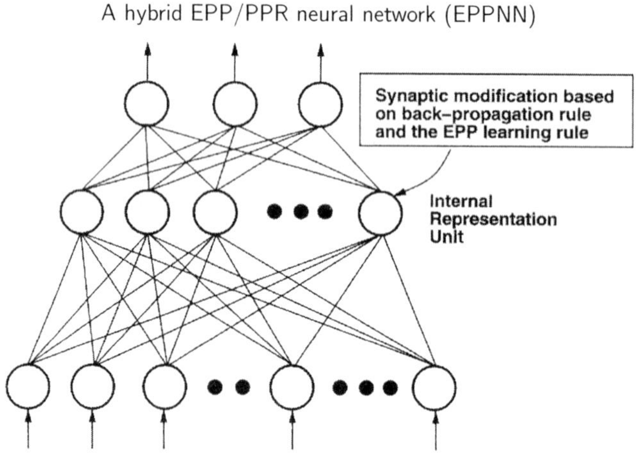

Figure 1: The modification of the hidden units' weights is achieved by back-propagation of the error from the output layer (via the chain rule) and by the gradient of the projection index.

Since our main interest is in reducing over-fitting for high dimensional problems, our underlying assumption is that the surface function to be estimated can be faithfully represented using a low-dimensional composition of sigmoidal functions, namely, using a feed-forward architecture in which the number of hidden units is *much smaller* than the number of input units. Therefore, the penalty term may be added to the hidden layer only; see Fig. 1. The synaptic modification equations for the hidden units' weights become

$$\frac{\partial w_{ij}}{\partial t} = -\epsilon \left[\frac{\partial \mathcal{E}(w,x)}{\partial w_{ij}} + \frac{\partial \rho(w_1,\ldots,w_n)}{\partial w_{ij}} + (\text{Contribution of cost/complexity terms}) \right], \tag{17}$$

where $\mathcal{E}$ is the error function and ρ is the explicit measure of goodness of projections (bias constraints), while the contribution of the cost/complexity terms (variance constraints) are also additively imposed.

3.3 Specific bias constraints

Applicability of such bias constraints has been demonstrated in various real-world applications. Entropy constraints have been used in image compression, with a penalty aimed at minimizing the entropy of the projected distributions [3]. BCM constraints have been used in face recognition [28] and more recently for partially occluded and blurred face recognition [43]. These constraints are also useful for acoustic signal classification from wavelet representations [23]. Kurtosis constraints have been used in conjunction with reconstruction to find sparse representations [38], and recently kurtosis and skewness have been found to be useful for neg-entropy calculations and independent components analysis; see [50] for a review.

4 Variance Control via Various Ensemble Averaging Methods

Error surfaces which are used to estimate the weights (parameters) of neural networks have in general many local minima. Thus, even with the same training set, different local minima are found when the learning algorithm starts from a different random initial values. These different local minima lead to somewhat independent predictors, and thus averaging over several experts can reduce the variance portion of the error. When a larger set of independent networks is needed but no more data is available (to make them independent), data reuse methods can be of help. Bootstrapping [7] has been very helpful, since, by resampling from the training data without replacement, the degree of independence among the training sets, and hence among the resulting sets of estimators, is increased, leading to improved ensemble results. Smoothed bootstrap [14] is potentially more useful since a wider range of sets of independent training samples can be generated. The smoothed bootstrap approach amounts to generating larger datasets by simulating the *true* noise in the data.

4.1 The Variance-Bias Dilemma

The motivation for simple averaging follows from a key observation regarding the bias/variance decomposition, namely the fact that ensemble averaging does not affect the bias portion of the error, but reduces the variance, when the estimators on which averaging is done are independent.

The classification problem is to estimate a function $f_\mathcal{D}(x)$ of observed data characteristics x, for predicting a class label y, based on a given training set $\mathcal{D} = \{(x_1,y_1),\ldots,(x_L,y_L)\}$, using some measure of the estimation error on $\mathcal{D}$. A good estimator will perform well not only on the training set, but also on new *validation* sets which were not used during estimation.

Evaluation of the performance of the estimator is commonly done via the mean squared error distance (MSE) by taking the expectation with respect to the (unknown) probability distribution P of y:

$$E[(y - f_\mathcal{D}(x))^2 | x, \mathcal{D}].$$

This can be decomposed into

$$E[(y - f_\mathcal{D}(x))^2 | x, \mathcal{D}] = E[(y - E[y|x])^2 | x, \mathcal{D}] + E[(f_\mathcal{D}(x) - E[y|x])^2].$$

The first term typically depends on neither the training data $\mathcal{D}$ nor the estimator $f_\mathcal{D}(x)$, it measures the amount of noise or variability of y given x. Hence f can be evaluated using

$$E[(f_\mathcal{D}(x) - E[y|x])^2].$$

The empirical mean squared error of f is given by

$$E_\mathcal{D}[(f_\mathcal{D}(x) - E[y|x])^2],$$

where $E_\mathcal{D}$ represents expectation with respect to all possible training sets $\mathcal{D}$ of fixed size.

To investigate further the MSE performance we decompose the error into bias and variance components [19] to obtain

$$E_\mathcal{D}[(f_\mathcal{D}(x) - E[y|x])^2] = (E_\mathcal{D}[f_\mathcal{D}(x)] - E[y|x])^2 + E_\mathcal{D}[(f_\mathcal{D}(x) - E_\mathcal{D}[f_\mathcal{D}(x)])^2]. \tag{18}$$

The first term on the right-hand side is called the bias term (strictly, the squared bias) of the estimator and the second term is called the variance term. When training on a fixed training set $\mathcal{D}$, reducing the bias with respect to this set may increase the variance of the estimator and contribute to poor generalization performance. This is known as the trade-off between variance and bias. Typically, variance is reduced by smoothing, but this may introduce bias since, for example, it may blur sharp peaks. Bias is reduced by incorporating prior knowledge. When prior knowledge is used also for smoothing, it is likely to reduce the overall MSE of the estimator.

When training neural networks such as multilayer perceptrons, the variance arises from two terms. The first term comes from inherent data randomness and the second term arises from the non-identifiability of the model, in that, for a given training dataset, there may be several local minima of the error surface.

Consider the ensemble average $\bar{f}$ of Q predictors, which in our case can be thought of as neural networks with different random initial weights which are trained on data with added Gaussian noise:

$$\bar{f}(x) = \frac{1}{Q} \sum_{i=1}^{Q} f_i(x).$$

These predictors are identically distributed, and thus the variance contribution to equation (18) becomes

$$
\begin{aligned}
E[(\bar{f} - E[\bar{f}])^2] &= E[(\frac{1}{Q} \sum f_i - E[\frac{1}{Q} \sum f_i])^2] \\
&= E[(\frac{1}{Q} \sum f_i)^2] + \left(E[\frac{1}{Q} \sum f_i] \right)^2 - 2E[\frac{1}{Q} \sum f_i E[\frac{1}{Q} \sum f_i]] \\
&= E[(\frac{1}{Q} \sum f_i)^2] - \left(E[\frac{1}{Q} \sum f_i] \right)^2;
\end{aligned}
\tag{19}
$$

we omit mention of x and $\mathcal{D}$ for clarity. The first term in (19) can be rewritten as

$$E[(\frac{1}{Q}\sum f_i)^2] = \frac{1}{Q^2}\sum E[f_i^2] + \frac{2}{Q^2}\sum_{i<j} E[f_i f_j],$$

and the second term gives

$$\left(E[\frac{1}{Q}\sum f_i]\right)^2 = \frac{1}{Q^2}\sum\left(E[f_i^2]\right)^2 + \frac{2}{Q^2}\sum_{i<j} E[f_i]E[f_j].$$

Plugging these equalities into (19) gives

$$E[(\bar{f} - E[\bar{f}])^2] = \frac{1}{Q^2}\sum\{E[f_i^2] - \left(E[f_i]\right)^2\} + \frac{2}{Q^2}\sum_{i<j}\{E[f_i f_j] - E[f_i]E[f_j]\}. \tag{20}$$

Set

$$\gamma = \text{Var}(f_i) + (Q-1)\max_{i,j}(E[f_i f_j] - E[f_i]E[f_j]).$$

It follows that[1]

$$\frac{1}{Q}\text{Var}(f_i) \le \text{Var}(\bar{f}) \le \frac{1}{Q}\gamma \le \max_i \text{Var}(f_i). \tag{21}$$

This analysis suggests a simple extrapolation to large values of Q by giving an upper bound of $1/Q\gamma$ to the variance behavior under many-network ensembles from small-size ensembles [36]. Note that

$$E[f_i f_j] - E[f_i]E[f_j] = E\left(\{f_i - E[f_i]\}\{f_j - E[f_j]\}\right).$$

Thus, the notion of independence can be understood as independence of the deviations of each predictor from the expected value of the predictor, which can be replaced, because of linearity, by

$$E\left(\{f_i - E[\bar{f}]\}\{f_j - E[\bar{f}]\}\right),$$

and is thus interpreted as an indication of the prediction variation around a common mean.

4.2 Exhaustive training

The analysis presented in Section 4.1 suggests that training an ensemble of predictors should be done in a different way from training single predictors. This is because an ensemble of predictors has a lower overall bias, and thus the optimal trade-off between variance and bias should correspond to a lower level of bias so as to balance the contribution to error from the lower variance. In neural networks, trained by methods such as iterative gradient descent, this is achieved by stopping the training process at a later point, thus overfitting the individual training dataset somewhat, thereby leading to lower bias but higher variance. Naftaly et al. [36], have demonstrated the effect of training on single and ensemble errors, using the well known sun-spots data [35]. After giving some technical details, we briefly review their results. As in [48], feed-forward, simple-recurrent [15] networks with 4 sigmoidal hidden units were used with data from 12 consecutive time points as inputs. In other words, the neural network was used as a nonlinear predictor of the number of sunspots in a given month, using the data from the 12 previous months as covariates/predictors. The prediction error was measured according to the average relative variance (ARV).

---

[1]We use the fact that $ab \le \frac{a^2+b^2}{2}$, thus, $E[f_i f_j] - E[f_i]E[f_j] = E\left(\{f_i - E[f_i]\}\{f_j - E[f_j]\}\right) \le \max_i \text{Var}(f_i).$

Naftaly et al. [36] presented a very simple way of estimating what the variance portion of the MSE will be for large ensemble sizes, based on the performance of small ensemble sizes: see Section 4.1. Figure 2 depicts results from [36] for two architectures. Values of ARV are shown as a function of the number of training epochs. The highest curve in each figure corresponds to $Q = 1$, i.e. the case of a single network. Below it, appear the curves of $Q = 2, 4, 10, 20$, followed by the extrapolation to $Q \to \infty$. The extrapolation over ensemble size is demonstrated in Fig. 2, where ARV values obtained for training time $t = 70$ and $t = 140$ KE for the test set are depicted as a function of $\frac{1}{Q}$. It is quite clear that a linear extrapolation is very satisfactory.

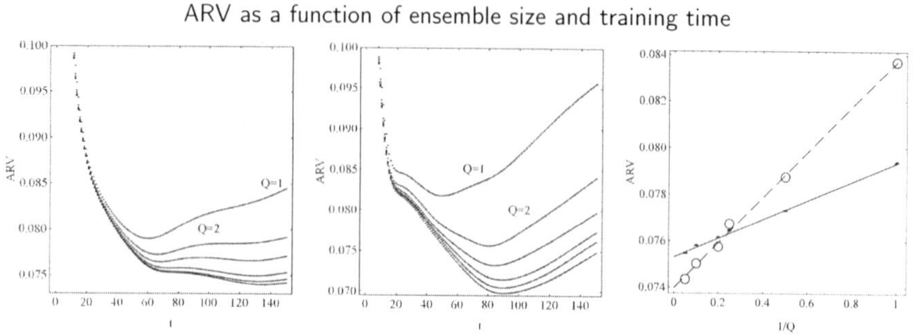

Figure 2: ARV vs. training time in kilo epochs for the sun-spots data (From [36]). Curves for two architectures are shown for different choices of ensemble sizes: $Q = 1, 2, 4, 10, 20$ from top to bottom. Far right, the two extrapolation curves obtained from the minima points of each ensemble size. Note the linearity of $1/Q$ and the different slopes.

4.3   Noise injection

In the previous section we have emphasized the reduction in the variance portion of the error resulting from ensemble averaging. This reduction was a result of the independence between the errors made by different predictors. While the use of initial random weights may lead to some independence, training on different datasets improves the independence even further. Bootstrapping [7] is most appropriate for small datasets since, by resampling with replacement from the training data, the independence between the training sets is increased, yet each predictor has more than a $1/Q$ fraction of the training set on which to train. Smoothed bootstrap [14] is potentially more useful since larger sets of independent training samples can be generated. The smoothed bootstrap approach amounts to generating larger datasets by simulating the *true* noise in the data. In this section, we demonstrate that training with added noise that is larger than the true data-noise, can still be helpful, as it increases the degree of independence between the training sets and, therefore, the degree of independence between predictors. A simple bootstrap procedure amounts to sampling with replacement from the training data and constructing several training sets, all of the same size as the original training set. Later, the variability between the sets of estimated parameters can be measured, and indicate the true variability of the estimates of model parameters. Furthermore, variability or error-bars of the predictions can also be estimated in this way.

One version of bootstrap involves estimation of a model of the form

$$y = f(x) + \epsilon, \tag{22}$$

for some parametric family to which f belongs, and a noise variable ϵ which is assumed to have small variance and zero mean. An estimate $\hat{f}$ of f is obtained from n training samples, leading to fitted residuals $\hat{\epsilon} = (\hat{\epsilon}_1, \ldots, \hat{\epsilon}_n)$. One can then sample n times with replacement from the ϵ_i, giving $\epsilon^* = (\epsilon_1^*, \ldots, \epsilon_n^*)$, and construct new samples of the form (x_i, y_i^*), in which ϵ_i is replaced by ϵ_i^* sampled from the above set. Clearly, this approach can be easily extended to a smoothed bootstrap version [14]. In such a case, one can increase the size of each bootstrap set, since because of the noise the different sets are sufficiently independent. It should be noted that, if $\hat{f}$ is biased, the noise variance may be over estimated.

For classification problems, the form

$$y = f(x + \epsilon), \tag{23}$$

may be more appropriate. In this case, applying noise injection to the inputs during training, one can improve the generalization properties of the estimator [42]. Bishop has shown that training with small amounts of noise is locally equivalent to regularization [5]. Here, we give a different interpretation of the addition of noise to the inputs during training, and view it as a regularizing parameter that controls, in conjunction with ensemble averaging, the capacity and the smoothness of the estimator. The major role of this noise is to push different estimators to different local minima and thereby produce a more independent set of estimators. Best performance is then achieved by averaging the estimators. For this regularization, the level of the noise may be larger than the 'true' level which can be indirectly estimated. Since we want to study the effect of bootstrapping with noise on the smoothness of the estimator, separately from the task of input noise estimation, we consider a highly nonlinear, noise-free classification problem, and show that, even in this extreme case, addition of noise during training improves results significantly.

We chose a problem that is very difficult for feed-forward neural networks to deal with. It is difficult because of the highly nonlinear nature of the decision boundaries, and the fact that these nonlinearities are easier to represent in terms of local radially symmetric functions rather than ridge functions such as those given by feed-forward sigmoidal functions. Since the training data are given with no noise, it seems unreasonable to train a network with noise, but we show that, even in this case, training with noise is a very effective approach for smoothing the estimator.

In the bootstrap ensemble with noise (BEN) [39], we push the idea of noise injection further. We observe that adding noise to the inputs increases the first term on the right-hand side of (20), in that it adds variance to each estimator, but it decreases the contribution of the second term as it increases the degree of independence between estimators. Instead of using the 'true' noise, estimated from the data, for bootstrap, we seek an optimal noise level which gives smallest contribution to the error from the sum of the two components of the variance. It is impossible to calculate the optimal variance of the Gaussian noise without knowing f explicitly, and therefore the value of this variance remains a regularization term, a parameter which has to be estimated so as to minimize the total contribution of the variance term to the total error measure. Furthermore, since the injection of noise increases the degree of independence between different training sets, we can use bootstrap samples that are larger than the original training set. This does not affect the bias, if the noise is symmetric around zero, but it can reduce the variance. Note that the bias contribution to the error is not affected by introducing the ensemble-average estimator, because of the linearity of the expectation operator.

It follows that the BEN approach has the potential to reduce the contribution of the variance term to the total error. We should therefore seek a different level of trade-off between the contribution of variance and bias. In other words, we are able to use large (unbiased) networks without being affected by the large variance associated with such networks. This observation implies that the estimation of optimal noise levels should not be based on the performance of a single estimator, but rather based on the ensemble performance. The large variance of each single network in the ensemble can be tempered with a regularization term such as weight decay [31, 40], but again the estimation of the optimal regularization factor should be based on the ensemble-averaged performance. Breiman [7] and Ripley [40] present compelling empirical evidence of the importance of weight decay as a single network stabilizer. Our results confirm this fact under the BEN model. In my mind, the reduction of variance via expert averaging is the the true blessing of multiple experts.

5 Conclusions

The curse of dimensionality is arguably the biggest obstacle which impedes model estimation in high dimensional data sets. We have discussed the relevance of the Central Limit Theorem for feature extraction in the form of linear projections. We have further extended the feature extraction to a hybrid architecture which performs feature extraction in conjunction with modeling the classification or regression problem. In this context we have briefly described the multi-task hybrid architecture. We believe that this approach is very useful for introducing prior knowledge into a model.

For variance control we have discussed multiple expert as a means to temper a collection of experts and achieve lower variance error. We have demonstrated how performance of many experts can be predicted from performance of a small number of experts so that model selection can be efficiently performed on a small number of experts. An additional hybrid architecture which is beyond the scope of this paper, is a combination of two different functional forms in a single architecture. Some discussion on that architecture can be found in [9]. Other extensions that have recently become popular are various mixtures of experts, with different experts, e.g. mixtures of trees [34].

References

[1] S. Amari, A. Cichocki, and H. H. Yang. A new learning algorithm for blind signal separation. In G. Tesauro, D. Touretzky, and T. Leen, editors, *Advances in Neural Information Processing Systems*, volume 8, pages 757–763. MIT Press, 1996.

[2] R. E. Bellman. *Adaptive Control Processes*. Princeton University Press, Princeton, NJ, 1961.

[3] M. Bichsel and P. Seitz. Minimum class entropy: A maximum information approach to layered netowrks. *Neural Networks*, 2:133–141, 1989.

[4] E. L. Bienenstock, L. N Cooper, and P. W. Munro. Theory for the development of neuron selectivity: orientation specificity and binocular interaction in visual cortex. *Journal Neuroscience*, 2:32–48, 1982.

[5] C. M. Bishop. Training with noise is equivalent to Tikhonov regularization. *Neural Computation*, 7(1):108–116, 1995.

[6] B. S. Blais, N. Intrator, H. Shouval, and L. N Cooper. Receptive field formation in natural scene environments: comparison of single cell learning rules. *Neural Computation*, 10(7):1797–1813, 1998.

[7] L. Breiman. Bagging predictors. *Machine Learning*, 24:123–140, 1996.

[8] J. S. Bridle and D. J. C. MacKay. Unsupervised classifiers, mutual information and 'Phantom Targets'. In J.E. Moody, S.J Hanson, and R.P. Lippmann, editors, *Advances in Neural Information Processing Systems*, volume 4, pages 1096–1101. Morgan Kaufmann, San Mateo, CA, 1992.

[9] S. Cohen and N. Intrator. A hybrid projection based and radial basis function architecture: Initial values and global optimization. *To appear in Special issue of PAA on Fusion of Multiple Classifiers*, 2001.

[10] P. Comon. Independent component analysis, a new concept? *Signal Processing*, 36:287–314, 1994.

[11] N. Cristianini and J. Shawe-Taylor. *An introduction to support vector machines and other kernel-based learning methods*. Cambridge University Press, 2000.

[12] P. Diaconis and D. Freedman. Asymptotics of graphical projection pursuit. *Annals of Statistics*, 12:793–815, 1984.

[13] D. Donoho. High-dimensional data analysis: The curses and blessings of dimensionality, August 2000. A talk given at the *Math Challenges of the 21st Century* meeting of AMS.

[14] B. Efron and R. Tibshirani. *An Introduction to the Bootstrap*. Chapman and Hall, New York, 1993.

[15] J. L. Elman and D. Zipser. Learning the hidden structure of speech. *Journal of the Acoustical Society of America*, 4(83):1615–1626, 1988.

[16] W. Feller. *An Introduction to Probability Theory and its Applications*, volume 1. John Wiley & Sons, New York, 2nd edition, 1957.

[17] J. H. Friedman. Exploratory projection pursuit. *Journal of the American Statistical Association*, 82:249–266, 1987.

[18] J. H. Friedman and J. W. Tukey. A projection pursuit algorithm for exploratory data analysis. *IEEE Transactions on Computers*, C(23):881–889, 1974.

[19] S. Geman, E. Bienenstock, and R. Doursat. Neural networks and the bias-variance dilemma. *Neural Computation*, 4:1–58, 1992.

[20] D. Gutfinger and J. Sklansky. Robust classifiers by mixed adaptation. *IEEE Transactions on Pattern Analysis and Machine Intelligence*, 13:552–567, 1991.

[21] P. Hall. Estimating the direction in which data set is most interesting. *Probab. Theory Rel. Fields*, 80:51–78, 1988.

[22] P. J. Huber. Projection pursuit. (with discussion). *The Annals of Statistics*, 13:435–475, 1985.

[23] Q. Huynh, L. N Cooper, N. Intrator, and H. Shouval. Classification of underwater mammals using feature extraction based on time-frequency analysis and bcm theory. *IEEE-Signal Processing*, 46(5):1202–1207, May 1998.

[24] A. Hyvarinen and E. Oja. Simple neuron models for independent component analysis. *Int. J. Neural Systems*, 7:671–687, 1996.

[25] N. Intrator. Combining exploratory projection pursuit and projection pursuit regression with application to neural networks. *Neural Computation*, 5(3):443–455, 1993.

[26] N. Intrator. Neuronal goals: Efficient coding and coincidence detection. In S. Amari, L. Xu, L. W. Chan, I. King, and K. S. Leung, editors, *Proceedings of ICONIP Hong Kong. Progress in Neural Information Processing*, volume 1, pages 29–34. Springer, Sep 18-21, Hong-Kong 1996.

[27] N. Intrator and L. N Cooper. Objective function formulation of the BCM theory of visual cortical plasticity: Statistical connections, stability conditions. *Neural Networks*, 5:3–17, 1992.

[28] N. Intrator, D. Reisfeld, and Y. Yeshurun. Face recognition using a hybrid supervised/unsupervised neural network. *Pattern Recognition Letters*, 17:67–76, 1996.

[29] M. C. Jones and R. Sibson. What is projection pursuit? (with discussion). *J. Roy. Statist. Soc.*, Ser. A(150):1–36, 1987.

[30] M. Kendall and A. Stuart. *The Advanced Theory of Statistics*, volume 1. MacMillan Publishing, New York, 1977.

[31] A. Krogh and J. A. Hertz. A simple weight decay can improve generalization. In J.E. Moody, S.J Hanson, and R.P. Lippmann, editors, *Advances in Neural Information Processing Systems*, volume 4, pages 950–957. Morgan Kaufmann, San Mateo, CA, 1992.

[32] J. B. Kruskal. Toward a practical method which helps uncover the structure of the set of multivariate observations by finding the linear transformation which optimizes a new 'index of condensation'. In R. C. Milton and J. A. Nelder, editors, *Statistical Computation*, pages 427–440. Academic Press, New York, 1969.

[33] J. B. Kruskal. Linear transformation of multivariate data to reveal clustering. In R. N. Shepard, A. K. Romney, and S. B. Nerlove, editors, *Multidimensional Scaling: Theory and Application in the Behavioral Sciences, 1, Theory*, pages 179–191. Seminar Press, New York and London, 1972.

[34] M. Meila and M. I. Jordan. Learning with mixtures of trees. *Journal of Machine Learning Research*, 1:1–48, 2000.

[35] P. M. Murphy and D. W. Aha. UCI Repository of machine learning databases, 1992. Department of Information and Computer Science. University of California at Irvine. `anonymous ftp from ics.uci.edu:/usr2/spool/ftp/pub/machine-learning-databases`.

[36] U. Naftaly, N. Intrator, and D. Horn. Optimal ensemble averaging of neural networks. *Network*, 8(3):283–296, 1997.

[37] S. J. Nowlan and G. E. Hinton. Simplifying neural networks by soft weight-sharing. *Neural Computation*, 4:473–493, 1992.

[38] B. A. Olshausen and D. J. Field. Emergence of simple cell receptive field properties by learning a sparse code for natural images. *Nature*, 381:607–609, 1996.

[39] Y. Raviv and N. Intrator. Bootstrapping with noise: An effective regularization technique. *Connection Science, Special issue on Combining Estimators*, 8:356–372, 1996.

[40] B. D. Ripley. *Pattern Recognition and Neural Networks*. Oxford Press, 1996.

[41] D. E. Rumelhart, G. E. Hinton, and R. J. Williams. Learning internal representations by error propagation. In D. E. Rumelhart and J. L. McClelland, editors, *Parallel Distributed Processing*, volume 1, pages 318–362. MIT Press, Cambridge, MA, 1986.

[42] J. Sietsma and R. J. F. Dow. Creating artificial neural networks that generalize. *Neural Networks*, 4:67–79, 1991.

[43] I. Stainvas and N. Intrator. Blurred face recognition via a hybrid network architecture. In *Proceedings Int. Conf. on Pattern Recognition*, volume 2, pages 809–812, 2000.

[44] A. Stuart and J. K. Ord. *Kendall's Advanced Theory of Statistics*. Edward Arnold, 1994.

[45] P. Switzer. Numerical classification. In V. Barnett, editor, *Geostatistics*. Plenum Press, New York, 1970.

[46] P. Viola and W. M. Wells. Alignment by maximization of mutual information. In *Fifth Intl. Conf. on Computer Vision*, pages 16–23, Cambridge, MA, 1995. IEEE.

[47] M. P. Wand. Fast computation of multivariate kernel estimators. *Journal of Computational and Graphical Statistics*, 3:433–445, 1994.

[48] A. S. Weigend, B. A. Huberman, and D. Rumelhart. Predicting the future: A connectionist approach. *Int. J. Neural Syst*, 1:193–209, 1990.

[49] M. Yamac. Can we do better by combining 'supervised' and 'nonsupervised' machine learning for pattern analysis. Ph.D. dissertation, Brown University, 1969.

[50] H. Yang and S. Amari. Adaptive on-line learning algorithms for blind separation – maximum entropy and minimum mutual information. *Neural Computation*, 9(7):1457–1482, 1997.

A kind of neural computing goes practical: TeraOPS, stored programmable, analog-and-logic visual microprocessors - a review

Tamás ROSKA

Analogical and Neural Computing Laboratory, Computer and Automation Research Institute
Hungarian Academy of Sciences and
Jedlik Laboratories, Péter Pázmány Catholic University,
Budapest, Hungary
Phone: +36 1 209 52 63, Fax: +36 1 209 52 64, email: roska@sztaki.hu

ABSTRACT

The analogic (analog and logic) cellular computer is based on the CNN Universal Machine (CNN-UM) architecture. It is a stored programmable spatial-temporal computer, its core is a Cellular Neural/nonlinear Network (CNN). Recent silicon implementations, as a focal plane array visual microprocessor show an unprecedented supercomputer speed on a single chip (a few TeraOPS). The sensors are integrated with the processors, each processor has its own sensor.

Stored programmability is a unique feature when we consider neural networks. Indeed, however, this is the key for broad acceptance and use.

We are introducing the basic notions, the computing architecture and some applications. The biological relevance and computational complexity issues are summarized as well.

INTRODUCTION

Cellular Neural/Nonlinear Networks (CNN) [1]-[2] are locally connected massively parallel alog array processors. Completing the base cells with local memories, sensors, analog and gical arithmetics, and control units leads to the CNN Universal Machine (CNN-UM [3]), the chitecture of a stored programmable visual microprocessor. Implementing this architecture on a igle 1cm^2 CMOS chip, an enormous computational power can be achieved reaching the order of raOPS (10^{12} equivalent digital operations per second). The computational capability makes it ssible to solve a wide range of problems, including the discrete-space solution of 2D partial fferential equations in microseconds and target detection and tracking with several 1k frames per cond. The building of various stored programmable sensor-computers now in the horizon. The iking similarity to the anatomy of many living sensory systems makes the CNN-UM a must for o-inspired computers and computing.

Recent books [e.g. 6,21,22] and more than thousand papers [4] are covering the broad area.

The CNN/UM defines a new computing paradigm on flows and related computational mplexity classes.

The application field of the CNN Technology is rich and also well developed. Many areas are covered in medical imaging (e.g. echocardiography analysis [30]), industrial quality control (e.g. texture segmentation [31], motion tracking [32]), etc.

2. THE CNN PARADIGM

A Cellular Neural/Nonlinear Network (CNN) is defined by two mathematical constructs [2]:

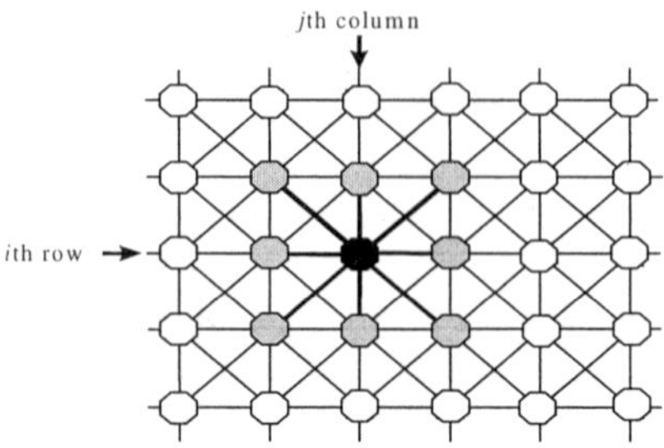

Figure 1 *A 2-dimensional CNN defined on a square grid with 3x3 neighborhood size.*

(i) A spatially discrete collection of continuous nonlinear dynamical systems called *cells*, where information can be encrypted into each cell via three independent variables called *input, threshold* and *initial state*.

(ii) A local (synaptic) *coupling law* relating one or more relevant variables of each cell to all neighboring cells located within a prescribed sphere of influence $S_{r(ij)}$ of radius *r* centered at *ij*.

Fig. 1 shows a 2D rectangular CNN composed of cells that are connected to their nearest neighbors. Due to its symmetry, regular structure and simplicity this type of arrangement (a rectangular grid) is primarily considered in all implementations.

In a two dimensional (*MxN*) CNN array the cell dynamics is described by the following nonlinear ordinary differential equation:

$$C\frac{d}{dt}x_{ij}(t) = -R^{-1}x_{ij}(t) + \sum_{kl \in S_r} A_{ij,kl}\, y_{kl}(t) + \sum_{kl \in S_r} B_{ij,kl}\, u_{kl} + z_{ij}$$

$$y_{ij}(t) = f(x_{ij}(t)) = 0.5\,(|x_{ij}(t)+1|-|x_{ij}(t)-1|)$$

where x_{ij}, u_{ij}, y_{ij} are the state, input and output voltage of the specified CNN cell, respectively. The state and output vary in time, the input is static (time independent), *ij* refers to a grid point associated with a cell on the 2D grid, and $kl \in \Sigma_r$ is a grid point in the neighborhood within the radius *r* of the cell *ij*. Term $A_{ij,kl}$ represents the linear feedback, $B_{ij,kl}$ the linear control, while z is the cell current (also referred to as bias or threshold) which could be space and time variant. The output characteristic *f* is a sigmoid-type piecewise-linear function.

CNNs with higher order base cells ("complex-cell" [5]) are also considered in latest architecture designs.

3. THE ANALOGIC CELLULAR COMPUTER ON FLOWS BASED ON THE CNN UIVERSAL MACHINE (CNN/UM) ARCHITECTUTE

We are defining algorithms on flows. The formal definition of the elementary operations is as follows [17].

Without loss of generality we will discuss 2D image flows, or video flows, the only discretization is in space.

Hence, a finite time image flow $\Phi(t)$ is defined as:

$$\Phi(t): \{\varphi_{ij}(t), \quad t \in T = [0, t_d]\}$$
$$1 \le i \le m \quad 1 \le j \le n$$

where m and n are positive integers, $t_d > 0$ (time duration), $\varphi_{ij}(t) \in C^1$ (continuously differentiable). For example, φ_{ij} may represent an input, state, or output of a cell (representing a pixel) in an $m \times n$ cell array, and $\varphi_{ij}(t)$ is bounded.

At $t = t^*$, $\quad \Phi(t^*)$ is an m x n *Picture* (a snapshot),

$$P: \{p_{ij} \in R^1\}, \quad |p_{ij}| \le p_{max} \in R^1 < \infty,$$ where p_{ij} is the pixel intensity.

Without loss of generality, we may assume that in a gray scale image black and white colors are represented by $+1$ and -1 (or $+1$ and 0). In this paper we will use the $+1$ and -1 convention. A color picture is represented by a combination of several color layers of m x n cell arrays, each layer is representing the intensity of the appropriate color component (e.g. R,G,B).

A binary picture can be called a *mask* M,

$$M: \quad m_{ij} \in \{1, -1\} \text{ or } \{1, 0\}$$

A sequence of snapshots at $t = t_0, t_0 + \Delta t, t_0 + 2\Delta t, \ldots$ is called *image sequence* or *video stream*. A spatial-temporal instruction set computer (StISC computer) operates on image flows, or image sequences, the elementary instruction is defined as

$$\Phi_{output}(t) := \quad \Psi(\Phi_{input}(t), \quad t \in T = [0, t_d] \quad (1)$$

Ψ *being a function on image flows or image sequences.* As an example, a video clip is transformed into another video clip.

A *functional F on an image flow* is defined as

$$P: = F(\Phi_{input}(t)) \qquad (2)$$

As an example, an image flow or a video clip is transformed into a picture showing the maximum intensity values in each pixel.

The output image could be a mask, M, as well, for example the mask pixel would be black if a change occurred in $\Phi(t)$.

If after $t = t_d$ the output is not settled, i.e. there exists at least one $ij \rightarrow \dot{\varphi}_{ij}(t) \neq 0$ then the spatial-temporal dynamics or the equivalent *spatial-temporal instruction is of non-equilibrium type*.

Now we have to define the formal definition of an algorithm of a Spatial-temporal Instruction Set Computer, called also a StISC computer (we refer to the CISC and RISC computers). In case of a digital Von Neumann Computer, running algorithms on integers, the formal definition of an algorithm on integers is the *μ-recursive function*. In our case of StISC machines, an algorithm on flows is defined by the *α-recursive function*.

The StISC Computer should perform
- non-equilibrium type spatial-temporal elementary instructions,
- spatial logic instructions on spatial masks, acting pixel-wise (e.g. a cellular automaton),
- spatial-temporal combination of image flows and or pictures pixel-wise, and
- algorithms (recursive functions) using the above three types of instructions.

Now we are in a position to define the new recursive function, the ***α-recursive function***. Algorithms of digital computers are defined mathematically via the **μ-recursive functions**.

The analogic spatial-temporal algorithms are defined via the **α-recursive function**.

These are defined by the
- initial settings of flows, pictures and masks: Φ (0), P, M;
- generating equilibrium and non-equilibrium PDE solutions via complex cell CNN via PDDE
$$: \Psi , \Phi (t) ;$$
- global minimization on the above;
- linear and logic combinations of functions and functionals defined above.

4. THE CNN UNIVERSAL MACHINE IS A MINIMAL ARCHITECTURE FOR A-RECURSIVE FUNCTIONS

The Turing Machine is a minimal architecture for the **μ**-recursive functions. Likewise, the CNN Universal Machine is a minimal architecture for the **α**-recursive functions. In many cases the LLU and LAOU can be implemented by special cells and templates, however, their presence is very practical for implementations (especially when logic instructions on multi-valued strings, like genetic instructions, or complex general I/O functions are defined. The additional building blocks to the Turing Machine that results in the Von Neumann Computer architecture made the digital computer practical when the stored programmability was introduced. To prove the Universality of the CNN-UM, we can implement all the elements of the **α**-recursive function step by step on the CNN Universal Machine.

5. COMPUTING POWER OF STISC MACHINES AND COMPUTATIONAL COMPLEXITY

In Table 1, the summary of properties of the three major classes of Universal Machines operating on integers (UMZ), on reals (UMR), and on flows (UMF) is shown. Related computational complexity results, including semantic complexity, can be found in [7,8,15,16,17,20,23]

To calculate a realistic computing power, in terms of the size of a problem, we have to define the basic operations implemented physically, via efficient hardware units. Here, Speed, dissipated Power, and physical Area (or volume) is the key measures.

We have calculated that the rough equivalent computing power of an ACE4k chip (a 4096-processor visual microprocessor) [26] is about a few TeraOPS (elementary operations are multiplication and addition).

If we are studying the calculation of this equivalent computing power in more details, it turns out that this *computing power depends heavily on the parameters of the problem, and not only on the size of the problem.*

The role of the accuracy, related to computational complexity is a delicate question. Not only in UMR, but also in UMF.

It is not easy to ask the good questions related to accuracy when studying locally connected dynamical systems, described in
- continuous time,
- continuous signal value,

- continuous interaction parameters, and
- discrete space.

Their Canonical Representations by multilayer Cellular (Neural) Nonlinear Networks (CNN) or
y the stored programmable CNN Universal Machine provides for the solid framework of
1athematical studies.

Table 1.

	Universal iterative Machine over Z	Universal (iterative) Machine over R	Universal, semi-iterative Machine over flows
	UMZ	**UMR**	**UMF**
I/O space	Z	R	F (flow on R^{nxn})
Elementary operators	Logic maps	Semi algebraic maps	Differential algebraic flows
Mode of operation	Iterative	Iterative	Semi iterative
Sphere of influence of elementary operators (instructions)	Local	Local	Global
Architecture	Turing Machine	Newton Machine	CNN Universal Machine
Typical computing models	Grammar	Basin of attraction Machine	2-3D differential and functional equations
	Partial recursive functions on Z	Register equations on R	α-recursive functions on F

6. DIFFERENT CNN-UM IMPLEMENTATIONS

Typical implementation types are the software with one processor, the FPGA, the dedicated
digital CMOS ASIC, (e.g. [35]), the analog (mixed-signal) CMOS (e.g. [25]-[27]), and the optical
(e.g. [28]). Although relying on digital CMOS implementation is the most straightforward from the
design point of view, the performance of these digital chips falls far from the analog and logic
versions that can reach with an 0.5 micron technology approximately TeraOPS: 10^{12} equivalent
digital operations per second. It should also be noted that optical implementations are still in the
experimental phase. Recent implementation with 128x128 processors on a chip with very efficient,
programmable focal plane optical sensors reach above 10 TeraOPS equivalent speed.

7. BIO-INSPIRED SENSORY COMPUTERS AND BIOLOGICAL MODELS

The anatomy and physiology of many living sensory systems can be programmed on the CNN-
UM. An outstanding example is the mammalian retina. A recent breakthrough in mammalian
retinal modeling [11] and the related CNN models show a good example of the genuine morphism
between these two areas [12].

Integrating sensor arrays with the CNN-UM based processors and introducing neuromorphic
adaptation, we have introduced the adaptive CNN-UM architecture, it is really a sensor-computer.

8. APPLICATIONS

During the last few years, more than thousand papers have been published on various aspects o
the CNN paradigm and the analogic cellular (CNN) computer. Many successful applications anc
application case studies have been proposed [29-34]. The availability of this technology througl
some start – up companies signals a new situation. The first commercial applications emerge.

9. ACKNOWLEDGEMENTS

The partial support of the Hungarian Academy of Sciences and the Office of Naval Research is
gratefully acknowledged.

REFERENCES

[1] L.O. Chua and L. Yang, "Cellular Neural Networks: Theory and Applications", *IEEE Transactions on Circuit,
and Systems*, Vol. 35, No. 10, pp. 1257-1290, October 1988.

[2] L.O. Chua and T. Roska, "The CNN Paradigm", *IEEE Transactions on Circuits and Systems - I*, Vol. 40, No. 3,
pp. 147-156, March 1993.

[3] T. Roska and L.O. Chua, "The CNN Universal Machine: An Analogic Array Computer", *IEEE Transactions of
Circuits and Systems - II*, vol. 40, pp. 163-173, March 1993.

[4] CNN BIBLIOGRAPHY: http://lab.analogic.sztaki.hu/ or http://www.ieee-cas.org/~cnnactc

[5] Cs. Rekeczky, T. Serrano-Gatarredona, T. Roska, and A. Rodríguez-Vázquez, "A Stored Program 2nd order/3
layer Complex Cell CNNM-UM*", Proc. 6th IEEE International Workshop on Cellular Neural Networks and thei,
Applications* CNNA 2000, pp. 213-218, Catania, May 2000.

[6] L. O. Chua, CNN: A Paradigm for Complexity, World Scientific, Singapore, 1998

[7] L. Blum, F. Cucker, M. Shub, S. Smale, Complexity and Real Computation, Springer Verlag, New York, 1988

[8] S. Smale, "Some remarks on the foundations of numerical analysis", *SIAM Review*, vol.30, pp.211-220, 1990

[9] T. Roska, L. O. Chua, D. Wolf, T. Kozek, R. Tetzlaff, F. Puffer, "Simulating nonlinear waves and partia,
differential equations via CNN - Part I. Basic Techniques*", IEEE Trans. on Circuits and Systems I
Fundamental Theory and Applications* Vol. 42, No.10, pp. 807-815, 1995

[10]Cs. Rekeczky and L.O. Chua, "Computing with Front Propagation: Active Contour and Skeleton Models ir
Continuous-Time CNN", *Journal of VLSI Signal Processing*, Special Issue: Spatiotemporal Signal Processing
with Analogic CNN Visual Microprocessors, Vol.23. No.2/3. pp.373-402, Kluwer, 1999

[11]B. Roska and F. S. Werblin, "Vertical interactions across ten parallel, stacked representations in the
mammalian retina", *Nature*, vol. 410, pp.583-587, 29 March , 2001

[12]F. Werblin, B. Roska, D. Bálya, Cs. Rekeczky, T. Roska, "Implementing a Retinal Visual Language in CNN: a
Neuromprphic Case Study*", Proc. IEEE ISCAS 2001*, Sydney, 2001

[13]I. Szatmári, "The Implementation of a Nonlinear Wave Metric for Image Analysis and Classification on the
64x64 I/O CNN-UM Chip", *Proceedings of IEEE Int. Workshop on Cellular Neural Networks and Thei,
Applications*, (CNNA'2000), pp. 395-400, Catania, 2000

[14]T. Roska, "Computer-Sensors: Spatial-Temporal Compu-ters for Analog Array Signals, Dynamically Integratec
with Sensors", *Journal of VLSI Signal Processing*, Special Issue: Spatiotemporal Signal Processing witr
Analogic CNN Visual Microprocessors, Vol.23. No.2/3. pp. 221-238, Kluwer, 1999

[15]E. Csuhaj-Varju, "Networks of language processors" In: Current Trends in Theoretical Computer Science
Entering the 21st Century. Eds. by G. Paun, G. Rozenberg and A. Salomaa, World Scientific Publishing Co.
Singapore, 2001, 771-790.

[16]G. Prószéky, G.: Psychological Reality and Mathematical Complexity in Computational Processing of Natura
Languages (Report, under Publication), 2001

[17]T. Roska, "Analogic Wave Computers*", Proc IEEE ISCAS 2001*, Sydney, 2001

[18]S. Espejo, R. Carmona, R. Domínguez-Castro and A. Rodríguez-Vázquez, "A CNN Universal Chip in CMOS
Technology", *International Journal of Circuit Theory and Applications*, vol. 24, pp. 93-109, 1996

[19]G. Liñán, P. Foldesy, S. Espejo, R. Domínguez-Castro and A. Rodríguez-Vázquez, "A 0.5µm CMOS 10^6 Transistors Analog Programmable Array Processor for Real-Time Image Processing". *Proc. of the 1999 European Solid-State Circuits Conference*, pp. 358-361, ISBN 2-86332- 246-X, September 1999

[20]M. Gilli, T. Roska, P. P. Civalleri, and L. O. Chua, "CNN dynamics represents a broader class than PDEs", Report DNS-4-2001, Comp. Aut.Res.Inst, Budapest, 2001

[21]T. Roska and A. Rodríguez-Vázquez (eds.), Toward the visual microprocessor- VLSI Design and the use of Cellular Neural network (CNN) Universal Machine Computers, J. Wiley, London, 2000

[22]L.O.Chua and T.Roska, Cellular Neural Networks and Visual Computing, Cambridge University Press, Cambridge, UK, 2002

[23]G.Chaitin, "Information theoretic Computational Complexity", *IEEE Trans. Information Theory*, Vol. IT/20, pp.10-15, 1974

[24]T. Roska, Á. Zarándy, S. Zöld, P. Földesy and P. Szolgay, "The Computational Infrastructure of Analogic CNN Computing - Part I: The CNN-UM Chip Prototyping System", *IEEE Trans. on Circuits and Systems* I: Vol. 46, pp. 261-268,1999

[25]Espejo, A.Rodriguez-Vázquez, R. A. Carmona, P. Földesy, Á. Zarándy, P. Szolgay, T. Szirányi, and T. Roska, "0.8µm CMOS Two Dimensional Programmable Mixed-Signal Focal-Plane Array Processor with On-Chip Binary Imaging and Instruction Storage", *IEEE Journal on Solid State Circuits*, Vol. 32. No. 7. pp.1013-1026, 1997.

[26]S. Espejo, R. Domínguez-Castro, G. Liñán, and Á. Rodriguez-Vázquez, "A 64x64 CNN universal chip with analog and digital I/O", 5th Int. Conf. Electronics, Circuits and Systems *(ICECS-98)*, Lisbon, pp. 203-206 1998.

[27]A. Paasio, A. Kananen and V. Porra, "A 176 x 144 processor binary I/O CNN-UM chip design", *Proc. Eur. Conf. Circuit Theory and Design - ECCTD'99 DAD*, Stresa, 1999

[28]Sz. Tőkés, L. Orzó, Cs.Rekeczky, T. Roska and Á. Zarándy, "An Optical CNN Implementation with Stored Programmability", *Proc. IEEE International Symposium on Circuits and Systems ISCAS 2000*, pp. 136-139, Geneva, June 2000.

[29]I. Szatmári, A. Schultz, Cs.Rekeczky, T. Kozek, T. Roska, and L. O. Chua, "Morphology and Autowave Metric on CNN Applied to Bubble-Debris Classification", *IEEE Trans. on Neural Networks*, Vol. 11, No. 6, pp.1385-1393, November 2000.

[30]Cs. Rekeczky, Á. Tahy, Z. Végh, and T. Roska, "CNN-based Spatio-temporal Nonlinear Filtering and Endocardial Boundary Detection in Echocardiography", *International Journal of Circuit Theory and Applications*, Vol. 27, pp. 171-207, 1999.

[31]T. Szirányi, M. Csapodi, "Texture Classification and Segmentation by Cellular Neural Network using Genetic Learning", *C. Vision and Image Understanding*, Vol. 71, No. 3, pp. 255-270, 1998.

[32]L. Czúni, T. Szirányi, "Motion Segmentation and Tracking with Edge Relaxation and Optimization using Fully Parallel Methods in the Cellular Nonlinear Network Architecture", *Real-Time Imaging*, (in press), 2001

[33]Cs. Rekeczky and L. O. Chua, "Computing with Front Propagation: Active Contour and Skeleton Models in Continuous-time CNN", *Journal of VLSI Signal Processing Systems*, Vol. 23, No. 2/3, pp. 373-402, November-December 1999.

[34]Á. Zarándy, F. Werblin, T. Roska, and L. O. Chua, "Spatial-logic Algorithms Using Basic Morphological Analogic CNN Operations", *International Journal of Circuit Theory and Applications*, Vol. 24, pp. 283-300, 1996.

[35]Á. Zarándy, P. Keresztes, T. Roska and P. Szolgay, "CASTLE: an Emulated Digital CNN Architecture: Design Issues, New Results", in *Proc. 5th Int. Conf. on Electronics, Circuits and Systems (ICECS'98)*, pp.199-202, Lisbon, September 1998.

[36]T.Roska and Á.Rodríguez-Vázquez, „Towards Visual Microprocessors", Proc. IEEE, July, 2002

Limitations and Future Trends in Neural Computation
S. Ablameyko et al. (Eds.)
IOS Press, 2003

On Pattern Formation in Cellular Neural Networks

Liviu Goraş

„Gh. Asachi" Technical University of Iasi, Faculty of Electronics and Telecommunications, Bd. Carol 11, Iasi 6600, Romania

Abstract. Cellular Neural Networks (CNN's) have recently received considerable attention due to their potential in high-speed image processing applications. An interesting behavior CNN's can exhibit is that of pattern formation. In this work we present several aspects regarding pattern formation in CNN's. First, we give a detailed description of the Turing pattern formation mechanism. We consider piecewise linear cell CNN's which can be analyzed using the decoupling technique – a powerful mechanism that allows significant insight into the dynamics of the CNN. Related to this topic we present the influence of boundary conditions, initial conditions and phase for patterns development. Next, we extend the theory to other architectures based on similar or different cells and various types of couplings. Finally, we present the possibility of using the root locus method to reflect the dynamics of CNN's.

1. Introduction

Since their invention [1,2], CNN's have been intensely investigated for their applications in fast image processing [3-14]. Inspired from biology, CNN's are homogeneous arrays of *identical and identically coupled* cells. The cells are, in general, nonlinear dynamic circuits characterized by input, state and output. The coupling between cells is local and algebraic, each cell being influenced through controlled sources or resistive grids by its closest neighbors. The image to be processed with CNN's is introduced through the input and/or the state of the cells, each cell of an N by M array corresponding to a pixel of the image.

The standard CNN cell [1] consists of an input source, an RC parallel circuit, a biasing source and a nonlinear (piecewise linear saturation type) controlled source, which converts the state of the cell into the output. The state of each cell is determined by the outputs (A template) and inputs (B template) of the neighboring¹cells through controlled sources. Two-port or even n-port cells can be used as well.

An interesting phenomenon, which has been shown to appear in CNN's, is that of pattern formation - a property that, perhaps, has not been yet enough exploited. Pattern will be the name for any stable equilibrium point.

---

¹ The neighborhood of the ij cell is considered to contain the ij cell as well.

Various connections with phenomena from other domains including biology have been made so far and interesting analogies have been established. Among them, pattern formation based on a mechanism similar to that proposed by Turing [15,16] to explain morphogenesis has been reported in two-grid coupled second order cell CNN's [17-19].

In the following, several results on pattern formation in CNN's are presented. The main topics refer to cells, interconnections, equations, mechanism of pattern formation and the influence of various factors as boundary conditions, initial conditions, and phase in the process of pattern formation.

2. Two-grid coupled CNN's

In the following we present a CNN architecture capable to produce patterns and in particular, Turing patterns. The architecture is based on second order two-port cells coupled by means of two resistive grids.

2.1. The Cells

In general, a cell consists of a *nonlinear resistive two port* characterized by the relations

$$i_1 = f(u,v)$$
$$i_2 = \tilde{g}(u,v) \tag{1}$$

where u and v are the port voltages and *two capacitors* as shown in Fig. 1.

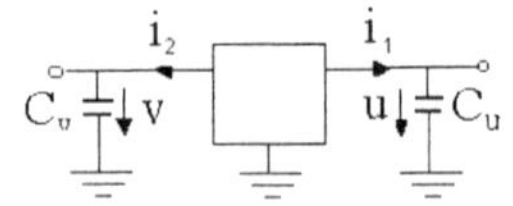

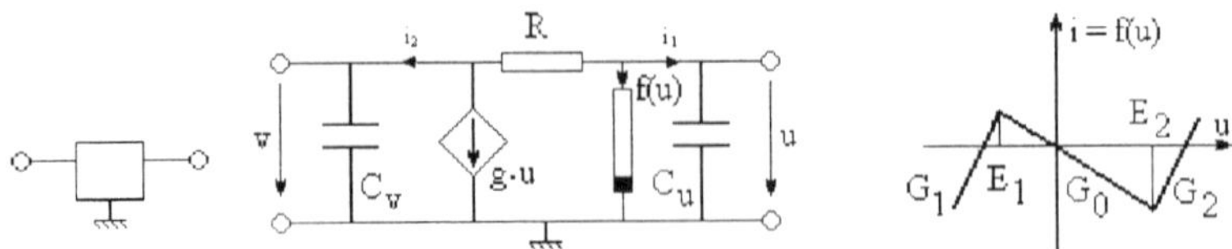

Fig. 1. *Two-port cell.*

The analysis is greatly simplified if the nonlinearity is piecewise linear. A cell consisting of four linear elements including a voltage controlled current source and a nonlinear resistor [20,21] is represented in Fig. 2 and is described by the equations:

$$i_1 = f(u,v) = -Gu - f(u) + Gv$$
$$i_2 = \tilde{g}(u,v)i_1 = (G-g)u - Gv \tag{2}$$

where the f(u) is the piecewise linear characteristic of the nonlinear resistor.

Fig. 2. *Two-port cell and i-v characteristic of the piecewise nonlinear resistor*

2.2. The interconnections

The CNN based on the above cell is built by connecting the cells using two resistive grids. The architecture is like a sandwich of cells between grids, in the sense that each grid connects similar ports. Controlled sources interconnections are possible as well and will be discussed later.

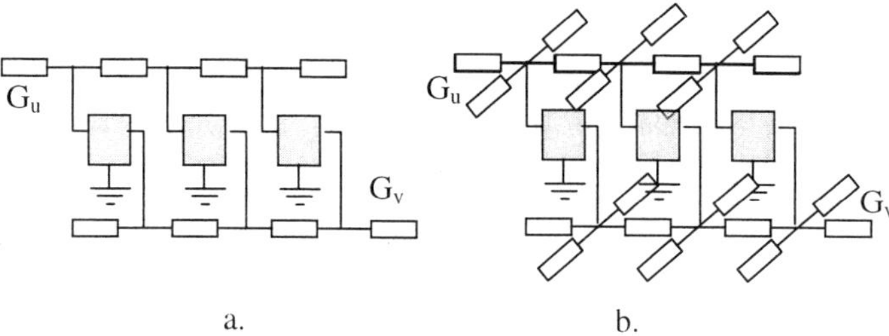

Fig. 3. *Sketch of a 1D two-grid coupled CNN architecture (a) and the way towards a 2D array (b).*

2.3. The equations

In the general case, the behavior of a 2D CNN composed of M×N cells is described by the following system of equations

$$C_u \frac{du_{ij}(t)}{dt} = f(u_{ij}, v_{ij}) + G_u \nabla^2 u_{ij}$$
$$C_v \frac{dv_{ij}(t)}{dt} = \tilde{g}(u_{ij}, v_{ij}) + G_v \nabla^2 v_{ij} \qquad i = 0,...,M-1, j = 0,...,N-1 \qquad (3)$$

where $\nabla^2 x_{ij} = x_{(i+1)j} + x_{(i-1)j} + x_{i(j+1)} + x_{i(j-1)} - 4x_{ij}$ is the Laplacean (which, for the 1-D case, has the form $\nabla^2 x_i = x_{i+1} + x_{i-1} - 2x_i$).

With the notations

$$\gamma = \frac{1}{C_u}; D_u = \frac{G_u}{C_u}; D_v = \frac{G_v}{C_v}; g(u_{ij}, v_{ij}) = \frac{C_u}{C_v} \tilde{g}(u_{ij}, v_{ij}) \qquad (4)$$

the equations become

$$\frac{du_{ij}(t)}{dt} = \gamma f(u_{ij}, v_{ij}) + D_u \nabla^2 u_{ij}$$
$$\frac{dv_{ij}(t)}{dt} = \gamma g(u_{ij}, v_{ij}) + D_v \nabla^2 v_{ij} \qquad i = 0,...,M-1, j = 0,...,N-1 \qquad (5)$$

Linearization of these equations gives

$$\frac{du_{ij}(t)}{dt} = \gamma(f_u u_{ij} + f_v v_{ij}) + D_u \nabla^2 u_{ij}$$
$$\frac{dv_{ij}(t)}{dt} = \gamma(g_u u_{ij} + g_v v_{ij}) + D_v \nabla^2 v_{ij} \qquad i = 0,...,M-1, j = 0,...,N-1 \qquad (6)$$

where f_u, f_v, g_u, g_v are the elements of the Jacobian matrix of $f(u,v)$ and $g(u,v)$, D_u and D_v are the diffusion coefficients and γ is a scaling coefficient. For the cell in Fig. 2, the above equation are valid for u-voltages within the interval $[E_1, E_2]$. In this case, the relations between the Jacobian parameters and the circuit elements are

$$f_u = -(G + G_0), f_v = G, g_u = \frac{C_u}{C_v}(G - g), g_v = -\frac{C_u}{C_v}G \qquad (7)$$

The saturation type piecewise linear shape for the cell nonlinearity is convenient from the implementation point of view as well as for the theoretical tractability. Thus, in the case when all cell voltages are in the central linear part of the nonlinear characteristics the analysis simplifies considerably due to linearity and symmetry (which is valid until at least one cell reaches saturation).

3. The decoupling technique

In the following we analyze a CNN made of piecewise nonlinear cells as shown in Fig. 2 and suppose that all voltages are within the central linear part of the cells characteristics. For the sake of simplicity we consider the 1D version of equations (6):

$$\frac{du_i(t)}{dt} = \gamma(f_u u_i + f_v v_i) + D_u \nabla^2 u_i$$
$$\frac{dv_i(t)}{dt} = \gamma(g_u u_i + g_v v_i) + D_v \nabla^2 v_i \qquad i = 0,...,M-1 \tag{8}$$

Using the notations from [18], we transform the system of equations by means of the change of variable

$$u_i(t) = \sum_{m=0}^{M-1} \Phi_M(i,m)\hat{u}_m(t)$$
$$v_i(t) = \sum_{m=0}^{M-1} \Phi_M(i,m)\hat{v}_m(t) \qquad i = 0,...,M-1 \tag{9}$$

where $\Phi_M(i,m)$ are eigenfunctions (dependent on the boundary conditions) of the 1D Laplacean i.e., $\nabla^2 \Phi_M(i,m) = -k_m^2 \Phi_M(i,m)$ and $-k_m^2$ are the eigenvalues, proportional to the square (or sum of squares) of sine functions [18].

If the set $\Phi_M(i,m)$ of M functions are orthogonal with respect to the scalar product in C^M, i.e.,

$$\sum_{i=0}^{M-1} \Phi_M^*(m,i)\Phi_M(i,n) = \delta_{mn} \tag{10}$$

$\hat{u}_m$ and $\hat{v}_m$ can be expressed, by means of the inversion formulas:

$$\hat{u}_m(t) = \sum_{i=0}^{M-1} \Phi_M^*(m,i)u_i(t) \tag{11}$$
$$\hat{v}_m(t) = \sum_{i=0}^{M-1} \Phi_M^*(m,i)v_i(t) \qquad m = 0,...,M-1$$

where

$$\Phi_M^*(m,i) = \Phi_M(i,m) \tag{12}$$

Making the change of variable and taking the scalar product of both sides of the equations, the dynamics of the 1D CNN is described by the following set of pairs of *decoupled* linear equations

$$\begin{bmatrix} \dot{\hat{u}}_m \\ \dot{\hat{v}}_m \end{bmatrix} = \left(\gamma \begin{bmatrix} f_u & f_v \\ g_u & g_v \end{bmatrix} - k_m^2 \begin{bmatrix} D_u & 0 \\ 0 & D_v \end{bmatrix} \right) \begin{bmatrix} \hat{u}_m \\ \hat{v}_m \end{bmatrix} \qquad m = 0,...,M-1 \tag{13}$$

Thus, the set of 2×M coupled differential equations in the u and v variables transforms into M sets of pairs of second order differential equations in the new variables - the amplitudes of the spatial components of the voltages.

The natural frequencies, λ_{m1} and λ_{m2} are the roots of the characteristic polynomials

$$\lambda_m^2 + \lambda_m[k_m^2(D_u + D_v) - \gamma(f_u + g_v)] + D_u D_v k_m^4$$
$$- \gamma(D_v f_u + D_u g_v)k_m^2 + (f_u g_v - f_v g_u) = 0 \qquad m = 0,...,M-1 \tag{14}$$

The solution of the 1-D CNN equations is thus

$$u_i(t) = \sum_{m=0}^{M-1} (a_m e^{\lambda_{m1}t} + b_m e^{\lambda_{m2}t}) \Phi_M(i,m)$$

$$v_i(t) = \sum_{m=0}^{M-1} (c_m e^{\lambda_{m1}t} + d_m e^{\lambda_{m2}t}) \Phi_M(i,m) \qquad i = 0,\dots,M-1 \qquad (15)$$

The integration constants satisfy the constraints

$$c_m = p_m a_m; \ d_m = q_m d_m \qquad (16)$$

where

$$p_m = \frac{\lambda_{m1} - \gamma f_u + D_u k_m^2}{\gamma f_v}; q_m = \frac{\lambda_{m2} - \gamma f_u + D_u k_m^2}{\gamma f_v} \qquad (17)$$

and can be expressed in terms of the initial conditions of the voltages in the two "layers' of
the CNN by means of the formulas

$$a_m = \frac{\hat{v}_m(0) - q_m \hat{u}_m(0)}{p_m - q_m}; \ b_m = \frac{\hat{v}_m(0) - p_m \hat{u}_m(0)}{q_m - p_m} \qquad (18)$$

Thus, the complete response of the CNN in terms of the spectrum of the initial
conditions with respect to the corresponding boundary conditions (which will be discussed
soon) can be expressed easily in terms of

$$\hat{u}_m(t) = \frac{\hat{v}_m(0) - q_m \hat{u}_m(0)}{p_m - q_m} e^{\lambda_{m1}t} + \frac{\hat{v}_m(0) - p_m \hat{u}_m(0)}{q_m - p_m} e^{\lambda_{m2}t}$$

$$\hat{v}_m(t) = p_m \frac{\hat{v}_m(0) - q_m \hat{u}_m(0)}{p_m - q_m} e^{\lambda_{m1}t} + q_m \frac{\hat{v}_m(0) - p_m \hat{u}_m(0)}{q_m - p_m} e^{\lambda_{m2}t} \qquad (19)$$

When biasing current sources are used at the u ports of the cells, the equations become

$$\begin{bmatrix} \dot{\hat{u}}_m(t) \\ \dot{\hat{v}}_m(t) \end{bmatrix} = \left(\gamma \begin{bmatrix} f_u & f_v \\ g_u & g_v \end{bmatrix} - k_m^2 \begin{bmatrix} D_u & 0 \\ 0 & D_v \end{bmatrix} \right) \begin{bmatrix} \hat{u}_m(t) \\ \hat{v}_m(t) \end{bmatrix} + \gamma \begin{bmatrix} \hat{J}_m \\ 0 \end{bmatrix} \qquad (20)$$

where $\hat{J}_m$ is the amplitude of the m-th spatial spectral component of the biasing source. In
this case the general form of the transient expressed in terms of the decoupled variables
[22] is

$$\begin{cases} \hat{u}_m(t) = a_m(\hat{J}_m, \hat{u}_m(0), \hat{v}_m(0)) e^{\lambda_{m1}t} + b_m(\hat{J}_m, \hat{u}_m(0), \hat{v}_m(0)) e^{\lambda_{m2}t} + f_1 \hat{J}_m \\ \hat{v}_m(t) = c_m(\hat{J}_m, \hat{u}_m(0), \hat{v}_m(0)) e^{\lambda_{m1}t} + d_m(\hat{J}_m, \hat{u}_m(0), \hat{v}_m(0)) e^{\lambda_{m2}t} + f_2 \hat{J}_m \end{cases} \qquad (21)$$

where f_1 and f_2 are:

$$\begin{cases} f_1 = \dfrac{-\gamma(\gamma g_v - k_m^2 D_v)}{(\gamma f_u - k_m^2 D_u)(\gamma g_v - k_m^2 D_v) - \gamma^2 f_v g_u} \\ f_2 = \dfrac{\gamma^2 g_u}{(\gamma f_u - k_m^2 D_u)(\gamma g_v - k_m^2 D_v) - \gamma^2 f_v g_u} \end{cases} \qquad (22)$$

The above results extend easily to the 2D case with the change of variable

$$u_{ij}(t) = \sum_{m=0}^{M-1} \sum_{n=0}^{N-1} \Phi_{MN}(i,j,m,n) \hat{u}_{mn}(t)$$

$$v_{ij}(t) = \sum_{m=0}^{M-1} \sum_{n=0}^{N-1} \Phi_{MN}(i,j,m,n) \hat{v}_{mn}(t) \qquad (23)$$

where $<\Phi_{MN}(i,j,m,n),\Phi_{MN}(i,j,p,q)>=\sum_{i=0}^{M-1}\sum_{j=0}^{N-1}\Phi^*_{MN}(m,n,i,j)\Phi_{MN}(i,j,p,q)=\delta_{mnpq}$.

3.1. Boundary conditions (BC's) and their influence on pattern formation

BC's reflect the way the cells on the edges of the array are connected and influence the behavior of the CNN. This influence will be bigger for smaller arrays going up to the aspect of allowing or not the development of a pattern. The spatial operator represented by the connection template (in our case the Laplacean) should be specified for the edge cells and the virtual cells around the array within the neighborhood radius.

The periodic and the zero-flux BC's are common in physics, biology, chemistry etc. but also in CNN implementation where they are considered as "natural". However, in the case of CNN's many other BC's may be imagined, some of them having no counterpart in physical, biological, chemical etc. problems but allowing analytical tractability [23,24].

In the table below we list the definition, the eigenvectors and eigenvalues for various BC's in the 1-D case. The results are useful to decouple the system of linear differential equations describing the CNN behavior in the central linear part.

Table 1. *Eigenvectors and eigenvalues for various BC's.*

Left/right	*Boundary conditions*	*Eigenvectors*	*Eigenvalues*
ring	$u(-1)=u(M-1)$ $u(M)=u(0)$	$e^{j\frac{2\pi}{M}mi}$	$-4\sin^2\dfrac{m\pi}{M}$
zero-flux zero-flux	$u(-1)=u(0)$ $u(M)=u(M-1)$	$\cos\dfrac{m(2i+1)\pi}{2M}$	$-4\sin^2\dfrac{m\pi}{2M}$
anti-zero flux anti-zero flux	$u(-1)=-u(0)$ $u(M)=-u(M-1)$	$\sin\dfrac{(m+1)(2i+1)\pi}{2M}$	$-4\sin^2\dfrac{(m+1)\pi}{2M}$
zero zero	$u(-1)=0$ $u(M)=0$	$\sin\dfrac{(m+1)(i+1)\pi}{M+1}$	$-4\sin^2\dfrac{(m+1)\pi}{2(M+1)}$
quasi zero flux quasi zero flux	$u(-1)=u(1)$ $u(M)=u(M-2)$	$\cos\dfrac{mi\pi}{M-1}$	$-4\sin^2\dfrac{m\pi}{2(M-1)}$
zero zero flux	$u(-1)=0$ $u(M)=u(M-1)$	$\sin\dfrac{(2m+1)(i+1)\pi}{2M+1}$	$-4\sin^2\dfrac{(2m+1)\pi}{2(2M+1)}$
anti-zero flux zero flux	$u(-1)=-u(0)$ $u(M)=u(M-1)$	$\sin\dfrac{(2m+1)(2i+1)\pi}{4M}$	$-4\sin^2\dfrac{(2m+1)\pi}{4M}$
zero quasi-zero flux	$u(-1)=0$ $u(M)=u(M-2)$	$\sin\dfrac{(2m+1)(i+1)\pi}{2M}$	$-4\sin^2\dfrac{(2m+1)\pi}{4M}$
anti-zero flux quasi-zero flux	$u(-1)=-u(0)$ $u(M)=u(M-2)$	$\sin\dfrac{(2m+1)(2i+1)\pi}{2(2M-1)}$	$-4\sin\dfrac{(2m+1)\pi}{2(2M-1)}$
zero anti-zero flux	$u(-1)=0$ $u(M)=-u(M-1)$	$\sin\dfrac{2(m+1)(i+1)\pi}{2M+1}$	$-4\sin^2\dfrac{(m+1)\pi}{2M+1}$

3.2. Dispersion curve

The dynamics of the CNN is significantly determined by the roots of the characteristic equations, even though the results are valid only for the linear central part. The crucial aspect regarding pattern formation is that, in certain conditions, at least one of the roots of the characteristic equation has positive real part. This will cause the corresponding spatial mode(s) to grow until some nonlinearity will limit the growth. The *dispersion curve* represents the real part of the temporal eigenvalues versus the spatial eigenvalues.

$$\text{Re } \lambda_{1,2}(k_m^2) = \text{Re } \{\gamma \frac{f_u + g_v}{2} - k_m^2 \frac{D_u + D_v}{2} + \sqrt{\left[\gamma \frac{(g_v - f_u)}{2} + k_m^2 \frac{D_u - D_v}{2}\right]^2 + \gamma^2 f_v g_u}\} \tag{24}$$

A typical dispersion curve is presented below.

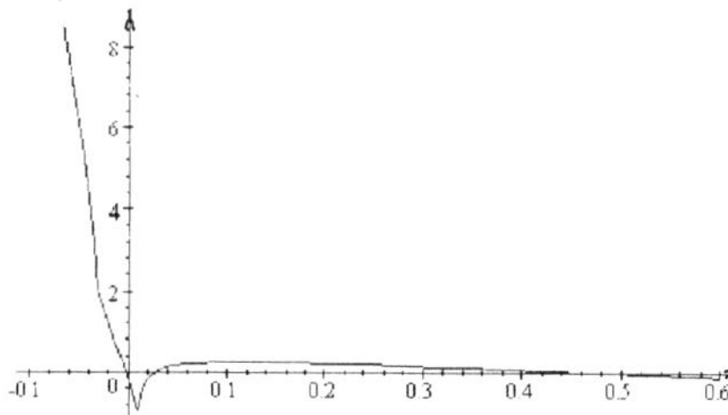

Fig. 4. *Typical dispersion curve.*

The curve has been computed for the following parameters: $\gamma=5$, $f_u=0.1$, $f_v=-1$, $g_u=0.1$, $g_v=-2$, $D_u=1$, $D_v=150$, $M=30$. The curve satisfies Turing conditions that will be discussed next as it exhibit a "band" of unstable modes.

4. Turing pattern formation mechanism

In principle, a pattern, i.e., a stable equilibrium points towards which the network emerges, can develop when the characteristic equation has at least one root with positive real part corresponding to a *nonzero* spatial frequency. Indeed, the instability of the zero spatial frequency spatial mode will determine that *all* cell go to either a positive or negative saturation value or simultaneously oscillate– situations which will not be called patterns.

An interesting situation is that when the origin is a **stable** equilibrium point for an isolated cell and an **unstable** equilibrium point for the whole array. The necessary conditions (Turing) that ensure the *instability* of an array built of *stable* cells linked together through resistive grids are [15,18]:

$$f_u + g_v < 0$$
$$f_u g_v - f_v g_u > 0$$
$$D_v f_u + D_u g_v > 0 \tag{25}$$
$$(D_v f_u - D_u g_v)^2 + 4 D_u D_v f_v g_u > 0$$

The first two conditions ensure the stability of an isolated cell while the last two, the potential instability of the array. In fact, Turing patterns in CNN's are dependent on the following aspects:

a – fulfillment of Turing conditions [18],

b – dispersion curve [18],

c – initial conditions [22],

d – boundary conditions [23,24],

e – biasing sources signal, when they exist [25].

Beside, the shape of the nonlinear characteristic of the cell resistor influences the pattern as well but this is an aspect that cannot be easily handled. However, it has been shown that the results of the linear theory fit remarkably well with the simulations especially for 1D arrays, which means that the nonlinearity plays mainly the role of limiting the growing process of the unstable spatial modes. In the 2D case, however, the linear theory is able to predicting the final pattern in fewer cases.

4.1. Qualitative Explanation of Reaction-Diffusion Phenomena in a 1D CNN

In the following we give an intuitive explanation of pattern formation emphasizing the reaction-diffusion mechanism used by Turing to explain morphogenesis on a chemical basis. We consider the array shown in Fig. 5 built with the cell in Fig. 2 and assume that the diffusion coefficients D_u and D_v of the u- and v-grid respectively satisfy the relation $D_u \ll D_v$; i.e., $R_u C_u \gg R_v C_v$ (implied by the Turing conditions). Suppose that the initial conditions are zero except for the voltage u_i that slightly increases. Through the R_u resistors the increase of u_i will slowly "diffuse" to the neighboring cells on the u-part. As a consequence the neighboring cells will have their u- voltages increased in the vicinity of cell i (local activation). At the same time, the voltage controlled source will determine the voltage of the opposite v-node to decrease; i.e., to become negative.

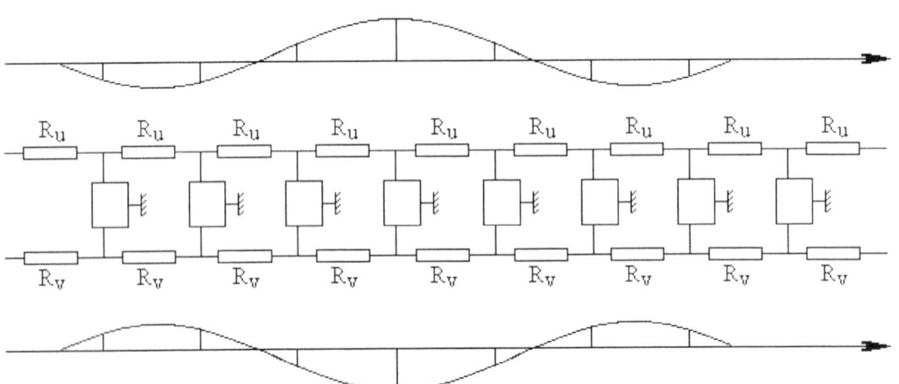

Fig. 5: 1D array exhibiting reaction-diffusion Turing pattern behavior.

Due to the much smaller value of the time constant of the v-grid, the negative voltage of the v_i node will propagate quickly on the v-side of the array (local activation again). At a greater distance of cell i, the negative voltage on the v-side of the array will determine, through the transversal resistors, the decrease of the opposite u-voltages which were not able to increase as a consequence of the slow propagation of the initial perturbation on the u-side (distance inhibition).

The voltage levels on the two sides of the array are sketched in Fig. 5 as well. The spatial wavelengths will be determined among other parameters by the ratios between the diffusion coefficients. Of course, this way of reasoning is only qualitative and it cannot replace rigorous calculations.

4.2. Boundary conditions in 2D CNN's

Extension of the results related to boundary conditions to the 2D case is straightforward. Denoting by $-k_m^2$, $-k_n^2$ and $-k_{mn}^2$ the spatial eigenvalues for the 1D and 2D case respectively and by $\phi_M(m,i)$, $\phi_N(n,i)$ and $\phi_{MN}(m,n;i,j)$ the corresponding eigenfunctions, the following relationships are satisfied [18]:

$$-k_{mn}^2 = -k_m^2 - k_n^2 \tag{26}$$

$$\Phi_{MN}(m,n,i,j) = \Phi_M(m,i)\Phi_N(n,j) \tag{27}$$

where M and N are the dimensions of the array m=0,...,M-1 and n=0,...,N-1. From the above relations it is apparent that, for a given dispersion curve, corresponding to a particular choice of the cell and diffusion parameters, the number and the position of the unstable modes can be controlled using various combinations of boundary conditions. Compared to the one-dimensional case, the number of possibilities is obviously much greater. Again, the control is more efficient in the case of small dimensional arrays. The analytical results corresponding to various BC's can be obtained using relations (27) and the results in Table 1. In the following, several simulations for various boundary and initial conditions are given. The parameters of the array and cells were: M=N=5, $G_1=G_2=-1$, $E_2=-E_1=1$, $f_u=-(G+G_0)=0.4$, $f_v=G=1/R=1$, $g_u=C_u(G-g)/C_v=-0.25$, $g_v=-C_uG/C_v=-0.5$, $\gamma=1/C_u=15$, $D_u=G_u/C_u=1.0$, $D_v=G_v/C_v=3.8$ (G_u and G_v are the conductances of the two resistive grids). The dispersion curve for this case is characterized by peak at 1.84915, $k_1^2=1.61056$, $k_2^2=2.11672$. The unstable modes and the corresponding real parts of the temporal eigenvalues for several types of BC's are given in Table 2.

Table 2. *Real part of the unstable modes for various BC's.*

$D_v=3.8$	Azf-Azf: Azf-Azf	Z-Z:Z-Z	Qzf-Qzf: Qzf-Qzf	Qzf-Qzf: Z-Z	Z-Zf: Azf-Qzf
m=0, n=1	$Re(\lambda)=0.378$	$Re(\lambda)=0.260$	--------------	$Re(\lambda)=0.039$	$Re(\lambda)=0.124$
m=0, n=2	$Re(\lambda)=0.028$	$Re(\lambda)=0.307$	$Re(\lambda)=0.362$	$Re(\lambda)=0.362$	$Re(\lambda)=0.261$
m=0, n=3	--------------	--------------	--------------	$Re(\lambda)=0.028$	--------------
m=1, n=0	$Re(\lambda)=0.378$	$Re(\lambda)=0.260$	--------------	--------------	--------------
m=1, n=1	**$Re(\lambda)=0.134$**	$Re(\lambda)=0.362$	$Re(\lambda)=0.199$	$Re(\lambda)=0.365$	$Re(\lambda)=0.376$
m=1, n=2	--------------	$Re(\lambda)=0.028$	$Re(\lambda)=0.205$	$Re(\lambda)=0.206$	$Re(\lambda)=0.010$
m=2, n=0	$Re(\lambda)=0.028$	$Re(\lambda)=0.307$	$Re(\lambda)=0.362$	$Re(\lambda)=0.307$	$Re(\lambda)=0.377$
m=2, n=1	--------------	$Re(\lambda)=0.028$	$Re(\lambda)=0.205$	$Re(\lambda)=0.028$	$Re(\lambda)=0.155$
m=3, n=0	--------------	--------------	--------------	--------------	$Re(\lambda)=0.051$

4.3. Patterns

Using random initial conditions and various BC's the following patterns have been obtained. The winning modes were generally those corresponding to the greatest real part of the temporal eigenvalues. However, in the case of Fig. 9, mode m=1, n=2 was obtained even though mode m=1, n=1 was expected.

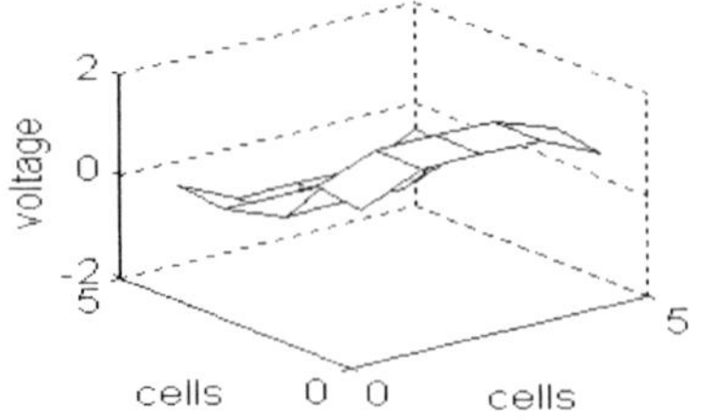

Fig. 6. *azf-azf:azf-azf, Dv=3.8, u side*

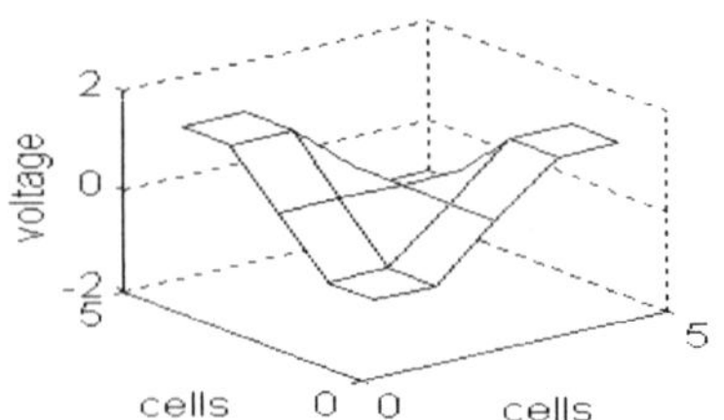

Fig. 7. *z-z:z-z, Dv=3.8, u side*

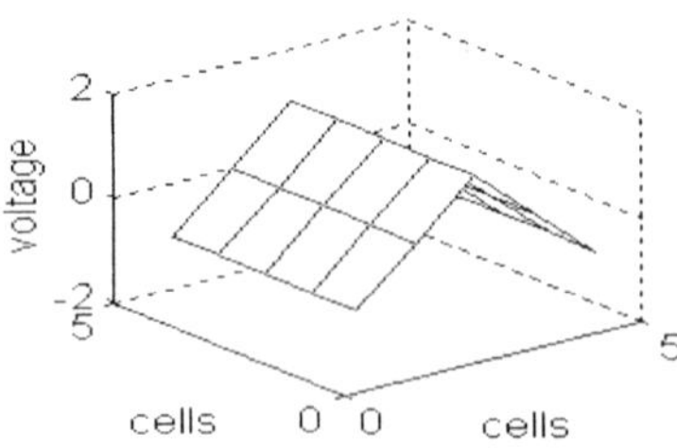

Fig. 8. *qzf-qzf:qzf-qzf, Dv=3.8, u side*

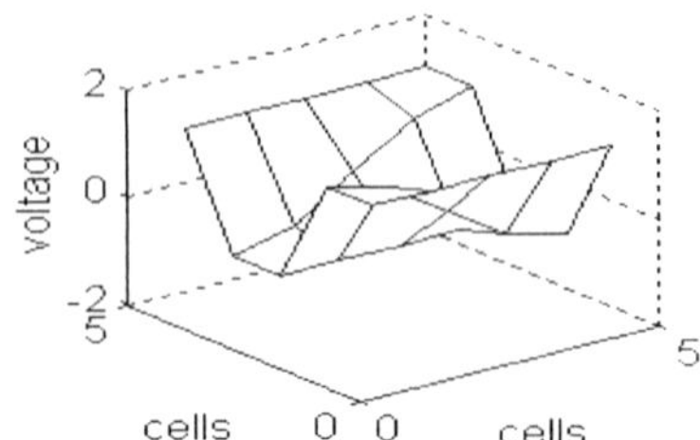

Fig. 9. *qzf-qzf:z-z, Dv=3.8, u side*

4.4. Mode suppression by initial conditions

The general form of the transient expressed in terms of the decoupled variables when no biasing is present is given by (20) where λ_{m1} and λ_{m2} are the roots of the characteristic equations. It is easy to observe that, with appropriate nonzero initial conditions, it is possible to suppress either of the two modes for each pair of spatial modes [22]. In particular, the above modes may be those with positive real part. In fact, when the Turing conditions are fulfilled, the band of unstable modes contains only real temporal eigenvalues. It is possible to suppress all unstable modes by means of appropriately pairing the initial conditions in the u- and the v-"layer" of the CNN. Alternatively, only part of the unstable modes may be suppressed. Stable modes may be suppressed as well.

4.5. Phase influence on mode competition

For initial conditions consisting of two pure spatial modes the technique of decoupling the differential equations predicts a race between the spatial modes which depends on their weight in the initial conditions and on the magnitude of the (positive) real parts of the corresponding temporal modes. The phase of the two spatial modes is irrelevant within linear theory. This statement is true as far as the amplification conditions for one mode are much more favorable than for the other one (in terms of amplitude ratio and eigenvalue real parts) [18,23]. However, when the competition is "tight", it has been found that the relative position (phase) of the two competing modes can influence the final pattern [26].

5. A Modified Architecture

Interesting patterns can be produced with a modified architecture consisting of cells coupled by resistive grids, this time over a specified number of nodes, k, as suggested in Fig. 10 (where rectangles are two-ports, straight lines are resistances and, for simplicity only 5 connections are shown). We will discuss only the 1D case, the extension to 2D being straightforward. The behavior of the CNN is described by the following state equations:

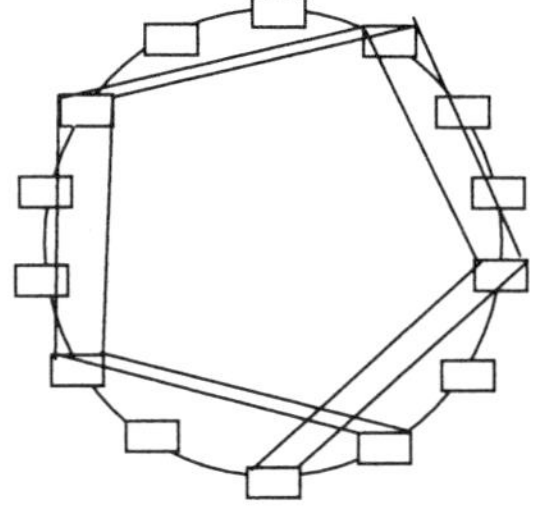

Fig. 10. *Sketch of the 1D architecture*

$$\frac{du_i(t)}{dt} = \gamma f(u_i, v_i) + D_u \nabla_k^2 u_i$$

$$\frac{dv_i(t)}{dt} = \gamma g(u_i, v_i) + D_v \nabla_k^2 v_i \qquad (28)$$

where $\nabla_k^2 x_i = x_{i+k} + x_{i-k} - 2x_i$ is the modified 1D Laplacean. Depending on the relationship between k and M (and N), the array dimension, various possibilities can be imagined. A special case is when k divides M, i.e., M=mk, with $m \in \mathbf{N}$. In this situation, the array consists of an interlaced combination of k independent sub-arrays.

The technique of equation decoupling used to predict the patterns (valid in the central linear regions of the cells characteristics) can be applied in this case as well. Various boundary conditions can be imagined but those allowing analytical treatment are ring (periodic) ones. For this special case it is easy to check that the eigenvectors are $e^{j\frac{2\pi}{M}mi}$ while the eigenvalues of the modified Laplacean are $-4\sin^2\frac{mk\pi}{M}$. Indeed

$$\nabla_k^2 e^{j\frac{2\pi}{M}mi} = -4\sin^2\left(\frac{mk\pi}{M}\right) e^{j\frac{2\pi}{M}mi} \qquad (29)$$

It is apparent that, when k divides M, the eigenvalues are identical to those of an array with M/k elements in a ring configuration.

We give below several computer simulation examples. In the first simulation we used a 1D array made of 58 cells with ring (periodic) boundary conditions and k=2. The CNN parameters were f_u=0.4, f_v=1, g_u=-0.25, g_v=-0.5, γ=3, D_u=1, D_v=3.8.

In Fig.11 the time evolution and the final pattern for the *u*- and *v*-"layers" of the array starting zero initial conditions except for $u_{15}(0)$=1 have been represented.

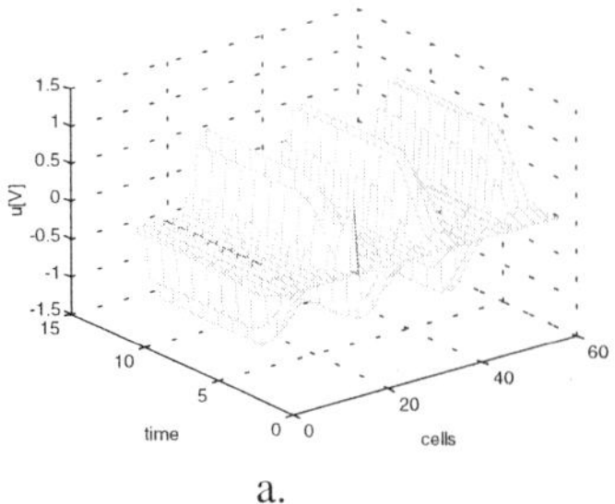

a.

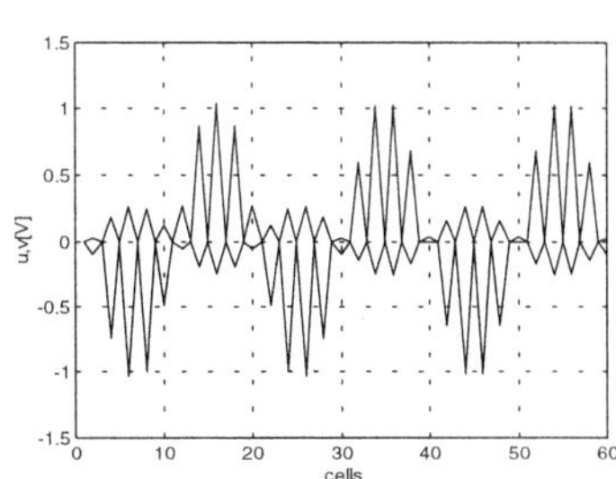

Fig. 11. *Time evolution (a) and final pattern (b) for the "u-layer" (M=58, k=2, $u_{15}(0)$=1).*

The simulations shown in Fig. 12 have been performed in the same conditions as above except for the number of cells that has been modified to 57. This time k=2 does no more divide M=57 and the shape of the pattern has been drastically changed.

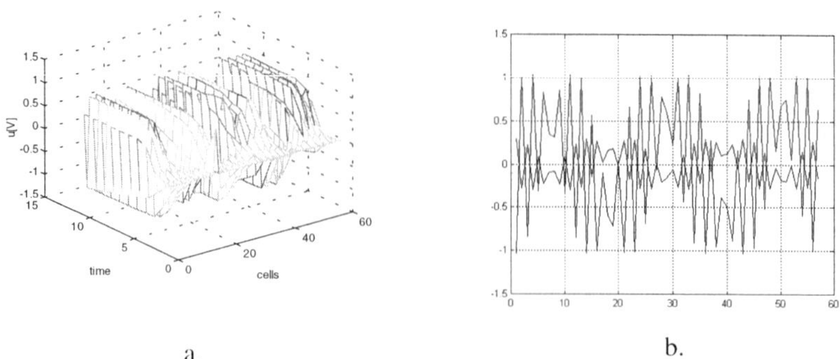

a.   b.

Fig. 12. *Time evolution (a) and final pattern (b) for the "u-layer" (M=57, k=2, $u_{15}(0)=1$).*

The above patterns show a high sensitivity to the change of the number of cells, under identical initial conditions. Such sensitivity seems to have not been observed so far for Turing patterns obtained in classical CNN's. It is apparent that the spatial spectrum is richer than in ordinary implementations, a fact that has been verified experimentally. Moreover, a remarkable property is the possibility of having interlaced patterns when k divides the number of cells.

6. Controlled sources coupled CNN's

In what follows we present several results concerning pattern formation in CNN's composed by cells coupled through controlled sources.

6.1. First order one-port cells – first order neighborhood CNN's

We consider an autonomous 1D CNN made of first order cells (Fig. 13) and first order neighborhood template and described, in the central linear part, by the equations:

$$\frac{du_i(t)}{dt} = -u_i + A_{-1}u_{i-1}(t) + A_0 u_i(t) + A_{+1}u_{i+1}(t) \qquad i = 0,...,M-1 \tag{30}$$

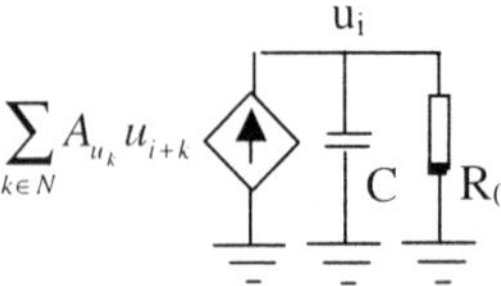

Fig. 13. *First-order cell.*

The shape of the nonlinear resistor is similar to that in Fig. 2 and $R_0C=1$. The cells are connected through voltage controlled current sources according to the A-template.

For ring BC's the spatial eigenfunctions have the form

$$\Phi_M(i,m) = e^{j(\omega(m)i + \varphi(m))} \tag{31}$$

and the eigenvalues are

$$K_{1D}(\omega(m)) = A_0 + (A_1 + A_{-1})\cos\omega(m) + j(A_1 - A_{-1})\sin\omega(m) \tag{32}$$

where $\omega(m) = e^{j\frac{2\pi}{M}mi}$. The spatial eigenvalues are in general complex and depend on the parameters of the template and on the mode they belong to.

For symmetric templates, $A_{-1} = A_1$, the spatial eigenvalues are real, $K_{1D}(\omega(m)) = A_0 + 2A_1\cos\omega(m)$. Using the change of variable:

$$u_i = \sum_{m=0}^{M-1} \Phi_M(i,m)\hat{u}_m \qquad i = 0,...,M-1 \tag{33}$$

where $\Phi_M(m,i)$ are the spatial exponential orthogonal functions presented above, we obtain the following set of first order decoupled equations:

$$\frac{d\,\hat{u}_m(t)}{dt} = (-1 + K_{1D})\hat{u}_m \qquad i = 0,...,M-1 \tag{34}$$

The roots of the characteristic equation are $\lambda(K_{1D}) = K_{1D} - 1$, so that the dispersion curve is a straight line.

6.2. Second order two-port cell – first order neighborhood CNN's

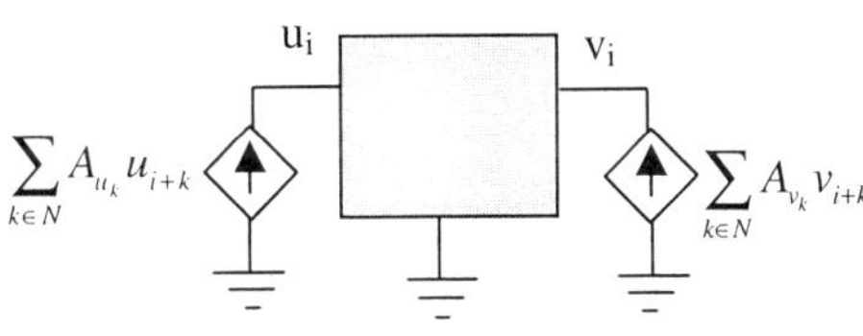

Fig. 14. *Two-port second order cell and first order template.*

In the following we consider an autonomous 1D CNN consisting of two-port cells terminated on capacitors, connected by means of two first order templates and ring BC's as sketched in Fig. 14. In the central linear part, the CNN is described by the following set of equations

$$\begin{cases} \dfrac{du_i(t)}{dt} = \gamma(f_u u_i + f_v v_i) + D_u A_{u1D}(u_i) \\[2mm] \dfrac{dv_i(t)}{dt} = \gamma(g_u u_i + g_v v_i) + D_v A_{v1D}(v_i) \end{cases} \qquad i = 0,...,M-1 \tag{35}$$

where A_{u1D} and A_{v1D} are the spatial operators for the state of the u and v layers respectively. D_u and D_v have been kept only as scaling coefficients for the two templates.

Using the decoupling technique by means of the change of variable (10), the following set of decoupled equations is obtained

$$\begin{bmatrix} \dot{\hat{u}}_m(t) \\ \dot{\hat{v}}_m(t) \end{bmatrix} = \left(\gamma \begin{bmatrix} f_u & f_v \\ g_u & g_v \end{bmatrix} + \begin{bmatrix} K_{1D} D_u & 0 \\ 0 & K_{1D}' D_v \end{bmatrix} \right) \begin{bmatrix} \hat{u}_m(t) \\ \hat{v}_m(t) \end{bmatrix} \qquad m = 0,...,M-1 \tag{36}$$

The general form of the solution is (14) where D_u and D_v are replaced by $D_u K_{1D}$ and $D_v K_{1D}'$ respectively and λ_{m1} and λ_{m2} are the solutions of the characteristic equation:

$$\lambda_m^2 - \lambda_m[\gamma(f_u + g_v) + D_u K_{1D} + D_v K_{1D}'] + D_u D_v K_{1D} K_{1D}'$$
$$+ \gamma(D_v K_{1D}' f_u + D_u K_{1D} g_v) + \gamma^2(f_u g_v - f_v g_u) = 0 \tag{37}$$

i.e.,

$$\lambda_{1,2}(K_{1D}, K_{1D}') = \gamma\frac{f_u + g_v}{2} + \frac{D_u K_{1D} + D_v K_{1D}'}{2} \pm \sqrt{\left[\gamma\frac{(g_v - f_u)}{2} - \frac{(D_u K_{1D} - D_v K_{1D}')}{2}\right]^2 + \gamma^2 f_v g_u} \tag{38}$$

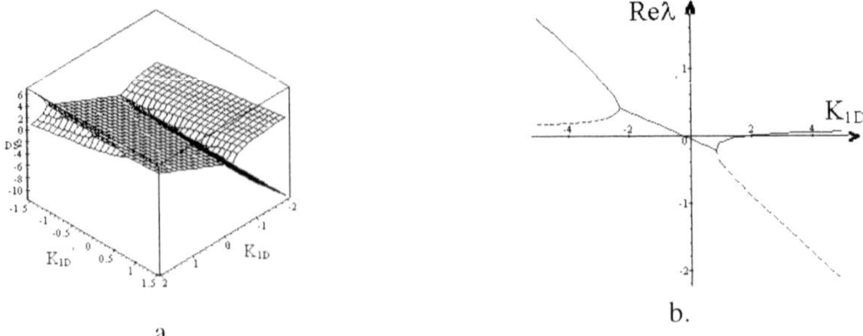

Fig. 15. *Real part of temporal eigenvalues vs spatial eigenvalues for different (a) and identical (b) symmetric templates.*

In general, K_{1D} and K_{1D}' have complex values. The roots of the characteristic equation can be real or complex. Patterns are associated to real positive part temporal eigenvalues. Typical forms for the real part of the temporal eigenvalues for symmetric templates, i.e., real spatial eigenvalues, are shown in Fig. 15. It is apparent that a spatial mode can have both temporal modes stable or unstable (real or complex conjugated) or one stable and another one unstable (real).

6.3. The decoupling between layers

When $\gamma^2 f_v g_u$ is small enough the behavior of the CNN is similar to that of two uncoupled CNNs made with first order cells, the roots of the characteristic equation being

$$\lambda_{m1} \cong \gamma f_u + D_u K_{1D}$$
$$\lambda_{m2} \cong \gamma g_v + D_v K_{1D} \tag{39}$$

and dependent only on the parameters of each layer. The "dispersion curve" for each first order cell CNN is a straight line with the slope dependent on D_u and D_v respectively

The dispersion curves/surfaces show that the CNN can be interpreted as a time variant spatial filter in the sense that the unstable spatial modes composing the initial conditions increase competitively (in a monotonic or oscillatory manner) in time while the stable ones decrease. When saturation is reached in at least one cell, the decoupling method is no more valid. The dispersion curves have generally three zones: a central one corresponding to complex roots and two lateral ones with (distinct) real roots.

Several relevant points on the dispersion curves are:

a) Extremities of the zone where the eigenvalues are complex conjugated:

$$K_{1D_{left}} = \frac{\gamma}{D_v - D_u}\left[(f_u - g_v) - 2\sqrt{-f_v g_u}\right]$$

$$K_{1D_{right}} = \frac{\gamma}{D_v - D_u}\left[(f_u - g_v) + 2\sqrt{-f_v g_u}\right] \tag{40}$$

b) Width of the middle zone (when it exists, i.e., when $f_v g_u < 0$):

$$\Delta K_{1D} = \frac{4\gamma\sqrt{-f_v g_u}}{D_v - D_u} \tag{41}$$

c) Coordinates of the center of the middle zone:

$$K_{1Dmiddle} = -\frac{\gamma}{D_u - D_v}\left(f_u - g_v\right)$$

$$\mathrm{Re}(K_{1Dmiddle}) = \frac{\gamma}{2(D_u - D_v)}\left(g_v D_u - f_u D_v\right)$$

(42)

d) Coordinates of the two extreme points, a maximum and a minimum (when they exist, i.e., $D_u - D_v \neq 0$ and $f_v g_u < 0$):

$$K_{1D_1} = \frac{\gamma}{D_u - D_v}\left(g_v - f_u - (D_u + D_v)\sqrt{\frac{-f_v g_u}{D_u D_v}}\right)$$

$$K_{1D_2} = \frac{\gamma}{D_u - D_v}\left(g_v - f_u + (D_u + D_v)\sqrt{\frac{-f_v g_u}{D_u D_v}}\right)$$

(43)

e) Real part of the temporal eigenvalue for the zero spatial frequency:

$$\mathrm{Re}(\lambda_{1,2}(0)) = \gamma f_u$$

(44)

f) Imaginary parts of the temporal eigenvalues

$$\mathrm{Im}\{\lambda_{1,2}(K_{1D}, K_{1D}')\} = \pm\sqrt{\left[\gamma\frac{(g_v - f_u)}{2} - \frac{(D_u K_{1D} - D_v K_{1D}')}{2}\right]^2 + \gamma^2 f_v g_u\}}$$

(45)

In the particular case when the templates for the two layers are $A_0 = 2$ and $A_{\pm 1} = -1$ and the cell parameters satisfy the constraints (26), Turing patterns are obtained. In this case, D_u and D_v are but scaling constants for the template parameters. (Here too, the number of parameters is greater then the number of degrees of freedom.)

6.4. The characteristic window

Using the above points, it is possible to design CNN's with specified behavior for a given domain of eigenvalues by observing that the cells determine the shape of the dispersion curves and the template defines a window for the "active" zone on it centered in A_0 and having $A_{-1} = A_1$ as width.

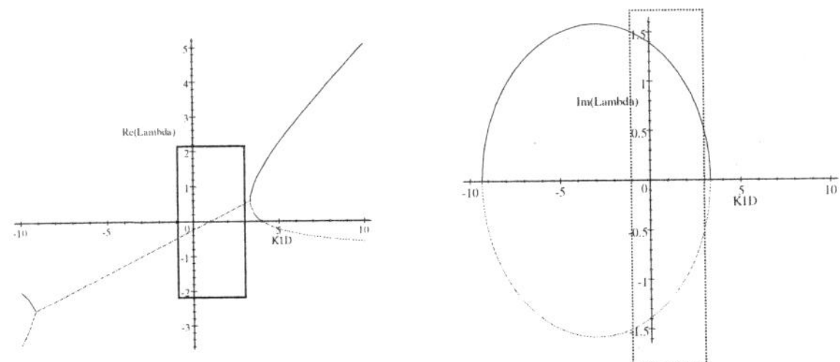

Fig. 16. *Windows on the real and imaginary parts of the temporal eigenvalues*

From the above dispersion curve one can see that various types of dynamics are possible according to the shape of the curves and the domain of the eigenvalues.

For the following set of parameters: $\gamma = 5$, $f_u = 0.1$, $g_u = 0.1$, $f_v = -1$, $g_v = -0.2$, $D_u = 0.5$, $D_v = 1$, $M = 40$, $u_{20}(0) = 0.1$, $A_0 = 1$, $A_{\pm 1} = 1$ and ring BC's, the results in Fig. 17 have been obtained.

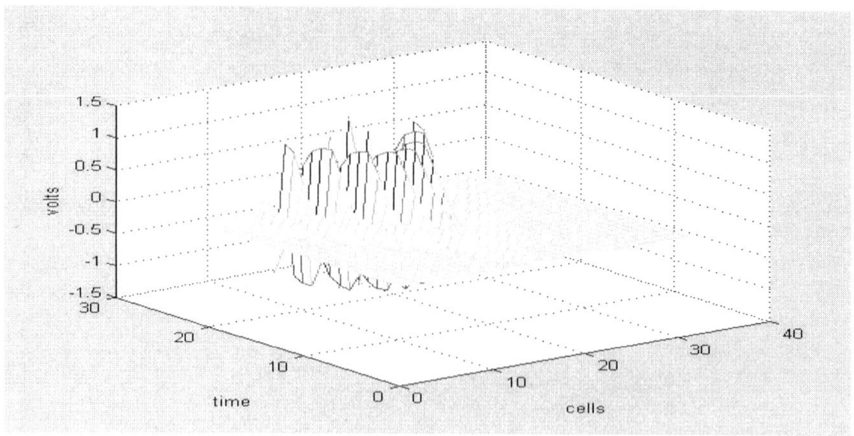

Fig. 17. *Time evolution for the u-cells.*

6.5. Oscillatory behavior

In the following we will consider a particular case of the dispersion curve characterized by a middle zone positioned on the real axis as shown in Fig. 18.

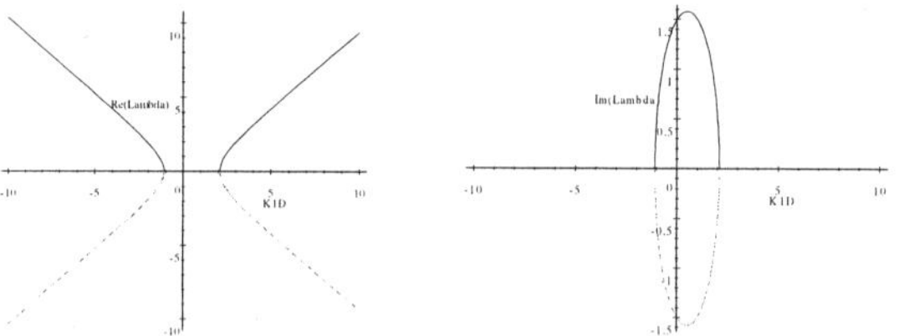

Fig. 18: *Dispersion curves and imaginary part of the temporal eigenvalues for the particular case $\gamma=5$, $f_u=-0.1$, $f_v=-0.1$, $g_u=1$, $g_v=0.1$, $D_u=1$, $D_v=-1$, $M=30$.*

As the center of the window is determined by A_0 and its width by $A_{\pm 1}$, it is possible to choose the template so that all eigenvalus be on the imaginary axis. In this care, the spatial harmonics of the signal represented by the initial conditions will oscillate in time with frequencies determined by the imaginary part of the dispersion curve.

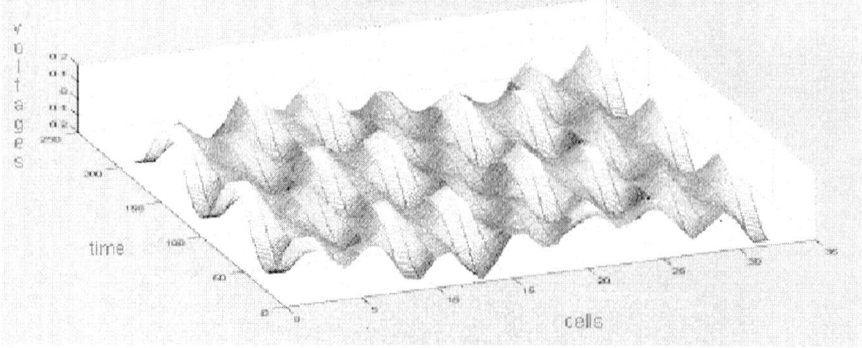

Fig. 19. *Time evolution of modes 3 and 13 for $A_0=0.5$ and $A_{\pm 1}=0.01$*

When the window width i.e., $A_{\pm 1}$ is small, which corresponds to weakly coupled cell, all the frequencies of oscillations are almost identical. This is the case when the center of the window is placed on $K_{1Dmiddle} = -\dfrac{\gamma}{D_u - D_v}(f_u - g_v)$ corresponding to the extreme values of the imaginary parts $\pm\gamma\sqrt{f_u g_v}$.

The simulation in Fig. 19 corresponds to temporal eigenvalues almost identical (A_0=0.5 and $A_{\pm1}$=0.01). The initial conditions were the sum of modes 3 and 13, both with amplitude 0.1. In this case, the imaginary parts are almost equal so that the whole pattern oscillate with the same frequency

Another case of interest is when the eigenvalues have an important variation within the window. This situation can be obtained choosing the window towards the extremities of the middle part of the dispersion curve. The simulation in Fig. 20 (A_0=0.88 and $A_{\pm1}$=0.1) corresponds to such a situation: the patterns changing its shape while oscillating.

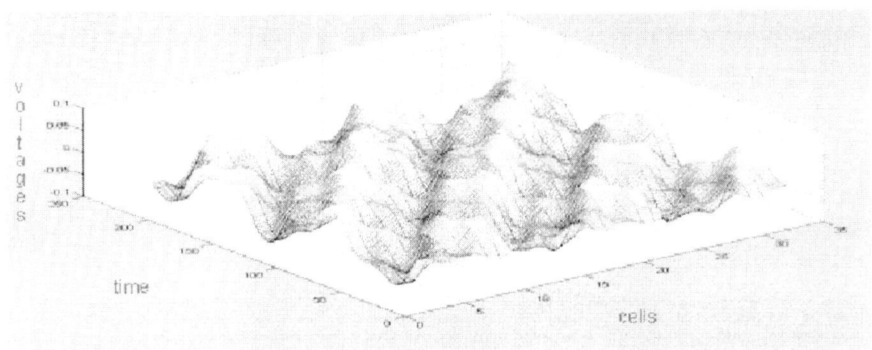

Fig. 20. *Time evolution of modes 3 and 13 for A$_0$=0.88 and A$_{\pm1}$=0.1.*

6.6. First order one-port cell – second order neighborhood CNN's

For the central linear part, the set of differential equations for the autonomous case is:

$$\frac{du_i(t)}{dt} = -u_i + A_{1D}^{r=2}(u_i), \quad i = 0,...,M-1 \tag{46}$$

where the spatial operator $A_{1D}^{r=2}$ is defined as

$$A_{1D}^{r=2}(u_i) = A_{-2}u_{i-2} + A_{-1}u_{i-1} + A_0u_i + A_1u_{i+1} + A_2u_{i+2} \tag{47}$$

and the spatial eigenvalues are:

$$K_{1D}^{r=2} = A_0 + (A_1 + A_{-1})\cos\omega(m) + (A_{-2} + A_2)\cos 2\omega(m) +$$
$$+ j(A_1 - A_{-1})\sin\omega(m) + j(A_2 - A_{-2})\sin 2\omega(m) \tag{48}$$

which, for the symmetric case are real.

$$K_{1D}^{r=2} = A_0^{r=2} + 2A_{\pm1}^{r=2}\cos\omega(m) + 2A_{\pm2}^{r=2}\cos 2\omega(m) \tag{49}$$

To make a comparison we cast (49) in the form:

$$K_{1D}^{r=2} = \alpha(K_{1D})^2 + \beta K_{1D} + \gamma \tag{50}$$

where $K_{1D} = A_0 + 2A_{\pm1}\cos\omega(m)$ are the eigenvalues for second order cell – first order neighborhood CNN's. Once A_0 and $A_{\pm1}$ have been adopted, the parameters α, β and γ can be determined uniquely in terms of $A_0^{r=2}$, $A_{\pm1}^{r=2}$ and $A_{\pm2}^{r=2}$.

For synthesis purposes the template can be determined using the following relations:

$$A_0^{r=2} = \alpha(A_0^2 + 2A_{\pm1}^2) + \beta A_0 + \gamma - 1$$
$$A_{\pm1}^{r=2} = 2\alpha A_0 A_{\pm1} + \beta A_{\pm1} \tag{51}$$
$$A_{\pm2}^{r=2} = \alpha A_{\pm1}^2$$

With the above notations, the dispersion curve is a parabola:

$$\mathrm{Re}(\lambda(K_{1D})) = \alpha(K_{1D})^2 + \beta K_{1D} + \gamma - 1 \tag{52}$$

which has a maximum for $\alpha<0$, a minimum for $\alpha>0$ and the extreme value,

$$\mathrm{Re}(\lambda(K_{1D})) = -\frac{\beta^2}{4\alpha} + \gamma - 1 \tag{53}$$

occurs for:

$$K_{1Dextrem} = \frac{-\beta}{2\alpha} \tag{54}$$

The parameter γ determines the position of the dispersion curve. It crosses the x-axis in the points:

$$K_{1Dleft} = \min\left\{\frac{1}{2\alpha}\left(-\beta \pm \sqrt{\beta^2 - 4\alpha(\gamma-1)}\right)\right\}$$
$$K_{1Dright} = \max\left\{\frac{1}{2\alpha}\left(-\beta \pm \sqrt{\beta^2 - 4\alpha(\gamma-1)}\right)\right\} \tag{55}$$

In order to have at least one mode with positive real part, the following conditions should be fulfilled:

$$\alpha<0 \text{ and } \beta^2 - 4\alpha(\gamma-1) > 0 \tag{56}$$

Summarizing, we point out that, in all cases, the cell parameters determine the dispersion curves while the template determines the center and the width of a window that selects the "active" region. In other words, there are two degrees of freedom, one related to the shape of the dispersion curve (determined by the cell parameters) and the other one, related to the position of the window (determined by the template parameters). Let us finally remark that the order of the decoupled equations is one for first order cell and two for second order cells. CNN's made with first order cells and second order neighborhood are somehow similar to second order two-port cell – first order template (which, however, exhibit more complex dynamics, including oscillations).

7. Further generalization

In the following the dynamics of a class of Cellular Neural Network (CNN) structures is analyzed. The class covers previously reported CNN structures as well as many new ones [27-29]. It is shown that the behavior of these structures can be analyzed, for the central linear part, using the decoupling technique based on discrete spatial transforms and the root locus method.

7.1. The CNN architecture

The CNN cells are supposed to be nonlinear (piecewise linear) dynamic one-ports, which for the central linear part behave linearly as a one-port admittance Y(s). In fact, the architecture is the generalization (for the central linear part) of the standard first order cell CNN [1] that is described by the well-known set of differential equations.

$$\frac{dx_{ij}(t)}{dt} = -x_{ij}(t) + \sum_{k,l \in Nb} A_{kl}\, y_{(i+k)(j+l)}(t) + \sum_{k,l \in Nb} B_{kl}\, u_{(i+k)(j+l)}(t) + I \tag{57}$$

$$y_{ij}(x_{i,j}) = \frac{1}{2}\left(|\,x_{ij} - 1| - |\,x_{ij} + 1|\right)$$

where Nb denotes the neighborhood, i=0,1,…,M-1, j=0,1,…,N-1, A and B are the cloning templates, I is a bias and y(x) expresses the nonlinear dependence between state and output.

The connection between cells corresponding to the template is realized by means of voltage controlled current sources and saturation type nonlinearity is used to bound the signals in the CNN. In the case of the standard CNN in the linear central part, the cell is described by the admittance $Y(s)=s+1-A_{0,0}$ while for the second order two-port cell CNN coupled with one layer, the admittance is [30] $Y(s) = \dfrac{s^2 + 2\alpha + \varpi_0^2}{s + \beta}$ where

$$\alpha = -\frac{\gamma}{2}(f_u + g_v),\ \beta = -\gamma\, g_v,\ \varpi_0^2 = \gamma^2 (f_u g_v - f_v g_u).$$

In the following, we will consider only autonomous CNN's working in the central linear part so that the B-template as well as the bias *I* will be zero. However, the stability results remain valid in the general case as well.

We consider the 1D CNN is described, in the linear central part, by the set of differential equations [31]:

$$Y(s)x(t) = \sum_{k \in N} A_k x_{i+k}(t) \tag{58}$$

where s=d/dt. In general, $Y(s) = \dfrac{Q(s)}{P(s)}$ where P(s) and Q(s) are polynomials in the variable s. Using the decoupling technique, i.e., the change of variables

$$x_i(t) = \sum_{m=0}^{M-1} \Phi_M(m,i)\hat{x}_m(t) \tag{59}$$

i=0,…,M-1, with eigenfunction $\Phi_M(m,i)$ of the form (ring BC's)

$$\Phi_M(\omega(m),\varphi(m),i) = e^{j(\omega(m)i + \varphi(m))} \tag{60}$$

in the general case, the action of the A template gives

$$\sum_{k \in N} A_k e^{j(\omega(m)i + \varphi(m))} = K_A e^{j(\omega(m)i + \varphi(m))} \tag{61}$$

where,

$$K_A = A_0 + \sum_{i=1}^{r}(A_i + A_{-i})\cos(i\omega(m)) + j\sum_{i=1}^{r}(A_i - A_{-i})\sin(i\omega(m)) \tag{62}$$

(here *r* is the radius of the neighborhood).

In particular, for first order neighborhood, the corresponding eigenvalues are (33). With the above change of variables, the equations decouple and have the following form

$$Y(s)\hat{x}_m(t) = K_A \hat{x}_m(t)$$
$$\frac{Q(s)}{P(s)}\hat{x}_m(t) = K_A \hat{x}_m(t) \tag{63}$$

The dynamics of the above equations is determined by the zeros of the following function

$$\frac{Q(s)}{P(s)} - K_A = 0 \tag{64}$$

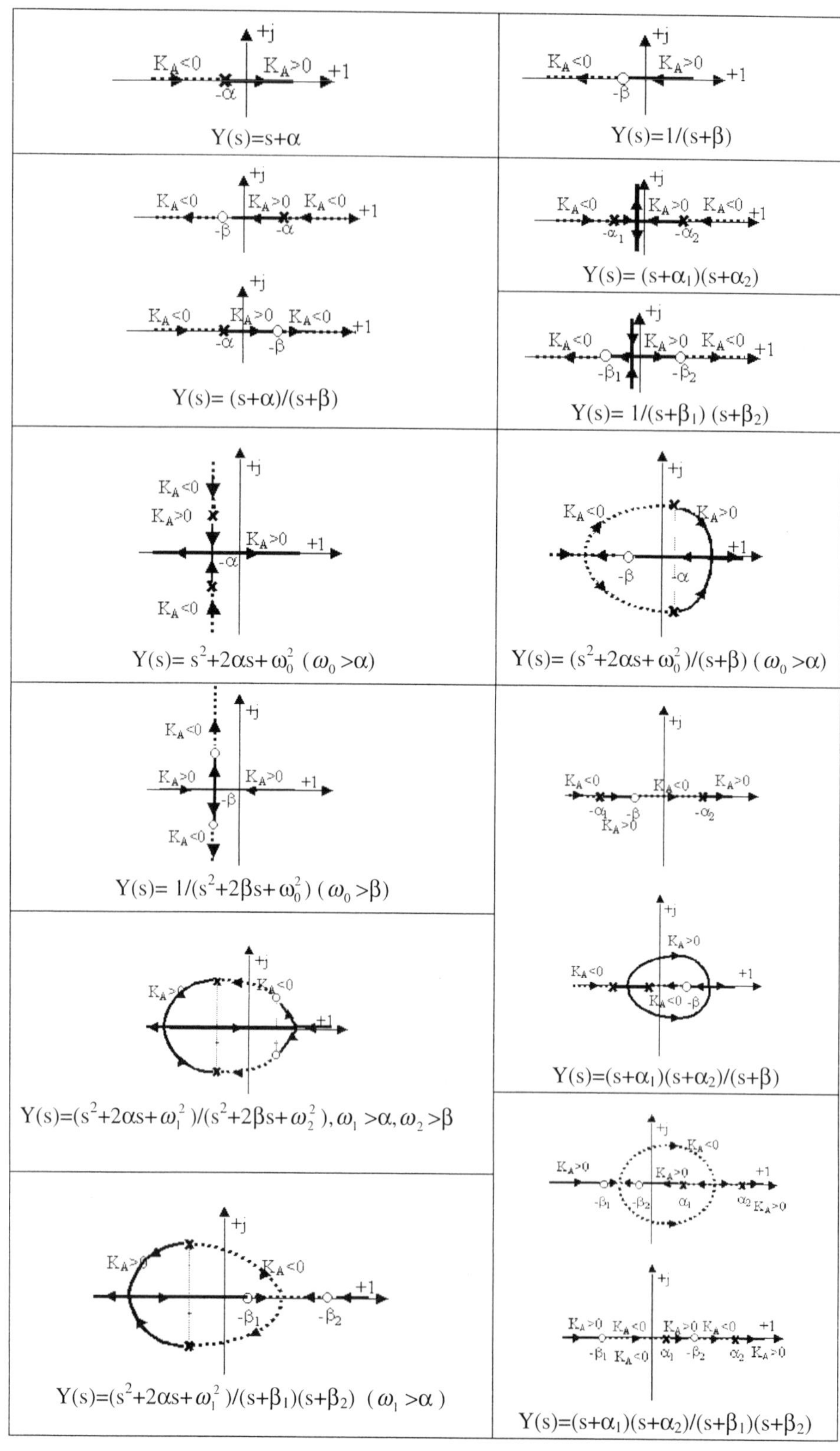

K_A<0   K_A>0   +1
-α
Y(s)=s+α

K_A<0   K_A>0   +1
-β
Y(s)=1/(s+β)

K_A<0   K_A>0   K_A<0   +1
-β   -α
K_A<0   K_A>0   K_A<0   +1
-α_1   -α_2
Y(s)= (s+α_1)(s+α_2)

K_A<0   K_A>0   K_A<0   +1
-α   -β
Y(s)= (s+α)/(s+β)

K_A<0   K_A>0   K_A<0   +1
-β_1   -β_2
Y(s)= 1/(s+β_1) (s+β_2)

K_A<0
K_A>0
K_A>0   +1
-α
K_A<0
Y(s)= s^2+2αs+ω_0^2 (ω_0 >α)

K_A<0   K_A>0
-β   α   +1
Y(s)= (s^2+2αs+ω_0^2)/(s+β) (ω_0 >α)

K_A<0
K_A>0   K_A>0   +1
-β
K_A<0
Y(s)= 1/(s^2+2βs+ω_0^2) (ω_0 >β)

K_A<0   K_A<0   K_A>0
-α_1 -β   -α_2
K_A>0
K_A>0
K_A<0   -β   +1
Y(s)=(s+α_1)(s+α_2)/(s+β)

K_A>0   K_A<0   +1
Y(s)=(s^2+2αs+ω_1^2)/(s^2+2βs+ω_2^2), ω_1 >α, ω_2 >β

K_A>0   K_A<0   +1
-β_1   α_1   α_2
K_A>0   K_A>0   K_A<0
-β_1   -β_2
Y(s)=(s^2+2αs+ω_1^2)/(s+β_1)(s+β_2) (ω_1 >α)

K_A>0 K_A<0 K_A>0 K_A<0   +1
-β_1 K_A<0 α_1 -β_2 α_2 K_A>0
Y(s)=(s+α_1)(s+α_2)/(s+β_1)(s+β_2)

which can be written as

$$1 - K_A \frac{P(s)}{Q(s)} = 0 \tag{65}$$

For symmetric templates, the above equation can be treated using the root locus method, as the eigenvalues are real:

$$K_A = A_0 + 2\sum_{i=1}^{r} A_i \cos(i\omega(m)) \tag{66}$$

In the table above we give some of the possible shapes of the root loci for several forms of the admittance Y(s). Using this tool combined with the window method it is easy to make an image of the array dynamics in the central linear part. Let us observe that when the denominator and the nominator exchange places, the shape of the roots locus remains the same. For the admittances in the table many particular cases can be considered, depending on the relative position of poles and zeros. We have represented only one or 2 situations for each type of admittance.

8. Concluding remarks

Pattern formation represents an interesting and intriguing behavior of CNN's, which seems to be worthwhile further studying. In this work, several analytical results concerning pattern formation have been presented. They are based on the decoupling technique, which, although intrinsically linear, give significant insight for pattern formation. The method puts into evidence the dynamics of the spectrum of the initial conditions with respect to some discrete spatial orthogonal functions. Patterns appear when at least one spatial mode is unstable. In certain cases this principle can be used for pattern recognition and feature extraction on the basis of mode competition and spatial selectivity. The study was focused on CNN's made with at most second order cells and templates with a special emphasis on Turing patterns. It has been also shown that more general CNN's can be analyzed using the decoupling technique and the root locus method.

Acknowledgments

The research on pattern formation presented in this work has been supported by the Fulbright Foundation, the Romanian National Council for Research in Higher Education under Grant CNCSIS 222 and by the Swiss National Science Foundation under Grant SCOPES 7RUPJ062381.

References

[1] L.O. Chua, L. Yang, "Cellular Neural Networks: Theory", IEEE Trans. Circuits Syst., vol. 35, no 10, pp. 1257-1272, October 1988.

[2] L.O. Chua, L. Yang, "Cellular Neural; Networks: Applications", IEEE Trans. Circuits Syst., vol. 35, no 10, pp 1273-1290, October 1988.

[3] T. Roska, J. Vanderwalle, Cellular Neural Networks, John Wiley & Sons, 1993.

[4] L.O. Chua, M. Hasler, G.S. Moschytz and J. Neirynck, "Autonomous Cellular Neural Networks: A Unified Paradigm for Pattern Formation and Active Wave Propagation, IEEE Trans. Circuits Syst, vol. 42, pp. 559-577, October 1995.

[5] K.R. Crounse, L.O. Chua – "Methods for Image Processing and Pattern Formation in Cellular Neural Networks – A Tutorial", IEEE Transactions on Circuits and Systems, Special Issue on Nonlinear Waves, Patterns and Spatio-Temporal Chaos in Dynamic Arrays, vol. 42, number 10, pp. 583-601, October 1995.

[6] T. Roska, L.O. Chua, "On a Framework of Complexity of Computation on Flows Implemented on the CNN Universal Machine" Technical Report, DNS-15-1995, Computer and Automation Institute, Budapest,.

[7] T. Roska, L.O. Chua, D. Wolf, T. Kozek, R. Tetzlaff, F. Puffer, "Simulating Nonlinear Waves and Partial Differential Equations via CNN – Part I: Basic Technique", IEEE Trans. Circuits Syst. I, vol.42, pp. 807-815, October 1995.

[8] T. Roska "Analogic CNN Computing: Architectural, Implementation and Algorithmic Advances – A Review", Proceedings of the Fifth IEEE International Workshop on Cellular Neural Networks and Their Applications, 14-17 April 1998, pp 3-10, London.

[9] L.O. Chua, T. Roska – "Cellular Neural Networks: Foundations and Primer", version 1.5, lecture notes for the course EE129 at U.C.Berkeley, 1997.

[10] A. Zarandy, T. Roska – "CNN Template Design Strategies and Fault Tolerant CNN Template Design – A Survey", Proc. of the European Conference on Circuit Theory and Design, ECCTD, pp 178-201, Budapest, 1997.

[11 K.R. Crounse, "Ph. Thesis: Image Processing Techniques for Cellular Neural Network Hardware", University of California, Berkeley, Fall, 1997.

[12] Bing J. Sheu. Kwang-Bo Cho, Wayene C Young, "Integration of Sensor/Processor under Cellular Neural Networks Paradigm for Multimedia Applications", Proceedings of the Fifth IEEE International Workshop on Cellular Neural Networks and Their Applications, 14-17 April 1998, pp 45-49, London, UK.

[13] *** - CNN Software Library (Templates and Algorithms) v. 7.3, Budapest, 1999.

[14] G. Linan, S. Espejo, R. Dominguez-Castro, A. Rodriguez-Vazquez, "The CNNUC3: An Analog I/O 64x64 CNN Universal Machine Chip Prototype with 7-bit Analog Accuracy", Proc. of the 6-th IEEE International Workshop on Cellular Neural Networks and Their Applications, pp. 201-206, May, 2000.

[15] A.M. Turing, "The Chemical Basis of Morphogenesis", Phil. Trans. Roy. Soc. Lond. B 237, pp.37-72, October 1952.

[16] J.D. Murray, Mathematical Biology, Springer-Verlag, Berlin Heidelberg, 1993.

[17] L. Goraş, L.O. Chua, D.M.W. Leenaerts, "Turing Patterns in CNN's-Part I: Once Over Lightly", IEEE Trans. Circuits Syst, vol.42, pp. 602-611, October 1995.

[18] L. Goraş, L.O. Chua, "Turing Patterns in CNN's - Part II: Equations and Behaviors", IEEE Trans. Circuits Syst, vol.42, pp. 612-626, October 1995.

[19] L. Goraş, L.O. Chua, L. Pivka, "Turing Patterns in CNN's - Part III: Computer Simulation Results", IEEE Trans. Circuits Syst, vol.42, pp. 627-636, October 1995.

[20] L. Goraş, L.O. Chua, Turing Patterns in CNN's Based on a New Cell, Proc. of the Fourth International Workshop on Cellular, Neural Networks and Their Applications, CNNA'96, pp.103-108, Seville, June 1996.

[21] T. Teodorescu, L. Goraş, "On the Dynamics of Turing Pattern Formation in 1D CNN's", Proc. SCS'97, Iasi, pp. 109-112, October 1997.

[22] L. Goraş, L.O. Chua, "On the Role of CNN Initial Conditions in Turing Pattern Formation", Proc. SCS'97, pp 105-108.

[23] L. Goraş, L.O. Chua, "On the Influence of CNN Boundary Conditions in Turing Pattern Formation", Proc. ECCTD'97, Budapest, pp. 383-388, 1997.

[24] L. Goraş, T. Teodorescu, "On CNN Boundary Conditions in Turing Pattern Formation", Proc. of the Fifth International Workshop on Cellular, Neural Networks and Their Applications, CNNA'98, pp.112-117, London, UK, 14-17 April, 1998.

[25] T. Teodorescu, V. Maiorescu, "Using Different Bias Current Sources for Controlling Turing Patterns", Proc. ECCTD'99, pp. 787-790, September, 1999, Stresa, Italy.

[26] L. Goraş, T. Teodorescu, A. Maiorescu, "Phase Influence on Mode Competition in Turing Pattern Formation", IEEE International workshop on Cellular Neural Networks and their Applications, Catania, Italia, May, 2000.

[27] L. Goraş, "A Modified CNN Architecture for Turing Patterns Generation", ECCTD, pp 791-794, Stresa, Italy, August 29-September 2, 1999.

[28] L. Goraş, T. Teodorescu, "On the Oscillatory Behavior of Second Order Cell 1D CNN's" Proc. ECCTD'01, vol. III pp. 273-276, Helsinki, 2001.

[29] T. Teodorescu, L. Goraş, "Cell and Template Order Influence on CNN Behavior: a Comparative Study", Proc. ECCTD'01, vol. III pp. 285-289, Helsinki, 2001.

[30] T. Teodorescu, L. Goraş, "Two Approaches for Studying Single Coupled Second Order Cell CNN's", Proc. SCS 2001, pp 453-456, Iaşi, 2001.

[31] L. Goraş, T. Teodorescu,, "On the Dynamics of a Class of CNN's", Proc. SCS 2001, pp 449-452, Iaşi, 2001.

Limitations and Future Trends in Neural Computation
S. Ablameyko et al. (Eds.)
IOS Press, 2003

Reliability of man-system interaction and theory of neural networks operations

Prof. Dr. Mirko NOVÁK, Prof. Zdeněk VOTRUBA

*Czech Technical University, Prague, Faculty of Transportation, Konviktská 20, 110
00 Prague 1; mirko@fd.cvut.cz, votruba@fd.cvut.cz; 00420602 242870, 00420608 346329*

Abstract

This paper concerns the problem of the reliability of interactions in complicated
artificial systems involving the combination of artificial- and human- based functional
blocks. Such composed systems are typical for many applications in present human society,
appearing in science, industry, business, finance, medical care, transportation, defense etc.
Though the significance of such systems is still higher, because they deal with still larger
amount of power, money and size of information and have the influence on still higher part
of human population, the failures of their operation causes very serious problems and quite
often is of really catastrophic character. Therefore, the requirements on their operation
reliability and safety are of extraordinary importance.

1. Introduction – the system structure

From the structural point of view, the heterogeneous systems can be of very different
character. However, almost all of them (even not really the all) involve some typical parts,
schematically shown in Fig. 1.

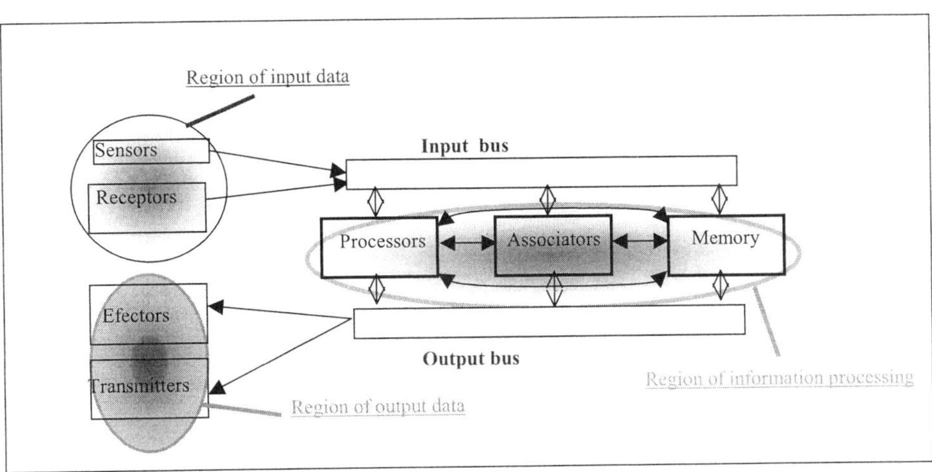

Fig. 1: Typical basic part of the system structure, appearing in many heterogeneous systems

Some parts mentioned in Fig.1 are specialized for handling with information I only. Some other, namely processors, efectors and transmitters can handle also the mass or energy. These parts, specialized for dealing with information I form the information subsystem of the respective heterogeneous system.

Any information subsystem consists of three main regions:

region of input data,

region of information processing and

region of output data.

Between the region of input data the input bus serves as the necessary interface similar as the output bus serves as interface between the region of information processing and the region of output data.

The existence of the information subsystem can be considered as the necessary (probably not as the sufficient) condition for the operation ability of any real heterogeneous system.

By another word:

It is hard to imagine any real heterogeneous system, operating reliable and safe without proper activity of its own information subsystem.

More over:

The quality of operation of information subsystem and its power determines (and limits) the quality of operation of the heterogeneous system under consideration as a whole.

In any complex heterogeneous system its own information subsystem represents therefore a part of special importance. One can postulate, that the reliability and safety of each system operation is proportional to the reliability and safety of its own information subsystem. Therefore, in general, the information subsystems are recognized at present as still more important object, which use is extremely important for all the aspects of the life of human society.

The axiom can be formulated:

Each system, natural or artificial, without respect to its physical nature, must involve and use its own information subsystem (or at least to share the use of activity of the information subsystem belonging to some other system).

Without proper function of such information subsystem any system cannot operate well, or even more, it cannot operate at all.

2. Reliability of artificial information systems

Let therefore artificial information systems here be considered only (however, certain from the further presented ideas can be applied also on natural [living] information systems).

Suppose that the information system under consideration realizes a set $F = \{F_k\}$, k – 1...K of system functions. These functions can be considered as the ratios among certain information I acting with the respective system. Of course, not all the partial system functions F_k of such an information system are of the same importance.

Therefore, the importance of each F_k can be measured by some value of importance merit $IM_k = <0,1>$. After the estimation of the values of IM_k is made, one can focus on the most significant of them.

Suppose further, that the set F depends on:

the structure St of the information system,

the vector X of N system parameters x_i, n = 1...N

the vector P of J independent variables p_j, j = 1...J

For the purpose of this study, the further assumption can be made because of simplicity:

the structure St of the system does not change with independent variables;

all the system parameters x_i can be expressed by real numbers;

from all possible independent variables p_j the time $p_j = t$ is considered as most important, because for any real system it acts as the only absolute uninfluenced independent variable.

This assumption is very often fulfilled with high accuracy. Nevertheless, if not, the respective modification of the further observations can be made without problems.

Each system, not only the information one, consists of certain number (often quite large) of particular functional blocks (further also FB only), realizing the partial system functions and interacting mutually. The existence of amorphous system involving no FB can appear exceptionally only. Among particular FBs in certain system the exchange of information is performed.

The structure St of mutual interaction among FBs can be fixed or can develop in the course of system operation (this is typical not only for living systems, but can be realized and successfully applied also in many sophisticated artificial systems).

Among the all the mentioned main kinds of functional blocks: receptors, processor, associators, memory, effectors and transmitters, various feed-forward and feed-back interactions exist. Because many of these basic functional blocks can in real information system appear to be operating in parallel, these interactions exist also among the individual functional blocks of all the mentioned kinds and the structure St of real information system can be therefore very often much more complicated.

3. Interfaces and synapses

When dealing with any heterogeneous system of the special importance are the interfaces (synapses[1] - this term is transposed from neurology and is now quite frequent in the theory of neural networks), which ensure the proper and in-time translation if information exchanged among such various functional blocks.

Suppose the interaction between two functional blocks FB_j and FB_k arranged so that the block FB_j supplies the output information $I_{j\ out}$, which is transmitted to the block FB_k as its input information $I_{k\ in}$. Such a procedure is performed by the use of two interaction supporting media, the interface If and the transmission path Tp.

The transmission path realizes the transmission of $I_{j\ out}$ to the input of the FB_k and we usually require that the respective transmission function Tp_{j-k} approaches 1 as much as possible.

The output information $I_{j\ out}$ from the functional block FB_j is formed on the base of some alphabet AB_j and with some grammar G_j. However, the functional block FB_k can able to understand the received information, only if it is written in its own alphabet AB_k and grammar G_k. This is quite frequent case.

If therefore the full understanding of the message transmitted from the functional block FB_j to the functional block FB_k is to be ensured, somewhere along the transmission path between FB_j and FB_k, the translation Tr of the message written in AB_j and G_j into the message written in AB_k and G_k has to be realized (see [3,4,5,6] e.g.).

This translation Tr can be provided either in only one location of the respective signal path or it also can be distributed along it in several places. In the later case, the individual translation functions can be realized simultaneously or subsequently.

---

[1] Synapses can be considered as special kind of functional blocks allowing proper interaction among other FB´s.

Usually, the first mentioned approach is much more common. Translation Tr is provided in the interface IF, which acts between two or more interacting FB´s.

This can be in the case of one directional interface, e.g..

The function of IF has different character, if it ensures the necessary translation in the case when the interaction between both interacting blocks is bi-directional.

In certain cases (especially in biological systems) the IF can be split into two parts, divided by shallow gap (cleft), bridged by special short transmission path.

In complicated heterogeneous systems interfaces can perform the necessary information translation also among more than only two mutually interacting FBs (such situation can be found quite often when analyzing the biological information systems, which are typically of very complicated heterogeneous nature).

The capability of certain information path in heterogeneous system to realize the requested information translation is called the translation-ability. This means that among all the considered interacting functional blocks the respective signal transmission paths must exist, in which the respective interfaces ensured the necessary information translations. Such a translation Tr must of course be realized with appropriate accuracy, reliability, safety and in requested time. Formulation of requirements on translation-ability (and inclusive on the respective interface function) belongs to one of most important problems in heterogeneous system design. In complicated systems also the mutual synchronization of function of all the interacting interfaces needs a special attention.

Let now turn the attention to the process of system functional homogenization (more detail discussion can be found e.g. in [5]).

Information is the most important entity in this process. The result is obvious – decisive role of language. Respective languages of the parts of the whole differ in theirs alphabets, grammars and semantics. Consequently, multilingual character of information exchange between individual functional blocks of the system, and object / environment respectively, arises [4,16,17,20,30].

Four basic classes of grammars should be recognized in this context: (*classes C and D are often referred as soft grammars*)

A: vocabulary–oriented grammars   (assorting of language. constructs)

B: Chomski grammars   (generation - rules)

C: grammars of similarity   (analysis of semantic similarity)

D: grammars of representation (comparison of process similarity and goals equivalence)

The *quality of multilingual translation* is the natural measure of the degree of homogenization. Integrity of the system is causally derived from the completeness or in some case completeness and efficiency, of translation.

Within the frame of system engineering, multilingual translation tasks [4,20,23,30,31] fit quite well to tackle this problem. Unfortunately, these tasks are at the very beginning of their study, understanding and implementation.

An important aspect of the multilingual translation ability is: the utilizing of limited resources and / or limited time to disposal.

Criterion of the effectivity should be the "Dynamics of the identity evolution" of the respective whole.

The homogenization of certain objects can be identified on more then one level, or their heterogeneity is of multi - dimensional nature.

That is the reason why there is a common need for universal means of homogenization processes recording.

We argue that the strong requirement of universality could be met by the general introduction of the concepts of object language translation in multi – lingual environment.

System theory and system engineering tools, even on the existing state-of the art level, offer concepts and approaches that are suitable for solving the tasks of homogenization of complex heterogeneous (hybrid) systems. These approaches should supplement or replace till this time prevailing attempts, based on intuition and experience.

Homogenization via multilingual translation has been presented in [14] as the approach with the highest degree of universality. To enable the utilization of this approach the concept of *pragmatic language* (see [31] e.g.) should be introduced.

The language of the real object is pragmatic one if (and only if) it can be *pragmatically translated* into the *language of identity* of the respective object in both directions. Pragmatic translation is the translation that is *acceptably degraded*, or it is joined with acceptable degradation of resources.

4. Heterogeneous systems interfaces reliability, safety and security

From the previous consideration it is evident that in all systems the problem of appropriate translation function Tr of all the respective interfaces is of top interest. When formulating the requirements on such translation function of the particular interface, one has to take into account the aspects of reliability, safety and security of the respective procedure.

All these three aspect are of an extraordinary importance and all have to be considered from the probabilistic and fuzzy point of view.

By the term <u>reliability</u> we understand here the probability, that the respective system function, in this case the particular translation will be realized in certain limits on its quality.

By <u>safety</u> we understand the probability that the realization of the respective system function (i.e. the respective translation) does not have negative influence[2] on realization of other functions of the system under consideration, or in general on other systems (including the human beings) existing in the environment [3].

By <u>security</u> we understand the probability that the content of translated information will not be open to any other information procedure[4].

The aspect of <u>translation reliability</u> requires before all that we need to determine:

The maximal acceptable error in translation function of the interface under consideration,

The instant in which the particular translation has to be realized in the course of the concert of all the mutual interacting interfaces activity,

The maximal acceptable delay between acceptance of the information submitted for translation into the particular interface and its transmitting in proper translated form into the respective interacting functional block,

The difference among the alphabets and grammars of the respective translated information.

<u>As concerns the first mentioned need</u>, the analysis of the system function sensitivity to the particular translation error has to be taken into account. It is evident, that in complicated hybrid system the significance of correct and accurate translation in certain its parts can be higher.

<u>As concerns the second mentioned need</u>, here one has to take into account that not all the translations realized in the system under consideration are often realized subsequently. Some partial translations can start in the same instant, especially if the parallel information processing is practiced in the particular case. All the partial information translation

---

[2] The requirement of "no negative influence" sound well, but in practice we almost ever have to accept the fact that there will be some negative influences of any realized system functions on something else. The reasonable specification of acceptable limits of such negative influence belongs to one of very important parts of the "art of system design".

[3] A wide and interesting discussion can be held as concerns the acceptable size of the environment, which has to be considered and also about its content. In extreme idealized approach in this environment the whole Universe can be considered, however for practical problems one has to restrict its size and content.

[4] This requirement needs to be considered in the course of time. In practice, after some time the requirements on translation security are significantly lowered.

procedures have therefore be done in certain specific schedule, forming the whole "translation concert", which optimal composition requires a very deep analysis.

As concerns the third mentioned need, one has to take into account that all the respective partial information translation are realized in real time and that they require some time. If in the " translation concert" under consideration requires subsequent translation processing, the condition that in proper instants all the input information have to be at disposal needs to be considered.

As concerns the fourth mentioned need, we have to take into account that the length of the partial information translation and its sensitivity to translation errors is in general proportional to the difference between the input and output alphabet and grammar. Also the fuzziness of the input information has to be taken into account.

The aspect of translation safety requires before all that we need to determine:

The sensitivity of other system function of the system under consideration on the particular translation procedure,

The effect of the particular information translation and its further dissemination on other systems (including the human beings) existing in the environment,

The effect of distortion of the particular information translation on other systems (including the human beings) existing in the environment.

As concerns the first mentioned need, not all from the whole set of information translation realized in the course of certain system operation have the same influence to other signal and information processing in general. Some of them influence the other translations more, some less. The analysis of the values of sensitivity $S^{Fk}_{tr\ i}$, where F_k is the system function under consideration and Tr_i is the particular translation is therefore of great importance. The knowledge of the values $S^{Fk}_{tr\ i}$ allow to determine, which translations have to be done with much more care. For the purpose of such an analysis a good part of the apparatus of the general sensitivity theory can be used, however some modifications will be suitable. These problems cannot be discussed here in detail unfortunately.

The knowledge of these sensitivities could be also used as starting point to solution of the problem if and in which manner the procedure of particular translation influence the activity of systems, existing and operating in the environment.

Similar approach can be used when solving the problem of maximal acceptable level of distortion ΔTr of particular information translation with respect to the correct activity of other systems (or humans) in the environment. Let us assume that the translation Tr itself depends on the set X_{IF} of N_{IF} interface parameters x_{IFi}, $i = 1,\ldots N_{IF}$ and on the vector P of J independent variables p_j, $j = 1,\ldots J$,

$$Tr = Tr(X_{IF},P) = I_{out}/I_{in},$$

where Tr represents the respective translation function realized in the interface under consideration and I_{out} and I_{in} are the output and input information processed in it.

Suppose further for simplicity that:

The respective signal transmission acting between the functional blacks FB_j and FB_k is ideal, i.e. that $Tp_{j-k} = 1$ and

From all the eventual independent variables p_j, which can have the influence on the particular interface acting between FB_j and FB_k only the time $p = t$ is considered as the most important.

Let now the interface parameter space X_{IF} be considered. The actual state of the vector of translation function Tr is in this space represented by a point, which in the course of time moves along certain trajectory Ψ_{Tr}, see the idealized Fig. 2 (sketched for the case $N_{IF} = 3$ only.

Here the point Tr_{t0} represents the initial value of translation function Tr, which suppose has acceptable function and therefore is inside the region $R_{A\ Tr}$ which represents the so called region of acceptability. However due the influence of the independent variable $p = t$ the value of Tr changes. If the respective vector $Tr(t_k)$ is still inside $R_{A\ Tr}$ (green case), the respective translation can be considered as acceptable for the understanding of the functional block FB_k to the information transmitted form the FB_j. However, when the values of Tr (t) crosses the boundaries of $R_{A\,Tr}$ (red case), the FB_k does not understand to what FB_j send. The system starts to fail its operation in such a case.

The problem remains, how to determine the boundaries of $R_{A\,Tr}$, and therefore also the maximal allowable deviation ΔTr_{j-k} of the translation of I_{jout} into I_{kin}. In many cases the value of ΔTr_{j-k} is significantly content dependent and varies with I_{jout}. In such cases the necessity of so called intelligent interfaces, which can modify their translation function according the content and the quality (level of distortion) of incoming information is evident.

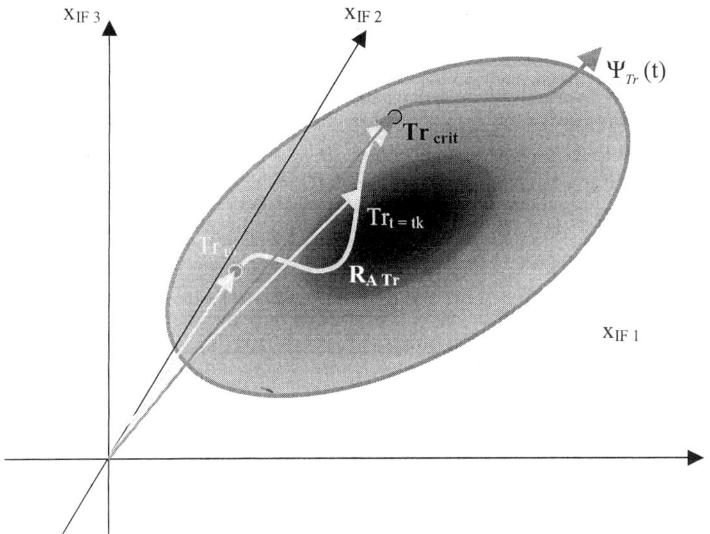

Fig. 2: The idealized trajectory Ψ_{Tr} in the interface parameter space of the translation vector Tr in the course of time p = t.

The aspect of <u>translation security</u> requires before all that we need to determine:

The maximal acceptable level of parasitic interactions among all the (non-functionally) interacting interfaces,

The time-dependence of requirements on translation security and the course of their subsequent decrease

<u>The first mentioned need</u> concerns the problem which part of information and energy can be spread around the interface realizing particular translation so that the security of the respective information procedure does not decrease under certain specified limit.

Of course, the requirements on translation security <u>do not remain still the same during the history of particular system activity.</u> Usually, they decrease in the course of time. Some secret information can be opened for broader distribution after some time.

As we have already mentioned, almost all the information procedures, and also the translations cannot be realized absolutely perfect. In any case we must accept the possibility that certain amount of errors and mistakes appear, which diminish the information content of the translated message and lower the probability that the receiving functional block will understand well the content of message. The faults appearing in the procedure of translation can be classified according to their significance for lowering this probability.

Before we try to start with classification of faults, we must take into account that there exist certain thresholds, below which the influence of translation faults can be neglected. This is due the ability of some interfaces to restore and reconstruct in certain manner the content of the translated information. Also some receiving functional blocks have the ability to accept and understand well certain information even if it is distorted. The dependence of the probability of well understanding the translated information on the scale and frequency of faults is therefore significantly nonlinear.

Let us propose to distinguish following main categories of the influence on the probability of the understanding to the translated information:

Negligible faults, which do not have any observable influence on the probability of understanding the translated information,

Slight faults, which have observable but neglect-able influence on the probability of understanding the translated information,

Serious faults, which have non neglect-able influence on the probability of understanding the translated information, and/or significant demands on system resources (energy/time),

Fatal faults, which causes the incapability of information translation at all.

More over, some information appearing at the outputs of certain functional blocks can be of fuzzy nature and its subsequent translation results therefore again in fuzzy statement.

For the safe procedure of information transmission, the improvement of translation reliability and safety is of great importance. In general, there are the following main approaches how to improve the translation reliability:

To realize the respective translation in more parallel paths comparing the results of particular translations and taking as correct that, which appears in majority.

To insert in the respective translation some hidden implicit code for translation reliability testing. This code cannot have, of course, any influence on the content of translated information.

To analyze the acceptable limits of possible information distortion in the course of translation and to predict the probability by which the particular translation approached these limits.

Extension of the last approach can be based on the basis of predictive diagnostics (see [1,2,9,11] e.g.) where one estimates the subsequently appearing distortions in the course of the translation procedure and corrects respectively its further steps. This is of special importance in the case of interactions in heterogeneous systems where the technical functional blocks interact with human subjects (see [7,8] e.g.).

No of these approaches is optimal, in general. They are therefore often combined. Doing this one has of course to take into account the requirements on translation speed, limits on translation cost, energy requirements etc.

For further research a very vast area opens here.

5. Reliability of artificial neural networks

Artificial neural networks as they are used today in many interesting and important applications represent only a very rough approximation of simplest information systems of living bodies. The reason is not only in the Mc Culloch – Pitts model of neuron, which is still dominantly used (probably because of its ingenious simplicity), but also in neglecting many auxiliary functions, which exist in natural neural networks helping to stabilize their function ability and therefore to improve their reliability. As result, the function reliability of artificial neural networks is naturally limited and serious attention has to be given to its improvement.

Analyzing the sources of possible faults in artificial neural networks operation, we can find the following factors as very significant:

A) High sensitivity of realized network functions to the changes of some parameters,

B) High redundancy of some artificial neural networks,

C) Non sufficient accuracy of adjusted values of some physically realized network parameters and their small time - and/or environmental stability,

D) Uncertainty of the artificial neural network actual training level.

As concerns the aspect A), some artificial neural network functions appear to be very sensitive to the change of network parameters, both of the network structure and of the used models of neurons. Therefore the analysis of these sensitivities is of great importance, especially in the case, when the particular artificial neural network is proposed for long time service or is applied in some critical point of artificial technical system. However, such an analysis requires a lot of computations, especially in the case of network composed of higher number of neurons. According to our experience, there are some places in artificial network structure, where one can expect higher values of these sensitivities. While in conventional linear electrical networks the theorem on sensitivity invariance is known to hold, saying that some weighted sum of network transfer function sensitivities is constant, nothing similar was proven up to now for artificial neural networks. Nevertheless, also here the practical experience tells us, that by insertion of redundant network components the sensitivity of realized network function sensitivity to changes of network parameters can be diminished – at least in certain cases. On the contrary, some classes of very complicated artificial neural network structures can be very sensitive. The explanation of this fact can be seen in uncertainty of the particular network position in the <u>training space $\Theta\,(m)$</u>.

By this term we mean the multidimensional space of all the particular network parameters w_i, i.e. the parameters of the respective network structure and also of models of all the used neurons, scaled by the sequence of training steps m (see Fig. 3). In the set of parameters w_i not only the synaptic weights acting among all neurons are to be involved, but also the parameters of individual neuron activation functions and their thresholds (suppose that the network structure does not change in the course of training).

The actual state of the artificial neural network training is represented by certain point in the space $\Theta\,(m)$. In the course of network training procedure this point moves along the training trajectory step by step from the initial position Θ_0. Suppose that this is already inside the space Θ_A of acceptable level of applied training-error criterion. The goal of the training procedure is to move the training vector near or inside the region Θ_{opt} of almost optimal training. Quite theoretically, the Θ_{opt} should be considered as a point, usually the surface of the values of training error criterion inside Θ_A is so flat, that one has consider the nonzero dimensions of Θ_{opt}.

Of course, the sketch shown in Fig. 3 is a highly idealized case only. Practically, both the shapes of Θ_A and Θ_{opt} could be quite complicated, each different from another and both often having two or more separate parts. This is one of reasons for the existence of the above-mentioned factor D).

If the training error criterion stops the training procedure when the vector Θ enters inside Θ_{opt}, we have no other information about the inside of Θ_{opt}.

Suppose now, that as result of the sufficiently realized training procedure, the vector Θ appears inside the region Θ_{opt} or at least in its close vicinity and that the respective network is able for to be used. If in the course of the network operation any change in its parameter values appears, the vector Θ moves from its trained position. However, because of the uncertainty of Θ_{opt}, there is hardly to say, whether the training stop condition will still be fulfilled.

One of perspective approached how to minimize such uncertainties is based on application of the principle of predictive diagnostics. The basic idea of this principle is known from the theory of system reliability:

One applies the suitable time-series prediction methods to estimate the further trajectory of the vector Θ in the network parameter space W caused by the parameter values changes, and satisfactory in advance derives from it the necessary hints for network values corrections.

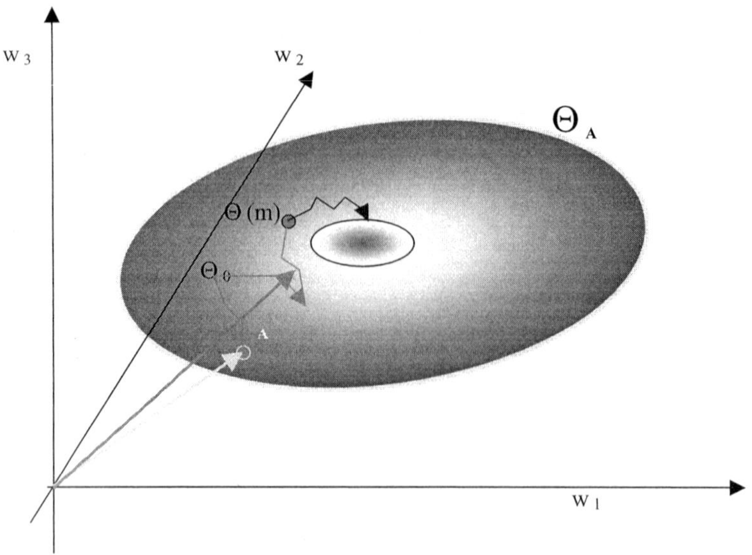

Fig. 3: The trajectory of the training vector in the training space Θ (m).

Of course, such a diagnostic and network repairing approach is applicable only if certain set of network parameter values can be corrected in the course of network operation. If no, the network operation must be broken for the time of network corrections.

Such principle of predictive diagnostics is important especially, when the respective artificial neural network is realized in microelectronic technologies, where there are considerably high limitations on the obtainable accuracy of parameter values. Of course, the design and practical realization of the respective sub-network ensuring the in time realization of the prediction and correction procedure can be very laborious and expensive task. Therefore, the careful economic calculation needs to be provided before.

6. References

[1]   Novák M.: Predictive diagnostics as a tool for improvement of transport system reliability (in Czech). Research report LSS No. 36/98, Faculty of Transportation Sciences CTU Prague, 1998

[2]   Novák M.: On reliability of prediction diagnostics (in Czech), Research report No. LSS-20/97, Faculty of Transportation Sciences CTU Prague, 1997

[3]   Novák M.: Theory of system tolerances, (in Czech), Academia, Prague, 1987

[4]   Vlček J.: Translation-ability as the principle of informatics, (in Czech), Seminary "Theoretical backgrounds of informatics", Faculty of Transportation Sciences CTU Prague, 1997

[5]   Votruba Z.: Parts of Stonier model and its analogy in natural sciences, (in Czech), Seminary "Theoretical backgrounds of informatics", Faculty of Transportation Sciences, Prague, 1997

[6]   Leso M., Votruba Z.: Reliability Estimator. Neural Network World. Vol. 9. 1999 No. 3, ISSN 1210-0552 Novák, Votruba: Reliability of man-system interaction and theory of neural networks operations 11

[7] Novák M.: Neural Network Approach for Man-System Interaction Reliability, CSC-IMACS '98, Pireus, Greece, October 26/28, 1998

[8] Faber J.: Associative Interneuronal biological Mechanisms, Neural Network World, Vol. 1, 1991, No. 1, 13-31

[9] Novák M.: Theory of Reliable Systems Based on Tolerance Prediction, Dexa'93, Prague, Czech Republic, September 6-8, 1993

[10] Votruba Z., Moos P.: Information Power, „CE&I" Technical University Košice, Herlany, Slovak Republic, October 1999, ISBN 80-88922-05-4

[11] Votruba Z., Novák M.: An Approach to the Analysis and Prediction of the Complex Heterogeneous Systems Evolution, Technical University Košice, Slovak Republic, October 2000

[12] Votruba Z.: Modeling of synaptic information function — proposal of the multilingual translation approach Neural Network World, vol. 11, 2001, No. 5

[13] Votruba Z.: Parts of Stonier model and its analogy in natural sciences, (in Czech), Seminary "Theoretical backgrounds of informatics", Faculty of Transportation Sciences, Prague, 1997

[14] Votruba Z., Novák M.: An Approach to the Analysis and Prediction of the Complex Heterogeneous Systems Evolution, „CE&I" Technical University Košice, Herlany, Slovak Republic, October 2000

[15] Novák M. et al.: Artificial Neuron Nets (Umělé neuronové sítě) (in Czech), C.H. Beck 1998 Praha, ISBN 80-7179-132-6

[16] Grmela A.: Neural Computing and Neural Science, Agces Publ., Prague, 1997, ISBN: 80-902329-0-6

[17] Votruba Z., Novák M.: On Homogenization of Heterogeneous Whole, Proc. CCSC Crete, July 2001

[18] Vlček J.: System Engineering, ed. ČVUT, Prague 1999. (in Czech)

[19] Stonier T.: Information and the Internal Structure of the Universe, Springer 1990

[20] Vlček J., Brandejský T., Moos P., Novák M., Votruba Z.: Proceedings of Seminar of Theoretical Backgrounds of Informatics – Information Power, problem study, Prague 2000 (in Czech), Institute of automation in Traffic and Telecommunication CTU in Prague, Faculty of Transportation Sciences

[21] Brillouin L.: Science and Information Theory, Academic Press, New York, 1956

[22] Prigogine I., Stengers I.: Order Out of Chaos, Bantam Books, Toronto, 1984

[23] Klir G. J.: Facets of System Sciences, Plenum, New York, 1991

[24] Novák M., Votruba Z.: System Theory Approach to the Hybrid System Lifetime Analysis and Prediction, CCSC'99 Athens 1999

[25] Manthey M.: The Phase Web Paradigm, Int. J. General Systems, Vol. 27(1-3)

[26] Deutsch D.: The Fabric of Reality, Allen Lane Penguin Press, New York 1997

[27] Vlček J. et al.: Reliability of Hybrid System, Research report No.: K614–01/2001 (in Czech) Institute of automation in Traffic and Telecommunication CTU in Prague, Faculty of Transportation Sciences

[28] Votruba Z.: Chaos and the Language of Object Identity, Seminar of Theoretical Backgrounds of Informatics (in Czech), Institute of automation in Traffic and Telecommunication CTU in Prague, Faculty of Transportation Sciences 13.3.2001 (revision 10.4.2001)

[29] Vlček J., Votruba Z.: Hybrid Systems in Transportation, (in Czech) Proc. Conference AUTOS 2001, Prague

[30] Vlček J.: Homogenization/Translation-ability/Efficiency/Criteria, Seminar of Theoretical Backgrounds of Informatics (in Czech), Institute of Control and Telematics CTU in Prague, Faculty of Transportation Sciences, 2001

[31] Vlček J.: A Sketch of the Hybrid System Constructive Theory Structure, Seminar of Theoretical Backgrounds of Informatics (in Czech), Institute of Control and Telematics, CTU in Prague, Faculty of Transportation Sciences, June 2001

From Neural Networks to Intelligent Systems: Selected Aspects of Training, Application and Evolution

Vladimir Golovko

Brest State Technical University, Moscowskaja 267,
224017 Brest, Republic of Belarus
gva@brpi.unibel.by

Abstract. This chapter examines different approaches to the design of neural network systems. It includes the efficient training algorithm for multilayer perceptron; neural network approach for chaotic time series processing and intelligent system for control of a mobile robot. Future directions and some challenges are discussed in the work.

1. Introduction

Development of artificial intelligent systems, which are capable to carry out functions of human beings, is an old dream of mankind. The ability of human beings to self-evolution, cognition and adaptation has large advantage in comparison with artificial systems. The advantage of computer systems is the high speed of the spreading of signals and the possibility to use a large volume of knowledge accumulated by humanity in various areas. The development of the artificial systems, which have ability to self-evolution, creates the conditions for evolution to a new computer generation.

Now mostly researches in the area of artificial intelligence are based on the theory of neural networks and are directed at the decision of concrete problems. There is a gradual accumulation of knowledge for building of universal neural computers. The neural networks have ability to training like human beings, but human beings in comparison with neural networks are capable also to evolution. It is the main limitation of neural networks.

Neural systems for decision of complex problems consist of different neural networks, which are combined in an intelligent system. Such systems are inherently parallel and many units carry out their computation at the same time. In accordance with [1] the intelligent system is called such a system, which can achieve complex goals in a complex environment. In order to achieve such goals it is necessary to predict the future. It will be one of key aspects of this chapter.

There are currently a lot of problems for designing of the neural system: effective training algorithms; the development of self-organizing and self-progressing systems; combination of the different neural networks in an intelligent system; etc. The solution of these problems is of great importance for the evolution of the contemporary computer systems.

The basic purpose of the report is to present the key ideas, approaches, algorithms for design of the neural systems, as well as limitations of the neural network approaches.

The rest of the chapter is organized as follows. In the Section 2 is developed the efficient training algorithm for multilayer perceptron. The benefit of the proposed method is that we can choose the training rate automatically. Section 3 presents the neural network approach for chaotic time series analysis and forecasting. As regards time series analysis we address two aspects, namely the definition of embedding parameters and the largest Lyapunov exponent. As for time series predicting, it is performed both on the level of emergent structures and on the level of individual data points. The future work in this area is discussed. In the Section 4 we describe the intelligent neural system for autonomous control of a mobile robot. Summary and discussion are given in Section 5.

2. The effective training algorithm for multilayer perceptron

Multilayer perceptron (MLP) is the most wide-spread among neural networks. Such a network is capable of approximating any function. Another important feature of MLP is the ability to generalization. Therefore MLP has a wide variety of application in different areas: classification, control, forecasting etc.

The most commonly training method of MLP is backpropagation algorithm (BP). In spite of the fact that BP is successfully used for different tasks, it has lacks such as slow convergence, non-stability of convergence and local minimum problems. Many efforts have been made to develop the efficient training methods using in BP variable training step size [2], layer by layer optimization [3] and using for training the Newton method [4], the Levenburg-Marguardt method [5], conjugate-gradient technique [6].

In this section a simple method is proposed for efficient training of MLP by combining BP and adaptive training step calculation technique (ATS). The ATS is used to find an optimal learning rate, which minimizes the training error. Compared to other training algorithms, the proposed approach is characterized by simplicity and efficiency. It can be applied also for training PCA (principal component analysis) and time delay Neural Networks [7,8]. Various numerical experiments are used to illustrate the potential of the suggested method.

2.1. Backpropagation technique

Let's examine the MLP structure. It is shown in Fig. 1 and consists of 3 layers.

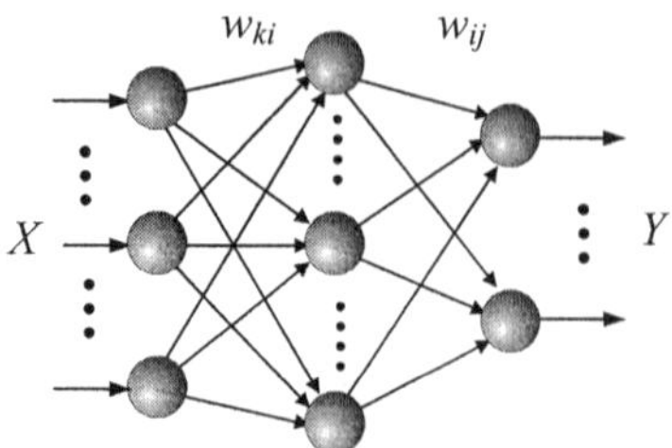

Fig. 1. The MLP structure

The *j*-th output unit is given by

$$y_j = F(S_j) \tag{1}$$

$$S_j = \sum_{i=1}^{P} w_{ij} y_i - T_j \tag{2}$$

The *i*-th hidden unit output is defined by the same way as follows:

$$y_i = F(S_i) \tag{3}$$

$$S_i = \sum_{k=1}^{P} w_{ki} x_k - T_i \tag{4}$$

where F is the activation function, S_j is weighted sum of the *j*-th neuron, w_{ij} is the weight from the *i*-th hidden unit to the *j*-th output unit, y_i is *i*-th hidden unit output, T_j is threshold of the *j*-th output neuron.

The *i*-th hidden unit output is defined by the same way as follows:

The purpose of the training MLP is to minimize the mean squared error (MSE):

$$E_s = \frac{1}{2} \sum_{k=1}^{L} \sum_{j=1}^{m} (y_j^k - d_j^k)^2 , \tag{5}$$

where L is the number of test patterns, d_j^k is desired *k*-th training sample. The weights and thresholds of MLP are updated iteratively in accordance with the following rule:

$$w_{ij}(t+1) = w_{ij}(t) - \alpha \frac{\partial E}{\partial w_{ij}(t)}, \quad T_j(t+1) = T_j(t) - \alpha \frac{\partial E}{\partial T_j(t)}, \tag{6}$$

The cost function E for one sample is defined by the expression:

$$E = \frac{1}{2} \sum_{j} (y_j - d_j)^2 , \tag{7}$$

Differentiating (7) with respect to w_{ij} and T_j we can get training rules for any layers i and j:

$$w_{ij}(t+1) = w_{ij}(t) - \alpha \gamma_j F'(S_j) y_i, \quad T_j(t+1) = T_j(t) + \alpha \gamma_j F'(S_j), \tag{8}$$

where $\gamma_j = \dfrac{\partial E}{\partial y_j}$ is error of *j*-th neuron. Before training the weights are initialized by small random values. The BP training rule (8) is repeated for all training samples until the acceptable squared error will be achieved (5).

2.2. Adaptive training step technique

As it has been mentioned before the BP has slow convergence to acceptable solution, non-stability of convergence and local minimum problems. It depends on choosing of the training rate. To choose of adaptive step it is possible to use the steepest descent method. Accordingly to it, the training step α for each layer is selected by means of minimizing the following expression:

$$\alpha(t) = \min_{j=1,m} E(y_j(t+1)), \tag{9}$$

The minimum of the function $E(y_j(t+1))$ must be located at a point, where

$$\frac{dE(y_j(t+1))}{d\alpha} = 0 \tag{10}$$

The last equation is not possible to decide, if we use the nonlinear function of activation.

Therefore many researches [9] apply the line search technique to find the minimum of the error function. However it is difficult task.

One way to avoid this problem is to use approximate decision of equation (10). Let's consider this approach.

The output value of the j-th neuron is defined by a nonlinear equation:

$$y_j(t+1) = F(S_j(t+1)),$$

$$S_j(t+1) = \sum_i y_i(t) w_{ij}(t+1) - T_j(t+1) \tag{11}$$

Substituting equation (6) in equation (11) we can get that

$$S_j(t+1) = \left(\sum_i y_i w_{ij} - T_j \right) - \alpha \left(\sum_i y_i \frac{\partial E}{\partial w_{ij}} - \frac{\partial E}{\partial T_j} \right). \tag{12}$$

Let

$$a_j = \sum_i y_i \frac{\partial E}{\partial w_{ij}} - \frac{\partial E}{\partial T_j}. \tag{13}$$

Then the expression (11) can be represented as follows:

$$S_j(t+1) = S_j(t) - \alpha a_j \tag{14}$$

and

$$y_j(t+1) = F(S_j(t) - \alpha a_j). \tag{15}$$

By using Taylor series expansion around $S_j(t)$ we can write

$$y_j(t+1) = F(S_j(t)) + F'(S_j(t))(S_j(t+1) - S_j(t)), \tag{16}$$

Substituting equation (14) in equation (16) we can get that

$$y_j(t+1) = F(S_j(t)) - \alpha F'(S_j(t)) a_j = y_j(t) - \alpha F'(S_j(t)) a_j \tag{17}$$

The error function associated with a single input pattern can be written as:

$$E = \frac{1}{2} \sum_j (y_j(t+1) - d_j)^2 \rightarrow \min \tag{18}$$

Then we have

$$\frac{\partial E}{\partial \alpha} = \sum_j (y_j(t) - d_j - \alpha F'(S_j(t)) a_j) \cdot (-F'(S_j(t)) a_j) = 0 \tag{19}$$

From last equation follows that

$$\alpha(t) = \frac{\sum_j (y_j(t) - d_j) F'(S_j) a_j}{\sum_j (a_j F'(S_j))^2} \tag{20}$$

It may be noted, that $\dfrac{\partial^2 E}{\partial \alpha^2} > 0$.

From this follows, that expression (20) minimizes the error function. Now let's find a_j. We must define for this purpose the following derivatives:

$$\frac{\partial E}{\partial w_{ij}} = \frac{\partial E}{\partial y_j} \cdot \frac{\partial y_j}{\partial S_j} \cdot \frac{\partial S_j}{\partial w_{ij}} = (y_j - d_j)F'(S_j)y_i \tag{21}$$

$$\frac{\partial E}{\partial T_j} = \frac{\partial E}{\partial y_j} \cdot \frac{\partial y_j}{\partial S_j} \cdot \frac{\partial S_j}{\partial T_j} = -(y_j - d_j)F'(S_j) \tag{22}$$

Substituting equations (21) and (22) in equation (13) we can get that

$$a_j = \left(1 + \sum_i y_i^2\right) \cdot (y_j - d_j) \cdot F'(S_j) \tag{23}$$

Assuming independence of neural network layers ($\gamma_j = y_j - d_j$), we can get the following approximate equation for adaptive training rate:

$$\alpha(t) = \frac{\sum_j (\gamma_j F'(S_j))^2}{\left(1 + \sum_i y_i^2\right)\sum_j \gamma_j^2 (F'(S_j))^4}, \tag{24}$$

where γ_j is error of j-th unit, which for hidden layer is computed as:

$$\gamma_j = \sum_{i=1}^m \gamma_i F'(S_i)w_{ji}, \tag{25}$$

where i is the next layer and j is the previous one.

Thus we got the common equation for adaptive training step calculation. Defining the values of $F'(S_j)$, we can get the adaptive step for different activation functions. For instance, if we use bipolar sigmoid function, then

$$F'(S_j) = \frac{1 - y_j^2}{2}. \tag{26}$$

It should be noted, that by using Taylor series decomposition around $S_j = 0$ we can get the following equation:

$$\alpha(t) = \frac{\sum_j \gamma_j^2 F'(S_j)}{F'(0) \cdot \left(1 + \sum_i y_i^2\right)\sum_j (\gamma_j F'(S_j))^2}, \tag{27}$$

where $F'(0) = \dfrac{\partial F}{\partial S_j}$ for $S_j = 0$.

ATS approach permits to choose step size for each layer and on each iteration of training algorithm. It should be noted, that for efficient training using ATS it is necessary to limit the ATS size [10], especially for real data. The limitation of step size may be defined both empirically and analytically [10]. An obvious advantage of ATS is computational simplicity. The next section illustrates the simulation results. Especially the proposed approach gives good results by using of binary data.

2.3. Simulation Results and Discussion

To assess the performance of the proposed learning technique experiments were conducted on standard problems of parity. Here the output of the MLP is required to be '1' if the input pattern contains an odd number of '1' and '0' otherwise. In this problem the most similar patterns, which differ by a single bit, require different answer. For simulation a three-layer MLP of size 4-4-1 is considered. The training set contains 16 samples. The average results are provided in the Table 1. Here NIT is the number of training iterations; MSE – mean square error. The simulation results demonstrate the efficiency of ATS technique. In contrast to standard approach, proposed technique permits to avoid the problem of choosing suitable training rate.

Table 1

NIT	MSE	Type of training step	Size of the training step
2100	0.0241	Constant	0.099
2100	0.0067	Constant	0.50
2100	0.0941	Constant	0.99
2100	0.0052	ATS	–

The experimental results show significant improvement in comparison with BP. The experiments for real data are considered in the next sections.

3. Neural network approach for chaotic time series processing

Problems concerning forecasting have existed for a very long time. People often have tried to predict the future. Traditional approach of time series analysis is based on linear mathematics. However, linearity is not too good tool for investigation of chaotic processes. In last years neural networks have been used to predict chaotic time series.

Chaotic behavior is characterized by highly sensitive to initial conditions and observed for many systems (stock market, EEG patterns of brainwave activity, central nervous system, etc.). The common test for chaos is calculation of the largest Lyapunov exponent, which should be positive. Chaos theory is currently very widely used in various areas and even in social sciences.

The key problem of chaotic time series is unpredictable on the long term, because error at the first step prediction is increased exponentially at time. Therefore the improvement of prediction accuracy is of great importance. It permits also to understand the behavior observed nonlinear system and to perform state space reconstruction, taking into account numerical data from complex system. It is based on an embedding theorem [11], which guarantees that a full knowledge of the behavior a system is contained in time series of any a one measurement. As a result the full multivariate phase space can be constructed from the single time series.

To apply the embedding theorem it is necessary to define a suitable embedding dimension and time delay. The estimation such parameters provide a maximum predictability of chaotic time series and can be used for choosing of optimal windows size (number of input units) in forecasting neural network. The processing of chaotic time series may be divided into three stages, which are shown in Fig. 2.

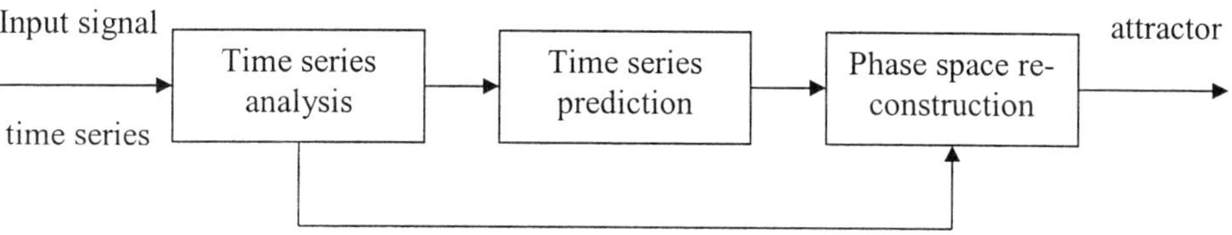

Fig. 2 Functional diagram of the data processing.

The first stage is time series analysis. As a result of this stage we can identify the chaotic behavior and estimate embedding parameters. Using the data from previous stage we can perform phase space reconstruction or build neural networks for optimal forecasting. In the next parts of this chapter are described both known and unknown approaches to chaotic time series processing.

3.1. Choosing of embedding delay

For the choosing the optimal time delay τ can be used the following approaches: autocorrelation function, mutual information, etc. The optimal time delay is typically chosen in accordance with first zero of autocorrelation function or first minimum of mutual information.

The mutual information can be defined as follows [12]:

$$I(\tau) = -\sum_{i,j} P_{ij}(\tau) \cdot \ln \frac{P_{ij}(\tau)}{P_i \cdot P_j}, \tag{28}$$

where P_i is the probability to find a time series value in the i-th interval, and $P_{ij}(\tau)$ is the joint probability that an observation is located in the i-th interval and the observation time τ later is located in the j-th interval.

Estimating τ by such a way, we can get the coordinates as independent as possible.

3.2. Embedding dimension

As stated earlier embedding dimension is applied for state space reconstruction and definition of window size for predicting neural networks. Suppose we have a given one-variable time series represented by the N values as follows:

$$x(t) = F\big(x(t-1), x(t-2), ..., x(t-k)\big), \ t = k + \overline{1, N}. \tag{29}$$

Takens proved that dynamic reconstruction is possible, if

$$m \geq 2[d] + 1, \tag{30}$$

where d is fractal dimension of original attractor, $[d]$ denotes the integer part of d and $k = m - 1 = 2d$ characterizes the window size.

In this case the reconstructed attractor embedded in the m-dimensional state space preserves important topological properties of the original attractor. There exist a lot of methods for estimating the embedding dimension m such as the false nearest neighbors, fractal dimension, principal component analysis and so on. Let's examine the false nearest neighbors approach [13]. It is based on idea, that geometrical properties of the original and reconstructed attractor must be preserved.

The algorithm of the false nearest method is the following:

1. Let $m=1$. Then we seek for each point $\bar{x}(i)$ in time series its nearest neighbor $\bar{x}(j)$ in m-dimensional space.
2. Calculate the distance $|\bar{x}(i) - \bar{x}(j)|$. After this we iterate both point and define
3. $R_i = \dfrac{|\bar{x}(i+1) - \bar{x}(j+1)|}{|\bar{x}(i) - \bar{x}(j)|}$
4. If $R_i > R_t$, where R_t is suitable threshold, then such a point is a false nearest neighbor. As a result we can get the number of the false nearest point P.
5. Calculate $\dfrac{P}{N}$ and repeat algorithm for $m=m+1$.
6. The algorithm is continued until $\dfrac{P}{N}$ is close to zero.

3.3. The largest Lyapunov exponent

As it is mentioned above the well-known test for chaos is calculation of the largest Lyapunov exponent, which characterizes sensitivity to initial conditions [14]. Such a Lyapunov exponent is statistical measure of divergence between two orbits starting from slightly different initial conditions. Let d_0 be initial divergence between two trajectories and d_n be divergence between such orbits after n steps. Then largest Lyapunov exponent is defined by

$$\lambda = \lim_{n \to \infty}\left(\frac{1}{n}\ln\frac{d_n}{d_0}\right) \tag{31}$$

Let's examine the different approaches for definition λ.

3.4. Analytical approach

The standard approach for computing λ is calculated as follows.

1. Starting from two points in the basin of attraction, separated by distance d_0. Usually d_0 is less the 10^{-8}.
2. Advance both orbits on one iteration ahead and calculate the new divergence between trajectories using Euclidian metric. As a result we evaluate $\ln d_1$.
3. We repeat the last step for n points and calculate $\ln d_2$, $\ln d_3$,..., $\ln d_n$.
4. Plot the graph $\ln d$ versus n.
5. Using method of least square we construct straight line of regression, taking into account only points, for which $\ln d < 0$. The slope of the regression line estimates the largest Lyapunov exponent.

Estimation λ by considered algorithm is a difficult task in general because initial divergence d_0 must be less then 10^{-8}. This condition may be performed using a large length of an experimental data. However, it is very problematic to reach for real data. Therefore the traditional approach has been limited in their applicability to many real world chaotic data. One way to avoid this problem is to use neural networks for computing largest Lyapunov exponent.

3.5. Neural network approach

The key idea of proposed method [15] is to compute by help of neural network divergence between two orbits on n step ahead, using iterative approach. Such a procedure can be represented as follows:

1. Train neural network using sliding window technique.
2. Select any point $x(\tau)$ from training set and form the following data point: $\{x(\tau), x(\tau-1),..., x(\tau-k+1)\}$, where k is window size.
3. Compute $\{x(\tau+1), x(\tau+2),..., x(\tau+n)\}$, using multistep prediction. $x(\tau+i)=F(x(\tau+i-1), x(\tau+i-2),..., x(\tau+i-k))$, where $i = \overline{1,n}$
4. Compute $x'(\tau) = x(\tau) + d_0$, where $d_0 \approx 10^{-8}$ and repeat step 3 in order to get $x(\tau+i)$, $i = \overline{1,n}$.
5. Define $\ln d_i = \ln|x'(\tau+i) - x(\tau+i)|$, $i = \overline{1,n}$ and mark point for which $\ln d_i < 0$.
6. Plot the graph $\ln d$ versus n.
7. Build line of regression for marked point and compute its slope, which equals to the largest Lyapunov exponent.

Let's examine numerical experiments for estimating λ using feed forward neural network. In the experiments, a neural network with 7 input, 5 hidden units and 1 output node is trained to predict Henon and Lorenz time series. The hidden units are based on neurons of the sigmoid function and output unit on neuron of the linear function of activation respectively. The back propagation algorithm with adaptive step is used for training of neural network. The training set consists of 1500 patterns for Henon and 930 patterns for Lorenz time series respectively. The mean square error for Henon time series is $5.92 \cdot 10^{-5}$ after 1000 iteration. Fig. 3 shows the graph $\ln d$ versus t and regression line, which characterizes the largest Lyapunov exponent. The estimated value $\hat{\lambda} = 0.43$ is close to the desired value 0.49. The mean square error for Lorenz time series is $9.2 \cdot 10^{-4}$ after 700 iterations. The regression line and function $\ln d$ from t is shown on Fig. 4.

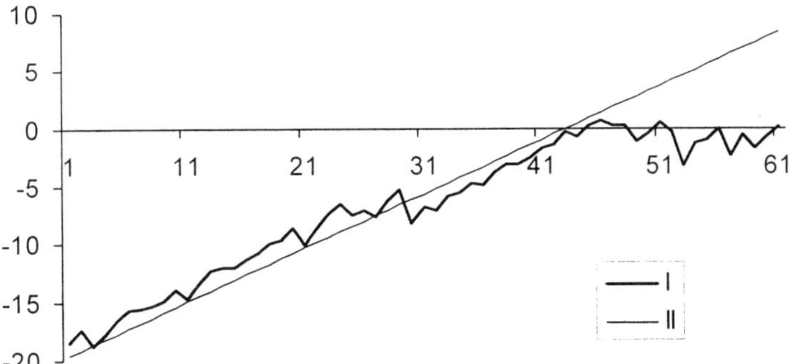

Fig. 3. I – the evolution of distance between two nearby orbits for Henon attractor;
II – regression line

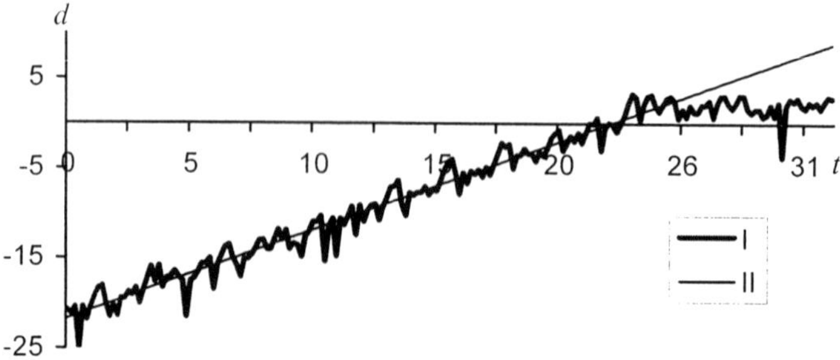

Fig. 4. I – the evolution of distance between two nearby orbits for Lorenz attractor;
II – regression line

The largest Lyapunov exponent is 0.98 (desired value is 0.906). We have seen, that neural network produced fairly accurate forecast.

As can be seen an obvious advantage of proposed approach in comparison with traditional is simplicity and accuracy.

3.6. Prediction and State Space Reconstruction

The *goal of time series prediction* on the level of the individual data points can be stated as follows: for a given sequence $x(1)$, $x(2)$,..., $x(l)$ it is necessary to find continuation $x(l+1)$, $x(l+2)$... The nonlinear predictive model can be presented, as

$$x(t) = F(x(t-1), x(t-2),...,x(t-k)), \qquad (32)$$

where $t = \overline{k+1, N}$, F – *nonlinear function*, provided by neural network nonlinear units and k is *size of the sliding window*, which is equal to number of time series elements simultaneously submitted to inputs of a neural network. The goal of prediction on the level of emergent structure is state space reconstruction.

As we noted before, for achievement of maximum predictability it is necessary to define embedding parameters. Let's examine applying feed-forward neural networks for chaotic time series forecasting and state space reconstruction. As the chaotic systems, which we want to model are the Lorenz and Henon attractors. The Lorenz attractor is defined by the three-coupled differential equations:

$$\frac{dx}{dt} = G(y-x), \quad \frac{dy}{dt} = -xz + rx - y, \quad \frac{dz}{dt} = xy - bz \qquad (33)$$

This system is chaotic for the parameter values $G=10$, $r=28$ and $b=8/3$.

We solved (33) using a 4-th order Runge-Kutta approach with a time step 0.01. Fig. 5 and Fig. 6 show Lorenz time series (x-axis) and 3-dimensional attractor respectively. Using the mutual information we can define that $\tau=0.16$. Analogously applying the method of false nearest neighbors we can get embedding dimension $m=5$. From this follows, that window size $k \geq m\text{-}1 = 4$.

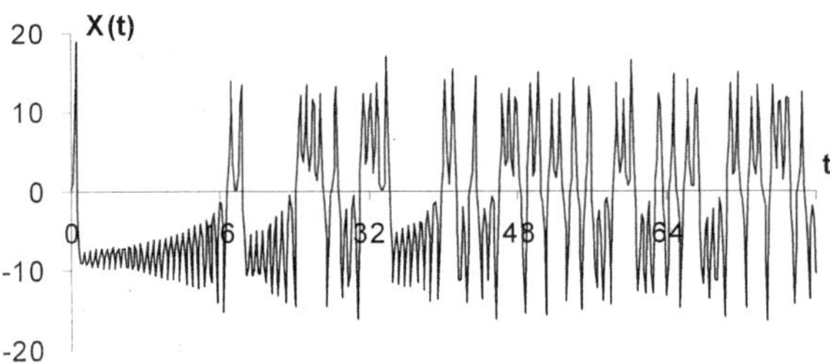

Fig. 5. Original Lorenz time series (*x*-axis)

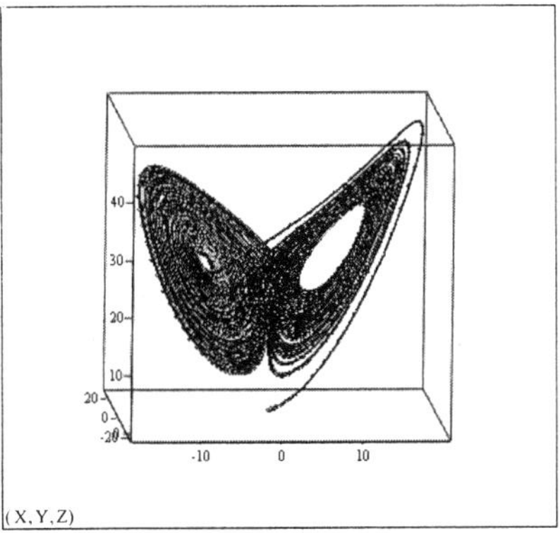

Fig. 6. Original Lorenz attractor

The Henon attractor is described by the following equations:

$$\begin{cases} x_{n+1} = 1 - \alpha x_n^2 + y_n \\ y_{n+1} = \beta x_n \end{cases},$$

(34)

where $\alpha=1.4$ and $\beta=0.3$ for chaotic behavior. Fig. 7 and Fig. 8 show the Henon time series (*x*-axis) and 2-dimensional original attractor.

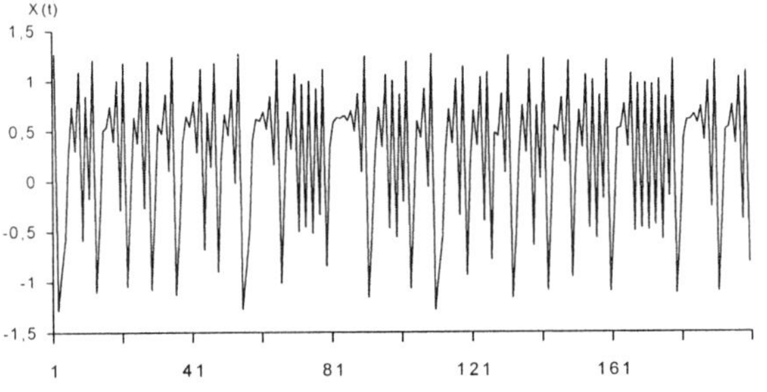

Fig. 7. The Henon time series (first 200 elements)

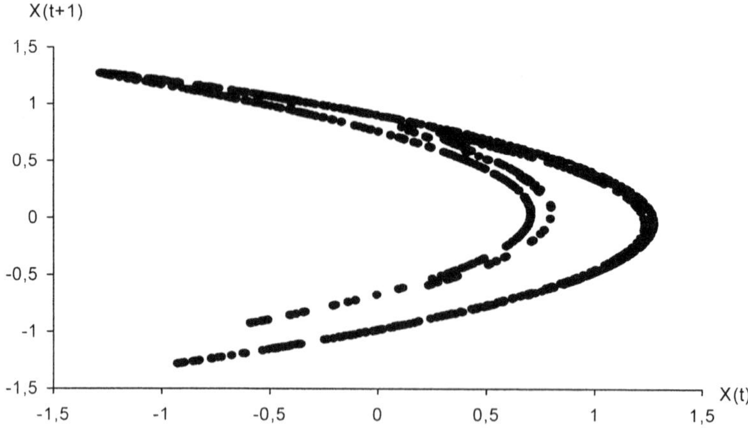

Fig. 8. Original Henon attractor constructed for 1500 elements

By analogy with mentioned above approach we can get that $k \geq 2$ and $\tau=1$. Let's examine forecasting of chaotic behavior by means of MLP.

We will use for the tests neural network with 7 input, 5 hidden and 1 linear output units. Notice, that hidden units use the sigmoid function of activation. The adaptive training rate is applied for training of neural network. The average results of experiments are represented in the Table 2. As can be seen the efficiency of proposed technique depends on limitation of training rate. As it is mentioned earlier, the limitation of step size may be defined analytically. In common case the experimental results show significant improvement over the traditional BP method.

Based on the iterative approach we predicted the Henon and Lorenz data for 1500 step ahead. The predicted Lorenz and the Henon attractors are shown in Fig. 9 and Fig. 10. As can be seen the neural network has the ability to capture the underlying properties of chaotic behavior and can be applied for state space reconstruction.

Table 2

Type of data	MSE	Type of training step	Size of the training step	ATS validation
Henon data	0.001998	Constant	0.01	–
	0.000587	Constant	0.49	–
	0.001217	Constant	0.99	–
	0.00129	ATS	–	<2.99
	0.000767	ATS	–	<0.99
	0.000099	ATS	–	<0.49
Lorenz data	0.0261	Constant	0.01	–
	0.0164	Constant	0.49	–
	0.0113	Constant	0.99	–
	0.0308	ATS	–	<2.99
	0.00756	ATS	–	<0.99
	0.0209	ATS	–	<0.49

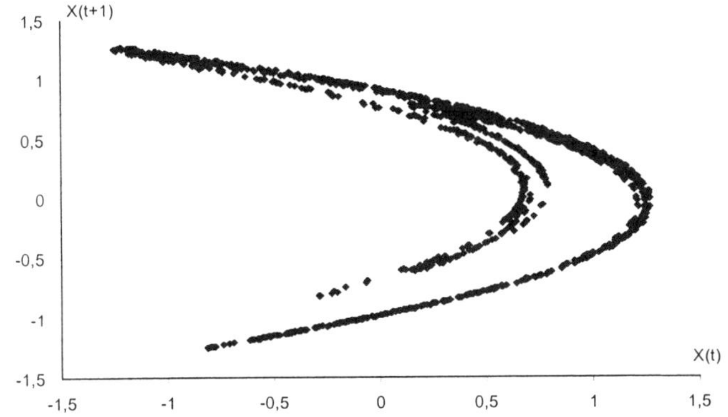

Fig. 9. Predicted Henon attractor constructed for 1500 predicting iterations

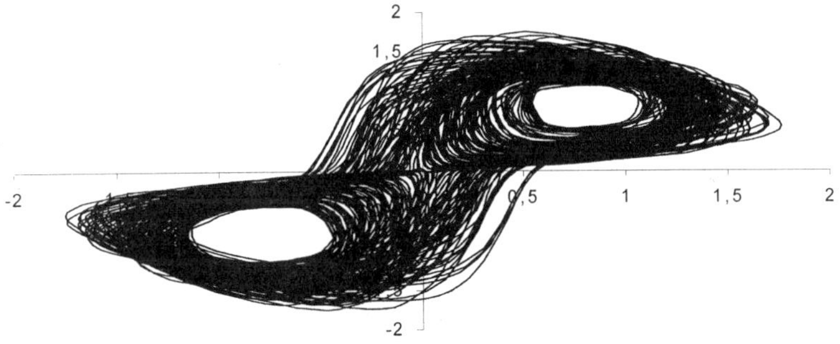

Fig. 10. Predicted Lorenz attractor constructed for 1500 predicting iterations

Thus the neural network permits to predict the behavior of complex system.

3.7. Horizon of prediction for chaotic time series

Horizon of prediction is characterized a range of time on which it is possible to perform precision forecasting. As it is mentioned before the chaotic data are unpredictable on the long term, because measurement error in the initial conditions grows exponentially in time. This sensitive dependence an initial conditions is defined by a positive Lyapunov exponent. Therefore the positive value of Lyapunov exponent determines the upper prediction limit. As is well known, the sum of positive Lyapunov exponent is equal to the Kolmogorov entropy. Then in accordance with chaos theory the horizon of prediction can be represented as follows [16]:

$$T \approx \frac{1}{K} \cdot \ln\left(\frac{1}{d_0}\right),$$ (35)

where $K = \sum_i \lambda_i$ is Kolmogorov entropy and $\lambda_i > 0$, d_0 is initial error of predicting.

In accordance with equation (35) the accurate prediction is possible only in range T. Thus, after training of neural network we can find horizon of predicting for initial point, starting with which one we perform forecasting.

3.8. The increase of predicting horizon

As it has been mentioned above, the horizon of prediction for chaotic behavior is limited in accordance with equation (35). One way to increase of predicting horizon is to retraining neural network. Let's examine proposed approach more detailed.

Suppose, that we trained neural network using training data set $X=\{x(1), x(2),.., x(N)\}$.

In accordance with predicting horizon we can perform accurate predicting on T point ahead. As a result we can define the following predicting points: $x(N+1)$, $x(N+2)$, ..., $x(N+T)$. The next step is to organize the new training data set, for instance, as follows: $X'=\{x(1), x(2),..., x(N+T)\}$. Training neural network for new data set we can increase predicting horizon. In order to test the ability of proposed approach to increase of predicting horizon, the experiments have been performed on Henon and Lorenz data. Table 3 and 4 show the comparative results of iterative and retraining approaches. The MSE_1 and MSE_2 are mean square error for the predicted points $x(N+1)$, $x(N+2)$, $x(N+3)$, $x(N+4)$ and $x(N+5)$, $x(N+6)$, $x(N+7)$, $x(N+8)$ respectively.

Table 3

Approach	NIT	Size of training set	MSE	T	MSE_1	MSE_2
Iterative approach	308	950	$3\cdot10^{-4}$	4	0.00022275	0.031198
Retraining approach	276	954	$3\cdot10^{-4}$	4	0.00003325	0.00804275

Table 4

Approach	Actual value	Desired value	Absolute error
Iterative approach	0.365621	0.363170	0.002451
	0.992627	1.002511	0.009884
	-0.274204	-0.298088	0.023884
	1.191078	1.176354	0.014724
	-1.101723	-1.026758	0.074965
	-0.363043	-0.123019	0.240024
	0.512435	0.670785	0.158350
	0.524174	0.333160	0.191014
Retraining approach	0.364677	0.363170	0.001507
	1.001295	1.002511	0.001216
	-0.288775	-0.298088	0.009313
	1.182933	1.176354	0.006579
	-1.046040	-1.026758	0.019282
	-0.247162	-0.123019	0.124143
	0.592083	0.670785	0.078702
	0.434126	0.333160	0.100966

Table 5 and 6 show the analogical results by using of Lorenz data.

Table 5

Approach	Actual value	Desired value	Absolute error
Iterative approach	-0.155480	-0.163600	0.008120
	-0.556713	-0.617800	0.061087
	-1.573766	-1.633100	0.059334
	-0.536221	-0.439700	0.096521
	0.085535	0.186400	0.100865
	0.237657	0.520500	0.282843
	0.719185	1.254000	0.534815
	1.509935	0.938200	0.571735
	0.461715	0.245600	0.216115
	-0.042810	0.230800	0.273610
Retraining approach	-0.169124	-0.163600	0.005524
	-0.613167	-0.617800	0.004633
	-1.598149	-1.633100	0.034951
	-0.430258	-0.439700	0.009442
	0.121533	0.186400	0.064867
	0.317614	0.520500	0.202886
	0.940051	1.254000	0.313949
	1.336355	0.938200	0.398155
	0.301510	0.245600	0.055910
	0.011798	0.230800	0.219002

Table 6

Approach	NIT	Size of training set	MSE	T	MSE_1	MSE_2
Iterative approach	1000	800	0.001357	5	0.0053618	0.1628954
Retraining approach	578	954	0.0014	5	0.0011142	0.0698684

As can be seen the retraining approach permits in common case to perform better prediction than iterative approach and to increase the horizon of predicting.

3.9. Future work

In the previous sections we examined the simple predicting approach, when for given time-series up to time N it is necessary to find the continuation of time series. The more complex problem is described as follows: given a d-dimensional chaotic system, which is defined by the d differential equations. However we have only one-dimensional observed data. Then the fundamental question is the following: Is it possible to define knowing only one coordinate of observed time series the others coordinates and how to do it?

One way to decide this problem may be the following. We can define the embedding dimension m and number of the factors d, which influence on this time series. In accordance with it we can construct the neural network which has m input and d output units and to apply the ICA (independent component analysis) or PCA methods. But experiments on Lorenz data shown, that these methods are not suitable for such a task. For instance, we try to mix the coordinates of the Lorenz data and after this to get the original sources. As a result traditional ICA is not able to do it. As a rule the ICA method gives the good results if we use non-gaussian (deterministic) data and PCA – on contrary. The chaotic data are more gaussian with comparison with other data. Therefore by using PCA we got better results in comparison with ICA on the level of the emergent structure. However it should be noted, that PCA also doesn't give the suitable decision of given problem on the level of individual point.

Therefore the next task is to develop a powerful tool for separation of chaotic time series and for getting using one-dimensional chaotic time series the others coordinates. It can permit to analyze the past and define the hidden factors.

4. Intelligent neural system for real-time navigation

As it is mentioned before, intelligent system is called such a system that can achieve complex goals in complex environment. One of the areas, where the creation of "an artificial brain" has large practical and theoretical importance, is the robotics. Mobile robots with capabilities to autonomously reach a target location despite of obstacles are designed for a broad range of applications. This section is focused on description of an intelligent neural system for the control of a mobile robot. Compared to other project activities, the proposed neural system has the ability for self-training and self-organizing and behaves itself as a person during orientation in environment.

4.1. The Control System architecture

The global architecture of the neural system is represented on Fig. 11. It consists of different neural modules, which are combined in an intelligent system. The neural system solves the following tasks: performs data fusion; reactive control of the mobile robot while moving in the unknown environment; the formation of the global route map in the process of the motion in the unknown environment; the choice of the optimal route and generating the direction of motion; The neural system must provide the following demands: robust control in case of inexact information from sensors; training with the supervisor; self-training and self-organizing; capability for real time action.

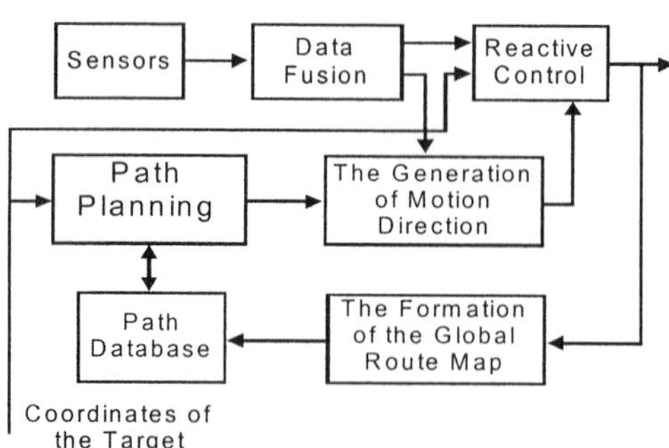

Fig. 11. The Control System architecture

One can see on Fig. 11 the information from different sensors is combined by data fusion module. As a result we have the local environment map. The local environment map is used for reactive control and for unpredicted obstacle avoidance, if the working environment is known.

Reactive control takes place if the working environment is unknown. In this case, the planning stage has no sense. The inputs to the neural system are the final goal position and the sensor data.

In the process of the robot motion the neural system memorizes the path. For this purpose is used the arrangement of the indicators from start point to target. Each indicator contains direction, which defines how the robot should reach next indicator, a distance between neighbor indicators etc. As a result of robot motion in the unknown environment mapping is performed. As a result of mapping the formation of the global route map and of path database takes place. The approach to the formation model of the environment is described in [17].

Now let's examine the case if the robot motion is performed in the known environment. In this case the path planning module identifies the optimal route for a specific motion action in the actual environment and generates the direction of the motion in the key points (indicators) of the path. For this purpose the path planning module uses a path database to choose an optimal solution allowing to reach the target with minimal cost. It is performed by original neural network presented in [16]. The neural system performs the reactive control between the key points of the possible route.

Such neural system has ability for self-training and self-organizing. In this case self-training and self-organizing is realized both on the reactive level and on the level of path planning. In the next section we will examine reactive system only.

4.2. General principles of obstacle avoidance

In the case of the reactive system only the current and target robot locations are known. We will examine the collision avoidance problem as the task of the robot motion in an indoor environment without collision with any obstacles in the absence of any prior knowledge about obstacle positions. The robot has to find the shortest path between the current and the goal position.

The input information of the reactive system is the data from different sensors. These data are processed by means of data fusion. As a result the local environment map is generated. This map is formed in the certain view radius and the angular range of $180°$: $OG=\{S(i),-90°{\leq}i{\leq}90°\}$, where $S(i)$ is the distance up to the obstacle if the angle between the current heading direction of the robot and the obstacle is equal to i grades.

The first task of the reactive system is the computing of the suitable passage of motion. Such a passage is considered to be the nearest to the target. It is obtained as a result of analysis of the local environment map. Such a passage is characterized both the linear (R_L, R_R) and angular distances to the obstacle (Fig. 12).

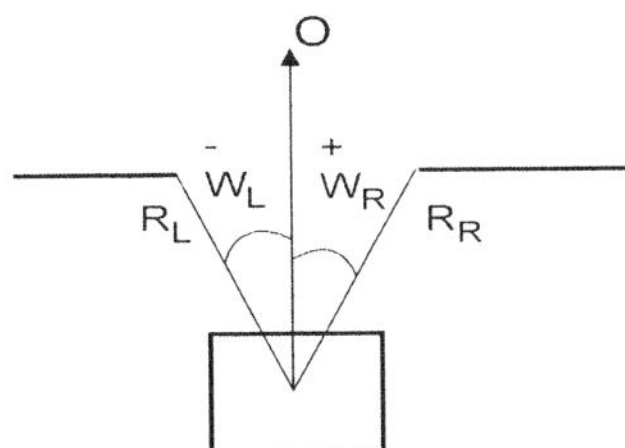

Fig. 12. The linear and angular characteristics of the passage:
O is the current heading direction

We use the dynamical network with fixed weights and the analytical approach for selecting the appropriate passage of motion. The structure and the algorithm of functioning of such a module were considered in [19].

The second task of the reactive system is the definition of the suitable direction in the selected passage of motion. The optimal direction is such a direction of motion, which ensures minimal angular distance to the target in the chosen interval of movement. The definition of such a direction is performed by way of analysis of the selected passage. For this we use the analytical and neural network approaches.

The analytical approach is used for control of the robot on large passage of motion, if $R_d>2d$, where R_d is the width of the chosen interval and d is the width of the robot. This approach is based on the analysis of the following data: angle α between the current and the target direction; angular (W_L, W_R) and linear (R_L, R_R) characteristics of the selected interval of motion. As a result we obtain the optimal direction of motion, which corresponds to the shortest path to the target.

Whenever the robot is moving obstacles have to be avoided. It is the complex problem, if the passage like door has a certain minimum size. In this case the inexact environment map can lead to the contact with an obstacle. The neural network approach is used for the robust control of the robot on the narrow passages of motion, if $R_d<2d$. If one trains a neural network to target output data in case of inexact input information it will provide the robust control of the robot. For these purposes we apply the backpropagation neural networks. The structure of the neural network module is shown in Fig. 13.

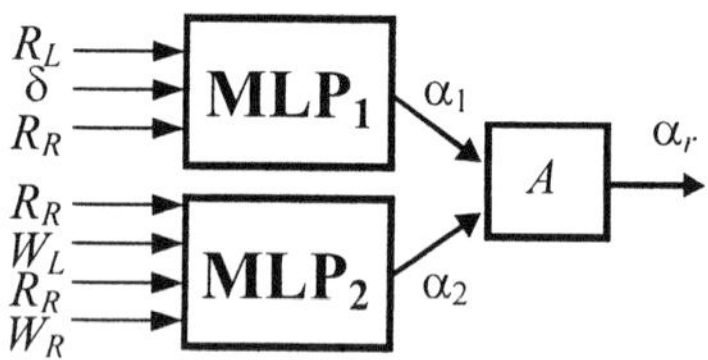

Fig. 13. The architecture of the neural networks module

It consists of two multilayer networks MLP_1 and MLP_2. The robust direction of the robot movement is formed by the arbiter. It should be noted, that $\alpha_r=\alpha_1$ if the robot moves in the space between various obstacles (through door posts, etc), and $\alpha_r=\alpha_2$ if the robot moves in the tunnel. Block MLP_1 forms the arc of the circumference as the trajectory what secures the exclusion of the collision of the robot with the left or right side of the obstacle during the maneuvers. Block MLP_2 uses the straight line as the trajectory, what provides the stable movement of the robot in tunnels. Linear (R_L, R_R) and angular (W_L, W_R, $\delta=W_L+W_R$) distances of the chosen interval of motion are used as the input data. We used the backpropagation algorithm with adaptive step for neural networks training. For the generation of training data set we use a simple approach [20], which is based on the rotation of selected interval of motion around the center of the robot. It permits to get different learning samples for training MLP_1 and MLP_2.

4.3. Module of precision control

The disadvantage of the previous approaches is that they do not take into account the distance from the side of the robot to the obstacle. As a result of performing the maneuvers by the robot there can be the collision with obstacles.

To maneuver without collisions it is necessary, that the side distance up to the obstacle were larger than the radius of the circle, circumscribed around the robot. If this condition is not fulfilled, the control of the robot performs the module of precision control (Fig. 14). In this case the angle of the turn of the robot in any direction is constant and is equal to a few grades.

The block F is intended for the conversion of the angular direction of driving α_r in a binary array. It is necessary for the control of the binary neural network. The block F performs the following functions:

$$Y_1 = \begin{cases} 1, & \text{if } \alpha_r > 0 \\ 0, & \text{otherwise} \end{cases}; \quad Y_2 = \begin{cases} 1, & \text{if } \alpha_r < 0 \\ 0, & \text{otherwise} \end{cases} \tag{36}$$

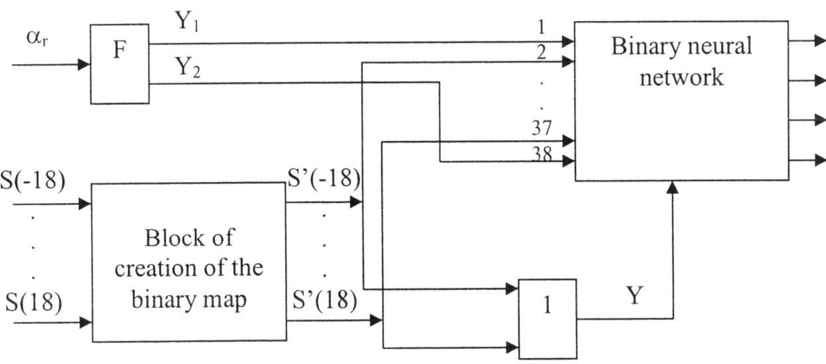

Fig. 14. Module of precision control.

The block of creation of the binary environment map is intended for generating the environment map of the given configuration (Fig. 15) and for the formation of the signal Y of the activation of the binary neural network.

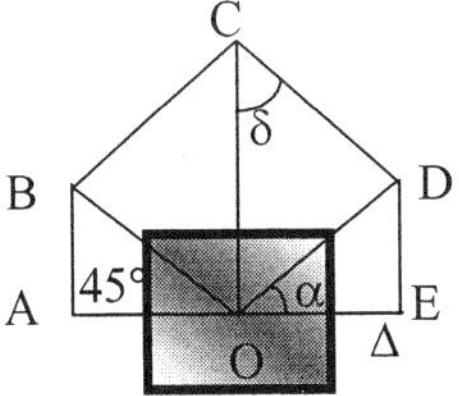

Fig. 15. Configuration of the environment map

Such a map is necessary for the control of the robot in situations, when the obstacle is too close (at the distance less than Δ) to the side of the robot. The block of creation of a binary environment map uses the compressed environment map consisting of 36 units as the input information. The technology of conversion is, that if the obstacle is in zone *ABCDE*, the appropriate units $S'(p)$ are installed in single values, otherwise in zero values (Fig. 16).

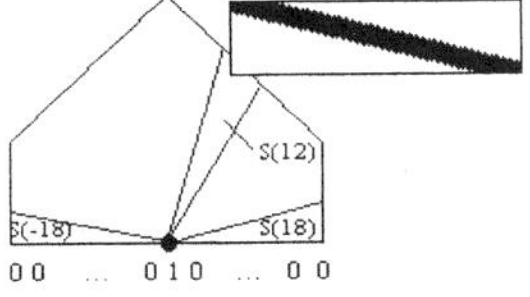

Fig. 16. The example of the binary environment map creation

As a result the binary array characterizes the presence of obstacles in the given area. This block consists of one layer of threshold neurons, each of which corresponds to the defined sector of the environment map.

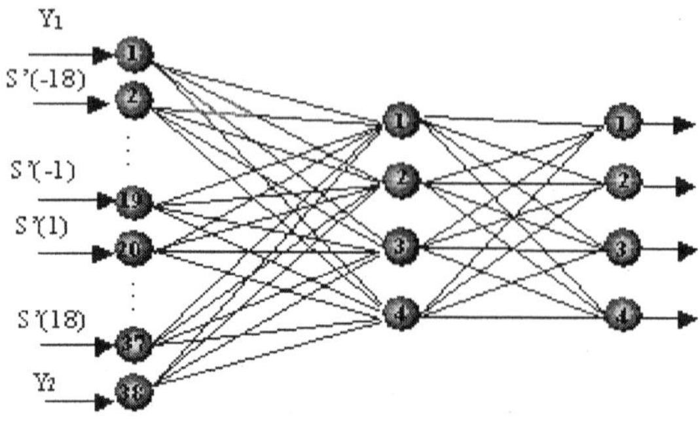

Fig. 17. The binary neural network

The binary neural network is intended for the control of the robot, when the turns on the large values can evolve into collision with the obstacle. Such a network represents the three-layer feed forward neural network (Fig. 17).

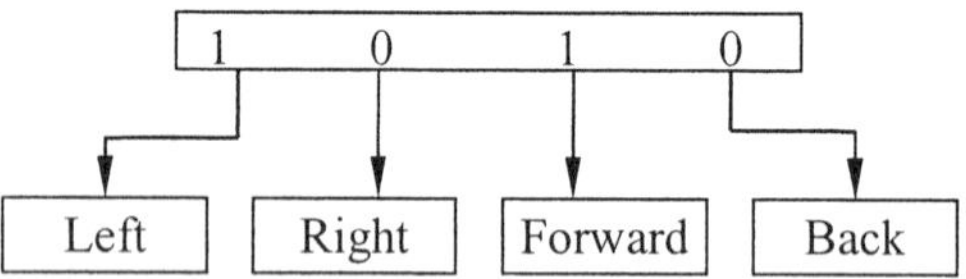

Fig. 18 Control commands of the robot

The sigmoid function is used as the function of activation of units. The commands of the robot are formed such a neural network: turn to the left (right) or move forward (back) (Fig. 18). Thus the turns are performed on a few grades, that exclusion collision of the robot with the obstacles. Also the signals Y_1 and Y_2 are used for the control of the binary network. So, if $Y_1=1$, that corresponds to $\alpha_r>0$, the binary network will form the command of turn to the right on the small value. Here α_r is the current direction of the robot, which is defined by analytical or neural network modules. Such an interaction between these modules provides the driving of the robot in the correct direction to the target. This is especially actually at the existence of the alternate paths of driving in narrow intervals. The binary network operates on the principle of overcoming the obstacle.

For training the binary network it is necessary to generate training sets. The generation of learning sampling is characterized by the simplicity and is performed by the logical way.

The training data for some situations are shown in table 7. For training the binary network the backpropagation algorithm was used.

Table 7

Input pattern	Output pattern
01100000000000000000000000000000000001	1010
10000000000000000000000000000000000000	0110
00000000000000000000000111111111111110	1000
00111111100000000000000000000011111100	0010
00000000000000000000000000000000000000	0010
01111111111111111111111111111111111110	0001

4.4. Self-training

One of the most important goals in the design and development of intelligent mobile robots is the ability of a vehicle to adapt to the environment. Life is full of situations, which are impossible to predict. In these cases the ability of a robot to self-training and self-organizing is of great importance. It permits the artificial system to progress without a person (self-progress). It is especially important, when the robot operates in the aggressive environment or on other planet.

As pointed out before the initial knowledge of the robot is determined by logical way. Such knowledge of the robot can be filled up and corrected through real-world experimentation. Then the task of the robot self-training is to train neural networks for providing the robust control on the narrow gap of motion in the process of robot functioning. For this the robot must collect itself the training data set. Such a process of self-organizing takes place through trial and error on the narrow passages of motion. The robot simply tries to find different actions for every situation and to collect the training samples. If the maneuver is carried out successfully the training data for the learning of the multilayer perceptron are formed. If the trial is not a success there is a return of the robot to the initial point for several steps back and the repetition of the maneuver.

We assume, that the control of the robot in regime of self-training is performed by means analytical module and module of precision control. The usage of the module of precision control in the regime of self-training gives an opportunity to decrease the number of mistakes while performing the maneuvers and consequently to accelerate the process of self-training. It should be noted, that self-training can take place both for obtaining new knowledge and for correction of the old knowledge. As a result the adaptation of the robot to the environment is provided.

4.5. Simulation and experimental results

For testing of the neural system the software has been developed which allows to simulate the robot motion. The training and simulation were performed in case of inexact data from the environment map. For example, the real location of the obstacles differs from the things the robot sees. The tests were carried out for various situations. However learning to target output data will neutralize these inexact data. It provides robust motion of the robot.

In these experiments the weights of the neural networks were initialized randomly and in process of interaction with the unknown environment the training of these networks was performed. For such training the backpropagation algorithm with adaptive rate was used.

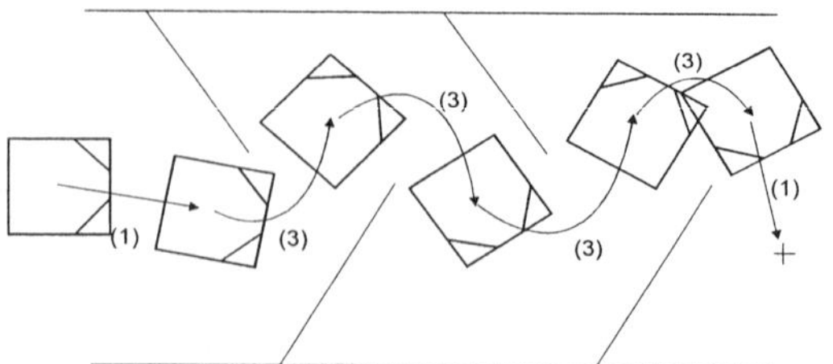

Fig. 19. "Slalom" task. (1)-Analytical module, (3)-MPL1

First of all the agent has to collect the training set by means trial and error and to apply the backpropagation algorithm for training. The inexact data from sensors were used for simulation. For instance the linear and angular distances to the obstacles were differed from real values. After self-training, the agent was tested in various situations. The slalom task is shown in Fig. 19. One can see, that the robot control is performed both by analytical module and MLP_1 module.

The online learning capabilities of our approach were investigated in a typical real-world environment by experiments, carried out in Laboratory of Robotics in Germany. Experiments was realized using Pioneer I and Walter mobile robots (Fig. 20 and 21)

Fig. 20. Pioneer I mobile robot

Fig. 21. "Walter" mobile robot

Pioneer's maximal velocity is 300 mm/s. It has 7 ultrasonic sensors (5 on the front of robot and 2 on the sides of robot). As a result of data fusion is formed the local environment map in the angular interval of 180° and in the review radius of 1.5 meter. The ultrasonic sensors report distances between 150 mm and 10 m. The mobile robot has been designed for indoor environments. An RS-232 cable interface is used to communicate between the SUN Sparc station with Sun Solaris installed and the robot microcomputer.

The robot "Walter" is the LABMATE® mobile robot (Fig. 21) with a video camera, infrared scanner and ultrasonic transducers. Its maximal velocity is 1000 mm/s. Different sensors have different perceptual characteristics. The SN288827 Polaroid ultrasonic sensors report distances between 300 mm and 10 m (frequency 45 kHz). As infrared scanner is used the RS2-180 (Leuze electronic). The mobile robot has been designed for indoor environments. An RS-232 radio-modem interface is used to communicate between the SUN Sparc station and the robot micro-computer.

The software for control of mobile robot was transferred to robot hardware. The experiments shown that the robots were able to pass through narrow openings (e.g. doorways) or narrow corridors without collisions, despite the inexact data from sensors. Thus the tests have shown a good confirmation to the theoretical results.

5. Summary and discussion

In this chapter we have addressed three key aspects of design and applying of neural networks, namely the efficient training algorithm for multilayer perceptron, neural network approaches for chaotic time series processing and intelligent neural system for autonomous control of a mobile robot. As can be seen the neural networks are powerful tool in different domains in comparison with traditional approaches. However, the neural networks have poor ability to self-progressing with purpose of adaptation to environment. So, for instance, the self-progressing and self-organization of the human beings is performed by means of interaction with environment as follows [21]. The source of the progressing of the individual organism is non-equilibrium state with outer and inner world, which appears as a result of influences from the environment. It brings excitement of the corresponding neural structures of the brain, which reconstruct themselves in such a way that to neutralize the arisen of non-equilibrium. It should be noted also that phenomenon of chaos influences greatly the process of ontogenesis and self-organizing of the organisms. Chaos corresponds to the highest point of creative process, when organism searches the suitable decision with purpose of adaptation to the environment. During this process takes place the infinite change of state until the solution of the problem in individual's opinion is found.

In comparison with it the traditional approach of design artificial systems is that the designed system must be located only in definite states. Such states characterize the area of stability. As a result it is limited the process of evolution of the artificial system. One way to decide this problem is to direct the instability to evolution of artificial system. At present time it is an open problem. From my point of view it can be performed combining neural networks and chaos theory. The neural networks are only the first step on the way of real artificial intelligence.

Acknowledgment

This work was supported by the INTAS within the following research projects: "Intelligent neural system for autonomous control of a mobile robot" and "Development of an Intelligent Sensing Instrumentation Structure".

References

[1] B. Goertzel, *The structure of Intelligence: A New mathematical model of mind.* Springer–Verlag, New York, 1993.

[2] X.-H. Yu and G.-A. Chen, *Efficient backpropagation learning using optimal learning rate and momentum.* Neural Networks, vol. 10, no. 3, pp. 517–527, 1997.

[3] G.-J. Wang and C.-C. Chen, *A fast multilayer neural-network training algorithm based on the layer-by-layer optimizing procedures.* IEEE Trans. Neural Networks, vol. 7, pp. 768–775, May 1996.

[4] R. Battiti, *First- and second-order methods for learning: Between steepest descent and Newton methods.* Neural Comput., vol. 4, pp. 141–166, 1992.

[5] T.H. Martin and B.M. Mohammad, *Training feedforward network with Marquardt algorithm.* IEEE Trans. Neural Networks, vol. 5, pp. 959–963, Nov. 1996.

[6] E.M. Johansson, F.U. Dowla, and D.M. Goodman, *Backpropagation learning for multilayer feedforward neural networks using the conjugate gradient method.* Int. J. Neural Systems, vol. 2, no. 4, pp. 291–302, 1992.

[7] V. Golovko, O. Ignatiuk, Y. Savitsky, T. Laopoulos, A. Sachenko, L. Grandinetti, *Unsupervised learning for dimensionality reduction //* Proc. of Second Int. ICSC Symposium on Engineering of Intelligent Systems EIS'2000, University of Paisley, Scotland, U.K. – 2000. – P. 140-144.

[8] V. Golovko. *Neurointelligence: theory and application. Book 1: Organization and training of the neural networks.* Brest State Technical University 1999, - 260p. (in Russian)

[9] S. Ahmed, J. Cross, A. Bouzerdoum. *A new self-adaptive backpropagation training method.* Proc. of Int. Joint Conf. on Neural Networks IJCNN'2000, Como, Italy. – 2000.

[10] V. Golovko, Y. Savitsky, T. Laopoulos, A. Sachenko, L. Grandinetti. *Technique of Learning Rate Estimation for Efficient Training of MLP //* Proc. of Int. Joint Conf. on Neural Networks IJCNN'2000, Como, Italy. – 2000. – pp. 323–329.

[11] F. Takens, *Detecting Strange attractors in fluid turbulence.* Springer-Verlag, Berlin, 1981.

[12] A. Fraser, H. Swinney. *Independent coordinates for strange attractors from mutual information.* Phys. Rev. A 33, 1134 (1986).

[13] M. Kennel, R. Brown, H. Abarbanel, *Determining embedding dimension for phase-space reconstruction using a geometrical construction.* Phys. Rev. A 45, 3403 (1992).

[14] H. Kantz. *A robust method to estimate the maximal Lyapunov exponent of a time series.* Phys. Lett. A 185, 77 (1994).

[15] V. Golovko, Y. Savitsky, N. Maniakov. *Modeling Nonlinear Dynamic using Multilayer Neural Networks.* Proceedings of the Workshop Intelligent Data Acquisition and Advanced Computing Systems: Technology and Applications. (IDAACS'2001), Foros, Ukraine, July 1-4 2001, pp. 197–202.

[16] H. Schuster. *Deterministic chaos. An introduction.* Physic-Verlag, Weinhheim, 1984, p.240.

[17] V. Golovko, V. Dimakov. *Self-Organizing Path Planning Control System for a Vehicle //* Proc. of Second Int. ICSC Symposium on Neural Computation NC'2000, Berlin, Germany, Publication by ICSC Academic Press. – 2000.

[18] V. Golovko, V. Dimakov. *The Neural Network of Best Path Planning //* In Proceedings of International Conference on Information Technologies for Education, Science and Business - Minsk, Belarus - 1999 - p. 220—222.

[19] V. Golovko, V. Dimakov. *Architecture of Neural System for Control of Autonomous Vehicles* // Preprints of the 3th IFAC Symposium on Intelligent Autonomous Vehicles (Spain, Madrid, March, 1998). – Oxford UK: Elsevier Science Ltd. – 1998. – V.1 – pp. 287–297.

[20] V. Golovko, O. Ignatiuk, V. Sauta. *An Approach to Mobile Robot Self-training* // Proceedings of the IV 2000, IEEE Intelligent Vehicles Symposium, 3-5 October 2000, Dearborn, Detroit, USA. pp. 608–613.

[21] V. Golovko. *Neural Networks: training, organization and application.* Moscow, Radiotechnica 2001, – 350 p.

Author Index

Ben-Hur, Asa	23
Buhmann, Joachim M.	115
Fishman, Shmuel	23
Golovko, Vladimir	219
Goras, Liviu	185
Gori, Marco	1
Haykin, Simon	95
Intrator, Nathan	163
Novák, Mirko	207
Pelillo, Marcello	71
Roska, Tamás	177
Siegelmann, Hava	23
Šíma, Jiří	45
Verleysen, Michel	141
Votruba, Zdeněk	207